Welcome to NEW Keystone

New Keystone has been specially designed to help you succeed in all areas of your school studies. This program will help you develop the English language skills you need for language arts, social studies, math, and science. You will discover new ways to use and build upon your language skills through your interactions with classmates, friends, teachers, and family members.

New Keystone includes a mix of many subjects. Each unit has four different reading selections that include literary excerpts, poems, and nonfiction articles about science, math, and social studies. These selections will help you understand the vocabulary and organization of different types of texts. They will also give you the tools you need to approach the content of the different subjects you take in school.

As you use this program, you will discover new words, use your background knowledge of the subjects presented, relate your knowledge to the new information, and take part in creative activities. You will learn strategies to help you understand readings better. You will work on activities that help you improve your English skills in grammar, word study, and spelling. Finally, you will be asked to demonstrate the listening, speaking, and writing skills you have learned through fun projects that are incorporated throughout the program.

Learning a language takes time, but just like learning to skateboard or learning to swim, it is fun! Whether you are learning English for the first time, or increasing your knowledge of English by adding academic or literary language to your vocabulary, you are giving yourself new choices for the future, and a better chance of succeeding in both your studies and in everyday life.

We hope you enjoy *New Keystone*, and we wish you success on every step of your learning journey.

NEW Keystone D

STUDENT EDITION
with Digital Resources

NEW
Keystone Ⓓ

Copyright © 2019 by Pearson Education, Inc.
All rights reserved. No part of this publication may be reproduced, stored in a retrieval system, or transmitted in any form or by any means, electronic, mechanical, photocopying, recording, or otherwise, without the prior permission of the publisher.
Pearson, 221 River Street, Hoboken, NJ 07030

Smithsonian American Art Museum contributors: Project director and writer:
Elizabeth K. Eder, Ph.D.; Writer: Mary Collins; Image research assistants: Laurel Fehrenbach, Katherine G. Stilwill, and Sally Otis; Rights and reproductions: Richard H. Sorensen and Leslie G. Green; Building photograph by Tim Hursley.

Cover credit: Colin Hawkins/Cultura/Getty Images

Library of Congress Cataloging-in-Publication Data
A catalog record for the print edition is available from the Library of Congress.

The publishers would like to recognize the contributions of our original Series Consultants, Anna Uhl Chamot, John De Mado, and Sharroky Hollie. This edition is published in memory of Dr. Chamot, an extraordinary educator, writer, and scholar.

Printed in the United States of America
ISBN-10: 0-13-523278-3 (with Digital Resources)
ISBN-13: 978-0-13-523278-1 (with Digital Resources)
      2 2019

www.english.com/keystone

Consultants and Reviewers

Sharena Adebiyi
Fulton County Schools
Stone City, GA, USA

Hien Chung
YOLA Education
Ho Chi Minh City, Vietnam

Carlos Eduardo Aguilar Cortés
Universidad de la Salle
Bogotá, Colombia

Jose Augusto Lugo
Cerros
Bogotá, Colombia

Jennifer Benavides
Garland ISD
Garland, TX, USA

Tracy Bunker
Shearer Charter School
Napa, CA, USA

Gabriela Cecilia Diaz
Grilli Canning College
Buenos Aires, Argentina

Dan Fichtner
UCLA Ed. Ext. TESOL Program
Redondo Beach, CA, USA

Trudy Freer-Alvarez
Houston ISD
Houston, TX, USA

Helena K. Gandell
Duval County
Jacksonville, FL, USA

Valeria Goluza
Grilli Canning College
Buenos Aires, Argentina

Glenda Harrell
Johnston County School Dist.
Smithfield, NC, USA

Michelle Land
Randolph Middle School
Randolph, NJ, USA

Joseph E. Leaf
Norristown Area High School
Norristown, PA, USA

Le Tue Minh
Wellspring International Bilingual School
Hanoi, Vietnam

Minh Phuong Nguyen
CIEM-Education
Hanoi, Vietnam

Richard Nickless
Kwong Chow School
Thailand

Ilona Olancin
Collier County Schools
Naples, FL, USA

Patricia Parroquiano
Gimnasio Campestre Reino Britanico
Bogotá, Colombia

Jeanne Perrin
Boston Unified School Dist.
Boston, MA, USA

Cheryl Quadrelli-Jones
Anaheim Union High School Dist.
Fullerton, CA, USA

Sergio Rivera
Liceo Hermano Miguel La Salle
Bogotá, Colombia

Mary Schmidt
Riverwood High School
Atlanta, GA, USA

Kampanart Thammaphati
Wattana Wittaya Academy
Thailand

Daniel Thatcher
Garland ISD
Garland, TX, USA

Denise Tiffany
West High School
Iowa City, IA, USA

Lisa Troute
Palm Beach County School Dist.
West Palm, FL, USA

Visual Literacy

Smithsonian American Art Museum

Dear Student,

At the end of each unit in this book, you will learn about some artists and artworks that relate to the theme you have just read about. These artworks are all in the Smithsonian American Art Museum in Washington, D.C. That means they belong to you, because the Smithsonian is America's collection. The artworks were created over a period of 300 years by artists who responded to their experiences in personal ways. Their world lives on through their artworks and, as viewers, we can understand them and ourselves in new ways. We discover that many of the things that concerned these artists still engage us today.

Looking at an artwork is different from reading a written history. Artists present few facts or dates. Instead, they offer emotional insights that come from their own lives and experiences. They make their own decisions about what matters, without worrying if others agree or disagree. This is a rare and useful kind of knowledge that we can all learn from. Artists inspire us to respond to our own lives with deeper insight.

There are two ways to approach art. One way is through the mind—studying the artist, learning about the subject, exploring the context in which the artwork was made, and forming a personal view. This way is deeply rewarding and expands your understanding of the world. The second way is through the senses—letting your imagination roam as you look at an artwork, losing yourself in colors and shapes, absorbing the meaning through your eyes. This way is called "aesthetic." The great thing about art is that an artwork may have many different meanings. You can decide what it means to you.

This brief introduction to American art will, I hope, lead to a lifetime of enjoyment and appreciation of art.

Elizabeth Broun
The Margaret and Terry Stent Director
Smithsonian American Art Museum

Glossary of Terms

You will find the following words useful when reading, writing, and talking about art.

abstract a style of art that does not represent things, animals, or people realistically

acrylic a type of paint that is made from ground pigments and certain chemicals

background part of the artwork that looks furthest away from the viewer

brushstroke the paint or ink left on the surface of an artwork by the paintbrush

canvas a type of heavy woven fabric used as a support for painting; another word for a painting

composition the way in which the different parts of an artwork are arranged

detail a small part of an artwork

evoke to produce a strong feeling or memory

figure the representation of a person or animal in an artwork

foreground part of the artwork that looks closest to the viewer

geometric a type of pattern that has straight lines or shapes such as squares, circles, etc.

mixed media different kinds of materials such as paint, fabric, objects, etc. that are used in a single artwork

oil a type of paint that is made from ground pigments and linseed oil

paintbrush a special brush used for painting

perception the way you understand something you see

pigment a finely powdered material (natural or man-made) that gives color to paint, ink, or dye

portrait an artwork that shows a specific person, group of people, or animal

print an artwork that has been made from a sheet of metal or a block of wood covered with a wet color and then pressed onto a flat surface like paper. Types of prints include lithographs, etchings, aquatints, etc.

symbol an image, shape, or object in an artwork that represents an idea

texture the way that a surface or material feels and how smooth or rough it looks

tone the shade of a particular color; the effect of light and shade with color

watercolor a type of paint that is made from ground pigments, gum, and glycerin and/or honey; another word for a painting done with this medium

Unit 1 Contents

Unit Preview

Unit Opener	**The Big Question: What is light?**	2

Reading 1: Myth

Prepare to Read	**Build Background**	4
	Literary Words: onomatopoeia, repetition, irony	5
	Academic Words: author, culture, text, tradition	6
	Word Study: Compound Words	7
	Reading Strategy: Predict	7
Reading Selection	**"Grandmother Spider Brings the Sun"** by Geri Keams	8
Review and Practice	**Listening and Speaking:** Reader's Theater and Response to Literature	14
Grammar	Order of Adjectives	16
	Italics, Repetition, and Other Devices Used for Emphasis or Effect	17
Writing	Describe a Character	18

Reading 2: Science

Prepare to Read	**Build Background**	20
	Key Words: concave, convex, opaque, translucent, transparent, wavelength	21
	Academic Words: interpret, transmit, virtual, visible	22
	Word Study: Words with /əl/ spelled -le and -el	23
	Reading Strategy: Skim	23
Reading Selection	**"Light"**	24
Review and Practice	**Listening and Speaking:** In Your Own Words and Read for Fluency	30
Grammar	Simple Present with *When* Clause for Facts	32
	Present Passive	33
Writing	Describe an Object	34

Reading 3: Short Story

Prepare to Read	**Build Background**	36
	Literary Words: imagery, setting, figurative language	37
	Academic Words: approached, despite, equivalent, visual	38
	Word Study: Antonyms	39
	Reading Strategy: Visualize	39

Reading Selection	"A Game of Light and Shade" by Arturo Vivante	40
Review and Practice	Listening and Speaking: *Reader's Theater* and *Response to Literature*	44
Grammar	Prepositions of Time and Place: *by, in, at, from, to, on*	46
	Prepositions Combined with Verbs	47
Writing	Describe a Place	48

Reading 4: Social Studies

Prepare to Read	Build Background	50
	Key Words: device, equipment, industry, investors, patented, tenacity	51
	Academic Words: contribution, rejected, injury, significant	52
	Word Study: Suffixes	53
	Reading Strategy: Use Visuals	53
Reading Selection	"Providing Light in the Darkness"	54
Review and Practice	Listening and Speaking: *In Your Own Words* and *Read for Fluency*	60
Grammar	Restrictive Relative Clauses	62
	Nonrestrictive Relative Clauses	63
Writing	Describe an Experience	64

Unit Wrap-Up

Link the Readings
  Critical Thinking 66
  Discussion 66
Media Literacy & Projects 67
Further Reading 67
Put It All Together
  Listening and Speaking Workshop: Description Guessing Game 68
  Writing Workshop: Write a Descriptive Essay 70
  Test Preparation 75
Smithsonian American Art Museum: The Language of Art
  Capturing the Power of Contrasts 76

Unit 2

Contents

Unit Preview

Unit Opener — **The Big Question: How are growth and change related?** 78

Reading 1: Science/Folktale

Prepare to Read
- Build Background 80
- Key Words: develop, embryo, germination, inactive, protective, straighten 81
- Academic Words: environment, function, potential, process ... 82
- Word Study: Related Words 83
- Reading Strategy: Recognize Sequence 83

Reading Selection
- "How Seeds and Plants Grow" 84
- "A Tale of Two Brothers" 86

Review and Practice
- Listening and Speaking: In Your Own Words and Read for Fluency 88

Grammar
- Sequence Words and Phrases 90
- Using Dashes to Explain or Clarify 91

Writing
- Write a Story with a Starter 92

Reading 2: Short Story

Prepare to Read
- Build Background 94
- Literary Words: point of view, plot, suspense 95
- Academic Words: affect, anticipation, discrimination, reaction 96
- Word Study: Homographs 97
- Reading Strategy: Compare and Contrast 97

Reading Selection
- "The Test" 98

Review and Practice
- Listening and Speaking: Reader's Theater and Response to Literature 102

Grammar
- Simple Past and Present Perfect 104
- Past Perfect: Active and Passive 105

Writing
- Rewrite a Familiar Story 106

Reading 3: Science

Prepare to Read
- Build Background 108
- Key Words: colony, decline, ecosystems, migrate, species, stable 109
- Academic Words: adapt, distribution, expand, prediction, region 110
- Word Study: Long a, i, o Spelling Patterns 111

	Reading Strategy: Scan	**111**
Reading Selection	**"Climate Change Puts Nature on the Move"**	**112**
Review and Practice	**Listening and Speaking:** *In Your Own Words* and *Read for Fluency*	**116**
Grammar	**Comparison Structures: Comparative Adjectives**	**118**
	Adjectives with *Too* **and** *Enough*	**119**
Writing	**Write a Personal Letter**	**120**

Reading 4: Short Story

Prepare to Read	**Build Background**	**122**
	Literary Words: *characterization, dialogue, sarcasm*	**123**
	Academic Words: *conduct, ignore, instruct, reluctance*	**124**
	Word Study: Idioms	**125**
	Reading Strategy: Make Inferences	**125**
Reading Selection	**"Abuela Invents the Zero" by Judith Ortiz Cofer**	**126**
Review and Practice	**Listening and Speaking:** *Reader's Theater* and *Response to Literature*	**132**
Grammar	*Have to* + Verb	**134**
	Conditional Sentences	**135**
Writing	**Write a Personal Narrative**	**136**

Unit Wrap-Up

Link the Readings
Critical Thinking	**138**
Discussion	**138**

Media Literacy & Projects ... **139**

Further Reading ... **139**

Put It All Together
Listening and Speaking Workshop: Skit	**140**
Writing Workshop: Fictional Narrative	**142**
Test Preparation	**147**

Smithsonian American Art Museum: The Language of Art
Cycles of Nature ... **148**

Unit 3

Contents

Unit Preview

Unit Opener **The Big Question:** How can we tell what's right? 150

Reading 1: Folktale

Prepare to Read	Build Background	152
	Literary Words: *moral, motivation*	153
	Academic Words: *adviser, collection, recognize, wisdom* ...	154
	Word Study: Irregular Plurals	155
	Reading Strategy: Identify Problems and Solutions	155
Reading Selection	"The Beggar King"	156
Review and Practice	Listening and Speaking: *Reader's Theater* and *Response to Literature*	162
Grammar	The Modal *must*	164
	The Modal *would* for Repeated Actions in the Past	165
Writing	Write a Review	166

Reading 2: Science

Prepare to Read	Build Background	168
	Key Words: *celestial, extinction, organisms, revolution, rover, terrestrial*	169
	Academic Words: *biased, debate, define, objectively*	170
	Word Study: Prefixes	171
	Reading Strategy: Distinguish Fact from Opinion	171
Reading Selection	"Mars: Pro and Con"	172
Review and Practice	Listening and Speaking: *In Your Own Words* and *Read for Fluency*	176
Grammar	Transition Words, Phrases, and Clauses (for Opinions) ...	178
	The Uses of the Modal *could*	179
Writing	Write a Letter to the Editor	180

Reading 3: Fable

Prepare to Read	Build Background	182
	Literary Words: *theme, moral, irony*	183
	Academic Words: *analyze, ethical, justify, principle*	184
	Word Study: Long and Short Vowels	185
	Reading Strategy: Identify the Purpose of a Fable	185

xii

Reading Selection	"The Golden Serpent" by Walter Dean Myers..........	186
Review and Practice	Listening and Speaking: *Reader's Theater* and *Response to Literature*	192
Grammar	Other Uses of *would* in the Past......................	194
	Subjunctive	195
Writing	Write a Persuasive Paragraph	196

Reading 4: Social Studies

Prepare to Read	Build Background....................................	198
	Key Words: athletes, capability, gender, marathon, racism, referee	199
	Academic Words: address, controversial, determined, witness	200
	Word Study: Synonyms...............................	201
	Reading Strategy: Summarize	201
Reading Selection	"When Is a Winner a Hero?"	202
Review and Practice	Listening and Speaking: *In Your Own Words* and *Read for Fluency*	206
Grammar	Superlative Adjectives	208
	Reciprocal and Reflexive Pronouns	209
Writing	Write an Advertisement..............................	210

Unit Wrap-Up

Link the Readings
  Critical Thinking 212
  Discussion 212
Media Literacy & Projects... 213
Further Reading 213
Put It All Together
  Listening and Speaking Workshop: Radio Commercial 214
  Writing Workshop: Speech.. 216
  Test Preparation 221
Smithsonian American Art Museum: The Language of Art
  That's Art? 222

Unit 4

Contents

Unit Preview

Unit Opener   **The Big Question: Can we think with the heart?** 224

Reading 1: Social Studies

Prepare to Read	Build Background	226
	Key Words: bitterness, defects, eventful, imitate, sensation, tangible	227
	Academic Words: communicate, concept, persistence, transformation	228
	Word Study: The Suffix -ful	229
	Reading Strategy: Identify Main Idea and Details	229
Reading Selection	from *The Story of My Life* by Helen Keller	230
Review and Practice	Listening and Speaking: *In Your Own Words* and *Read for Fluency*	236
Grammar	Possessive Adjectives	238
	Adjectives and Adjectival Phrases	239
Writing	Write a Critique	240

Reading 2: Play

Prepare to Read	Build Background	242
	Literary Words: narrator, soliloquy, stage directions	243
	Academic Words: abandon, alternative, circumstances, conflict, convince	244
	Word Study: Synonyms	245
	Reading Strategy: Analyze Text Structure	245
Reading Selection	*To Capture the Wild Horse*	246
Review and Practice	Listening and Speaking: *Dramatic Reading* and *Response to Literature*	250
Grammar	Simple and Compound Sentences	252
	Complex and Compound-Complex Sentences	253
Writing	Write a Summary	254

Reading 3: Social Studies

Prepare to Read	Build Background	256
	Key Words: arteries, cholesterol, circulation, nutrients, organs, sensations	257
	Academic Words: contribute, evaluate, function, source, struggle	258
	Word Study: Related Words	259
	Reading Strategy: Monitor Comprehension	259

Reading Selection	"The Heart's Wisdom"	260
	"Nourishing Your Heart and Your Brain"	265
Review and Practice	**Listening and Speaking:** *In Your Own Words* and *Read for Fluency*	266
Grammar	Imperatives	268
	Adverb Phrases and Clauses to Describe a Process	269
Writing	Write Instructions	270

Reading 4: Short Story

Prepare to Read	Build Background	272
	Literary Words: *characterization, figurative language, symbol*	273
	Academic Words: *bond, devoted, mutual, significance*	274
	Word Study: The /z/ Sound	275
	Reading Strategy: Recognize and Analyze Cultural Context	275
Reading Selection	"Ginger for the Heart" by Paul Yee	276
Review and Practice	**Listening and Speaking:** *Reader's Theater* and *Response to Literature*	280
Grammar	Present and Past Perfect	282
	Adjective Phrases (*-ing, -ed*)	283
Writing	Write a Critical Analysis	284

Unit Wrap-Up

Link the Readings
Critical Thinking	286
Discussion	286

Media Literacy & Projects	287
Further Reading	287

Put It All Together
Listening and Speaking Workshop: How-To Demonstration	288
Writing Workshop: Expository Essay	290
Test Preparation	295

Smithsonian American Art Museum: The Language of Art
Bonding or Breaking	296

Unit 5 Contents

Unit Preview

Unit Opener   **The Big Question:**
What can we learn from times of war?........ 298

Reading 1: Social Studies

Prepare to Read	**Build Background**................................	300
	Key Words: alliance, armistice, assassination, civilians, surrendered, trenches................................	301
	Academic Words: neutral, resources, technology, tension, vehicle................................	302
	Word Study: Roots................................	303
	Reading Strategy: Identify Cause and Effect............	303
Reading Selection	"World War I"................................	304
Review and Practice	**Listening and Speaking:** In Your Own Words and Read for Fluency................................	310
Grammar	**Appositives**................................	312
	Prepositions of Time: in, on, at, by, before, and until.....	313
Writing	**Write a Cause and Effect Paragraph**................	314

Reading 2: Poetry, Song, Prose

Prepare to Read	**Build Background**................................	316
	Literary Words: extended metaphor, figurative language, personification................................	317
	Academic Words: context, create, impact, similar.........	318
	Word Study: Homophones................................	319
	Reading Strategy: Recognize Historical Context.........	319
Reading Selection	"In Flanders Fields"................................	320
	"Anthem for Doomed Youth"......................	321
	"Three Wonderful Letters from Home"..............	322
	"Letter Home"................................	323
Review and Practice	**Listening and Speaking:** Dramatic Reading and Response to Literature................................	324
Grammar	**Contrast**................................	326
	Pronouns and Antecedents........................	327
Writing	**Write to Compare and Contrast**....................	328

Reading 3: Social Studies

Prepare to Read	**Build Background**................................	330
	Key Words: consulate, diplomat, heroism, honor, lecture, refugees................................	331

	Academic Words: document, estimate, exploits, integrity, sympathetic	332
	Word Study: The Suffix -ness	333
	Reading Strategy: Draw Conclusions	333
Reading Selection	"In the Name of His Father" by Fred Tasker	334
Review and Practice	**Listening and Speaking:** In Your Own Words and Read for Fluency	338
Grammar	Passive	340
	Using Quotations	341
Writing	Write a News Article	342

Reading 4: Poetry

Prepare to Read	Build Background	344
	Literary Words: sonnet, ballad, symbol, imagery	345
	Academic Words: bond, indicate, tragic, universal	346
	Word Study: Spelling Long e	347
	Reading Strategy: Read Aloud	347
Reading Selection	"Sonnet to My Brother, a Soldier"	348
	"He Died at His Post" by J.W. Holman	349
Review and Practice	**Listening and Speaking:** Dramatic Reading and Response to Literature	350
Grammar	Comparison Structures	352
	Inverted Word Order in Poems	353
Writing	Write to Support a Position	354

Unit Wrap-Up

Link the Readings
  Critical Thinking 356
  Discussion 356
Media Literacy & Projects 357
Further Reading 357
Put It All Together
  Listening and Speaking Workshop: Oral Report 358
  Writing Workshop: Expository Essay: News Article 360
  Test Preparation 365
Smithsonian American Art Museum: The Language of Art
  Citizens on the Home Front 366

Unit 6

Contents

Unit Preview

Unit Opener ❓ **The Big Question:**
What makes animals so amazing? 368

Reading 1: Short Story

Prepare to Read	Build Background	370
	Literary Words: *archetype, protagonist, antagonist, foil* ...	371
	Academic Words: *attached, complexity, consequence, thrive*	372
	Word Study: Suffixes	373
	Reading Strategy: Connect Ideas	373
Reading Selection	"The Talking Bird"	374
Review and Practice	Listening and Speaking: *Reader's Theater* and *Response to Literature*	378
Grammar	Reduction of Adjective Clauses to Adjective Phrases	380
	Inverted Word Order in Prose	381
Writing	Write an Introductory Paragraph	382

Reading 2: Science

Prepare to Read	Build Background	384
	Key Words: *echolocation, mammals, nocturnal, prey, the wild, wingspan*	385
	Academic Words: *accurate, beneficial, features, ignorance* ..	386
	Word Study: Compound Words	387
	Reading Strategy: Evaluate New Information	387
Reading Selection	"Getting to Know Real Bats" by Laurence Pringle	388
Review and Practice	Listening and Speaking: *In Your Own Words* and *Read for Fluency*	394
Grammar	Relative Pronouns as Subjects	396
	Noun Clauses with *that*	397
Writing	Write Classifying Paragraphs	398

Reading 3: Poetry

Prepare to Read	Build Background	400
	Literary Words: *figurative language, imagery, metaphor, simile*	401
	Academic Words: *appreciation, attitude, category, vehicle* ...	402
	Word Study: Words with Double Letters	403
	Reading Strategy: Read Aloud	403

Reading Selection	"**A Narrow Fellow in the Grass**" by Emily Dickinson	404
	"**Daybreak**" by Galway Kinnell	406
	"**Birdfoot's Grandpa**" by Joseph Bruchac	407
Review and Practice	Listening and Speaking: *Dramatic Reading* and *Response to Literature*	408
Grammar	Typical and Atypical Word Order	410
	Simple Past (Irregular) and Past Progressive	411
Writing	Support the Main Idea	412

Reading 4: Novel

Prepare to Read	Build Background	414
	Literary Words: setting, point of view, flashback, foreshadowing	415
	Academic Words: abandon, committed, resist, reveal	416
	Word Study: Frequently Misspelled Words	417
	Reading Strategy: Sequence	417
Reading Selection	from **White Fang** by Jack London	418
Review and Practice	Listening and Speaking: *Reader's Theater* and *Response to Literature*	424
Grammar	Gerunds	426
	Infinitives	427
	Using Quotation Marks for Exact Words	428
	Quotation Marks: Terms, Expressions, and Titles	429
Writing	Write an Interpretive Response	430

Unit Wrap-Up

Link the Readings
Critical Thinking	432
Discussion	432

Media Literacy & Projects	433
Further Reading	433

Put It All Together
Listening and Speaking Workshop: TV Documentary	434
Writing Workshop: Research Report	436
Test Preparation	443

Smithsonian American Art Museum: The Language of Art
Animals in Human Society	444

Unit 1

What is light?

THE BIG QUESTION

This unit is about light and the absence of light. You'll find out what light is and how it behaves. You'll read stories showing different ways in which light is important to us. Reading, writing, and talking about this topic will give you practice using academic language and help you become a better student.

Reading 1
Myth

"Grandmother Spider Brings the Sun" retold by Geri Keams

Reading Strategy
Predict

Reading 2
Science

"Light"

Reading Strategy
Skim

Reading 3
Short Story

"A Game of Light and Shade" by Arturo Vivante

Reading Strategy
Visualize

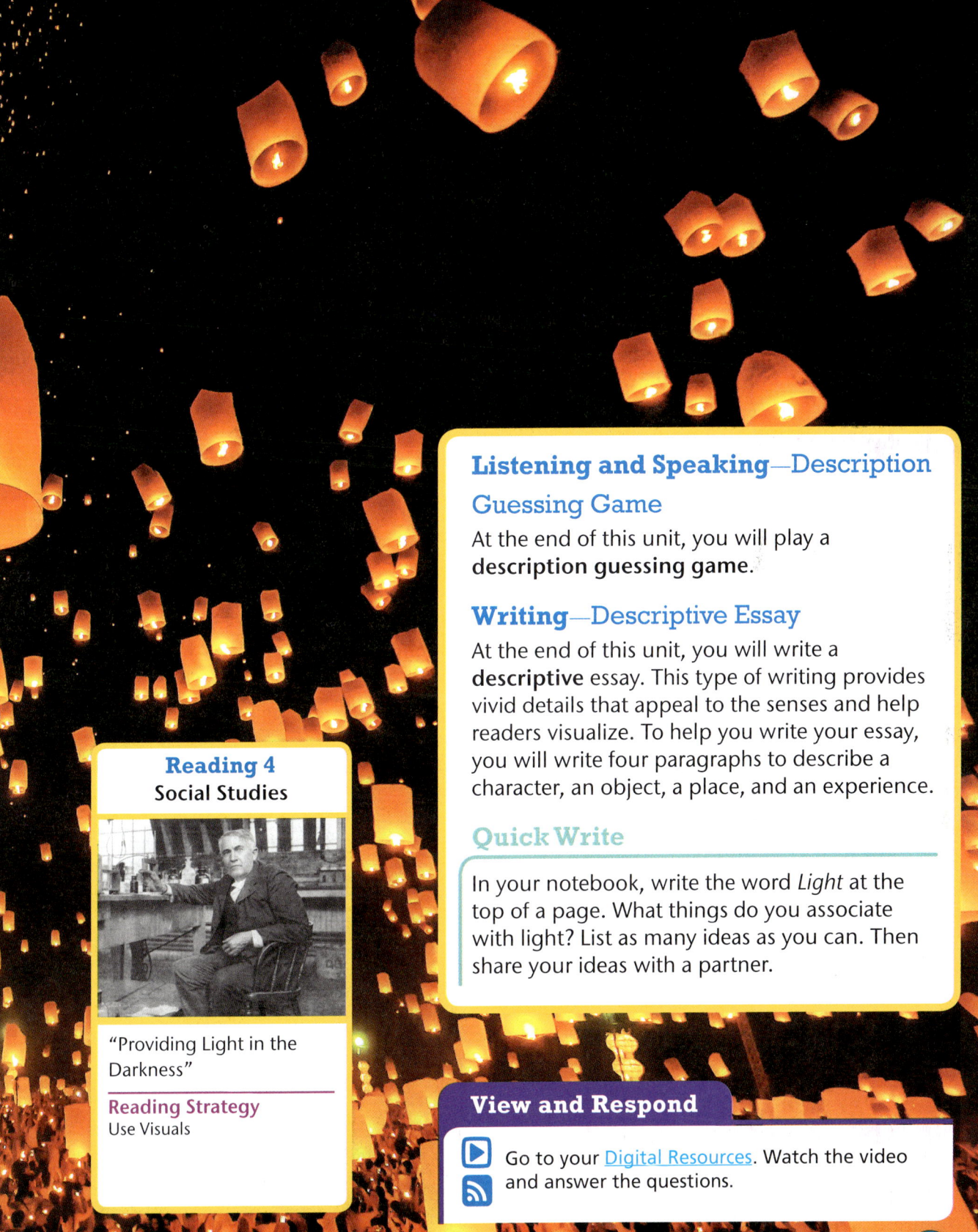

Listening and Speaking—Description
Guessing Game

At the end of this unit, you will play a **description guessing game**.

Writing—Descriptive Essay

At the end of this unit, you will write a **descriptive** essay. This type of writing provides vivid details that appeal to the senses and help readers visualize. To help you write your essay, you will write four paragraphs to describe a character, an object, a place, and an experience.

Quick Write

In your notebook, write the word *Light* at the top of a page. What things do you associate with light? List as many ideas as you can. Then share your ideas with a partner.

Reading 4
Social Studies

"Providing Light in the Darkness"

Reading Strategy
Use Visuals

View and Respond

Go to your Digital Resources. Watch the video and answer the questions.

Reading 1

Prepare to Read

What You Will Learn

Reading
- Vocabulary building: *Literary terms, word study*
- Reading strategy: *Predict*
- Text type: *Literature (myth)*

Grammar
- Order of adjectives
- Italics, repetition, and other devices used for emphasis and effect

Writing
- Describe a character

THE BIG QUESTION

What is light? Light often represents different things in literature. For example, it might stand for knowledge or hope. Why do you think this is so? Can you think of some other examples? Discuss with a partner.

Build Background

In this unit you will read a myth called **"Grandmother Spider Brings the Sun."** Myths are fictional tales that explain how things in nature came to be or describe the actions of gods or heroes. People probably created myths as a way of explaining things they didn't understand about the world around them.

Different ancient cultures each had their own myths. People told these myths to their children generation after generation. Because myths were passed down orally, or by word of mouth, we say that they are part of the oral tradition. Luckily for us, many myths have been written down.

The myth you are about to read comes to us from the Native American people known as the Cherokee. It explains some facts about the natural world in an amusing way.

Many cultures have told myths about the northern lights, or aurora borealis. In China, the myth was that the light was created by dragons fighting. In France, seeing the lights predicted war.

Vocabulary

Learn Literary Words

Literary Words
onomatopoeia
repetition
irony

As part of the oral tradition, "Grandmother Spider Brings the Sun" is written the way a storyteller would tell it.

One way that storytellers make a story interesting to hear is through words that imitate sounds. The word *Whoosh!* sounds like the noise water makes when poured on a fire. We call the use of words that imitate sounds **onomatopoeia**. Other examples of onomatopoeia include the words *buzz, click, jingle, bang,* and *boom*.

Another technique storytellers use is **repetition**. In the story you are about to read, the character Coyote says, "Calm down, calm down, calm down." Here, repetition shows how coyote is feeling about the situation. Repetition can also be used for emphasis or to create humor.

Irony is the difference between what the reader expects to happen and what actually happens in a story. Writers include ironic situations in stories to create surprise or amusement. In "Grandmother Spider Brings the Sun," the author ends the story with an ironic situation.

Listening Tip

Myths were passed down from generation to generation by word of mouth. They were meant to be listened to. As you read and listen to the examples of onomatopoeia and repetition, think about how these devices helped storytellers retell a myth. How did the devices also make myths memorable for those who listened to them?

Practice

Work with a partner. Take turns reading the lines below aloud. Identify the examples as *onomatopoeia* or *repetition*. Then write a sentence using onomatopoeia and a sentence using repetition in your notebook.

1. The frog jumped into the pond with a loud splash. __onomatopoeia__
2. "Please, please, please don't chase me anymore," cried the frightened rabbit. _____
3. There was nothing to do but listen to the pitter-patter of the rain. _____
4. The coyote raised his head and howled. _____
5. After the game was over, the little girl cheered, "I won! I won! I won! I won!" _____
6. "Wait! Wait! Wait!" the boy said, as he ran to catch up. _____

Reading 1 5

Reading 1

Learn Academic Words

Study the **purple** words and their meanings. You will find these words useful when talking and writing about literature. Write each word and its meaning in your notebook. After you read "Grandmother Spider Brings the Sun," try to use these words to respond to the text.

Academic Words
- author
- culture
- text
- tradition

author = someone who writes a book, story, article, or play	➡	Geri Keams is the **author** who retold the myth you are about to read.
culture = the art, literature, music, beliefs, and practices of a particular group of people	➡	Myths in the Cherokee **culture** include animal characters.
text = the words in a printed piece of writing	➡	Colorful illustrations go with the **text** of this story.
tradition = a belief, custom, or way of doing something that has existed for a long time	➡	Telling stories is a Cherokee **tradition**.

Practice

Work with a partner to answer these questions. Try to include the **purple** word in your answer. Write the sentences in your notebook.

1. Who is your favorite **author**?
2. Which celebrations are common in your **culture**?
3. Do you prefer reading **text** with illustrations or without them?
4. What **tradition** is important to you and your family?

Reading Skill

Which question words are used in the Practice activity? What information does each question word ask for? What kind of information will you give to answer each question?

◀ Making clay pots is a tradition in the Cherokee culture.

Word Study: Compound Words

A compound word is made up of more than one word. Some compound words are written as one word, as in *sunshine*. Some are written as two words, as in *peanut butter*. Some are written with hyphens between the words, as in *mother-in-law*.

Practice

Work with a partner. Combine words from Column A with words from Column B to form compound words. Write the words in Column C. Use a dictionary to find out whether the words are written as one word or two. None of these words is hyphenated.

A	B	C
1. any	brush	
2. every	plane	
3. high	off	
4. grand	school	
5. some	cycle	
6. tooth	one	
7. air	father	
8. motor	thing	
9. show	body	

▲ In Japan, a man teaches his granddaughter about bonsai trees. Growing and trimming bonsai trees is a tradition in Japan.

Reading Strategy Predict

Predicting as you read helps you stay focused. It also helps you understand a text better. Before you read, predict, or guess, what the story will be about. You can also make new predictions as you're reading. To predict, follow these steps:

- Look at the title and predict what might happen.
- Pause from time to time and think about what will happen next.
- Look for clues in the story and illustrations.
- Think about your own experiences and what you already know about myths.
- If you discover your prediction was not correct, make a new one.

As you read "Grandmother Spider Brings the Sun," stop from time to time and check to see if your prediction was correct. Did you learn anything new that made you want to change your prediction?

Reading 1
Literature
Myth

Set a purpose for reading This myth is about light. Read to discover a traditional Cherokee explanation for where light came from.

Grandmother Spider Brings the Sun

A Cherokee myth retold by Geri Keams

A long time ago it is said that half the world had the sun, but the other side of the world was very dark. It was so dark that all the animals were always bumping into each other and getting lost.

Wolf lived on this side of the world. He was tired of everybody bumping into him and asking him for directions, for you see, Wolf could see in the nighttime.

Wolf gathered all the animals together in a big cave. He got up in front of them and crossed his arms, and he said, "I am tired of everybody bumping into me and asking me for directions."

"I have an idea," he said. "I think we should go to the other side of the world and ask them for a piece of their sun. I think if we're nice, they'll give us a piece."

Another animal jumped up. This was Coyote, known as the trickster because he lies and cheats and steals.

Coyote said, "No, no, no, no, no! I don't think we should be so nice! If they're so nice, how come they haven't *offered* us a piece of their sun?"

The other animals nodded in agreement.

"I have a better idea," Coyote said. "I think we should sneak over there and just *steal* a piece."

"*Steal* a piece!" said Wolf. "What are you talking about, Coyote?"

"Calm down, calm down, calm down," Coyote said. "We're not going to steal a *big* piece. We'll only take a *little* piece. They'll never even miss it."

And that is what they decided to do.

Then all the animals began asking, "Who is going to go to the other side of the world? How will they get there?" Everybody had an idea, but none seemed quite right.

Then from the back of the room came a small voice. "Hey, I'll go! I'll go!"

Wolf said, "Who is that? Come down here. I can't see you."

Down to the front of the room came a little round animal with chubby cheeks. He was shy and quiet. He stood up in front of all the animals, and as he looked at all those hundreds of eyes looking back at him, he got kind of scared.

He looked out over the crowd of animals and he said in his timid voice, "Hi. M-m-m-my name is Possum. I think I can go to the other side of the world. You see, I've got these long, sharp claws, and I think I can dig a tunnel. And when I go *all* the way to the other side of the world, I'll take a piece of the sun and I'll hide it in my big, bushy tail."

And Wolf said, "Oh, a tunnel! That's the best idea yet!"

So Possum went to the big wall of dirt at the back of the cave, stuck in his sharp claws, and began to dig and dig and dig and dig, faster and faster and faster and faster. Possum disappeared inside the tunnel, and soon he had gone all the way to the other side of the world.

Reading Skill

Play the audio. Listen for patterns of intonation. Listen to the way a character's voice rises and falls. Notice which character is the trickster. Think about the effect of how the trickster speaks.

✓ LITERARY CHECK

What effect does the **repetition** of the word *no* have here?

Before You Go On

1. What method do the animals decide upon to get part of the sun?
2. What makes Possum qualified for the task?

👤 On Your Own

Do you think Coyote's idea is better than Wolf's? Why or why not?

Now, Possum had never seen the sun, so when he popped out on the other side, the light hit his eyes, and he was blinded. His eyes got all squinty and he rubbed them with his dirty fists, saying, "Hey! I can't see!" Well, you know, Possum's eyes have been squinty and ringed with dirt ever since.

Possum struggled over to the sun, took a little piece, and put it inside his big ol' bushy tail. Then he turned around and came running back down the tunnel.

Possum ran faster and faster and faster and faster. Something started to get hot inside his tail, but Possum kept running, faster and faster.

That something got hotter, and Possum kept running faster, and he soon ran into the room where all the animals were waiting. They all saw smoke coming out of his tail, and they screamed, "Possum! Your tail! Your tail!" and threw water on him. *Whoosh! Whoosh! Whoosh!* The light was gone.

When the smoke had cleared, Wolf looked up and said, "Oh, no, Possum! Look at your tail! It's all skinny!"

And you know, Possum's tail has been this way ever since.

Wolf said, "We still don't have any sun. What are we going to do now?"

A loud voice from the back of the room said, "Send me! I'll go!"

Down to the front stormed a large bird with long black feathers all over his body, and a crown of feathers on top of his head. He held his head high and stuck his chest out as he marched importantly past the other animals. You see, this bird was a show-off. He thought he was the most beautiful bird alive.

He stood up in front of all the animal people and he said, "It's me, Big Bad Buzzard. I'll go to the other side of the world and it won't take me long at all, but I wouldn't be so dumb as to hide the light in my tail. I'm gonna hide it in my beautiful crown of feathers."

Buzzard jumped into the tunnel and soared through the darkness, and it didn't take long at all until he came out on the other side.

Buzzard took a little piece of sun, put it inside his crown of feathers, turned around, and soared back down the tunnel faster and faster and faster and faster. As he came down the tunnel, something started to get hot on top of his head.

Buzzard soared faster and faster, and something got hotter and hotter.

Faster he soared, and soon he came into the room where all the animals were waiting. They looked up, and they saw smoke coming from Buzzard's head. "Oh, no! Buzzard! Your head! Your head!" They got water and *Whoosh! Whoosh! Whoosh!* The light went out.

Wolf looked up and said, "Buzzard! You're bald!"

All of Buzzard's feathers crackled and fell down to the ground. Big Bad Buzzard got so shy and quiet that he ran and hid in the back of the room. And you know, Buzzard has been bald ever since, and he still doesn't like anybody looking at him.

> **✓ LITERARY CHECK**
> What effect does the **repetition** of the word *faster* have here?

> **Listening Tip**
> Play the audio. As you listen, notice how some words imitate sounds, and how other words and phrases are repeated. How do these make the myth memorable to you?

> **✓ LITERARY CHECK**
> Which word in the last paragraph is an example of **onomatopoeia**?

Wolf said, "Possum's burned his tail off and now Buzzard's bald, and we still don't have any sun. What are we going to do now?"

A tiny voice from up above said, "Send me, I'll go! Hey, send me, I'll go! I'll go!"

Wolf looked all around, but he couldn't tell where the voice was coming from. "Who is that? Where are you? Come down where I can see you."

Down from the corner of the ceiling squeaked the tiny voice: "Send *meeeeeee!*"

And right there in front of Wolf landed a tiny spider. The spider looked up and Wolf looked down, and Wolf said, "Oh, no! Not you, Grandma! You can't go to the other side of the world. You're too old—and besides that, you're too slow!"

Well, this was Grandmother Spider. She had done many things to help the animals in her long life. She crossed her little arms and said, "I know I'm old. You don't have to tell me I'm old. But I want to help my people one more time. I need a piece of clay about so big, and you'll get me a piece, won't you, son?"

Before You Go On

1. Did you predict the first two animals would fail? Explain.
2. Why does Wolf say Grandma can't go? Do you think he's right?

On Your Own

How do you predict Grandmother Spider will use the clay? What does this say about her?

Wolf went and got Grandmother Spider a piece of clay, and she sat in the middle of the room and began to **chant**. Soon she had worked the clay into a little bowl.

She picked up that beautiful clay bowl and disappeared inside the tunnel. They say it took Grandma Spider a long, long, long, long time to get to the other side of the world.

The Sun Guards were out now. They knew somebody was trying to steal some of their sun, and they stood in a tight circle around it. They weren't going to let anybody through.

The Sun Guards were mean-looking monsters. They had fire coming out of their heads. They had fire coming out of their mouths: *Hissssss!* And they held their weapons, ready for a fight.

But Grandmother Spider was so tiny that they didn't even see her. She sneaked between them, went up to the sun, took a little piece, put it in her clay bowl, and sneaked back past the Sun Guards.

Reading Skill

Notice any words or phrases and their definitions at the bottom of a page. As you read them in the text, use the definitions to help you understand them.

---

chant, sing words on one tone

She came back down the tunnel *very* slowly. It took her a long, long, long, long time to get to her side of the world. And as she got closer, something happened. The light inside her bowl began to grow. The little rays stretched out of the bowl.

As she came out of the tunnel into the cave, that ball of light was growing. She could hardly even carry it.

All the animals came running to help Grandmother Spider: blind Possum and bald Buzzard, Wolf and Coyote and Bear and Deer and all the others. But that ball of light just kept getting bigger and bigger and bigger and bigger, and it got so big that the animals had to squeeze it out of the cave, and as it squeezed out into the world it bounced up into the sky: *Boingggg!*

It is said that from that day on, whenever Grandmother Spider would spin her web, the shape of the sun would be at the center. And you see, Grandmother Spider spins her web that way to this very day.

✓ LITERARY CHECK

What **irony** do you find in the fact that Grandmother Spider is able to bring the sun?

Before You Go On

1. Why doesn't Grandmother Spider fear the Sun Guards?
2. What explanation does this myth give for the shape of a spider web?

👤 On Your Own

What does this myth suggest about age and size?

About the Author

Geri Keams is an author, storyteller, and actress. Born and raised in the Navajo Nation in Arizona, Keams grew up without television, herding sheep and weaving rugs with her grandmother. Also a storyteller, Keams's grandmother taught her grandchildren the importance of preserving and sharing the stories of Native-American peoples. Keams tells Native American stories in order to encourage others to explore these cultures and to help keep them alive.

Reading 1

Review and Practice

Reader's Theater

Act out the following scene in small groups.

Buzzard: What a bad, bad day I had! I took a piece of sun and zoomed back down the tunnel. I felt so good. But then I felt something hot on top of my head. Suddenly I heard, "Buzzard! Your head! Your head!" Then *Whoosh! Whoosh! Whoosh!* The fire went out, and I was soaking wet. Now, as you can see, I'm bald. My beautiful feathers are gone! Please don't look at me.

Possum: You call that bad? As soon as the light hit my eyes, I was blinded. But even though I could hardly see, I took a piece of sun and ran back down the tunnel. I felt something getting hot inside my tail, but I kept running, faster and faster. Then I heard, "Possum! Your tail! Your tail!" And someone threw water on me. *Whoosh! Whoosh! Whoosh!* When the fire went out, my tail was all skinny. My big bushy tail is naked. And my eyes are all squinty!

Wolf: At least we have sunlight now, and we can all see where we're going!

Possum: You mean everyone *except me* can see.

Wolf: Well, yes, I guess you're right, Possum.

> **Speaking Tip**
>
> Consider how your character feels about what's happened as you say that character's lines.

Comprehension

Recall

1. What is Wolf tired of? What does he propose the animals do?
2. What does Coyote say about Wolf's idea?

Comprehend

3. How does Buzzard's character change in the story? Summarize what happened to him.
4. According to Cherokee myth, why do certain animals look the way they do?

Analyze

5. Which character from the text does the myth make you respect the most? Explain your answer.
6. What are two techniques or literary devices that the author uses to show that this is a story meant to be told aloud?

Connect

7. To this day, when the Cherokee people make clay bowls, it reminds them of Grandmother Spider's journey. What items in your culture remind you of a story in your culture's history?
8. What does this myth explain about the natural world? What do you think about this explanation? How do you think people long ago reacted to it?

Discussion

Discuss with a partner or in a small group.

Why do you think the tradition of oral storytelling still survives?

 What is light? Having sunlight will change how the animals live. It will bring them warmth and the ability to see things more clearly. In what ways does the light in this story represent more than just physical comfort and convenience? How is light important to you in your life?

> **Listening Tip**
>
> Listen carefully to other people's ideas so that you can add new information or insights.

Response to Literature

Write a newspaper article explaining what happened to "the dark side of the world" where the creatures lived before and after the sun came back. To help you with your article, role-play interviews with animal witnesses and the Sun Guards in a small group. Use responses to the interview in your article. When you have finished your newspaper article, read it aloud to the class.

▲ Creating and using clay bowls is a tradition in many cultures.

Reading 1 | 15

Reading 1
Grammar

Order of Adjectives

We often use more than one adjective to describe a noun. The adjectives must be placed in a certain order according to type. Study the different types of adjectives and their correct order.

Adjectives					Noun
Opinion	Size	Age	Color	Material	
beautiful		new		clay	bowl
	big		brown		bear
favorite		old		wool	scarf
	long		black		feathers

Example: We visited an interesting small white clay home in Taos, New Mexico, which uses only solar power.

Practice A
6

Circle the correct phrase to complete each sentence.

1. Lou made a **beautiful new clay** / **clay beautiful new** bowl.
2. We live in a **stone white** / **white stone** house.
3. Do you have any **wool large** / **large wool** blankets?
4. We took pictures of the **brown small** / **small brown** bear.
5. That bird has **beautiful blue** / **blue beautiful** feathers.
6. My grandfather gave me his favorite **old gold** / **gold old** watch.

Practice B

Work with a partner. Use each group of words to write sentences with more than one adjective. Use the chart above to help you place the adjectives in the correct order. Write the sentences in your notebook.

1. old / long / yellow **raincoat**
2. rubber / black / ugly **boots**
3. new / green / tiny **leaves**
4. huge / brick / red **building**
5. clear / plastic / large **bottle**
6. blue / cotton / favorite **t-shirt**

Grammar Skill
When a noun is used to describe another noun, it functions as an adjective and comes directly before the noun it describes. Example: *a big new* **glass** *building.*

Grammar Check
✓ Can you create new sentences using the correct **order of adjectives** with the words in the chart? Example: *I have a beautiful old wool scarf.*

Apply
Work with a partner. Choose items you see in your classroom and list adjectives to describe the items. Then make sentences about the items. Be sure to put the adjectives in the correct order. Example: *David is wearing a cool new black sweatshirt.*

▲ A Native-American clay bowl

Italics, Repetition, and Other Devices Used for Emphasis or Effect

Sometimes writers set words in a special way, especially in a story that has dialogue. For example, they may use italics, repetition, or other ways to create an effect, such as by using all capital letters. Look at the chart below.

Example	Device	Purpose
Coyote said, "We're not going to steal a *big* piece. We'll only take a *llllle* piece."	italics	for emphasis
… they screamed, "Possum! Your tail! Your tail!" and threw water on him. *Whoosh! Whoosh! Whoosh!*	italics	to show what something sounds like
Coyote said, "No, no, no, no, no! I don't think we should be so nice! …"	repetition	for emphasis
"Hi. M-m-m-my name is Possum…."	repetition	to show how someone speaks
"We're OVER HERE!"	capital letters	for emphasis

Grammar Skill
Notice that you might sometimes see a combination of techniques used. Example: "The bird sang *tweet, tweet, tweet*!"

Practice A

Underline the use of italics or repetition for effect.

1. Coyote said, "I think we should sneak over there and just <u>steal</u> a piece."
2. The tiny voice squeaked: "Send *meeeeeee!*"
3. They had fire coming out of their mouths: *Hissssss!*
4. It took Grandma Spider a long, long, long, long time to get there.
5. It bounced up into the sky: *Boingggg!*

Grammar Check
✓ When you use **italics** or **repetition** for effect, what punctuation mark can you use for an even greater effect?

Practice B

Match the sentence halves to make complete sentences. Write the letter.

1. When he opened the old door, he heard ___*a*___
2. When I won first prize, I exclaimed, _____
3. The firefighter found her when she cried, _____
4. My little brother insisted, _____
5. The bell woke us with its _____

a. *Screeeech!*
b. *Clang! Clang! Clang!*
c. "I won, I won, I won!"
d. "HELP! I'M OVER HERE!"
e. "I'm not a *baby* anymore!"

Apply
Work with a partner. Choose animals or items that make sounds. Then, make sentences about the sounds. Use italics, repetition, and/or capital letters for effect.
Example: *We knew there were bees when we heard: Bzzzz!*

Reading 1 17

> Reading 1
Writing

Describe a Character

At the end of this unit, you will describe a character. To do this, you'll need to learn some of the skills authors use in descriptive writing. To describe a character, writers give details about the character's physical traits, or how the character looks. For example: *Buzzard has long black feathers all over his body.* A writer also gives details about the character's personal traits, or the qualities of a character. For example: *Buzzard thinks he is the most beautiful bird alive.*

> **Writing Prompt**
> Write a paragraph describing a character from a story, movie, or TV show. Give details that describe the character's physical and personal traits. When you use more than one adjective to describe the character, make sure that the adjectives are in the correct order.

1 Prewrite Begin by choosing a character from a story, movie, or TV show.

- Close your eyes and visualize the character. Think of your character's physical traits.
- Complete a chart with examples of the character's physical traits and personal traits.
- Think about how the character's physical or personal traits are important to the story, movie, or TV show.

Here's a word web created by a student named Bruno. He listed his ideas on a word web.

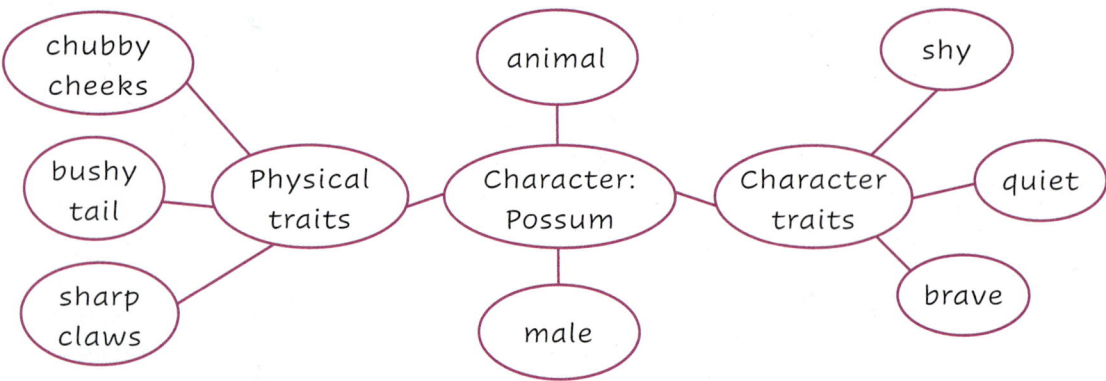

18 Unit 1

② **Draft** Use your word web to help you write a first draft.
- Describe the character's physical traits and personal traits.
- Use adjectives to describe the character.
- Be sure to use the correct order when you use more than one adjective.

③ **Revise** Read over your draft. Look for places where the writing is unclear or needs improvement. Complete (✓) the Writing Checklist to help you identify problems. Then revise your draft, using the editing and proofreading marks listed on page 467.

④ **Edit and Proofread** Copy your revised draft onto a clean sheet of paper. Read it again. Correct any errors in grammar, word usage, spelling, and mechanics.

⑤ **Publish** Prepare a clean copy of your final draft. Share your descriptions with the class. Save your work. You'll need to refer to it in the Writing Workshop at the end of the unit.

> **Writing Checklist**
>
> **Ideas:**
> ☐ I described my character clearly.
>
> **Word Choice:**
> ☐ I used descriptive details, including adjectives, to reveal my character's physical and personal traits.
>
> **Conventions:**
> ☐ When I used more than one adjective, I used the correct order.

Bruno Arbogast

Possum

Possum is a character in "Grandmother Spider Brings the Sun." He is a little round animal with cute chubby cheeks. Though shy and quiet, Possum is brave enough to volunteer to go to the other side of the world to steal a piece of the sun. He plans to use his sharp claws to dig a tunnel and his bushy tail as a hiding place for the piece of sun. He speeds through the long dark tunnel, but as soon as he pops out, the bright light blinds him. But does that stop him? No. Possum manages to get a bit of the sun, but his tail catches fire. His friends put out the fire, and they end up with no sun. But Possum's valiant efforts do pay off because Grandmother Spider is able to use the tunnel he dug to retrieve a piece of the sun.

Reading 2

Prepare to Read

What You Will Learn

Reading
- Vocabulary building: *Context, dictionary skills, word study*
- Reading strategy: *Skim*
- Text type: *Informational text (science)*

Grammar
- Simple present with *when* clauses for facts
- Present passive

Writing
- Describe an object

THE BIG QUESTION

What is light? What do you know about light? Where does it come from? How do you use it every day? What are some of the main sources of light?

In your notebook, make a K-W-L-H chart like the one below. Work in small groups. Complete the first column with information you know about light. Use the questions above as a guide. Then complete the second column with what you want to know about light. As you read the text, you can complete the third column with the new information you are learning. Complete the fourth column by telling how you learned the new information.

K What do I **know**?	W What do I **want** to know?	L What did I **learn**?	H **How** did I learn it?

Build Background

"**Light**" is a science article that tells what light is and how it behaves. Have you ever seen waves moving across the ocean? Different kinds of energy can move through air, water, and even solid materials in the form of waves. In this article you will read about electromagnetic waves. These are the waves that make up light. The article explains how light waves travel and what happens when light waves reflect off objects. It also explains how mirrors work.

Natural and artificial light work with mirrors to illuminate The Hall of Mirrors at the Palace of Versailles in France. ▼

Vocabulary

Listening and Speaking: Key Words

Read these sentences aloud with a partner. Use the context to figure out the meaning of the highlighted words. Use a dictionary, the glossary, or a thesaurus to determine or confirm your answers. Then write each word and its meaning in your notebook.

Key Words
- concave
- convex
- opaque
- translucent
- transparent
- wavelength

1. A concave mirror curves inward and makes an image seem larger.
2. The side mirrors on a car are convex. They curve outward and make other cars reflected in them seem closer and smaller than they really are.
3. We cannot see through walls because they are opaque.
4. A translucent object, such as a sheet of notebook paper, allows some light to pass through it.
5. It is possible to see through a window because the glass is transparent.
6. Because radio waves are longer than X rays, we say they have a longer wavelength.

Practice

Choose a word from the box above to complete each sentence. Then take turns reading the sentences aloud with a partner.

1. A _____ mirror curves outward and makes objects appear smaller.
2. Because a leaf is _____, we can see light coming through it.
3. X rays have a shorter _____ than radio waves.
4. A _____ mirror makes the reflected image appear larger than it is.
5. A brick wall is _____, so light does not pass through it.
6. Clear plastic is an example of a _____ material.

▲ Which of these marbles are opaque? Which are translucent? Are there any transparent ones?

Reading 2

Listening and Speaking: Academic Words

Study the purple words and their meanings. You will find these words useful when talking and writing about informational texts. Write each word and its meaning in your notebook, then say the words aloud with a partner. After you read "Light," try to use these words to respond to the text.

Academic Words
- interpret
- transmit
- virtual
- visible

interpret = explain or decide what something means	→	Your brain will **interpret** different wavelengths of light as different colors.
transmit = pass something through	→	You can **transmit** light through glass.
virtual = able to be seen but not real	→	What you see in a mirror is a **virtual** image.
visible = able to be seen	→	Light waves are the only electromagnetic waves that are **visible**.

Practice

Work with a partner to rewrite the sentences. Use the purple word in each new sentence. Then write the sentences in your notebook.

1. The brain will see the longest wavelengths of visible light as the color red. (interpret)
2. You can pass light through water. (transmit)
3. When you see yourself in the mirror, you are looking at this kind of image. (virtual)
4. These kind of light waves can be seen. (visible)

▲ When transmitted through water, light refracts, or bends. This makes objects in the water look different from how they look in the air.

Word Study: Words with /əl/ spelled -le and -el

Many words end with the /əl/ sound that you hear at the end of the word *pickle*. This sound is often spelled *le* or *el*. Here are some examples.

-le	Definition	-el	Definition
visible		angel	
brittle		camel	
little		bagel	
angle		vessel	
ample		gravel	
nimble		scalpel	

Practice

Work with a partner. Say a word from the chart, and ask your partner to spell it aloud. Then have your partner say the next word. Continue until you can spell all of the words correctly. Then use a dictionary to look up the meaning of each word. Write a definition for each word.

Reading Strategy — Skim

Skimming a text helps you get a general understanding of what the text is about. To skim a text, follow these steps:

- Look at the title and the images and captions. What do they tell you?
- Look at the headings for each section of text. What do the headings tell you?
- Read the first paragraph quickly. Then read the first sentence of the paragraphs that follow.
- Now read all the paragraphs quickly. Don't stop at words you don't know—skip over them.
- After you skim the text, try to summarize what you learned before you go back and read it again more carefully.

As you read "Light," skim the text quickly to see what it's about. Think about the subject and what you already know about it. What do you think you will learn?

Reading 2
Informational Text
Science

Set a purpose for reading What is light and how does it behave?

Light

How Does Light Travel?

Light travels from the sun to Earth in waves. These waves, called **electromagnetic waves**, are a form of energy that can travel through space. We talk about electromagnetic waves in terms of the length of the wave, or wavelength.

The electromagnetic spectrum is the name for the whole range of electromagnetic waves. It is organized by wavelength, from the longest electromagnetic waves to the shortest. The longest waves in the spectrum are radio waves. Then come microwaves, infrared rays, visible light, ultraviolet rays, X rays, and gamma rays. (See Figure 1.)

---

electromagnetic waves, waves that form when an electric field couples with a magnetic field; the waves that make up light

> **Reading Skill**
> To understand the boldface words, read the definitions at the bottom of the text. After you read, write your own sentences with the words in your notebook.

▼ When white light passes through a prism, it separates into colors.

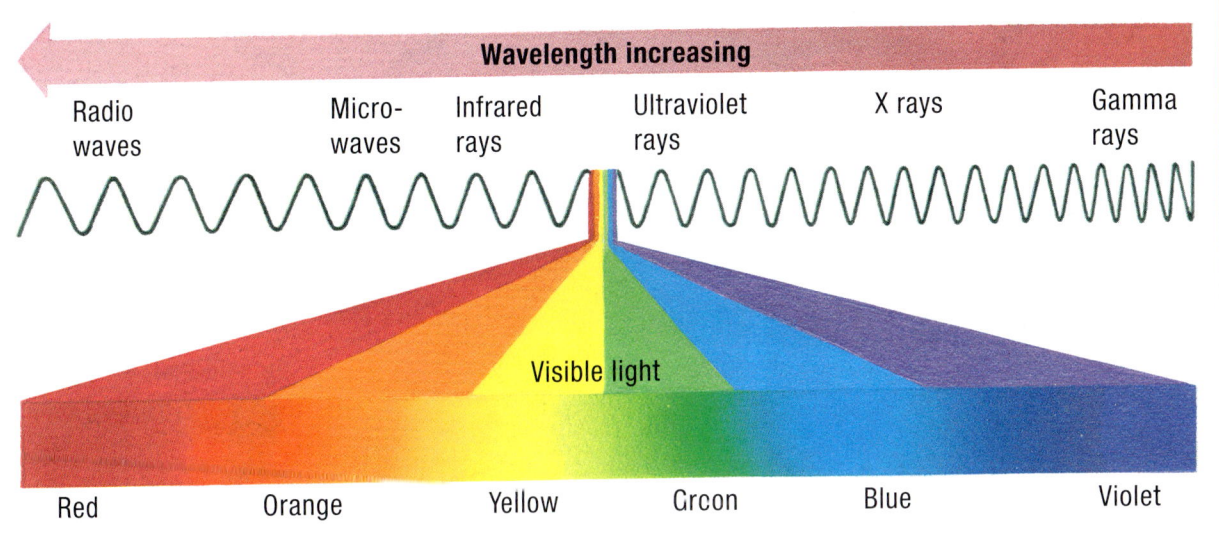

Wavelength increasing

Radio waves | Micro-waves | Infrared rays | Ultraviolet rays | X rays | Gamma rays

Visible light

Red | Orange | Yellow | Green | Blue | Violet

▲ Figure 1. The electromagnetic spectrum

Visible light is the only part of the electromagnetic spectrum that people can see. Visible light is just a small part of the electromagnetic spectrum. It is located between infrared rays and ultraviolet rays. Visible light is a mixture of all the colors we can see in a rainbow: red, orange, yellow, green, blue, and violet. When our eyes take in different wavelengths of light, we see different colors. We see the longest wavelengths of visible light as red. We see the shortest wavelengths as violet.

◀ Visible light is only a small part of the electromagnetic spectrum, but it includes all the colors the eye can see.

What Happens When Light Strikes Objects?

When light strikes an object, the light can be reflected, or bounced off the object. The light might also be absorbed, or taken in by the object. Or the light can be transmitted, or passed through the object.

Objects that you cannot see through, such as wood and metal, are called **opaque**. When light strikes an opaque object, the light is either reflected or absorbed. You cannot see through an opaque object because light cannot pass through it. A glass object is **transparent**. When light strikes it, the light is allowed to pass through. As a result, you can see through the glass object.

Before You Go On

1. Which electromagnetic waves have the longest wavelength? The shortest wavelength?
2. How can you use what you know about light to explain the difference between opaque and transparent objects?

On Your Own

What are some transparent objects you use every day?

Reading 2 **25**

▲ Gold nuggets

▲ A lens with a landscape behind it

▲ A piece of amber with an insect trapped inside

Other objects are **translucent**. When light strikes them, only some light passes through. When you look through a translucent object, you can see something behind it, but you cannot see the details clearly. Look at the pictures above. Which objects are opaque? Which are transparent? Which is translucent?

Reading Skill

Read the caption for each photograph. This will help you understand both the visual and the reading.

What Is Reflection?

All objects reflect some light. This means that light bounces off the objects. However, different objects reflect light in different ways.

Some objects allow you to see a reflection—or image—of something. For example, when you look at a mirror or a pool of water, you can see a reflection of yourself.

Other objects do not do this. For example, when you look at a wool sweater or a painted wall, you see only the object itself. What you see when you look at an object depends on how its surface reflects light.

To show how light travels and reflects, we can use straight lines to represent light rays. When **parallel** rays of light hit a smooth, or even, surface, all the rays are reflected at the same angle. This is called regular reflection. For example, when you look at a mirror, you see your own reflection. The light rays from your body hit the smooth surface of the mirror and are reflected regularly. (See Figure 2 on page 27.)

---

parallel, two lines that stay the same distance apart and never touch

▶ Your image in a mirror is caused by rays of light that reflect regularly from the mirror.

26 Unit 1

When parallel rays of light hit a bumpy, or uneven, surface, each ray is reflected at a different angle. This is called diffuse reflection. Most objects reflect light diffusely because their surfaces are not completely smooth. For example, a wall may look smooth. But if you look carefully, you will see that its surface has many small bumps. These bumps cause the light to scatter, or to be reflected at different angles. (See Figure 3.)

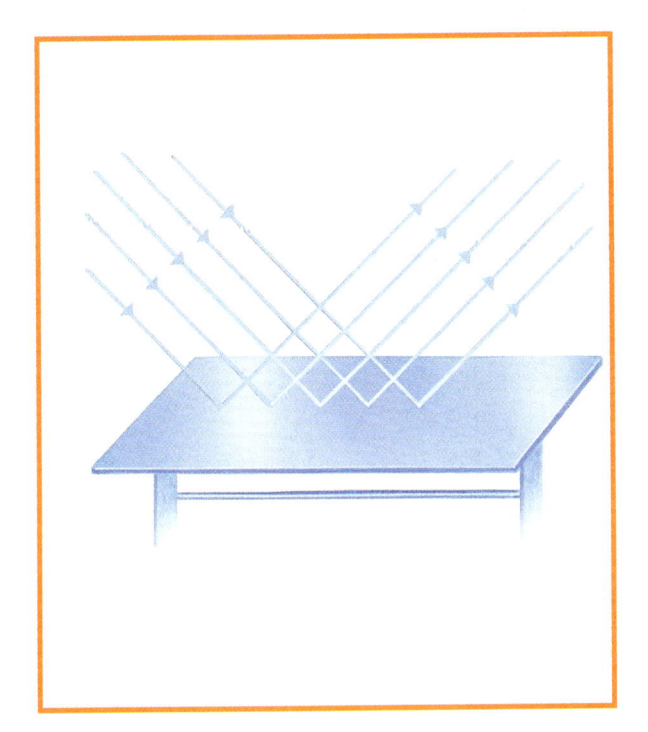

▲ Figure 2. When parallel rays of light strike a smooth surface, the reflection is regular.

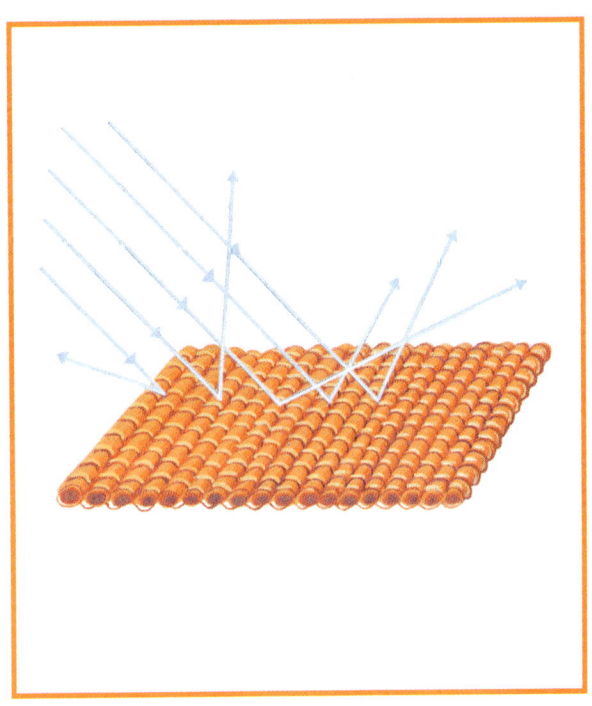

▲ Figure 3. When parallel rays of light strike an uneven surface, the reflection is diffuse.

How Do Mirrors Work?

A mirror is a sheet of glass that has a smooth, silver-colored coating on one side. Glass is transparent, so light passes through it. However, the silver coating behind the glass is opaque. When light rays pass through the glass, they hit the smooth surface of the silver coating and all the rays are reflected regularly. The result is that you see an image in the mirror. An image is a copy of an object and is formed by reflected rays of light.

Mirrors can have a flat or curved shape. The shape of a mirror determines how the image will look. An image in a mirror can be the same size as the object, or it can be larger or smaller—depending on the mirror's shape.

Before You Go On

1. What happens when light strikes the surface of a translucent object?
2. Which occurs more often—diffuse reflection or regular reflection? Why?

On Your Own

Have you ever seen your reflection in things other than mirrors? Explain.

Reading 2

A plane mirror has a flat surface. When you look into a plane mirror, you see an image that is the same size as you are. Your image appears to be the same distance behind the mirror as you are in front of it. The image you see in a plane mirror is called a virtual image. *Virtual* images are right side up, or upright. Virtual means something you can see but does not really exist. You can't reach behind a mirror and touch your image.

Figure 4 shows how a plane mirror forms a virtual image of a dancer. Light rays reflected from the dancer strike the mirror. (The green and orange arrows show light rays from the top and bottom of the dancer.) The mirror reflects the rays toward the dancer's eyes. The brain **assumes** that the reflected rays have reached the eyes in a straight line.

The rays are reflected, but the brain interprets the rays as if they had come from behind the mirror. The dashed lines show the points from which the rays appear to come. Since the dashed lines appear to come from behind the mirror, this is where the dancer's image appears to be located.

---

assumes, thinks that something is true; imagines

Plane mirror

Dancer

Image

▲ Figure 4. A plane mirror forms a virtual image.

28 Unit 1

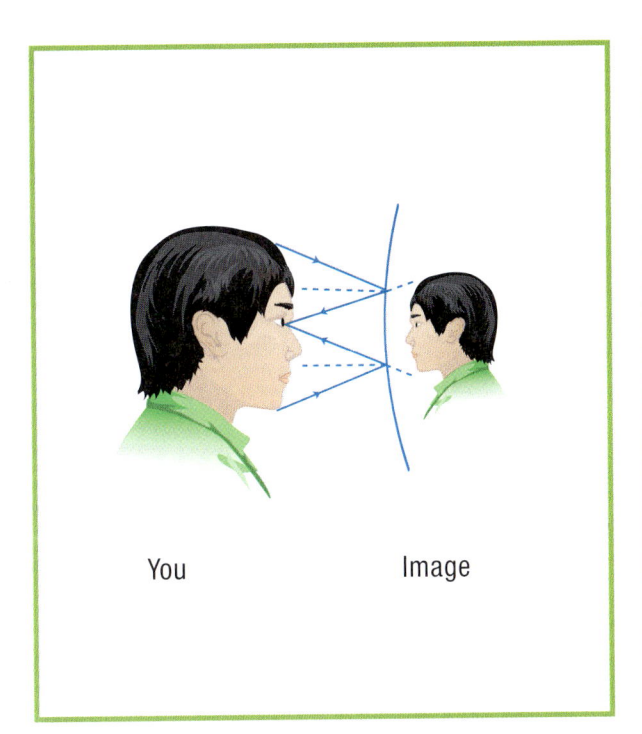

▲ Figure 5. An image reflected in a convex mirror

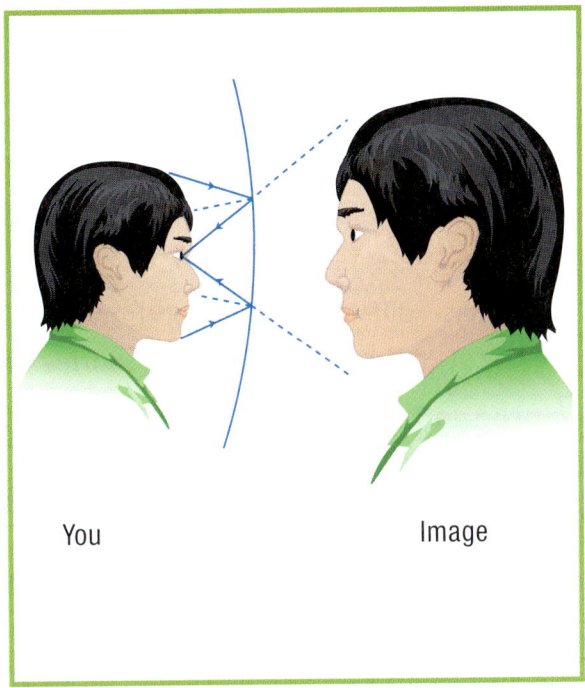

▲ Figure 6. An image reflected in a concave mirror

Curved mirrors behave as though they were many, many little flat mirrors placed side by side, each at a slight angle to the one next to it. Unlike plane mirrors, curved mirrors create reflected images that are not the same size as the object being reflected. The images also appear farther away from or closer to the mirror than the object really is.

A **convex** mirror has a surface that curves outward. When you look into a convex mirror, the image you see is smaller than you are. And it appears closer to the mirror than you really are. (See Figure 5.)

A **concave** mirror has a surface that curves inward. When you look into a concave mirror, the image you see of yourself appears larger than you really are. It also appears farther away from the mirror than you are actually standing. (See Figure 6.)

Concave and convex mirrors are both useful in their own ways. Because concave mirrors enlarge the image, people use them when they are putting on makeup or shaving. Concave mirrors are also used as reflectors in flashlights and headlights. Convex mirrors let you see a large distance and a wide field of view, so they are used as rearview mirrors in cars and buses. They are also used as security mirrors in stores.

Before You Go On

1. What does *virtual* mean? What is a virtual image?
2. Describe the image created by a concave mirror.

On Your Own

Observe your reflection in different types of surfaces: a flat mirror, the back or a spoon, the front of a spoon, a mirrored building. How does your reflection change? Why?

Reading 2

Review and Practice

Comprehension

Recall
1. What are six different kinds of electromagnetic waves?
2. Which color of visible light has the shortest wavelength?

Comprehend
3. When you look at something, what parts of your body interpret the image?
4. Why do convex and concave mirrors have different uses? Name one use for each and tell why it is used rather than the other.

Analyze
5. Would the author of this article agree with this statement: "The image you see in a mirror exists only in your brain." Explain how such an image is virtual and not real.
6. If light did not reflect off objects, would we be able to see anything? Why or why not?

Connect
7. How would life be different if there were no mirrors? Explain.
8. As you go about your day, notice ways in which we use transparent materials. Keep a list and share it with a partner.

In Your Own Words

Imagine you are teaching someone about how light transmits and behaves. Tell this person five important facts that you learned by reading "Light." Write your ideas in your notebook and read them aloud to a partner. Use the images in the reading to help you explain the information. Then listen to your partner's ideas.

Discussion

Discuss with a partner or in a small group.

What will you remember about light after reading this selection? Why?

What is light? After reading the selection, how would you explain what light is? What did you learn that was new about light? Explain.

> **Listening Tip**
>
> As you listen to others, use phrases to show you are listening, such as *I see. / I understand. / That's true.*

Read for Fluency

It is often easier to read a text if you understand the difficult words and phrases. Work with a partner. Choose a paragraph from the reading. Identify the words and phrases you do not know or have trouble pronouncing. Look up the difficult words in a dictionary.

Take turns pronouncing the words and phrases with your partner. If necessary, ask your teacher to model the correct pronunciation. Then take turns reading the paragraph aloud and giving each other feedback.

Extension

The painting *Portrait of Giovanni Arnolfini and His Wife* uses a mirror in an interesting way. Look at the detail of the painting below. You can see the husband and wife's backs, and two other people, reflected in the mirror. Look again at the mirror. Is this a virtual image? Would you say it is flat, concave, or convex? Why? Discuss your ideas and reasons with a partner.

▲ *Portrait of Giovanni Arnolfini and His Wife*, Jan van Eyck, Flemish, 1434

◄ A detail of the mirror in the painting

Reading 2

Grammar

Simple Present with *When* Clauses for Facts

Adverb clauses of time show when something happens and can be used to express facts. An adverb clause of time begins with a time expression, such as *when*. In scientific writing, time clauses with *when* and the simple present express scientific facts.

When an adverb clause begins a sentence, use a comma. When an adverb clause ends the sentence, do not use a comma.

> **Grammar Skill**
>
> Some other adverbial expressions of time are *before, after, since, until, whenever, while.*

Adverb clause at the beginning	Adverb clause at the end
When light strikes an object, the light bounces off.	The light bounces off **when light strikes an object**.
When you look in the mirror, you see your reflection.	You see your reflection **when you look in the mirror**.

Practice A (WB 14)

Match a phrase from the first column with one from the second column to make a sentence. Write the letter.

1. When you look into a mirror, __d__
2. When white light passes through a prism, _____
3. When you look into a concave mirror, _____
4. When our eyes take in different wavelengths of light, _____
5. When light strikes a translucent object, _____

a. only some light passes through.
b. you look bigger than you really are.
c. we see different colors.
d. you see your reflection.
e. it separates into colors.

> **Grammar Check**
>
> ✓ When do you use a comma with *when* clauses?

Practice B

Complete the sentences. Use your own ideas.

1. When you drop a mirror, ____it breaks____.
2. When you turn off the lights, _____.
3. Most students eat lunch when _____.
4. I do my homework when _____.
5. I use a flashlight when _____.

> **Apply**
>
> Work with a partner. Write adverb clauses of time beginning with *when* in your notebook. Then write statements of fact with the adverb clauses of time.
>
> Example: *When it is 9:00, the bell rings.*

Present Passive

Writers use the passive form when the focus is on the receiver, not the performer, of an action. To form the present passive, use the verb *be* + the past participle.

> Each ray **is reflected** at a different angle.
>
> All the rays **are reflected** regularly.

The form of *be* must agree with the subject. Use *is* with singular subjects, such as *each ray*, and *are* with plural subjects, such as *all the rays*.

Form regular past participles by adding *-d* or *-ed* to the base form of the verb. Memorize irregular past participles like the ones below.

Base Form of Verb	Simple Past	Past Participle
show	showed	shown
grow	grew	grown
write	wrote	written

Grammar Skill

When using the passive, use a *by*-phrase to indicate the performer of the action. For example: *For effect, concave mirrors were used by the movie actors.* When the performer of the action is unimportant or unknown, omit the *by*-phrase.

Grammar Check

✓ How is the **passive** formed?

Practice A WB 15

Circle the correct form of *be* to complete each sentence. Then, underline the subject.

1. The electromagnetic spectrum **is** / are organized by wavelength.
2. These waves **is** / **are** called electromagnetic waves.
3. Electromagnetic waves **is** / **are** formed when an electric field couples with a magnetic field.
4. The electromagnetic spectrum **is** / **are** shown in the text.

Practice B

Complete each sentence with the correct present passive form of the verb in parentheses.

1. The homework assignment ____is written____ (write) on the board.
2. Textbooks _____ (provide) for all students.
3. Peaches and pears _____ (grow) on that farm.
4. The mail _____ (deliver) every day except Sunday.

Apply

Work with a partner. Find two images in this unit and create a sentence using the passive in the simple present for each. Share your ideas with the class.

Reading 2

Reading 2

Writing

Describe an Object

You will write a description of an object. To do this, you will need to use sensory details, or words that describe how something looks, sounds, feels, smells, or tastes. To describe a mirror, you might use *flat, smooth, silver,* and *shiny*. The words *flat* and *smooth* appeal to the sense of touch. The words *silver* and *shiny* appeal to the sense of sight.

> **Writing Prompt**
>
> Write a paragraph describing an object. Choose an object that you can describe by appealing to at least two senses. You can choose a man-made object, such as a blanket or a work of art. Or you can choose a natural object, such as a tree or a flower. List your ideas in a Sensory Details chart like the one below. Be sure to use the simple present with *when* clauses correctly.

1 Prewrite Begin by thinking of an object to describe.

WB 16

- Close your eyes and visualize the object. Think about how it looks, sounds, feels, smells, or tastes.
- Think about what details you want to focus on.
- Complete a chart with sensory details about the object.

Here's a two-column Sensory Details chart created by a student named Min Jun.

\	Kaleidoscope: Sensory Details
Sight	colored glass translucent material at end small eyehole shapes and colors in a pattern symmetrical image
Sound	soft swishing sounds as bits of glass move
Touch	smooth tube
Smell	none
Taste	none

Unit 1

② **Draft** Use your chart to help you write a first draft.
- Add the sensory details from your chart. Put them in an order that makes sense.
- Make sure you use the simple present with *when* clauses to relate facts.

③ **Revise** Read over your draft. Look for places where the writing is unclear or needs improvement. Complete (✓) the Writing Checklist to help you identify problems. Then revise your draft, using the editing and proofreading marks listed on page 467.

④ **Edit and Proofread** Copy your revised draft onto a clean sheet of paper. Read it again. Correct any errors in grammar, word usage, spelling, and mechanics.

⑤ **Publish** Prepare your final draft. Share your description with your teacher and classmates.

> **Writing Checklist**
>
> **Word Choice:**
> ☐ I used details that appeal to the senses.
>
> **Conventions:**
> ☐ I used *when* clauses with the simple present correctly.

Min Jun Synn

A Kaleidoscope

A kaleidoscope is a smooth tube containing pieces of colored glass. One end is covered with a translucent material. The other end has a small eyehole. When you look into the kaleidoscope, you see shapes and colors arranged in a pattern that radiates out from a center point. When you turn the kaleidoscope, the bits of colored glass shift randomly, changing the pattern. You can hear them make soft swishing sounds as they move. Even though the pattern keeps changing, the image stays symmetrical. What creates the symmetry? The mirrors inside the kaleidoscope do. Light passes through the translucent material and the colored glass, and then it reflects off the mirrors in a symmetrical way. With each turn of the kaleidoscope, another fascinating pattern is created.

Reading 3

Prepare to Read

What You Will Learn

Reading
- Vocabulary building: *Literary terms, word study*
- Reading strategy: *Visualize*
- Text type: *Literature (short story)*

Grammar
- Prepositions of time and place: *by, in, at, from, to, on*
- Prepositions combined with verbs

Writing
- Describe a place

THE BIG QUESTION

What is light? Discuss with a partner: How are we affected by light? Is light more than just a source of energy that allows us to see? Explain.

Build Background

The next reading is a short story called **"A Game of Light and Shade."** The narrator, the person who tells the story, is a curious man who finds out that things are not always as they appear.

▼ Piazza del Campo in Siena, Italy

Vocabulary 🎧

Learn Literary Words

Literary Words
- imagery
- setting
- figurative language

Imagery is descriptive language that appeals to the senses. Writers create imagery by using sensory details, helping the reader see, hear, touch, smell, or taste what is being described. Here is part of a poem called "Velvet Shoes" by Elinor Wylie. Which of your senses does the language appeal to?

> Let us walk in the white snow
>   In a soundless space;
> With footsteps quiet and slow,
>   At a tranquil pace,
>   Under veils of white lace.

The words *white snow* and *veils of white lace* appeal to your senses of sight and touch. The words *soundless space* and *footsteps quiet and slow* appeal to your sense of hearing. The poet's use of imagery helps us feel the peacefulness, hear the quietness, and see the beauty of the scene.

The **setting** is the time and place of the action in a literary work. The time might be the year, the season, the day, or the hour. The place might be a city, a forest, a garden, or a kitchen. In "A Game of Light and Shade," the setting is a tower in Siena, Italy, on a sunny winter day.

Writers also engage their readers through **figurative language**—a writer's unique way of creatively using language to give the reader an idea or a feeling. A writer who wants to describe the snowy scene in the photo can engage the reader with figurative language by using this simile: "The trees looked like they had suddenly grown into old men overnight, with shocks of bright white hair on their heads." What is being compared?

Practice 📖 WB 17

Work with a partner to describe your classroom. What do you see as you look around? What sounds do you hear? Does it smell like chalk or sharpened pencils? List sensory details in your notebook. Then use the details to write your description in a paragraph. Share your work with the class.

▲ Every writer will have a unique way of describing this wintry setting and the feelings created by the snowy scene.

Reading 3

Reading 3

Listening and Speaking: Academic Words

Study the **purple** words and their meanings. You will find these words useful when talking and writing about literature. Write each word and its meaning in your notebook, then say the words aloud with a partner. After you read "A Game of Light and Shade," try to use these words to respond to the text.

Academic Words
- approached
- despite
- equivalent
- visual

approached = moved closer to	I **approached** the scared cat carefully, so it wouldn't run away.
despite = in spite of; regardless of	It is possible to enjoy the sunshine **despite** the cold weather.
equivalent = something that has the same value or importance	How many Euros is the **equivalent** of five U.S. dollars?
visual = relating to seeing or sight	Enjoying a beautiful view is an example of a **visual** experience.

Practice

Work with a partner to rewrite the sentences. Use the **purple** word in each new sentence. Write the sentences in your notebook.

1. I went over to the police officer to ask him a question. (**approached**)
2. I enjoyed the party even though I knew only one person there. (**despite**)
3. Ten Euros does not have the same value as ten U.S. dollars. (**equivalent**)
4. Looking at photos is an activity relating to sight. (**visual**)

▼ A hiker carefully approaches a dark cave—who knows what's inside?

Word Study: Antonyms

Antonyms are words that have opposite or nearly opposite meanings. Word pairs such as *up/down, sunny/shady,* and *light/dark* are examples of antonyms. As you read, you can use antonyms as context clues to help you figure out the meaning of unfamiliar words.

> I was fully expecting my day to be **dull**; instead, to my delight, it turned out to be **fascinating**.

Suppose you knew the word *dull* but not *fascinating*. The word *instead* tells you that what follows is in opposition, so *fascinating* means nearly the opposite of *dull*. Other words that signal opposition include *but, yet, however, in contrast,* and *on the other hand*.

Practice

Work with a partner. Write the words *inside, empty, heavy, narrow,* and *strong* in your notebook. Write an antonym for each word. Use a dictionary, if necessary. Then write a sentence for each pair of antonyms. Include a signal word or phrase in each sentence.

Light and *dark* are antonyms.

Reading Strategy: Visualize

Visualizing helps you understand an author's description. When you visualize, you make pictures in your mind of what you are reading. To visualize, follow these steps:

- Pay special attention to descriptive words and figurative language.
- Stop from time to time to picture in your mind the characters, places, and events described in the text.
- Think about how the author helped you create mental pictures.

As you read "A Game of Light and Shade," notice the words the author uses to describe the characters, setting, and events. How does visualizing help you understand the story?

Reading 3

Reading 3

Literature
Short Story

Set a purpose for reading Most of the time we perceive light by using our sense of sight. Can we perceive light using other senses?

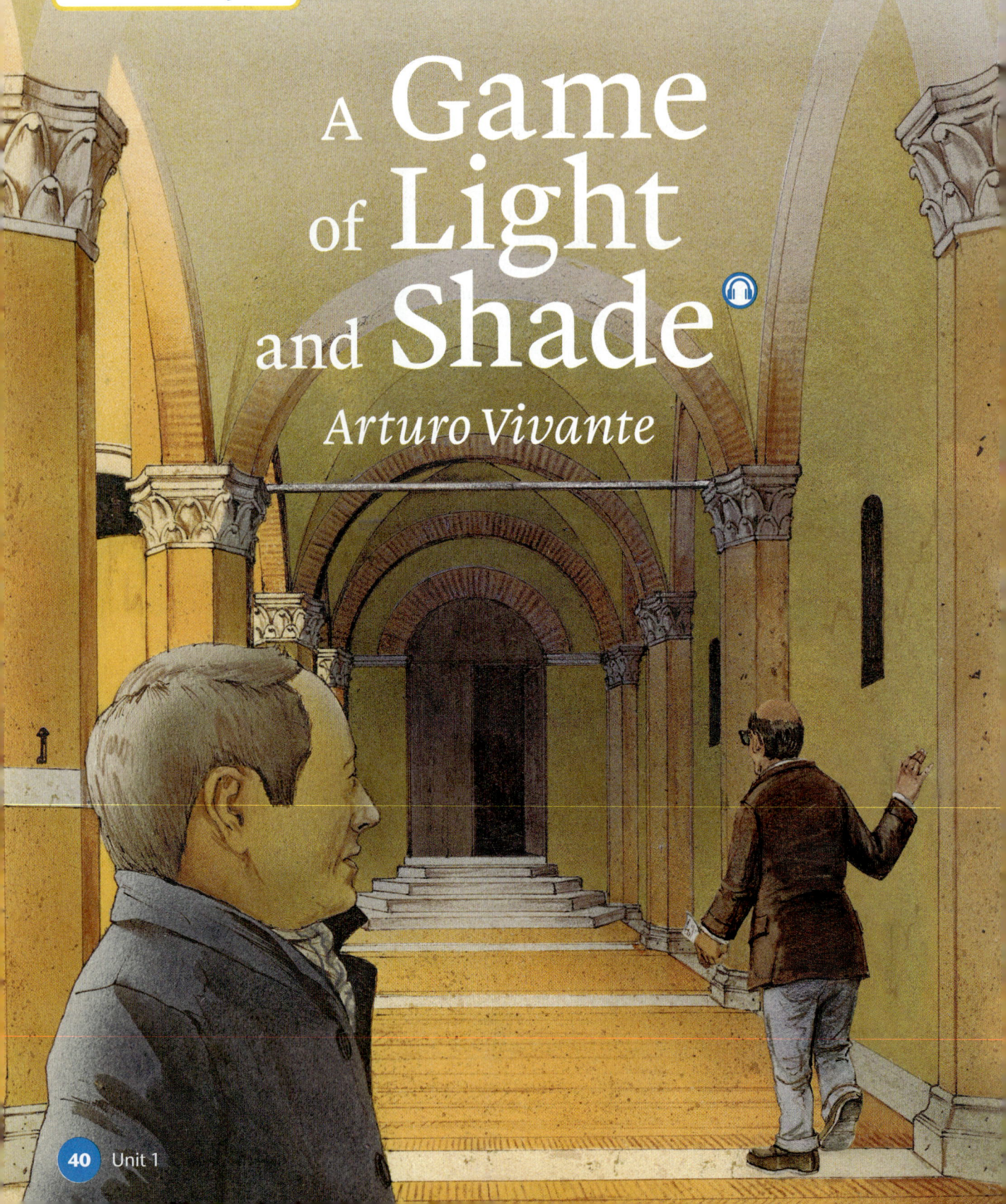

A Game of Light and Shade

Arturo Vivante

It was a sunny winter day. I had gone up and down the tower, and felt pleased with myself for having taken this initiative, when, outside the little door at the foot, a blind man came toward me. He was a pale, thin man, with sparse black hair and dark glasses that gave him an **impenetrable** look. He kept close to the inner wall of the courtyard, grazing it with his arm. On reaching the door, he touched the **jamb** and sharply turned inside. In a moment, he disappeared up the staircase. I stood still, looking at the empty space left by the open door, and at the little plaque that said "To the Tower" nailed to the wall. I felt **compelled** to follow.

I didn't follow closely. I caught up with him in the ticket office. There I was surprised to see the attendant selling him a ticket as though he were any other visitor. The man **fumbled** for it, sweeping a little space of desk with his hand until he had it, but the attendant didn't seem to take any notice. Then, with the ticket in one hand and touching the wall with the fingers of the other, he reached the staircase leading to the terrace.

I stood by the desk, watching him until he was out of earshot. "That man is blind," I said to the attendant, and expected him to show some concern, but he just looked at me with his sleepy eyes. He was a heavy man who seemed all one piece with his chair and desk. "He's blind," I repeated.

He looked at me vacantly.

"What would a blind man want to climb up the tower for?" I asked.

He didn't answer.

"Not the view certainly," I said. "Perhaps he wants to jump."

His mouth opened a little. Should he do something? The weight of things was against him. He didn't stir. "Well, let's hope not," he said, and looked down at the crossword puzzle he had begun.

The blind man was now out of sight. I turned toward the staircase.

"The ticket," the attendant said, rising from his chair. It seemed the only thing that could move him.

I handed him a fifty-**lira** piece, and he detached a ticket from his book. Then I hurried up the staircase.

The man hadn't gone as far as I imagined. Much less time had passed than I thought. A third of the way up the tower, I heard his step. I slowed down and followed him at a little distance. He went up slowly, and stopped from time to time. When he got to the terrace, I was a dozen steps behind. But as I reached it, he wasn't to be seen. I dashed to the first corner of the bell tower, around the next, and saw him.

---

impenetrable, difficult to understand
jamb, the side of a door or window
compelled, forced
fumbled, felt around for something in an awkward way
lira, the form of money used in Italy before the euro

✓ LITERARY CHECK
How does the author establish the **setting** in the first two sentences?

Word Skill
If you don't know a word, use the context of the sentence to understand the meaning.

✓ LITERARY CHECK
What **imagery** in this paragraph helps you visualize the attendant? Support your responses with evidence from the text.

Before You Go On
1. What does the narrator notice about the man who comes toward him?
2. What is the narrator afraid that the blind man will do?

On Your Own
From the title and what's happening so far, what is the mood of the story? What do you think is going to happen next?

Reading 3   41

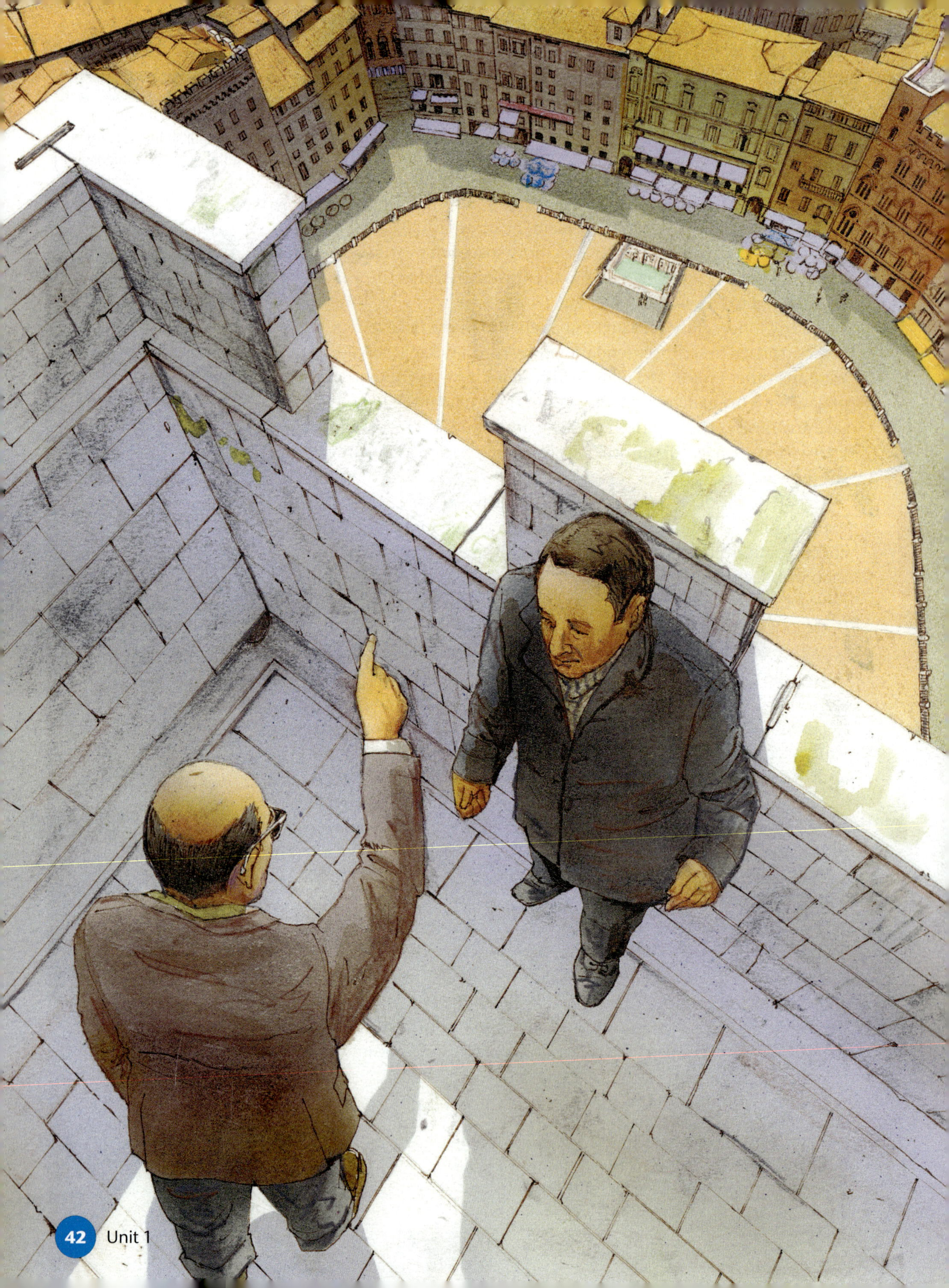

At last, after ten minutes, I approached him. "Excuse me," I said with the greatest courtesy I could summon, "but I am very curious to know why you came up."

"You'd never guess," he said.

"Not the view, I take it, or the fresh air on this winter day."

"No," he said, and he assumed the amused expression of one who poses a puzzle.

"Tell me," I said.

He smiled. "Perhaps, coming up the stairs, you will have noticed—and yet, not being blind, perhaps you won't—how not just light but sun pours into the tower through the narrow, slitlike windows here and there, so that one can feel the change—the cool staircase suddenly becomes quite warm, even in winter—and how up here behind the **merlons** there is shade, but as soon as one goes opposite a **crenel** one finds the sun. In all of Siena there is no place so good as this for feeling the contrast between light and shade. It isn't the first time that I've come up."

He stepped into the shade. "I am in the shade," he said. "There is a merlon there." He moved into the sunlight. "Now I am opposite a crenel," he said. We went down the bell tower. "An arch is there," he said.

"You never miss. And the sun isn't even very strong," I said.

"Strong enough," he said, and added, "Now I'm behind a bell."

Coming back down onto the terrace, he went around it. "Light, shade, light, shade," he said, and seemed as pleased as a child who, in a game of hopscotch, jumps from square to square.

We went down the tower together. "A window there," he said, up near the top. "Another window," he said, when we were halfway down.

I left him, gladdened as one can only be by the sunlight.

---

merlons, solid parts of a fortress wall
crenel, cut-out part of a fortress wall

✓ LITERARY CHECK

How does the writer use **figurative language** to describe the blind man's excitement? What comparison does the writer use?

Before You Go On

1. Why does the blind man say the narrator would never guess his reason for going up the tower? Explain.

2. Do you think the narrator respects the blind man? Why or why not?

On Your Own

What do you think the narrator learns from the blind man? Explain.

About the Author

Arturo Vivante was born in Italy in 1923. He earned his medical degree and practiced medicine in Rome for a number of years before he moved to the United States. For over fifty years Vivante was a full-time writer of fiction, especially short stories, over 70 of which were published in *The New Yorker* magazine. "A Game of Light and Shade" comes from his book *Run to the Waterfall*.

Reading 3

Review and Practice

Reader's Theater 🎧

Act out this scene between the attendant and the blind man.

Attendant: [*looks up from crossword*] Say, do you know a six-letter word for an opening between two merlons?

Blind man: I do! That word is *crenel*, *c-r-e-n-e-l*. There are some on top of this very tower, if you'd like to see them.

Attendant: Uh, no, thanks. I'll take your word for it.

Blind man: Do go up on a sunny day. There's no better spot for enjoying the contrast between light and shade.

Attendant: I'm not sure I understand. Aren't you going up to the tower to enjoy the view?

Blind man: [*smiles*] I cannot enjoy the view the way you do since I am blind. But I can *feel* things. The sun shines through the crenels, so that I feel its warmth when I'm opposite one. When I step behind a merlon, I feel the cool shade. Light, shade. Light, shade. You see?

Attendant: [*smiles faintly*] Yeah, I think I do see.

> **Speaking Tip**
>
> As you act out this scene, pay attention to commas (,). Pause after a comma.

Comprehension 📘 21

Recall

1. Before he approached the blind man, what did the narrator do at the tower?
2. How does the narrator say he feels at the beginning of the story?

Comprehend

3. Why does the blind man climb the tower?
4. How does the blind man enjoy the contrast between light and shade despite his blindness?

Analyze

5. Why do you think the author uses the word *game* in the title?
6. How is the narrator affected by his talk with the blind man?

Connect

7. Have you ever visited a place where you could experience sensations caused by light and shadows? Describe the place.
8. Would you enjoy speaking with the blind man about his experiences at the tower? Explain.

> **Reading Skill**
>
> Information questions begin with *wh-* words such as *what*, *why*, *where*, *when*, and *how*. These questions ask for information. Yes/no questions begin with *do/did*, *have/had*, or *is/are* and ask for a *yes* or *no* answer.

Discussion

Discuss with a partner or in a small group.

1. Discuss the meaning of the last line of the story, "I left him, gladdened as one can only be by the sunlight."
2. How do you think the narrator's conversation with the blind man will affect the narrator's experience the next time he climbs the tower? Explain.

What is light? The blind man was able to "see" the light by feeling the warmth of it on his skin. Do you think that blind people can have experiences that are equivalent to, although different from, the visual experiences of sighted people? Explain.

> **Listening Tip**
>
> If you don't understand something a speaker says, you can say, "I don't understand. Can you explain, please?" or "Would you repeat that, please?"

Response to Literature

Think about an experience that you shared with another person. Think about how your experience was different from the other person's experience of the same event. Write a paragraph about the experience from the other person's point of view.

▲ Walls with merlons and crenels

Reading 3

Reading 3

Grammar

Prepositions of Time and Place: *by, in, at, from, to, on*

The prepositions *by, in, at, from, to,* and *on* can be used to indicate place or location. They can also show time. Look at the examples in the chart below.

Preposition	Place	Time
in	in the ticket office	in winter
at	at the tower	at noon
on	on the staircase	on Monday
by	by the open door	by ten o'clock
from/to	from the top to the bottom	from nine o'clock to noon

> **Grammar Skill**
> A preposition is always followed by a noun, a pronoun, or a noun phrase.

Practice A

Circle the correct word to complete each sentence.

1. It's warm even (in) / **at** winter.
2. They met every day **on** / **at** noon.
3. He was standing **by** / **to** the open door.
4. They both climbed the stairs **to** / **from** the top of the tower.
5. The attendant **in** / **to** the ticket office didn't seem concerned.
6. The man went there **on** / **at** Monday.

> **Grammar Check**
> ✓ Which **prepositions** can be used for either time or place?

Practice B

Use your own words to complete each sentence. Use the preposition correctly.

1. It's *at* [place] ___the top of the tower___.
2. It's *in* [time] _____.
3. The party will be over *by* [time] _____.
4. It's the ticket *from* [place] _____.
5. The event is *on* [place] _____.
6. The movie is *at* [time] _____.

> **Apply**
> Work with a partner. Complete each item in Practice B, using the prepositions differently. For example, for 1, write a sentence using time instead of place (*It's at nine o'clock.*)

46 Unit 1

Prepositions Combined with Verbs

Certain prepositions often appear with certain verbs. Certain prepositions also combine with *be* + adjective. Some examples of verb + preposition from the story are:

> He <u>looked</u> **at** me vacantly. (look at)
> The man <u>fumbled (or looked)</u> **for** it. (fumble for, look for)
> What would a blind man want to <u>climb</u> **up** the tower for? (climb up)

These *be* + adjective + preposition combinations are used to tell about the story:

> The blind man <u>was excited</u> **about** his experience at the tower. (be excited about)
> The narrator <u>was afraid</u> **of** his motivation. (be afraid of)
> The narrator <u>was curious</u> **about** the blind man. (be curious about)
> The narrator <u>was aware</u> **of** his blindness. (be aware of)
> It's amazing that light and shade <u>were responsible</u> **for** the man's joy. (be responsible for)

Grammar Skill
It's good to know common phrasal verbs (a verb combined with one or more prepositions) like *look into* (investigate), *look over* (examine), and *look up* (find information) so that you can use them correctly.

Grammar Check
✓ What is one **preposition** that is often **combined with the verb** *be* and an adjective?

Practice A

Circle the correct preposition to complete each sentence.
1. We climbed (down) / at the mountain and hiked home.
2. The sunlight was responsible for / in our good mood.
3. We looked for / down flowers and leaves during the hike.
4. My dad fumbled at / for his keys when we got to the car.
5. I was curious about / on an animal we saw on the hike.
6. On the drive home, I looked at / about the flowers we collected.

Practice B

Complete the sentences. Use a preposition and your own ideas. Underline the preposition.
1. I'm curious <u>about</u> your vacation. Tell me everything!
2. I'm pleased _____
3. I'm excited _____
4. I'm responsible _____
5. I'm aware _____
6. I'm afraid _____

Apply
Work with a partner. Use prepositions combined with verbs and adjectives to talk about the story.

Example: *I **was curious about** why the blind man was at the tower.*

Reading 3

Writing

Describe a Place

You have learned to use sensory details when you write a description. When you describe a place, it is important to use spatial order. Choose a type of spatial order that makes sense for the place you are describing. For example, to describe a tower, you might start with the entrance at ground level, continue with the stairway leading up, and then finish with the lookout at the top. To describe your bedroom, you might start with the doorway and allow your eye to move around the room from left to right, describing all the important things you see.

> **Writing Prompt**
>
> Write a descriptive paragraph about a favorite place. You might choose a nature preserve, a resort, a park, or a room in your home. Use sensory details to help readers experience what the place is like. Then arrange your details, using the type of spatial order that makes sense for your topic. Be sure to use prepositions of place and time correctly.

1 **Prewrite** Begin by thinking of a place you want to describe. WB 24

- Draw a sketch of the place. Include details that show where things are and label them.
- Using your drawing and labels, make notes about where they are in relation to each other.
- Arrange the things in spatial order. How will you lead your reader through the place? Try different orders. Which order makes the most sense?

Here's a flow chart created by a student named Jia. Notice how she used spatial order.

Approaching the beach

↓

Standing at the water's edge

↓

In the water

2 **Draft** Use your flow chart to help you write a first draft.
- Keep in mind your purpose for writing.
- Use sensory details and spatial order.
- Use prepositions of place and time correctly.

3 **Revise** Read over your draft. Look for places where the writing is unclear or needs improvement. Complete (✓) the Writing Checklist to help you identify problems. Then revise your draft, using the editing and proofreading marks listed on page 467.

4 **Edit and Proofread** Copy your revised draft onto a clean sheet of paper. Read it again. Correct any errors in grammar, word usage, spelling, and mechanics.

5 **Publish** Prepare your final draft. Share your descriptive paragraph with your teacher and classmates.

> **Writing Checklist**
>
> **Word Choice:**
> ☐ I used sensory details to describe a place.
>
> **Organization:**
> ☐ I organized my details using spatial order.
>
> **Conventions:**
> ☐ I used prepositions of place and time correctly.

Jia Kace

Sun and Sand

The best place to enjoy the sun on a hot day is at the beach. Even approaching the beach from a busy street or burning your feet on the sand on your way to the water is exhilarating. You can't wait to dip your toes in the cold wetness. As your feet dig into the soft folds of sand, you hear nothing but a seagull flying over you and the rumble of the surf. You run across the wet sand to cool the soles of your feet. Then you watch the sand slowly dry up until the next wave hits. You take a deep breath of salty air. At last, you take a running jump in the water, feeling ecstatic as you plunge under the water's surface. When you pop up, the sun kisses your cheeks and you feel that you want to stay right where you are for as long as you live.

▲ A beach in Fiji

Reading 4

Prepare to Read

What You Will Learn

Reading
- Vocabulary building: *Context, dictionary skills, word study*
- Text type: *Informational text (social studies)*

Grammar
- Restrictive relative clauses
- Nonrestrictive relative clauses

Writing
- Write a procedural document

THE BIG QUESTION

What is light? In this section, you will connect the Big Question to an article about Thomas Edison's inventions, focusing on the light bulb. Before you begin, discuss with a partner:
- What were people's lives like before the invention of electric light?

Build Background

Informational texts, such as newspaper or magazine articles, give facts about a topic. Some texts tell what happened or explain why it happened. Others tell how to do something or make something. For example, the article that you will read, **"Providing Light in the Darkness,"** tells about how Thomas Edison came to invent the light bulb. The article explains how Edison became an inventor and invented many useful things.

▶ Thomas Edison in his laboratory

Vocabulary

Listening and Speaking: Key Words

Read these sentences aloud with a partner. Use the context to figure out the meaning of the highlighted words. Use a dictionary, the glossary, or a thesaurus to determine or confirm your answers. Then write each word and its meaning in your notebook.

Key Words
- device
- equipment
- industry
- investors
- patented
- tenacity

1. A Global Positioning System (GPS) is a **device** that helps you find directions.
2. A camera is a photographer's most important piece of **equipment**.
3. The work of an inventor can lead to an entirely new **industry**.
4. Many new companies rely on **investors** to start their businesses.
5. A **patent** is a document that shows only one person can make or sell something.
6. My brother has a lot of **tenacity**. He studies day and night.

Practice

Choose a word from the box above to complete each sentence. Then take turns reading the sentences aloud with a partner.

1. We have special _____ for camping, such as a gas stove.
2. Many people working in the movie _____ live in Hollywood.
3. Some people wear a _____ that shows them how many steps they take each day.
4. You need a lot of _____ to get a graduate degree.
5. He hopes _____ will provide money for his new project.
6. You should get a _____ for your new invention.

Reading 4

Listening and Speaking: Academic Words

Study the purple words and their meanings. You will find these words useful when talking and writing about an informational text that is also biographical. Write each word and its meaning in your notebook, then say the words aloud with a partner. After you read "Providing Light in the Darkness," try to use these words to respond to the text.

Academic Words
- contribution
- rejected
- injury
- significant

Word	Example
contribution = something a person gives to the world that helps and is positive	Tasha made a valuable **contribution** to our project.
rejected = not chosen	The company **rejected** his application because he didn't have any computer skills.
injury = some damage caused to a body	Because of a knee **injury**, she could no longer play soccer, so she began swimming.
significant = important; meaningful	Marie Curie was a **significant** inventor who discovered radioactivity and won two Nobel Prizes.

Practice
WB 26

Work with a partner to answer these questions. Try to include the purple word in your answer. Write the sentences in your notebook.

1. What **contribution** have you or someone you know made to your community?
2. What are some ways that a person might be **rejected**?
3. What is an **injury** an athlete can have?
4. Describe an object that is **significant** to you or someone you know. Why is this object important?

52 Unit 1

Word Study: Suffixes

A suffix is a letter or group of letters that, when added to the end of a word, forms a new word. Words ending in *e* + a suffix usually follow certain spelling rules.

To add a suffix to a word ending in *e*, note whether the suffix begins with a consonant or vowel. If it begins with a consonant, usually you do not drop the *e*. If the suffix begins with a vowel, usually you do drop the *e*.

taste + -ful = tasteful   improve + -ment = improvement
successful + -ly = successfully

danger + -ous = dangerous   like + able = likable
express + -ion = expression

There are some exceptions, such as *mileage* and *agreeable*.

mile + -age = mileage   agree + -able = agreeable

Practice

Add the suffixes to the words below. Write the new words. Then write a sentence with each word in your notebook.

1. reject + -ion
2. comfort + -able
3. announce + -ment
4. advise + -able
5. power + -ful
6. close + -ly

Reading Strategy: Use Visuals

Using visuals helps you understand a text better. Visuals include art, photos, diagrams, charts, figures, and maps. To use visuals, follow these steps:

- Look at each visual. Ask yourself what it shows and how it will help you understand the text.
- Read the titles, headings, labels, and captions for each visual.
- If you come across a difficult word or idea, check to see whether it is represented in a visual. This will help your comprehension.

Look closely at each visual from "Providing Light in the Darkness." What type of visual is each image? Does the visual have a title, heading, and/or caption? Which part of the text does each visual help you understand? What types of visuals do the first three readings in this unit include?

Reading 4

Reading 4

**Informational Text
Social Studies**

Set a purpose for reading As you read, think about how Edison kept trying and trying even though he failed many times. What were his successes? What were his failures? What was Edison's attitude towards "failure"?

Providing LIGHT in the DARKNESS

You may have said it yourself when you have a great idea—"a light bulb turned on." But have you ever wondered where the expression came from? To trace the origin of the light bulb as a symbol of ingenuity, you'd have to travel back in time to the late 1880s. At that time, people lit their homes at night with only candles, torches, and gas lamps. Using fire to create light could be quite dangerous. For 50 years, scientists and inventors had been trying to create a light bulb that was powered by heat, and not fire.

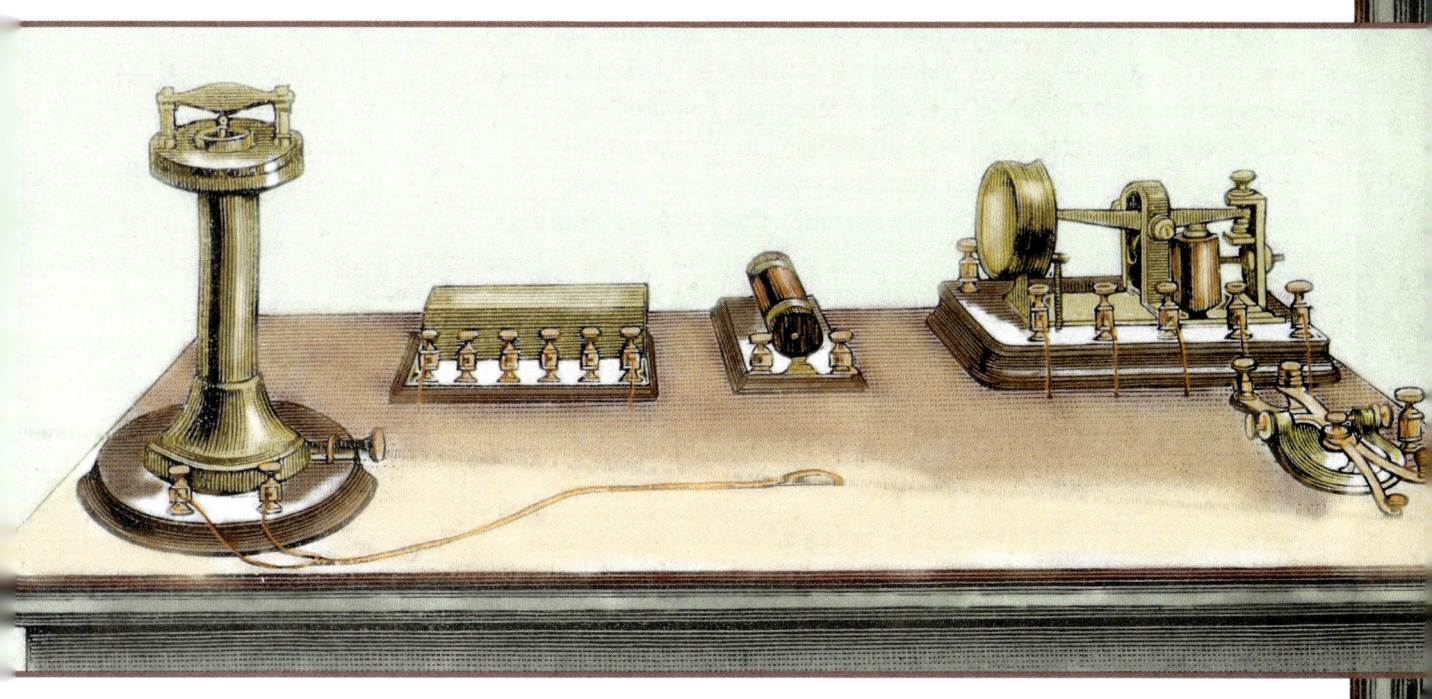

▲ Working as a telegraph operator, Edison improved the technology, creating the phonoplex telegraph seen here.

Enter Thomas Edison, a mostly self-taught inventor and businessman, who devoted himself to finding a safe, inexpensive, and long-lasting incandescent light bulb. While previous inventors had made great strides, it was Edison who expanded on their ideas to make it happen. And it was Edison who developed the first electric network, bringing electric light to the masses.

Always an Inventor

Thomas Alva Edison was born in Milan, Ohio, in 1847. An inquisitive and restless student, he left school after only 12 weeks. At the age of twelve, he became a newspaper boy on a train. He worked on the Grand Trunk Railroad, going back and forth between two cities in Michigan and selling papers to the travelers. By the time he was fifteen, he had gone beyond selling somebody else's newspapers. He was publishing his own, *The Weekly Herald*, right on the train. It was the first newspaper ever printed on a moving train.

Edison took advantage of his access to the railroad and used a baggage car to set up a small laboratory. There, he would experiment with chemicals, a somewhat risky undertaking. In fact, one day, as he was mixing some volatile chemicals, he started a small fire, which spiraled out of control. It spread to the entire car and created a pungent burning smell. The conductor, who had no idea about what Edison was doing in the baggage car, smelled the fire and barged in, hitting Edison on the head in the excitement. While they managed to put out the fire, Edison was banned from making and selling newspapers inside the train cars and had to publish and sell his newspapers outside of the train cars.

Before You Go On

1. What did people use to light their homes before the invention of the light bulb?
2. How old was Edison when he came up with his first patented invention?

On Your Own

How do you think Edison's early life contributed to his becoming an inventor?

Reading 4

At the age of sixteen, Edison became a telegraph operator. This work gave him the chance to travel. He went around the country, taking jobs here and there. He became a very good telegraph operator. He also made improvements to the telegraph equipment that he used.

Edison came up with his first patented invention when he was twenty-one. It was an electrical vote recorder. It was meant for use by members of Congress.

Every member would have a small switch that could be flipped to vote "yes" or "no" on an issue. Edison thought that the device would speed up the voting process. And it probably would have. However, members of Congress did not want to change the way they had always voted, so they never used Edison's switch.

Successful Inventions

Edison's second invention was more successful. He was twenty-three when he invented the stock ticker. At the time, business people learned about stock prices on the New York Stock Exchange from "runners." Runners had to run back and forth from the stock exchange to the business offices, and that took time. In contrast, Edison's device reported the prices of stocks instantly, over wires.

Seven years later, Edison made some important improvements to Alexander Graham Bell's invention, the telephone. His improvements worked so well that people began to install telephones in offices and homes for the first time. It was really the beginning of the telephone industry. Edison also began work on the phonograph. That invention eventually led to the recording industry.

With the phonograph and telephone successfully launched, Edison turned from sound to light. Light became what the great inventor was most famous for.

Edison was thirty-one when he began work on a small electric light for home use. His invention was remarkably clever, but the light bulb was just a small part of what Edison had on his mind. His thinking went far beyond how to light up a single home. He could imagine a future where electricity was distributed throughout an entire city. A central power station would generate the electricity, and a vast network of wires and cables would distribute it to every factory, office, and home that was part of the network. And of course, every factory, office, and home would need small electric light bulbs. People would have light when and where they wanted it.

Edison established the Edison Electric Light Company and found investors who were willing to back him. The truth was, though, he did not even have an electric light bulb yet. Between 1878 and 1880, Edison and his team had come up with 3,000 different theories in their quest to perfect the first incandescent light bulb.

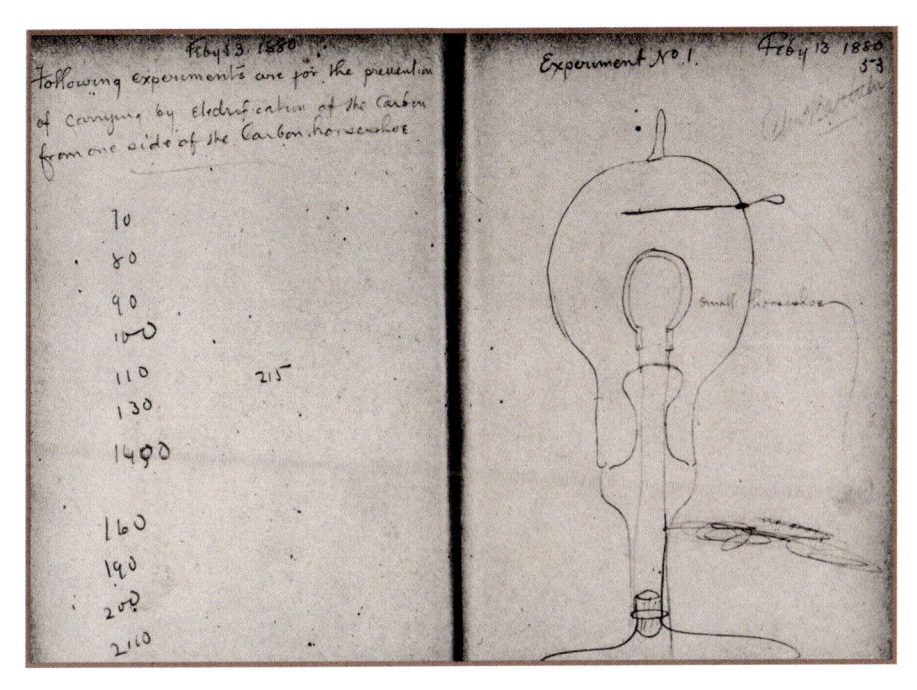

◀ An early sketch of Edison's light bulb

A Promise He Had to Keep

Edison was never shy when it came to telling the world about his accomplishments, and sometimes did so even before he had actually accomplished them. Such was the case when he announced his new electric light to the New York newspapers. The announcement brought him quite a lot of attention. He was famous. Now all he had to do was invent the product! Edison and his staff went to work. They began with the bulb itself. They found that the most difficult part was the "element," the part inside the bulb that lights up when electricity passes through it. It was a real puzzle to find something that would light up without burning up. Eventually, the element would be made of wire. However, in the early days, inventors tried almost everything. After experimenting unsuccessfully with more than 6,000 materials, Edison and his team finally settled on specially treated bamboo.

When the bulb was ready, Edison and his team turned their attention to creating a system that would bring electricity to the bulb. Edison spurred on his team with characteristic **tenacity**. Here's the way Edison described the work:

> *My laboratory was a scene of feverish activity, and we worked incessantly, regardless of day, night, Sunday, or holiday . . . . We accomplished a great deal in a short space of time, and before Christmas of 1879 I had already lighted up my laboratory and office, my house and several other houses . . . and some twenty street lights.*

By the time they had finished, they had done more than simply create a light bulb. As with the telephone and the phonograph, they had created a new industry. Edison's tenacity had paid off.

Before You Go On

1. Why do you think Edison announced his inventions before he had them ready?
2. What was the biggest challenge for Edison's team in creating the light bulb? How was it solved?

On Your Own

What qualities do you think the people on Edison's team had?

▲ Thomas Edison perfected the phonograph after five sleepless days and nights. He is shown here with his phonograph, listening through early headphones.

A Positive Attitude Despite Failures

Even before he developed the light bulb, Edison was a very successful inventor. However, later in life, Edison completed several inventions that were not as well received. In 1895, Edison tried to combine film and sound to make "talking" movies. He created the kinetophone, which allowed people to watch a motion picture through a peephole. The viewer listened to sound played on a phonograph while they watched the film. Edison abandoned the idea in 1915 due to lack of interest. In 1899, Edison formed a concrete company with the idea of building cement cabinets, pianos, and even houses. But concrete was too expensive, and the idea never took off.

Yet Edison had a good attitude toward his failures: "I have not failed 10,000 times—I've successfully found 10,000 ways that will not work."

By the end of his life, Edison had secured an astounding 1,093 patents. Of these, 389 were related to light and power alone.

Edison was an inventor rather than a scientist. He was driven by the need to create things he thought people needed and would buy—and made long lists of them. For example, his desire to perfect the electric light bulb came from his recognition that gas lamps were too expensive and dangerous to illuminate every home. Not all of his inventions succeeded, but his willingness to try and try again changed the world, as we know it.

▲ Thomas Edison did not succeed on his own. In this photo taken about 1880, he stands in front of his Menlo Park, N.J., laboratory, with the engineers and technicians who made his success possible.

Before You Go On

1. Which of Edison's inventions were not very successful?
2. What kinds of things did Edison make lists of?

On Your Own

What do you think is most remarkable about Edison? Explain.

Reading 4

Review and Practice

Comprehension

Recall
1. What are two **devices** related to sound that Edison invented?
2. What was Edison's first major contribution to society?

Comprehend
3. Which of Edison's inventions were rejected by the public?
4. Why was Edison such a success? What did his inventions lead to? Explain.

Analyze
5. What qualities of Edison's made him the successful inventor that he was? Explain.
6. How important an inventor do you think the author thought Edison was? Explain.

Connect
7. What do you think was Edison's greatest success? Explain.
8. From what you read about Edison, what advice would you give about being successful in life? Explain.

In Your Own Words

Imagine you are a newspaper reporter describing one of Edison's inventions. Choose an invention. How would you describe the invention? What interesting details would you share about it? How would it change people's lives? Write your ideas in your notebook and read them aloud to a partner. Then listen to your partner's ideas.

Speaking Skill

Present your ideas clearly; pause for a few seconds between each main point. Ask your partner for feedback. Can he or she understand everything you are saying?

Discussion

Work with a partner or in a small group.
- Which of Edison's inventions do you think was the most significant? Why?
- Do you think that failure is necessary for success? Explain.

What is light? Think back to the discussions you've had about light. How important was Edison's invention in these discussions?

> **Listening Skill**
>
> Listen carefully to your classmates. Identify the important ideas. Retell these ideas in your own words to confirm that you have understood them correctly.

Read for Fluency

When we read aloud to communicate meaning, we group words into phrases, pause or slow down to make important points, and emphasize important words. Pause for a short time when you reach a comma and for a longer time when you reach a period. Pay attention to rising and falling intonation at the end of sentences.

Work with a partner. Choose a paragraph from the reading. Discuss which words seem important for communicating meaning. Practice pronouncing difficult words. Take turns reading the paragraph aloud and giving each other feedback.

Extension

Now that you have read about Edison's inventions, go online to find additional information about inventions related to light. Choose an article about an inventor and his or her inventions. Read the article and summarize it in your notebook. Be sure to include the title and source of the original article.

◀ Inventor and scientist Nikola Tesla in his lab with his *magnifying transmitter high voltage generator*, **which produces bolts of electricity, December 1899**

Reading 4
Grammar

Restrictive Relative Clauses

A relative clause describes a noun and begins with a relative pronoun. Use *who* and *that* to describe people. Use *that* and *which* to describe places and things.

Restrictive clauses tell us which person, place, or thing a noun refers to. A restrictive clause is necessary: an idea would not make sense without it.

> **Grammar Skill**
> If you have to ask what a sentence means, it may need a restrictive clause with necessary information.

Example	Meaning
Edison finally found the few investors **who / that were willing to back him.**	The relative clause refers to *investors*.
The company distributed power to homes, businesses, and factories **which / that were part of the network.**	The relative clause refers to *homes, businesses, and factories.*

Do not use commas before and after a restrictive clause.

Practice A

Circle the correct word to complete each sentence.

1. Ms. Smith is the one teacher (**that**) / which everybody likes.
2. The light bulb is the invention **that** / **who** Edison is most famous for.
3. The manager wants to hire people **who** / **which** have tenacity.
4. This is the chapter **who** / **which** we have to read for homework.
5. The inventions **who** / **which** Edison created have changed the world.

> **Grammar Check**
> ✓ Does the relative pronoun *that* in a **restrictive clause** refer to people, things, or both?

Practice B

Underline the restrictive relative clause in each sentence. Circle the person, place, or thing the relative clause refers to.

1. This is one of the (sketches) that Edison made.
2. Bell was the inventor who created the telephone.
3. Runners were workers that ran between the stock exchange and businesses.
4. The stock ticker appealed especially to people who wanted to learn about stock price changes quickly.
5. In the early 1900s, Mary Anderson invented a device which wiped water from car windshields.

> **Apply**
> Work with a partner. Describe a person or thing using restrictive clauses, but do not tell who or what the person or thing is. Your partner guesses.
>
> Example: A: *She is the classmate who always wears blue jeans.*
> B: *Is it Rosa?*

Nonrestrictive Relative Clauses

A nonrestrictive relative clause gives extra information, but the meaning is clear without it. Look at the examples. They use nonrestrictive relative clauses to combine two shorter sentences with *who* or *which*. Notice that commas are used with nonrestrictive clauses.

Two Shorter Sentences	Combined Sentences with *who* or *which*
Edison brought electric light to the masses. Edison developed the first electric network.	Edison, **who developed the first electric network**, brought electric light to the masses.
He invented the kinetophone. The kinetophone allowed people to watch a film through a peephole.	He invented the kinetophone, **which allowed people to watch a film through a peephole**.

> **Grammar Skill**
>
> Note that the relative pronoun *that* cannot be used with nonrestrictive relative clauses. As with restrictive clauses, use *who* to refer to people and *which* to refer to things.

Practice A

Add commas to the nonrestrictive relative clause in each sentence.

1. The phonograph**,** which Edison invented**,** eventually led to the recording industry.
2. Edison who left school at an early age became very successful.
3. The Edison Electrical Light Company which Edison established created many inventions.
4. The electrical vote recorder which Edison patented when he was twenty-one was meant for use by members of Congress.
5. The members of Congress who did not want to change the way they voted never used the electrical vote recorder.

> **Grammar Check**
>
> ✓ What punctuation do you use with **nonrestrictive relative clauses**?

Practice B

Combine two sentences to make one sentence using nonrestrictive relative clauses. Write the sentences in your notebook.

1. I am reading a book about Edison. Edison is my favorite inventor.

    I am reading a book about Edison, who is my favorite inventor.

2. I like my smartphone. The smartphone is an important device.
3. My uncle is an inventor. My uncle works for the post office.
4. No one has invented a time machine. A time machine would allow people to travel through time.
5. Shunpei Yamazaki has patented over 2,000 inventions. Shunpei Yamazaki is a talented inventor.

> **Apply**
>
> Work with a partner. Write simple sentences in your notebook about people or things. Then add extra information about them using nonrestrictive relative clauses.
>
> Example: *Our teacher is very friendly. Our teacher, who is always smiling, is very friendly.*

Reading 4
Writing

Describe an Experience

So far in this unit, you have described a character, an object, and a place. Now, you will describe an experience. When you describe an experience, you give the reader a general impression about what happened. You may include sensory details. You can organize your ideas using chronological order (the order in which events happened) or order of importance.

> **Writing Prompt**
>
> Write a descriptive paragraph about an important event or experience in your life. Consider these examples: performing for an audience, learning how to do something new, or helping a friend when you weren't in the mood. Include at least one relative clause. Check that you have used the relative clause (or clauses) correctly.

1 Prewrite Begin by thinking of the experience you want to describe.

- Make a list of experiences that you might want to write about.
- Choose an experience and think about the best way to organize the story: chronological order or order of importance?
- Arrange the events in the order you have chosen.

A student named Santos decided to organize his paragraph in chronological order and listed his ideas on a flow chart.

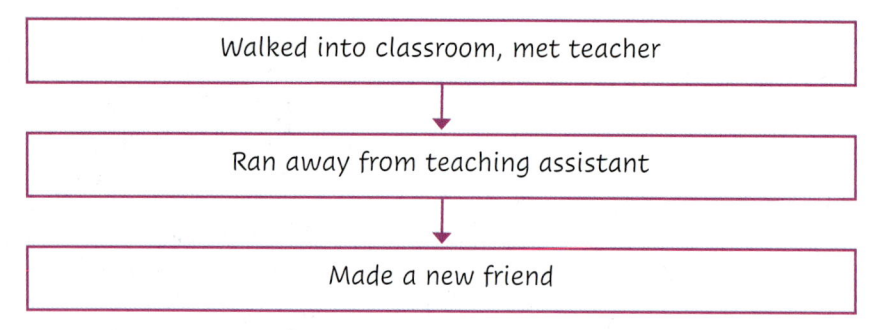

Walked into classroom, met teacher
↓
Ran away from teaching assistant
↓
Made a new friend

Unit 1

② Draft Use your flow chart to help you write a first draft.
- Remember to give a general idea of what happened.
- Use your flow chart to help you organize your ideas.
- Be sure to use restrictive and nonrestrictive clauses correctly.

③ Revise Read over your draft. Look for places where the writing is unclear or needs improvement. Complete (✓) the Writing Checklist to help you identify problems. Then revise your draft, using the editing and proofreading marks listed on page 467.

④ Edit and Proofread Copy your revised draft onto a clean sheet of paper. Read it again. Correct any errors in grammar, word usage, spelling, and mechanics.

⑤ Publish Prepare your final draft. Share your story with your teacher and classmates.

Writing Checklist

Ideas:
☐ I gave the reader a general impression of my experience.

Organization:
☐ I chose an appropriate order to describe my experience.

Conventions:
☐ I used restrictive and/or nonrestrictive clauses correctly.

Santos Rivera III

My First Day of School

My first day of kindergarten was September 9, 2009. I was expecting torture. The day officially began when I walked into what seemed like a giant classroom. I looked around and got a glimpse of my teacher, who looked like an angel. But I knew better. I was terrified. Suddenly, her second-in-command, the assistant teacher, began moving toward me. I ran away without waiting for her to introduce herself. The torture was becoming real. Somehow I made it through a math lesson and story time, until, finally, it was play time. I looked around anxiously, wondering what to do, when a boy named Ralph came over and said hello. We built things out of blocks together and quickly became friends. For the first time that day, I realized that I didn't need to be afraid. I finally saw that school wasn't so bad after all.

Reading 4

Link the Readings

Critical Thinking

What logical connections can you make between the ideas and details in the readings in this unit? Although the readings do not all have the same purpose, they share a common theme and reflect a range of viewpoints. Complete the chart below. Be prepared to support your responses with evidence from each of the texts.

Title of Reading	Purpose	Big Question Link
"Grandmother Spider Brings the Sun"		Only a wise and clever animal could harness light.
"Light"	to inform	
"A Game of Light and Shade"		
"Providing Light in the Darkness"		

Discussion

Work with a partner or in a small group.

- From the readings, what is the most important thing you learned about light? Which reading would you recommend to someone who wants to appreciate light more? Why?

What is light? What different perspectives did the readings give you about light? Which interested you the most? Why? Discuss with a partner.

Fluency Check

Work with a partner. Choose a paragraph from one of the readings. Take turns reading it for one minute. Count the total number of words you read. Practice saying the words you had trouble reading. Take turns reading the paragraph three more times. Did you read more words each time? Record the number of words you read each time.

	1st Reading	2nd Reading	3rd Reading	4th Reading
Number of Words				

Media Literacy & Projects

Work with a partner or in a small group. Choose one of these projects.

1. Write a myth about a natural feature or event, such as a river, a beach, lightning, or a tornado. Explain how this feature or event came about. Tell your myth aloud to the class.

2. Make a short video about light. Film for 10–20 seconds without sound. Then, watch the video and write a description of it in your notebook. Describe what you notice about light. Take turns sharing your videos and asking questions about them.

3. In this unit, you have explored light. Think about sound. Create a word web in your notebook with all of the ideas you can think of related to sound.

4. What's the next big invention? Do some online research on what scientists, engineers, and inventors have been working on in the fields of technology, the environment, or any area that interests you. Take notes in your notebook. Discuss your ideas with your class. Make a class Top 10 list of the most interesting new inventions.

Further Reading

Choose from these reading suggestions. Practice reading silently for longer and longer periods.

The Phantom of the Opera, Gaston LeRoux
This book tells the intriguing tale of something or someone that lurks in the shadows of the Paris Opera House, drawing a young soprano into a world of music and danger.

Light (Experimenting with Science), Antonellia Meiani
The experiments in this book offer hands-on experience with the mysteries of light, including reflection, refraction, and colors.

Thomas Alva Edison: Inventing the Electric Age, Gene Adair
This biography of Edison feels like an adventure—just like Edison's life. The book explores Edison's contributions with text and images.

Echo, Pam Muñoz Ryan
In this historic fairytale, Otto meets three mysterious sisters in a dark forest, beginning a quest. Decades later, three teens continue the quest to help people in their lives.

Put It All Together

Listening & Speaking Workshop

Description Guessing Game

You will give an oral description of a person, thing, place, or experience for your classmates to guess.

① Think About It

Review the readings in this unit, focusing on the descriptions of people, things, places, and experiences. For example, reread the descriptions of the attendant in "A Game of Light and Shade" and of the animal characters in "Grandmother Spider Brings the Sun."

Next, discuss the descriptions in a small group. What made them vivid? Which words helped you visualize what the author was describing? Then work together to develop a list of people, things, places, and experiences you could describe. Write down your ideas. Here are some examples:

- A piece of fruit
- An animal
- A famous person
- An interesting place you have visited
- An experience that you had playing your favorite sport

Choose a topic from your group's list, but don't tell anyone what it is. Your classmates will try to guess your topic after you present your description.

② Gather and Organize Information

Write down the details you could use in your description. It may help you to close your eyes and visualize the person, place, thing, or experience you are going to describe.

Research Go to the library, look at pictures, or use the internet to get ideas or find information. Take notes on what you find.

Order Your Notes Choose a logical way to organize your ideas—for example, spatial order. List your ideas in a graphic organizer.

Use Visuals Make a drawing or find a photograph that illustrates what you are describing. You will show the drawing or photograph to the class after someone guesses it correctly. Do not show it to anyone beforehand.

③ Practice and Present

Use your graphic organizer to begin practicing your presentation. Then practice talking to an audience without any notes. You may want to look in a mirror as you talk or give your presentation for a friend or family member. See if anyone can guess your topic from your description. Keep practicing until you have to look at your notes only occasionally. To make your presentation richer and more interesting, use a variety of grammatical structures, sentence lengths, sentence types, and connecting words.

Deliver Your Presentation Look at your audience as you speak. When you're finished, invite students to guess your topic. After someone guesses correctly, or if no one guesses correctly, show your drawing or photo.

④ Evaluate the Presentation

You will improve your skills as a speaker and as a listener by evaluating each presentation you give and hear. Complete (✓) this checklist to help you judge your presentation and the presentations of your classmates.

- ☐ Did the description include vivid details?
- ☐ Could you visualize what was being described?
- ☐ Did the speaker speak too fast or too slow, talk too loud or too low?
- ☐ Did you enjoy the presentation?
- ☐ Are there ways the speaker could improve the presentation?

Listening Tips

Listen for clues to the speaker's topic. Try to figure out right away if the topic is a person, place, thing, or experience. Then you can get more specific.

Take notes as you listen. Taking notes helps you to listen attentively and think critically. Pay attention to the speaker's tone of voice and gestures.

Strengthen Your Social Language

Describing things clearly helps you communicate your ideas. Go to your Digital Resources and do the activity for this unit. This activity will require you to use and reuse descriptive language in other meaningful writing activities.

Put It All Together

Writing Workshop

Descriptive Essay

In this workshop, you will write a descriptive essay. In a descriptive essay, the writer creates a vivid picture in the reader's mind of a person, place, thing, or experience. A descriptive essay begins with a paragraph that introduces the topic. The writer develops the topic in three or more body paragraphs and ends with a strong concluding paragraph. Descriptive essays contain sensory details that appeal to the five senses. Descriptive essays also include precise, interesting words.

Writing Prompt

Write a five-paragraph descriptive essay about a special person, place, thing, or experience in your life. Use vivid and specific words, including ones that appeal to the senses. When you use more than one adjective to describe a noun, be sure to use the correct order.

① Prewrite Close your eyes and see what images come to mind. Is there an object that you and your family members use and love? Is there an experience you will never forget? Brainstorm a list of possible topics. Choose someone or something that you can describe vividly and enthusiastically.

List and Organize Ideas and Details Use a graphic organizer such as a sensory-details chart or a word web to organize your ideas. A student named Ruth decided to write a descriptive essay about a beautiful summer day at an amusement park. Here is the sensory-details chart she prepared:

Sight	Sound	Taste	Touch	Smell
serene grays shiny yellows blazing pink and blue	bangs pops	sweet cotton candy	warmth	sunscreen popcorn

Unit 1

② Draft

Use the model on pages 72–73 and your graphic organizer to help you write a first draft. Remember to include an introductory paragraph, three body paragraphs, and a concluding paragraph.

③ Revise

Read over your draft. As you do so, complete (✓) the Six Traits of Writing Checklist. Use the questions to help you revise your essay.

Six Traits of Writing Checklist

- ☐ **Ideas:** Do my sensory details create pictures in readers' minds?
- ☐ **Organization:** Are my ideas presented in an order that makes sense?
- ☐ **Voice:** Does my writing convey enthusiasm for my topic?
- ☐ **Word Choice:** Are my words precise and lively enough?
- ☐ **Sentence Fluency:** Do my sentences flow smoothly?
- ☐ **Conventions:** Does my writing follow the rules of grammar, usage, and mechanics?

Put It All Together

Here are the changes Ruth plans to make when she revises her first draft:

Summer Light

On a beautiful day last July, I went with my friends to visit an amusement park near our homes. We wanted to go on some rides and enjoy ourselves in the summer sunshine. our trip turned out to be a wonderful experience.

Everything that afternoon seemed to glow in the suns ^golden^ rays. My eye muscels became tired from squinting in the brightness! Each surface and object reflected a different hue. A man who stood near the ferris wheel held a cluster of blazing pink and blue objects. It took me a while to realize that he was the cotton-candy man. The ferris wheel combined serene grays and shiny yellows. Just looking at the candy, I could feel the airy layers of sweetness ^melt^ in my mouth.

^Nearby,^ A family was picnicking on the green lush grass. I could smell their sunscreen and their turkey sandwiches. The father and little boy had turned their faces up toward the sky They clearly liked the warmth of the sun on their skin.

Revised to add detail and correct spelling.

Revised to improve organization.

Revised to add detail with active verb.

Revised to add detail and put adjectives in correct order.

When the sunlight at last began to fade‸I gathered my friends to start home. Suddenly, I heard bangs and pops and noticed green glitter. I turned around to see ‸multicolored fireworks. The colored light seemed to rain down on the grass and viewers. ⟨I started to reach out to touch the colors, and then I realized that I'd look too foolish!⟩ I was completely at a loss for words.

(inserted: *sprinkling down the face of my friend Sam*)
(inserted: *an eruption of*)

I left the amusement park that night with a new appreciation for the things I take for granted. Thinking about every‿thing I had felt, seen heard, tasted, and smelled gave me a sense of clarity and understanding. Every day I realize all over again that every‿thing in the world is beautiful—you just need the light to be able to see it.

Revised to correct comma error.	
Revised to add detail and vivid description.	
Revised to improve organization.	
Revised to correct error in mechanics.	

④ Edit and Proofread Check your work for errors in grammar, usage, mechanics, and spelling. Then trade essays with a partner and complete (✓) the Peer Review Checklist below to give each other constructive feedback. Edit your final draft in response to feedback from your partner and your teacher.

WB 33

Peer Review Checklist

☐ Does the first paragraph introduce the topic?
☐ Do the three body paragraphs focus on different aspects of the topic?
☐ Are the ideas presented in an order that makes sense?
☐ Does the description include sensory details?
☐ Does the concluding paragraph sum up the main ideas?
☐ Is it clear how the writer changed?
☐ Could changes be made to improve the essay?

Here are the changes Ruth decided to make in her final draft as a result of her peer review:

Put It All Together

Ruth Kace

Summer Light

On a beautiful day last July, I went with my friends to visit an amusement park near our homes. We wanted to go on some rides and enjoy ourselves in the summer sunshine. our trip turned out to be a wonderful experience.

Everything that afternoon seemed to glow in the suns golden rays. My eye muscles became tired from squinting in the brightness! Each surface and object reflected a different hue. The ferris wheel combined serene grays and shiny yellows. A man who stood near the ferris wheel held a cluster of blazing pink and blue objects. It took me a while to realize that he was the cotton-candy man. Just looking at the candy, I could feel the airy layers of sweetness melt in my mouth.

Nearby, a family was picnicking on the lush green grass. I could smell their sunscreen and their turkey sandwiches. The father and little boy had turned their faces up toward the sky They clearly liked the warmth of the sun on their skin.

When the sunlight at last began to fade, I gathered my friends to start home. Suddenly, I heard bangs and pops and noticed green glitter sprinkling down the face of my friend Sam. I turned around to see an eruption of multicolored fireworks. The colored light seemed to rain down on the grass and viewers. I was completely at a loss for words. I started to reach out to touch the colors, and then I realized that I'd look too foolish!

I left the amusement park that night with a new appreciation for the things I take for granted. Thinking about everything I had felt, seen heard, tasted, and smelled gave me a sense of clarity and understanding. Every day I realize all over again that everything in the world is beautiful—you just need the light to be able to see it.

Revised to correct an error in mechanics.

Revised to correct an error in mechanics.

Revised to correct an error in mechanics.

Revised to correct an error in mechanics.

5 **Publish** Obtain feedback from your teacher and classmates; then prepare your final draft. Share your essay with the class.

WB 34

Test Preparation

Unit 1 Practice

Read the passage and the tips. Answer the questions.

Where the Sun Never Sets

Although it is the same sun that shines upon the same Earth throughout the globe and throughout the year, a single person situated at a different point of the globe experiences light and dark, day and night, in extraordinarily different ways. There are places where the daytime and nighttime hours are always the same. There are places where the sun doesn't shine at all for days and places where the sun doesn't set at all for days. This is because of the shape and tilt of the Earth as well as the way in which the Earth orbits the sun on its 365.25 day course.

At the equator, day and night are each exactly twelve hours long. This never changes, regardless of the season. The equatorial region does not experience a change at the summer (June 21) and winter (December 21) solstices like North America does. In the United States, the days are shortened until the winter solstice (the shortest day of the year) and lengthen from then until the summer solstice (the longest day of the year).

In the Arctic Circle, however, something else occurs during the solstices. In Barrow, Alaska, for example, the sun doesn't set for days around the summer solstice. During the winter solstice in Barrow, the sun never rises. Your location on Earth and the time of year can mean an endless summer day or an endless winter night.

1 Based on the information in the passage, what causes Barrow, Alaska, to experience long periods of daylight?

 A Its extreme temperatures
 B Its geographic location
 C Its weather patterns
 D Its relative distance from the equator

2 According to the passage, what is unusual about days and nights at the equator?

 A The hours of sunlight and darkness are always equal.
 B It is the part of Earth farthest away from the sun.
 C Its longer days contribute to its hot climate.
 D The summer and winter solstices occur there.

Taking Tests
You will often take tests to show what you know. Study the tips below to help you improve your test-taking skills.

Tip
Some answers state correct information from the passage, but don't answer the question. Read the question carefully and all the answer choices to make sure you choose the answer that contains the information asked for.

Tip
Determining the main idea of the passage helps to guide you through questions that ask about key facts from the passage.

WB 35–36

Visual Literacy

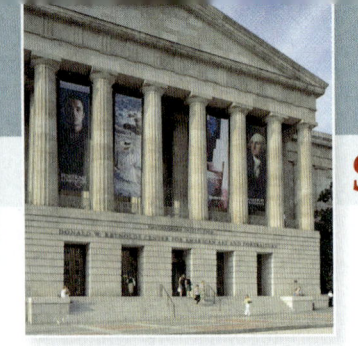

Smithsonian American Art Museum

Capturing the Power of Contrasts

Sometimes life is easier if we can put things in categories: black or white, light or shadow, good or evil. Such clean dividing lines often help us make decisions. Artists often use strong contrasts in their work to create a mood or make a point. They appeal to the viewer's need for simple, bold storylines.

Edward Hopper, *Ryder's House* (1933)

In *Ryder's House*, Edward Hopper painted outdoors and captured a typical New England house in a natural landscape. Hopper chose to paint a particular view of the two-story structure that emphasized the house's massiveness. The sharp horizontal lines of the rectangular building are repeated in the small hills of grass in the foreground and the sky and clouds above. This contrast gives the viewer the feeling that the house stands firmly in the field.

The simple, sun-washed, white building projects a feeling of stability that Americans appreciated in the 1930s, when the country was in a terrible economic depression. Hopper's use of light and shadow in *Ryder's House* creates a dramatic effect where many of us might see none.

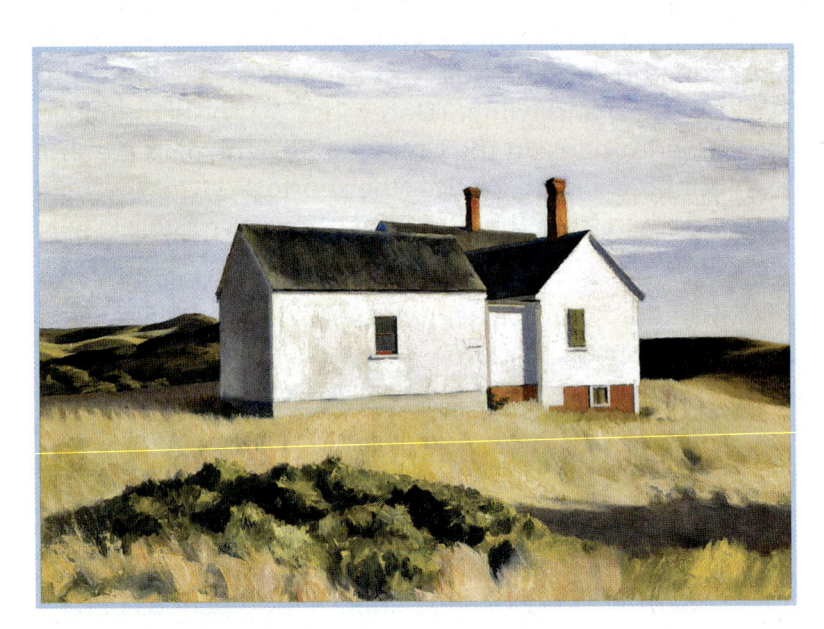

▲ Edward Hopper, *Ryder's House*, 1933, oil, 36⅛ x 50 in., Smithsonian American Art Museum

Arthur Dove, *Sun* (1943)

Solar waves of heat roll toward Earth in Arthur Dove's landscape painting *Sun*. The artist used warm yellow-orange colors to capture the sun's heat and light and darker tones to represent our planet's gravitational pull. The circle of the sun is reflected on Earth's surface in the bottom right of the painting. This further emphasizes the connection between the planet and its source of life-giving light. The broad band of colors and the repetition of tones give this painting a joyful energy, as though we can feel the sunny rays coming down on us. Dove himself spent most of his lifetime outdoors. In many of his paintings, he celebrates his love for the natural world.

▲ Arthur Dove, *Sun*, 1943, wax emulsion, 24 x 32 in., Smithsonian American Art Museum

Robert Sperry, *Plate #753* (1986)

In *Plate #753*, artist Robert Sperry plays with light and shadow on a piece of stoneware. First, he painted it with black glaze. Then he used white liquid clay, called slip, to decorate it with spirals and strong brushstrokes down the center. The end result was a huge, 4-foot plate with different surface textures. Because he used only black and white, which are contrasting colors, the artist captured a rhythmic energy.

Robert Sperry, *Plate #753*, ▶ 1986, stoneware, 4 x 27⅝ in. diam., Smithsonian American Art Museum

Hopper, Dove, and Sperry all understood the power of contrasts: light against dark, sharp lines against soft backgrounds. Their work makes us think more deeply about the energy that radiates from everything, whether it is a house, the sun, or a piece of stoneware.

Discuss What You Learned

1. How do these three artists use light and shadow to create contrasts in their artworks?
2. If you were to create an artwork that showed contrast between light and dark, what would it look like?

BIG QUESTION
Why do you think contrasts between objects often create powerful artworks?

37–38

Unit 1

Unit 2

How are growth and change related?

THE BiG QUESTION

This unit is about ways in which people and things grow and change. You'll find out how seeds grow. You'll read about young people growing up and plants and animals migrating. Reading, writing, and talking about these topics will give you practice using academic language and help you become a better student.

Reading 1
Science/Folktale

- "How Seeds and Plants Grow"
- "A Tale of Two Brothers"

Reading Strategy
Recognize sequence

Reading 2
Short Story

"The Test"

Reading Strategy
Compare and contrast

Reading 3
Science

"Climate Change Puts Nature on the Move"

Reading Strategy
Scan

Listening and Speaking—Skit

At the end of this unit, you and your classmates will create and perform a **skit**.

Writing—Narrative

At the end of this unit, you'll write a **fictional narrative**. This type of writing is a story that you create. To help you write your fictional narrative, you will write a story with a starter, rewrite a familiar story, write a personal letter, and write a personal narrative.

Quick Write

Write *Growing up* in your notebook. Create a word web with words you associate with growing up.

Reading 4
Short Story

"Abuela Invents the Zero"
by Judith Ortiz Cofer

Reading Strategy
Make inferences

View and Respond

Go to your Digital Resources. Watch the video and answer the questions.

Reading 1

Prepare to Read

What You Will Learn

Reading
- Vocabulary building: *Context, dictionary skills, word study*
- Reading strategy: *Recognize sequence*
- Text type: *Informational text (science); Folktale*

Grammar
- Sequence words and phrases
- Using dashes to explain or clarify

Writing
- Write a story with a starter

THE BIG QUESTION

How are growth and change related? What do you know about the life cycle of plants? How do plants change as they grow? Talk with a partner about changes plants go through, such as a seed sprouting, a flower blooming, or leaves changing color.

Build Background

"How Seeds and Plants Grow" is a science article that explains what happens inside a seed when it germinates, or first begins to grow. The folktale **"A Tale of Two Brothers"** is from Korea. It is about two brothers' different experiences planting magic melon seeds. Many folktales involve magic seeds or plants. For example, in "Jack and the Beanstalk," Jack plants a magic seed that grows into a giant beanstalk. In "Cinderella," Cinderella's fairy godmother turns a pumpkin into a golden carriage. What stories do you know about magic plants? List the tales in your notebook and discuss them with a partner.

▲ Melons like the ones these men have grown are important in the story "A Tale of Two Brothers."

Vocabulary

Learn Key Words

Key Words
- develop
- embryo
- germination
- inactive
- protective
- straighten

Read these sentences. Use the context to figure out the meaning of the highlighted words. Use a dictionary, the glossary, or a thesaurus to determine or confirm your answers. Then write each word and its meaning in your notebook.

1. Seeds **develop** into plants only when conditions are right and the seeds have all they need in order to grow.
2. The **embryo** is the part of the seed that becomes the plant.
3. **Germination** is the stage at which the embryo inside a seed first begins to grow.
4. When a seed is **inactive**, it does not grow.
5. The **protective** covering on a seed, called the seed coat, keeps the seed from being harmed or drying out.
6. Plant stems **straighten** as they grow toward the sun.

Practice

WB 39

Choose a word from the box above to complete each sentence. Then take turns reading the sentences aloud with a partner.

1. The stage at which a seed first begins to grow is called _____.
2. The seed was _____ because we had not planted it or watered it.
3. Most trees _____ as they grow.
4. The hard _____ covering of a seed is called the seed coat.
5. The _____ contains all the basic parts of a plant.
6. Not all seeds _____ into plants.

▲ A seed develops into a plant.

Reading 1

Reading 1

Listening and Speaking: Academic Words

Study the purple words and their meanings. You will find these words useful when talking and writing about informational texts. Write each word and its meaning in your notebook, then say the words aloud with a partner. After you read "How Seeds and Plants Grow," try to use these words to respond to the text.

Academic Words
- environment
- function
- potential
- process

environment = the land, water, and air in which plants live	A rain forest is a wet **environment**. A desert is a dry **environment**.
function = the usual purpose of a thing	Each stage in a seed's growth has a **function**. For example, when the seed coat breaks open, the roots grow downward.
potential = the possibility that something will develop in a positive way	The internet has the **potential** to create many more jobs around the world.
process = a series of actions, developments, or changes that happen in a sequence	Germination is a **process** that a seed goes through when it first begins to grow.

Practice

WB 40

Work with a partner to answer these questions. Try to include the purple word in your answer. Write the sentences in your notebook.

1. What kind of **environment** does a cactus live in?
2. What do you think is the **function** of the embryo?
3. What does a plant seed that is properly cared for have the **potential** to become?
4. In what way is writing a **process**?

▲ A cactus in bloom

82 Unit 2

Word Study: Related Words

Related words are words in the same word family. They share the same base word and have related meanings. Look at similarities and differences among the related words below.

> **protect** (verb) to prevent someone or something from being harmed
> **protection** (noun) the act of protecting or the state of being protected
> **protective** (adjective) used or intended for protection

Once you know the meaning of a base word, you can make a guess about the meanings of other words in that family. Try to memorize the meanings of as many suffixes as possible. This will help when you are trying to understand the meanings of related words.

Practice 🔖 41

Work with a partner. Copy the words in the box below into your notebook. Write the part of speech and the meaning of each word. Then check your work in a dictionary

action	correction	production
active	corrective	productive

Reading Strategy | Recognize Sequence

Recognizing sequence will help you understand the order of events in a text. To recognize sequence, follow these steps as you read:

- Look for words that show sequence, such as *first, then, next, finally, last, while, during,* and *after.*
- Look for time expressions, such as *every morning, yesterday, in the spring, next February,* and *on Jan 10, 2010.*
- You may wish to track the events in a sequence-of-events chart.

As you read "How Seeds and Plants Grow" and "A Tale of Two Brothers," notice the sequence in which things happen.

🔖 42

Reading 1   83

Reading 1
Informational Text
Science

Set a purpose for reading Think about how plants change as they grow. What happens inside a seed as it first begins to grow?

How Seeds and Plants Grow 🎧

Parts of a Seed

Most plants produce new plants from seeds. A seed is like a tiny package. It contains the beginning of a very young plant inside a protective covering.

A seed has three important parts—an embryo, stored food, and a seed coat. The embryo contains the basic parts from which a young plant will develop—roots, stems, and leaves. Stored food keeps the young plant alive until it can make its own food through **photosynthesis**. Seeds contain one or two seed leaves, called cotyledons. In some plants, food is stored in the cotyledons.

The outer protective covering of a seed is called the seed coat. The seed coat is like a plastic wrap; it protects the embryo and stored food from drying out. This protection is necessary because a seed may be inactive—may not begin to grow—for weeks, months, or even years.

Then, when conditions are right, the embryo inside a seed suddenly becomes active and begins to grow. The time when the embryo first begins to grow is called germination.

▲ A young bean plant

▲ Bean seed (Outside / Inside — Epicotyl, Seed coat, Hypocotyl, Redicle, Hilum, Cotyledon, Endosperm, First true leaves)

---

photosynthesis, process by which a plant makes food in its leaves

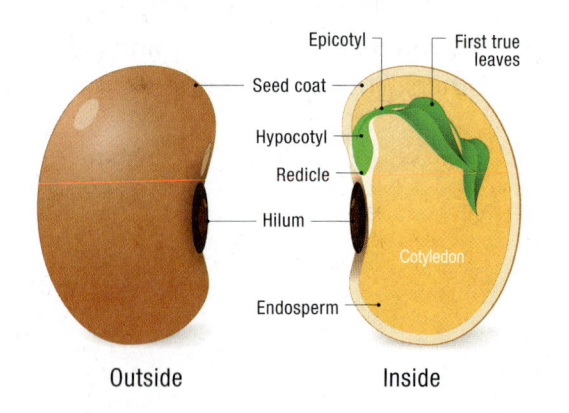

84 Unit 2

Germination

During germination, the seed absorbs water from the environment. Then the embryo uses its stored food to begin to grow. The seed coat breaks open, and the embryo's roots grow downward. Then its stem and leaves grow upward. As the stem grows longer, it breaks out of the ground. Once it is above the ground, the stem **straightens** up toward the sunlight, and the first leaves appear on the stem. When the young plant produces its first leaves, it can begin to make its own food by photosynthesis.

Reading Skill

To help you understand the reading, study the titles and headings. This will help you identify the most important ideas.

Germination of a Runner Bean

1.
2.
3.
4.

Before You Go On

1. What are three important parts of a seed?
2. What is the first thing that happens during germination?

On Your Own

Why do you think knowing about how seeds and plants grow could help people grow healthier plants?

Reading 1

Literature
Folktale

Set a purpose for reading Read this folktale about two brothers who each plant a magic seed. Why do they get such different results?

A Tale of Two Brothers
A Korean folktale

Long ago, there were two brothers named Heungbu and Nolbu, who lived with their father on a rice farm in Korea. When their father grew old and sick, Heungbu, who was the younger brother, said, "Brother, we must take care of our father." Every day, Heungbu brought his father food and tea and medicine, but Nolbu, the older brother, was too busy going out to parties and seeing friends.

After their father died, Heungbu said, "Papa said we should work together on the farm and share the **profits**."

"Surely you misunderstood!" said Nolbu. "The farm is all mine, for I am the elder brother, but do not worry, I will give you a plot of your own."

Nolbu gave Heungbu a tiny, shaded plot of land where rice would not grow, and Heungbu became very poor. Nolbu, on the other hand, enjoyed a good **harvest** each year and lived a comfortable life.

One winter day when Heungbu was in his yard, he noticed a swallow hobbling around on a broken leg, so he brought the bird indoors and wrapped its broken leg to help it heal.

Reading Skill

Take turns reading aloud with a partner. As you listen, use the visuals to help clarify words or ideas. Discuss these words or ideas with your partner to gain understanding.

---

profits, money that you gain by selling something or doing business
harvest, the time when crops are gathered from the field

86 Unit 2

When spring came, the swallow returned and dropped a seed at Heungbu's feet. Heungbu understood that the seed was a thank-you gift and planted it. Soon, a flower-filled vine sprung up, and within a week, the flowers turned into huge melons. As Heungbu cut one open, he could almost taste the juicy sweet fruit but, to his surprise, the inside of the melon had no fruit at all. Instead, it was filled with gold and **gemstones**. He cut open the other melons and found riches in every one. He had become a wealthy man!

Soon, Nolbu heard about his brother's great wealth, and he demanded to know how it happened. After hearing the story, Nolbu went out into his yard, caught a swallow, and broke its leg, ignoring the bird's cries of pain. Nolbu then wrapped the bird's leg in cloth the way his brother had done.

The swallow came back a few days later and dropped a seed at Nolbu's feet. "Finally, I will be rich!" Nolbu thought.

Nolbu planted the seed and, very soon, had his own vine of melons, but when he cut into one, muddy water came rushing out of it, destroying his rice farm and his home.

---

gemstones, valuable stones that have been cut into a particular shape

Before You Go On

1. What did Heungbu do when he noticed an injured bird?
2. What did Nolbu find inside his melon?

On Your Own

What do you think is the lesson that can be learned from the folktale? Explain.

> Reading 1

Review and Practice

Comprehension

Recall
1. What is the function of the seed coat?
2. Who took care of the brothers' father when he grew old and sick?

Comprehend
3. What are three basic parts of a plant?
4. Why was the content of the brothers' melons different? Explain.

Analyze
5. *Photo* is a Greek root, or word part, meaning "light." Given this information, what conclusion can you draw about the process of photosynthesis?
6. There is a saying, "You reap what you sow." It means that what you harvest reflects what you planted and the energy you put into growing it. How does this saying apply to the folktale?

Connect
7. Which selection did you enjoy more? Which one did you learn more from? Explain.
8. Which brother would you want as a friend? Explain.

▲ Plants use the process of photosynthesis to make food from the energy of the sun.

In Your Own Words

Work with a partner. In your own words, explain how a seed germinates and becomes a plant. Include as many new vocabulary words as possible. Ask your partner to listen carefully to your explanation. Are there any key points that you missed? Did you use the vocabulary words correctly?

> **Speaking Tip**
>
> Write important ideas on note cards. Review your notes before you begin speaking.

88 Unit 2

Discussion

Discuss with a partner or in a small group.

1. Why do you think the science article is included with the folktale in this unit? Explain.
2. Do you think Nolbu deserved what happened to him? Explain.

❓ **How are growth and change related?** Which selection do you think addresses the Big Question better: the science article or the folktale? Explain.

> **Listening Tip**
>
> Respect your classmates. Listen politely, even if you disagree with a person's ideas.

Read for Fluency

It is often easier to read a text if you understand the difficult words and phrases. Work with a partner. Choose a paragraph from the reading. Identify the words and phrases you do not know or have trouble pronouncing. Look up the difficult words in a dictionary.

Take turns pronouncing the words and phrases with your partner. If necessary, ask your teacher to model the correct pronunciation. Then take turns reading the paragraph aloud. Give each other feedback on your reading.

Extension

Use the internet or go to the library to get information about forests that are in danger of disappearing. What causes deforestation? What problems can result from deforestation? What can be done to help solve the problem?

Prepare a short oral report on the topic. Include drawings, posters, or photographs to help your audience understand the information better. Present your report to the class.

This spruce-tree seedling was planted as part of a reforestation program.

Reading 1

Grammar

Sequence Words and Phrases

Sequence words help the reader connect events in an informational text or in a story, such as in the folktale "A Tale of Two Brothers."

Sequence words help you follow the order of events in a story.

Sequence words and expressions include *first, then, next, after that, afterward, following that, last,* and *finally*. A comma follows all sequence words at the beginning of a clause or sentence except for *then*.

Practice A

Here are the events from the first half of "A Tale of Two Brothers." Circle the correct sequence words or phrases.

1. **First,** / **Then** Heungbu bound the swallow's leg.
2. **First,** / **Then** the swallow's leg healed, and Heungbu set it free.
3. **Next,** / **Finally,** the swallow dropped a melon seed at Heungbu's feet, so Heungbu planted it.
4. **Afterward,** / **Last,** a big melon vine grew from the seed.
5. **Following that,** / **Last,** Heungbu cut the melon open, and gemstones tumbled out.
6. **Finally,** / **First,** Nolbu heard about what happened with Heungbu's melons.

Practice B

"How Seeds and Plants Grow" is a science article that explains the process of germination.

Turn to page 85. In your notebook, write captions for the photographs shown. Use the text for information. Start your captions with sequence words. Share your captions with a partner.

Grammar Skill

In your writing, in place of sequence words such as *next* and *then*, you can spell out ordinal numbers to indicate steps: *second, third, fourth,* and so on.

Grammar Check

✓ What follows most **sequence words** at the beginning of a sentence?

Apply

Think about a task you are good at. Explain how to do it to your partner. Use sequence words.

Using Dashes to Explain or Clarify

Dashes (—) can take the place of colons, commas and parentheses in some sentences, if you want to explain, clarify, or emphasize a certain point.

Example	Purpose
The embryo within a seed contains the basic parts from which a young plant will develop—roots, stems, and leaves.	To clarify the word *parts*. Here, a dash replaces a colon.
This protection is necessary because a seed may be inactive—may not begin to grow—for weeks, months, or even years.	To explain the meaning of *may be inactive*. Here, dashes replace parentheses or commas.

The last sentence could be punctuated differently to emphasize the time aspect: *This protection is necessary because a seed may be inactive (may not begin to grow) for weeks, months—or even years.*

> **Grammar Skill**
> You can use dashes to set off text in the middle or at the end of a sentence.

> **Grammar Check**
> ✓ What are two ways **dashes** can be used?

Practice A

Rewrite each sentence below in your notebook. Add the missing dashes to emphasize, set off information, or provide a definition. Then circle the word or phrase in the sentence that is explained by the use of dashes.

1. We grew three kinds of beans kidney beans, lima beans, and navy beans.
2. In "A Tale of Two Brothers," Heungbu finds gemstones in his melon a gift from the bird he saved.
3. Seeds contain one or two cotyledons leaves where food is stored.

Practice B

Rewrite the sentences below in your notebook. Include the phrase in parentheses by using one or two dashes.

1. There are many uses for seeds. (growing new plants, feeding animals, eating)
2. The seed coat is like plastic wrap. (the outer protective covering)
3. Heungbu and Nolbu have very different personalities. (two brothers in a Korean folktale)

> **Apply**
> As you work through this unit, highlight examples of dash usage. What is the purpose of each use of dashes?

Reading 1
Writing

Write a Story with a Starter

At the end of this unit, you will write a fictional narrative. To do this, you will need to learn skills that writers use to write fictional narratives, or stories. Most stories include a series of events. The events make up the story's plot. The writer presents the story events in an order that makes the most sense. In "A Tale of Two Brothers," the events are in chronological order, or time order. The author uses sequence words and phrases like *a few days later* and *Soon* to make the relationships clear.

> **Writing Prompt**
>
> Write a fictional narrative. Begin your story with the following starter: *It was the most incredible thing I'd ever seen in nature.* Use sequence and time words and phrases to present the story events in a logical order.

① Prewrite Begin by thinking of the story starter and the events that you'll include in your story.

WB 46

- Close your eyes and visualize your story. Imagine what might happen in it.

- Write events on sticky notes or slips of paper. You don't have to think about the order now. Just write different events that happen.

- Next, arrange the events in a story order. Try different orders. What order makes the most sense?

Here's a flow chart created by a student named Thomas. He used this story starter: *I had never seen such an amazing plant*. He visualized a plant wrapping its tentacles around him. Then he used the flow chart to put the story events in order.

First, I worked my arm free.

↓

Next, I made an opening in the vegetation.

↓

Finally free, I heard a voice.

92 Unit 2

② **Draft** Use your flow chart to help you write a first draft.
- Use the story starter to lead into your story events.
- Describe the incredible thing in nature that your story is about.
- Use sequence and time words and phrases to present the events of your story in order.

③ **Revise** Read over your draft. Look for places where the writing is unclear or needs improvement. Complete (✓) the Writing Checklist to help you identify problems. Then, revise your draft, using the editing and proofreading marks listed on page 467.

④ **Edit and Proofread** Check your work for errors in grammar, usage, mechanics, and spelling. Trade papers with a partner to obtain feedback. Edit your final draft in response to feedback from your partner and your teacher.

⑤ **Publish** Prepare a clean copy of your final draft. Share your story with the class. Save your work. You'll need to refer to it in the Writing Workshop at the end of the unit.

> **Writing Checklist**
>
> **Ideas:**
> ☐ I narrated a story that included a sequence of events in logical order.
>
> **Word Choice:**
> ☐ I used sequence words and phrases to show the order of events.
>
> **Conventions:**
> ☐ I used commas correctly to set off sequence and time words and phrases where appropriate.

Thomas Kasterine

An Amazing Plant

I had never seen such an amazing plant. Its smooth, curling leaves seemed to reach out to me. I wanted badly to touch it. Suddenly, its tentacles—its long, curling stems—shot out and wrapped themselves around me. I tried to break loose, but I was trapped. I started to panic. Then I got an idea. First, I worked my arm free of the tangle. Next, I made an opening in the vegetation near my pants pocket. I pulled out my knife and cut randomly at the leaves and stems. Finally, when I was free, I heard a voice. "You, there!" It was a park ranger. "Have you ever seen such an amazing plant?" I shook my head. The ranger smiled and explained that people should never touch this species of plant because it was becoming rare. I turned and looked at the plant. It was in perfect condition, just as it was when I first saw it. Had it all been a daydream?

Reading 2

Prepare to Read

What You Will Learn

Reading
- Vocabulary building: *Literary terms, word study*
- Reading strategy: *Compare and contrast*
- Text type: *Literature (short story)*

Grammar
- Simple past and present perfect
- Past perfect active and passive

Writing
- Rewrite a familiar story

❓ THE BIG QUESTION

How are growth and change related? Societies grow and change at different rates. What might cause societies to change quickly? What would cause them to stay the same or to change slowly? Discuss with a partner or in small groups. What kinds of experiences can make people grow and change in terms of their emotions and understanding? Discuss with a partner or in small groups.

Build Background

This reading is a short story called **"The Test."** The story is historical fiction. It deals with discrimination, inequality, and rights for African Americans at a bleak time in U.S. history—which was beginning to change, though slowly.

When African Americans were brought to the United States as slaves, they were not allowed to learn to read or write. Slavery was abolished, and African Americans were considered citizens in the 1860s. However, African Americans still faced many barriers to education and voting rights.

Before 1965, people in southern states who wanted to vote often had to take tests to show that they could read or write. Some people used these tests to discriminate against African Americans.

The short story "The Test" takes place in the southern state of Louisiana in the 1960s. While the setting and some of the references, such as the ones made about Ruby Bridges, are real, the characters—Lucas, Mama, and Gramps—are fictional.

◀ Ruby Bridges was six when her parents fought in court for her to be able to go to the school of her choice.

Vocabulary

Learn Literary Words

In a narrative, the person telling the story is called the *narrator*. The narrator tells the story from a particular **point of view**. This means that the reader views things however the narrator describes them. Sometimes the narrator is a character in the story. Then the narrator assumes the first-person point of view, telling the story using the pronouns *I* and *my*. In the short story "The Test," the main character, Lucas, narrates the story.

Because Lucas is the narrator, readers understand the **plot** from his point of view. The plot is the sequence of connected events that make up a story. The events in the short story "The Test" make up its plot.

Plot development can be divided into two categories: linear and nonlinear. In "The Test," the plot development is linear, meaning the plot is described in chronological order. In a nonlinear story, the events are not described in time order.

Suspense is a feeling of uncertainty about the outcome of events in a story. Writers often create suspense by keeping readers wondering how a situation is going to turn out.

> **Literary Words**
> point of view
> plot
> suspense

Practice

Think of a TV show or movie that contains an element of suspense. Describe the plot and the point of view, then focus on what the element of suspense is in the show or movie. Fill in the boxes below with the information before you begin writing your description.

Title

Point of View

Element of Suspense

Reading 2

Listening and Speaking: Academic Words

Study the **purple** words and their meanings. You will find these words useful when talking and writing about literature. Write each word and its meaning in your notebook, then say the words aloud with a partner. After you read "The Test," try to use these words to respond to the text.

Academic Words
- affect
- anticipation
- discrimination
- reaction

Word	Example
affect = cause a person to feel strong emotions	She pretended that the bad news did not **affect** her in order to appear strong.
anticipation = a feeling of excitement because something good or fun is going to happen	We were filled with **anticipation** as we waited for the show to start.
discrimination = the practice of treating one group of people differently from another in an unfair way	Laws against **discrimination** help prevent various groups from being treated unfairly.
reaction = something you say or do because of what has happened or been said to you	His **reaction** to my joke was not what I had hoped. Instead of laughing, he groaned.

Practice

Work with a partner to answer these questions. Try to include the **purple** word in your answer. Write in your notebook.

1. Do you think it is acceptable to show how things **affect** you? Explain.
2. In what ways can **anticipation** sometimes lead to disappointment?
3. Which organizations work to help end **discrimination**?
4. What would your **reaction** be if you found out you had won a contest?

▲ This 1870 print celebrates the 15th Amendment, but the amendment did not end voting discrimination.

Word Study: Homographs

Some words in English are spelled alike but have different meanings. These words are called *homographs*. There are several ways to figure out the meaning of a homograph. Here are some suggestions:
- Check to see how the word is used. What part of speech is it?
- Look at the other words in the sentence for context clues.
- Use a dictionary to find the correct definition.

The chart below includes some examples of homographs.

Homograph	Part of Speech	Meaning
last	adjective	final
last	verb	to have a duration of time
change	noun	something new; a new situation
change	noun	metal coins

Practice
W|B 49

The following homographs appear in the short story "The Test": *pop, clear, sense, hand*. Find and underline each word in the reading. Then copy the context sentences into your notebook. Ask yourself how the word is used in the sentence. What is another meaning of the same word? Use a dictionary to find the meaning used in the context sentence. Record it in your notebook.

Reading Strategy | Compare and Contrast

Comparing and contrasting helps you to understand ideas in a text. When you compare, you see how things are similar. When you contrast, you see how things are different. To compare and contrast, ask yourself the following questions as you read:
- How are the characters and events in this story similar to people and events in my own life?
- How are the characters and events in this story different from the people and events in my own life?
- How are the characters' ideas about the events similar?
- How are the characters' ideas about the events different?

As you read the short story "The Test," answer the questions listed above by comparing and contrasting.

W|B 50

Reading 2   97

Reading 2

Literature
Short Story

Set a purpose for reading Read this story to find out about some of the obstacles African Americans faced as they attempted to practice their right to vote. What does Lucas and his family do?

THE Test

The narrator is Lucas, a 13-year-old African-American boy in Louisiana in the 1960s. He lives with his mother, Mama, and his 71-year-old grandfather, Gramps. In this story, the family accompanies Gramps as he takes a literacy test in order to register as a voter.

"I never **dared** try before," Gramps said. He pushed my history book across the table at me. "And now look. I can read."

I was so proud I felt like I was going to pop. "You read better than some of the kids in my class," I said. "You're going to **ace** that test."

My mother made a small sound, one that I knew meant "We'll see." She gave the supper one last stir. "Time to eat," she said. "Clear that book away, Lucas, and wash your hands."

"Yes, ma'am." I wanted to ask her if we could do something to celebrate Gramps's accomplishment, but the look in her eye made me hold my tongue. Over the last four years, she'd seen too many disappointments to celebrate before anything was settled and certain. I remembered her watching and worrying as little Ruby Bridges had walked to school, **clutching** her books in front of her. "Some people don't like change," Mama had said.

But I knew change was on the wind. I had caught Mama **peeking** at my math book the week before. Now Gramps could read. And once he passed the **literacy** test, he was going to be able to vote.

I sat down and tucked into my food. "Can I go with you tomorrow?" I asked between bites.

Mama and Gramps exchanged a look. "You know I don't like you missing school," Mama said.

"He can be my good luck charm," Gramps said.

Mama sighed. "All right. Just this once."

---

dared, tried something difficult or scary
ace, to do very well
clutching, holding something very tight
peeking, looking at something quickly and secretly
literacy, the ability to read and write

98 Unit 2

The next morning, we all dressed in our **Sunday best** and caught the streetcar. My hands sweated, but Gramps looked calm. Mama fanned herself and stared out the streetcar window.

At the office, Gramps took off his hat. "My name is William Johnson. I want to register to vote," he said in a deep, clear voice.

The clerk, a young man in a white short-sleeved shirt and skinny dark tie, said, "You need to take the test."

"I know. I am ready."

"Ten minutes. Thirty questions. If you get one question wrong, you fail. Do you understand?"

"I do."

The clerk glanced at Mama and me. "They have to wait out here."

He went to a file cabinet and got a sheet of paper. He motioned for Gramps to follow. Gramps nodded at us. Mama clasped my wrist.

I patted her hand. "He's a good reader," I whispered. "He'll do fine."

She watched Gramps and the clerk go into a side room. "Change comes slow, Lucas. We've **made strides**, but we still have a long way to go."

The clerk left the door open so he could watch Gramps take the test.

We took two of the hard wooden seats in the waiting area, and I craned my neck to see over the counter. I wanted to see Gramps right away when he came out of that room triumphant, a brand-new voter.

Ten minutes takes a long time when you're waiting. The clerk busied himself with other tasks. A woman typed rapidly, the clatter of the typewriter rattling my nerves.

Sunday best, formal clothes that people might wear to go to church
made strides, made progress

✓ LITERARY CHECK

How can you tell that the story is being told from the first-person **point of view**? How does this point of view shape the story?

✓ LITERARY CHECK

How does the **suspense** start to build here?

Before You Go On

1. What did Gramps learn to do?
2. Why is Lucas missing school today?

👤 On Your Own

Why do you think Lucas is so anxious? What do you think is going to happen?

Reading 2

Unexpectedly, Gramps strode out of the side room and handed the test to the clerk. "Thank you for your time," he said. Then, back stiff and straight, he walked past the counter, into the waiting area, and right past us out the door.

> **✓ LITERARY CHECK**
> How is the **plot** building?

Mama and I trailed after him. "Gramps! Wait!" I called.

"Hush!" Mama ordered. As we hurried after Gramps in silence, questions knocked against my teeth.

At the streetcar stop, Gramps turned to face us. "I did not finish the test," he said.

"What? Why?" I burst out. "But you can read—."

"That was no kind of reading test, Lucas," Gramps said. "The questions on that test made no sense. Underline this letter, circle that letter. Write this word backwards and put a dot over what would have been its second letter— if it were written forward. That test doesn't care if you are a good citizen. That test doesn't want you to pass."

Fury boiled up inside me. "That's not right! They just say you need to be able to read." I turned away back toward the building, but Mama grabbed my arm.

"Don't you dare go back in there, Lucas," she said. "**Making a scene** won't help anybody."

---

making a scene, creating a lot of noise through argument and drama

"But—" I began.

"I told you, change comes slow," Mama said. "It will come. But not today." She glanced at Gramps. His face was set hard, and his eyes gleamed. At first, I thought that gleam was tears, but then I realized it was something else.

"Let's go home. We've got plans to make."

"We?" I asked.

He nodded and looked at Mama. "You've been thinking about going back to school."

Her eyes widened. "Aha!" I exclaimed. "You *were* looking at my math book!"

"Hush, child," Mama said.

Gramps continued, "I think it's time. You never graduated high school. You should go back and get your diploma."

Mama stammered, "But—how will we **make ends meet**?"

"Well, I'm old, but I'm not dead," Gramps said. "I'll go back to work. You both go to school. You are both whip smart. And you need to be smart, because I need you to help fight. I need you both to help **do away with** these tests and everything that keeps us from voting."

Mama looked uncertain, but I took her hand. "I'll help you," I said.

The clang of the bell heralded the arrival of the streetcar. I followed Mama onboard, realizing that things for our family were going to change. Maybe slowly, but they *would* change.

---

make ends meet, to make enough money to pay for the basic necessities

do away with, to eliminate

Before You Go On

1. Why did Gramps leave the test suddenly?
2. What does Gramps decide the family will do?

On Your Own

How do you think the family is going to change now? Explain.

Reading 2

Review and Practice

Reader's Theater

In pairs, act out the following scene between Lucas and Mama.

Lucas: Mama, I don't understand why Gramps didn't pass the test. It wasn't fair!
Mama: What do you mean, Lucas?
Lucas: They told him he had to learn to read. And he did! But they gave him an unfair test! They never told him there would be questions that didn't focus on reading.
Mama: I know, Lucas. He didn't know. We didn't know.
Lucas: But it's not fair!
Mama: I know, Lucas. But sometimes life isn't fair. We try to change things so they are more fair. But change comes slowly.
Lucas: I don't want things to be unfair. What can we do?
Mama: Well, as Gramps said, you can get a good education. Get a good job. Then when you grow up maybe you can help make things more fair for people like us.
Lucas: What do you mean?
Mama: Well, if you get a good education and a good job—more people will listen to you. Then you can make good changes happen.

> **Speaking Tip**
>
> Speak slowly and clearly. Self-correct, as necessary. Adjust your tone of voice to match the emotions the characters are feeling.

Comprehension

Recall

1. Why does Lucas feel proud of Gramps?
2. What does Lucas want to tell the people at the office after Gramps explains why he didn't finish the test?

Comprehend

3. How do Gramps and Lucas feel the day before the test? What do you think each anticipates will happen? Why?
4. How does Mama's feeling about the test differ from those of her father and her son?

Analyze

5. What does Gramps mean when he says "That test doesn't want you to pass."? Do you think he's right? Explain.
6. How do the characters feel about change? Do their feelings

Connect

7. Do you think the title of the story was effective? Explain.
8. Which story character do you identify with more? Explain.

Discussion

Discuss with a partner or in a small group.

1. Do you think Lucas might react differently to discrimination in the future? Explain.
2. What are some of the challenges this family might face as they put their plan into action?
3. **How does the story show how growth and change are related? Explain.** How do you think the test affected Gramps? How do you think it affected Mama and Lucas? How might it have changed them?

Listening Skill

Listen carefully to your classmates to understand their main points. Also listen for details that support or help clarify others' main points.

Response to Literature

WB 51

With a partner, talk about Gramps's, Mama's, and Lucas's experiences in the story. The family makes plans for the future. What do you think happens next? Think about the next meaningful event for one of the characters. Write a dialogue between the character and one or two others. You may choose to introduce a new character, such as a teacher or another family member.

Reading 2
Grammar

Simple Past and Present Perfect

The simple past is used to show that an action began and ended at a definite time in the past.

The present perfect is used to show that an action began in the past but has no definite end. Form the present perfect with *have* or *has* + the past participle.

Verb	Simple Past	Present Perfect
travel	She **traveled** a long way yesterday.	She **has traveled** all over the world.

The present perfect is also used to show that an action began in the past and continues into the present.

Verb	Simple Past	Present Perfect
work	My father **worked** late last night.	My father **has worked** there since 2013.

Many verbs are irregular in the simple past and the present perfect.

Practice A

Circle the correct words or phrases in boldface to complete the sentences.

1. I **went** / **have gone** to the movies last weekend.
2. We **lived** / **have lived** here for two years.
3. My sister **wrote** / **has written** an essay last night.
4. My sister **keeps** / **has kept** a journal since she was four.

Grammar Skill

Some verbs are irregular and you need to memorize them.

Verb	Simple Past	Present Perfect
come	came	has/have **come**
forget	forgot	has/have **forgotten**
know	knew	has/have **known**

Grammar Check

✓ Do the **simple past** and the **present perfect** always use the same verb form?

Practice B

Complete the paragraph with the simple past or the present perfect of the verb in parentheses.

I ____have lived____ in San Diego for many years now. I _____ (move) here from China in 2017 because my father _____ (take) a new job. At first, it _____ (be) difficult, but now it _____ (became) easier. I _____ (make) many new friends at my new school, but my best friend is Allison.

Apply

Talk with a partner about where you have traveled and what you did there.

Past Perfect: Active and Passive

Use the past perfect to indicate that something happened (or did not happen) in the past, prior to another event. Study the sentences in the chart below. The form of a verb in the past perfect is *had* (+ *not* / *never*) + *past participle*.

Past Perfect Example	Meaning
Gramps **had studied** for weeks before taking the literacy test.	Gramps studied before taking the test.
Lucas **had caught** Mama peeking at his math book once before.	Lucas found his mother looking at the book.

A past perfect sentence can be in the active or the passive.

Look at the active and passive sentences. Notice that the passive of the past perfect is *had* (+ *not* / *never*) + *been* + *past participle*.

Active	Passive
By the time we got home, we **had created** a new plan.	By the time we got home, a new plan **had been created**.
I **had not gotten** some books.	I **had not been given** some books.

Grammar Skill
The passive form is sometimes used with a *by* phrase to indicate the doer of the action. **Example:** The garden was planted **by volunteers.**

Practice A

Identify each boldfaced phrase as *passive* or *active*.

1. _____ I **had finished** my homework early.
2. _____ There were no oranges left. They **had** all **been eaten**.
3. _____ When I got there, classes **had started**.

Grammar Check
✓ What are some time words and phrases that can be used with the **past perfect** in both the **active** and **passive**?

Practice B

Complete the sentences with the correct past perfect form of the verb in parentheses.

1. All the books _____ to the library at the end of the year. (return)
2. I _____ they would be able to visit. (hope)
3. The actor _____ a large sum of money before he quit the film. (pay)

Apply
Work with a partner to find two past perfect sentences in this unit (Readings 1 and 2) and identify them as active or passive. Restate the active sentences as passive and the passive sentences as active.

Reading 2

Reading 2
Writing

Rewrite a Familiar Story

At the end of this unit, you will write a fictional narrative. In this lesson, you are going to write a familiar story from a different point of view. When you tell a story, you can tell it from a character's or someone outside of the story's point of view. The story you just read is told from one of the character's point of view. But the story could be narrated from the point of view of another character in the story.

> **Writing Prompt**
>
> Choose a familiar story that you know well or can refer to. Decide on a new point of view for the story—one that is different from that of the original story. Be sure to use verbs in the simple past correctly.

1 Prewrite Choose a story that you want to retell.

WB 54

- Choose a new narrator—a character or someone outside the story.
- Decide how your narrator's point of view will be different from the original narrator's.

Here's a chart created by a student named Linda about the point of view used in "The Test" and the new point of view she is going to use.

Event	Lucas's point of view	Mama's point of view
Gramps learns to read.	Now Gramps will be able to vote.	Cautious, not too optimistic
Gramps comes out of office	What is going on? I want answers!	We must stay calm.

② **Draft** Use your chart to help you write a first draft.
- Keep in mind your narrator's point of view.
- Choose words to convey the new narrator's point of view, including feelings about what's happening.
- Remember to adjust pronouns, as needed, for new point of view.
- Be sure to use simple past correctly.

Writing Checklist

Voice:
☐ I used a voice that reflects the narrator's point of view.

Conventions:
☐ I used the simple past correctly.

③ **Revise** Read over your draft. As you do so, complete (✓) the Writing Checklist. Use the questions in the Writing Checklist to help you revise your story. Then, revise your draft, using the editing and proofreading marks listed on page 467.

④ **Edit and Proofread** Check your work for errors in grammar, usage, mechanics, and spelling. Trade papers with a partner to obtain feedback. Edit your final draft in response to feedback from your partner and your teacher.

⑤ **Publish** Prepare a clean copy of your final draft. Share your story with the class. Save your work. You'll need to refer to it in the Writing Workshop at the end of the unit.

Here is Linda's rewrite of "The Test." Notice the changes in the story because of the new point of view.

Linda Chang

<u>The Test</u>

I was happy and proud when my father learned to read. But I knew that change comes slowly, so I didn't want to get too excited. My father hadn't been given any educational opportunities, but if he passed the literacy test, he would be able to vote. I know how unfair life can be. This was such an important event that I agreed to let Lucas skip school. I thought it would be important for him to experience this and, hopefully, celebrate. But I didn't want him to be too hopeful. When my dad came out of the office, I could tell something was wrong. I had to stop Lucas from making a scene. I understood why Lucas was so upset, but I know that making a scene never helps. On our way back home, we all talked about making a new plan to help change come for our family.

Reading 3

Prepare to Read

What You Will Learn

Reading
- Vocabulary building: *Context, dictionary skills, word study*
- Reading strategy: *Scan*
- Text type: *Informational text (science)*

Grammar
- Comparison structures: Comparative adjectives
- Adjectives with *too* and *enough* + infinitive

Writing
- Write a personal letter

❓ THE BIG QUESTION

How are growth and change related? Think of a place you know that is affected by changes in climate. How does climate change affect the organisms—the plants and animals—in that place? How does it affect the people? Discuss your ideas with a partner.

▲ In Africa, drier conditions caused by climate change have affected the wildebeest's migration and range.

Build Background

This reading is a science article called **"Climate Change Puts Nature on the Move."** It presents factual information about how climate change has affected animals, plants, and people. The image below is a graph—a picture that uses lines or curves to show the relationship between numbers or measurements that change.

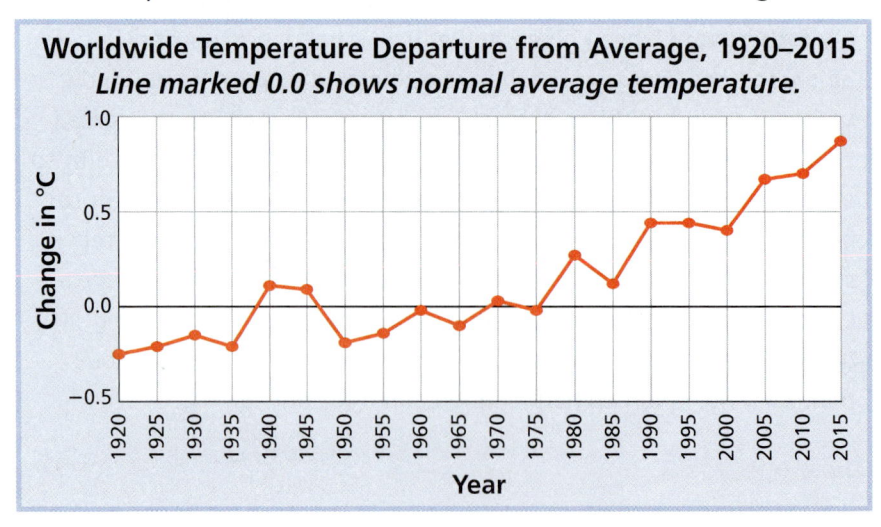

▶ This graph shows that the Earth has been warming slowly for over 100 years. The red line shows some temperatures rising and falling, but the overall trend is a warming climate.

Worldwide Temperature Departure from Average, 1920–2015
Line marked 0.0 shows normal average temperature.

Vocabulary

Listening and Speaking: Key Words

Read these sentences aloud with a partner. Use the context to figure out the meaning of the highlighted words. Use a dictionary, the glossary, or a thesaurus to determine or confirm your answers. Then write each word and its meaning in your notebook.

Key Words
- colony
- decline
- ecosystems
- migrate
- species
- stable

1. The field was pockmarked with holes, a sign of a ground squirrel **colony**.
2. There has been a large **decline** in the number of penguins in some parts of Antarctica.
3. All living things are part of **ecosystems** that exist in the sea or on the land.
4. We are studying how birds **migrate**. They move to warmer climates in the winter.
5. Most bird **species** can fly, but penguins cannot.
6. After years of change, the fish's population has become **stable**.

Practice

Complete the sentences with a word from the box above. Then take turns reading the sentences aloud with a partner.

1. Animals _____ to find enough food and water.
2. The tundra and the desert are among the world's driest _____.
3. There has been a(n) _____ in the number of polar bears in the Arctic—there are fewer and fewer of them.
4. The scientists tracked the group of wolves to understand if their population was _____ or decreasing.
5. Several _____ of fish, such as the blue walleye, have died out, or become extinct.
6. The class noticed a large _____ of bees living in a nest near the school.

▲ Wild geese migrate from north to south in the winter and south to north in the summer.

Reading 3

Reading 3

Listening and Speaking: Academic Words

Study the **purple** words and their meanings. You will find these words useful when talking and writing about informational texts. Write each word and its meaning in your notebook, then say the words aloud with a partner. After you read "Climate Change Puts Nature on the Move," try to use these words to respond to the text.

Academic Words
- adapt
- distribution
- expand
- prediction
- region

adapt = to gradually change behavior in order to become successful	Some species have shifted where they feed in order to **adapt** to environmental changes.
distribution = scattering or spreading of something over an area	This map shows the **distribution** of people in the country.
expand = become larger, or to make something become larger	We will **expand** our search for your missing key and look all over the house for it.
prediction = statement that something is going to happen	Do you have a **prediction** about your final grade in this class?
region = fairly large area of a state or country, usually without exact limits	The southern **region** of the United States is warmer than the northern region.

Practice

WB 56

Work with a partner to answer these questions. Try to include the **purple** word in your answer. Write the sentences in your notebook.

1. Describe the population **distribution** in your area. Where do most people live? Where do few people live?
2. Do you think the population in your area will **expand** in the next ten years? Explain.
3. What **prediction** can you make about the weather this weekend?
4. What **region** of your country do you live in?
5. Describe a time when you have had to **adapt** to a new situation. What strategies did you use? How did you change?

People move, or migrate, to other regions for different reasons.

Word Study: Long *a*, *i*, *o* Spelling Patterns

Long vowel sounds can be spelled in different ways. The chart below shows the different spelling patterns for the long vowels *a*, *i*, and *o*.

Long *a*	Long *i*	Long *o*
a_e: state, same, rate, decade, age, migrate	**i_e**: decline, nine, five	**o_e**: home, alone
ai, ay: remained, stay, today	**igh**: right, slightly, higher	**ow**: shows, owner, widow, lower

Practice

Work with a partner. Take turns reading aloud the words in the box. After you say a word, identify the long vowel sound and its spelling. Then choose five words and write a sentence for each.

always	flowing	mine	safe	tight
bright	grain	paint	shape	tiles
crow	hides	play	sight	window
drive	late	revive	stone	write

Reading Strategy — Scan

Scanning helps you find information you need quickly. When you scan, you read for particular kinds of information, such as names, dates, numbers, and facts. To scan, follow these steps:

- Look at the title, visuals, captions, and labels to see if they contain the information you need.
- Start reading the beginning of the text. Move your eyes quickly over the lines. Don't stop at words you don't know.
- Look for key words related to the information you want to find.
- Stop scanning and begin reading as soon as you find any of the key words or ideas you're looking for.

Before you read "Climate Change Puts Nature on the Move," use the scanning strategy to find three key pieces of information that you want to know and think might be in an article like this one.

Reading 3

Informational Text
Science/Social Studies

Set a purpose for reading As you read this science and social studies article, consider this question: How is climate change affecting plants, animals, and people?

Climate Change Puts Nature on the Move

You may not have taken too much notice of the planet's changing climate, but nature sure has. Around the world, **organisms** large and small are changing their behavior, diets, and home ranges in response to changing temperatures. A scientific study of 4,000 different species of animals and plants discovered that half of them are now on the move.

Moving is nothing new for Earth's living things; they have moved from place to place for millions of years. Many birds spend their winters close to the equator and their summers near the poles. Land animals, such as caribou, and ocean animals, such as whales, migrate hundreds and hundreds of miles from their feeding grounds to the places where they give birth to their young.

However, scientists are observing changes to those established patterns. Regions that were once perfect **habitats** have now become too hot for the organisms that live there. Faced with warmer temperatures, animals must either move or adapt to survive. For many, adapting means changing patterns and behaviors that kept them alive for years. Among the living things that are affected are penguins, moose, and, yes, even people.

organisms, living things, such as plants or animals
habitats, places where plants or animals live

▲ Due to climate change, many animals and birds, such as the white stork, have shifted their migration patterns.

Penguins in Peril

The effects of climate change are more pronounced at the poles than elsewhere. This is not good news for polar animals that are well adapted to cold climates. The Adélie penguin, which nests in colonies on the Antarctic Peninsula, is among the polar species that are struggling.

Over the last 40 years, the temperature along the peninsula has increased by 9 degrees F, causing the sea ice to form later and melt sooner. The temperature change had caused the penguins' main **prey**, silverfish, to leave, following their own prey to different areas. As a result, not only are the penguins that are nesting on the Antarctic Peninsula struggling to find food, but they also are facing warmer temperatures, which bring rain that can flood nests and kill chicks.

As the Adélies decline on the Antarctic Peninsula, another species of penguin, the Gentoo penguin, has been moving into this part of the Adélies' **range**. Gentoos consume a more varied diet than Adélie penguins. Also, they are larger than Adélies and can dive deeper to find food. However, that doesn't mean that warmer temperatures are good for penguins; it just means that some species may be able to adjust to changing conditions better than others.

There is some good news for the Adélies: The penguin colonies in locations that are being less affected by climate change are remaining stable or even growing. As long as these safe havens remain, the Adélies will survive.

---

prey, an animal that is hunted by another animal
range, the area of land where a species can live

▼ A group of **Adélie** penguins hunting and diving for fish in the Antarctic.

Before You Go On

1. Why are some animals changing where they migrate?
2. How have Earth's rising temperatures affected the Adélie penguin?

On Your Own

What other species that you know of might be affected by climate change?

Reading 3

Shrubs, Moose, and Caribou

Around the world, climate change is altering the makeup of ecosystems. Every living thing on Earth is part of an ecosystem, a web of life in which each part affects, and is affected by, every other part. The plants that grow in an area are eaten by certain animals that have adapted to eating them. When those plants change, the animals are affected. When plants spread to new areas, the animals that eat them follow their source of food.

The North Slope, the far northern part of Alaska, U.S.A., is far beyond the tree line, the northernmost limit where trees grow and thrive. Most of the North Slope is tundra, home to low-growing plants. Caribou, which are related to deer, live on the tundra because they have adapted to eat these plants.

Climate change has altered the North Slope's ecosystem. Because of warmer temperatures, shrubs like willow and alder are spreading through the river valleys, and with them have come moose. Once limited to the tree line because they could find no food on the tundra, moose have spread about 400 kilometers north from their northernmost limit in 1880.

However, the story is different for the caribou. Some research has found that the arrival of the shrubs has reduced the kinds of plants that the caribou need to survive; the caribou cannot eat the woody shrubs that moose feast upon.

What will happen to the moose and the caribou? Will the moose replace the caribou, like the Gentoo penguins are replacing the Adélies? It's too soon to tell, but scientists are watching the situation closely.

Life Is on the Move

In addition to penguins, shrubs, and moose, thousands more species of animals and plants are responding to warmer global temperatures by moving. Scientists have discovered that all life on the planet is shifting away from the **equator** toward the cooler poles. Land animals and plants are moving toward the poles at a rate of 16 kilometers per decade. In the ocean, the migration is even faster than on land, with species moving at a rate of 71 kilometers per decade.

---

equator, the line that divides the Earth into the Northern and Southern Hemispheres

◀ When shrubs like willow grow lower in the valleys, they attract moose.

◀ The floodgates in Rotterdam can open and close to help control the water during tides and storms.

Movement toward the poles is only part of the story. Animals and plants are also moving up mountains and diving deeper into the ocean to find cooler temperatures. The patterns of life on Earth are changing rapidly to adjust to hotter and more challenging living conditions.

People Are Moving, Too

Are humans immune to the effects of climate change? No; humans are being affected, too. Increasing temperatures will lead to greater and more severe **flooding** in coastal areas. By 2100, sea level may rise as much as 2 meters. This will happen for two reasons. First, water expands when it is warmer because heat makes water molecules move faster and spread apart. Second, much of the water that is currently frozen in ice at the poles will melt and become part of the ocean.

In some places, people are already being forced to move. In Alaska, residents of 31 coastal villages must move because ice no longer forms a protective barrier. As a result, storms have **eroded** the land where their houses stand, making it unsafe to remain. Similarly, in the Pacific Ocean, rising seas have already covered five islands. On other low Pacific islands, like Kiribati, the Maldives, and Tuvalu, people are already making plans to move. Major cities will be especially vulnerable. In Shanghai alone, 17.5 million people may need to migrate out of flood zones by 2100. Other cities, such as Miami in the United States, are also at risk, as are nations that have many low-lying areas, such as Bangladesh.

Elsewhere, people have started preparing for the changes brought about by climate change. And they've learned from those who live in places that have experience dealing with flooding. Because two-thirds of the Netherlands is already at or below sea level, people there have built garages, lakes, parks, fields, and canals that can hold water during storms or when tides are high. Engineers have constructed 21-meter-tall **floodgates** to protect the major port in Rotterdam.

Climate change is a reality, and all living things—including people—will need to find ways to cope with rising temperatures and sea levels.

---

flooding, a large amount of water covering the land
eroded, destroyed over time by natural forces
floodgates, gates that can be opened or closed to let water in or keep it out

Before You Go On

1. How are ecosystems affected by climate change?
2. How is climate change affecting people? Give an example.

👤 On Your Own

How is your area being affected by climate change?

Reading 3 115

Reading 3

Review and Practice

Comprehension

Recall
1. What is causing living things to move on our planet?
2. What is one species that has been affected by climate change? How?

Comprehend
3. How can an animal that has expanded its habitat affect other plants and animals in the area?
4. What regions are most affected by climate change?

Analyze
5. From what you read in the article, what predictions can you make about the future of the Adélie penguin, the moose, and the caribou?
6. Why are leaders from other coastal cities visiting the Netherlands?

Connect
7. What do you think is the greatest impact of climate change? Explain.
8. What do you think is the author of this article's viewpoint about climate change?

▲ Seagulls feast on any fish that escape this feeding humpback whale. If the range of the whale changes, it can affect the seagulls.

In Your Own Words

Tell a partner some facts you learned about climate change and migration. Before you begin speaking, you may wish to write sentences using some of the words and phrases below.

adapt	equator	prey
caribou	flooding	poles
climate change	habitat	range
ecosystems	organisms	sea level
erosion	penguins	survive

Speaking Tip
You may wish to use the images in this reading to help explain the main ideas and details presented in the text.

Discussion

Discuss with a partner or in a small group.

Climate change continues to affect migration. How do you think that warming temperatures will affect animals, plants, and people five years from now?

? **How are growth and change related?** How would you answer the Big Question, based on what you read in this article? Explain.

> **Listening Tip**
> If you have a question, wait until the speaker has finished speaking before asking it.

Read for Fluency

When we read aloud to communicate meaning, we group words into phrases, pause or slow down to make important points, and emphasize important words. Pause for a short time after a comma and for a longer time after a period. Pay attention to rising and falling intonation at the end of sentences.

Work with a partner. Choose a paragraph from the reading. Discuss which words seem important for communicating meaning. Practice pronouncing difficult words. Take turns reading the paragraph aloud and giving each other feedback.

Extension

WB 59

Now that you have read about how climate change affects migration patterns, go online to find additional information on this topic. Choose an article, read it, and summarize it. Be sure to include the title and source. Does the information in the article change or confirm your reaction to the text you just read? Explain how.

◀ Deforestation—the cutting down of trees—has affected moth and butterfly migration patterns.

Reading 3

Grammar

Comparison Structures: Comparative Adjectives

A comparative adjective compares one thing to another. Comparative adjectives are formed in different ways, depending on the adjective that they are based on. Using the word *than* also clarifies the comparison. Here are the rules to follow to form comparative adjectives.

> **Grammar Skill**
>
> Irregular comparatives must be memorized.
> much → more
> good → better
> little → less

Example	Rule
Warmer habitats are near the equator.	Most one-syllable adverbs, add *-er*: [warm].
Birds are **larger than** insects.	Most one-syllable adjectives ending in *-e*, add *-r*: [large].
Hotter climates are near the equator.	Most one-syllable adjectives with a consonant-vowel-consonant pattern, double final consonant, add *-er*: [hot].
Climate change will lead to **more severe** flooding.	Adjectives of two or more syllables, add *more*: [severe].
So far, our family has been **luckier than** most.	Adjectives ending in *-y*, change *-y* to *-ier*: [lucky].
Last night's storm was **worse than** others.	Memorize irregular forms: *bad* → *worse*.

Practice A

Complete the sentences with the correct comparative form of the adjective in parentheses.

1. India is _____ than Canada. (warm)
2. The place is _____ than it was five years ago. (safe)
3. Coastal areas are _____ to live in than they were five years ago. (dangerous)

> **Grammar Check**
>
> ✓ When do writers use *than* with **comparative adjectives**?

Practice B

Complete the sentences with the correct comparative form of the adjective in parentheses and the word *than*.

1. The altitude of a mountain peak is ____higher than____ sea level. (high)
2. Mild temperatures are _____ extremely hot temperatures. (comfortable)
3. Flooding at sea level is _____ in the mountains. (bad)

> **Apply**
>
> Look at the graph on page 108 and make comparisons with a partner. **Example:** Global temperatures in 2010 are **higher** than they were in 1960.

Adjectives with *Too* and *Enough*

Writers often use *too* and *enough* with adjectives to indicate a degree, as in *too hot*, meaning "hotter than necessary or desired." Study these examples:

Sentence	Meaning
The air is **too cold for animals.**	Animals cannot live in air this cold.
The water was **warm enough** for the fish to thrive.	This water was a good temperature that was sufficiently warm for fish to thrive.

Writers use *not* and *enough* with an adjective to mean not as much as needed. In this case, *not* + adjective + *enough* has the opposite meaning from *too* + adjective. The examples below have the same meaning.

too + adjective	*not* + adjective + *enough*
Some climates are **too hot** for these organisms.	Some climates are **not cool enough** for these organisms.

Writers sometimes follow expressions with *too* and *not . . . enough* with infinitives to clarify a result.

> There is **not enough** food **to last**.
> Their habitats are becoming **too hot to live in**.

> **Grammar Skill**
>
> Use an infinitive after *too* or *enough* to show a situation: *The soup is too hot. The soup is too hot to eat now.*

Practice A

61

Circle the correct phrases to complete the sentences.

1. Wear a coat. It's too **cold / cold enough** to go out in a T-shirt.
2. The ladder is **too short / short enough**. It doesn't reach the roof.
3. Marco can lift that heavy stone. He is **too strong / strong enough**.
4. You must be 18 to see that movie. You are only 16, so you are not **too old / old enough**.

Practice B

Complete the sentences with *too* or *enough* and one of these adjectives: *light, salty, sweet*.

1. This box is _____. I can carry it easily.
2. Waiter, please take back this soup. It is _____ to eat.
3. I don't want any more sugar in my tea. It is _____.

> **Grammar Check**
>
> ✓ When do writers use the infinitive with *too* and *enough*?

> **Apply**
>
> Write a sentence using *too* to show degree, such as *It's too early to eat lunch*. Then work with a partner and rewrite each other's sentences with *enough*: *It's early enough to eat lunch.*

Reading 3

Reading 3
Writing

Write a Personal Letter

In this unit, you have been learning about narrative writing. In this lesson, you will write a narrative in the form of a personal letter to a friend or a family member. In a personal letter, you tell the reader a story about a memorable event or experience in your life. A personal letter has five parts: the date, the greeting, the body, the closing, and the signature. It is in the body of the letter that you include details about the event or experience.

> **Writing Prompt**
>
> Write a personal letter to a friend or a family member about a memorable event or experience. Choose an event or an experience you had that you can write a story about. Include adjectives with *too* and *enough* and comparative structures where possible.

1 Prewrite Choose an interesting event or experience you had.

- Think about why this event or experience was important to you.
- Ask yourself who would enjoy reading about it.
- List your ideas in a graphic organizer.

Here is a graphic organizer created by a student named Adrian for a letter describing his move to a new place.

Date: September 21, 2019

Greeting: Dear Alex,

Body: Everything is different here.
Met Ricardo.
He likes to play soccer so we practice together.
I'm going to try out for the team.

Closing: Take care,
Signature: Adrian

---

120 Unit 2

2 **Draft** Use your organizer to help you write a first draft.
- Keep in mind the person who will read your letter and your purpose for writing it.
- Remember to include all five parts of a friendly letter.
- Be sure to include adjectives with *too* and *enough* and comparative structures correctly.

3 **Revise** Read over your draft. As you do so, complete (✓) the Writing Checklist. Use the questions in the Writing Checklist to help you revise your story. Then, revise your draft, using the editing and proofreading marks listed on page 467.

4 **Edit and Proofread** Check your work for errors in grammar, usage, mechanics, and spelling. Trade papers with a partner to obtain feedback. Edit your final draft in response to feedback from your partner and your teacher.

5 **Publish** Prepare a clean copy of your final draft. Share your letter with the class. Save your work. You'll need to refer to it in the Writing Workshop at the end of the unit.

> **Writing Checklist**
>
> **Ideas:**
> ☐ The ideas and events in my letter are clear.
>
> **Word Choice:**
> ☐ I used descriptive words to help my reader understand my message.
>
> **Sentence Fluency:**
> ☐ I used a variety of sentence types and patterns.
>
> **Conventions:**
> ☐ I used comparative structures correctly.

Here is Adrian's letter to Alex. Notice how he used comparison structures.

September 21, 2019

Dear Alex,

   How's it going, buddy? Man, everything is different here. I get lost on the way to all my classes and nobody eats lunch together! I've been thinking about our lunchtime pick-up soccer games. I think I found a way to make my life more interesting—or at least interesting enough! I met a kid named Ricardo. I was doing some practice drills out in the field when he called out to me, "Hey, man, pass!" For a second, I was too surprised to react, since I've barely spoken to anyone at this school. But once I understood that he wanted to play, I passed him the ball and we took turns trying to score on each other. Just like you and I used to, we set up our backpacks as goal markers and spent lunch hour training. We're supposed to meet up again tomorrow, so I'll keep you posted. Maybe you can visit and we can all hang out.

                                          Take care,
                                          Adrian

Reading 4

Prepare to Read

What You Will Learn

Reading
- Vocabulary building: *Literary terms, word study*
- Reading strategy: *Make inferences*
- Text type: *Literature (short story)*

Grammar
- *Have to* + verb
- Conditional sentences

Writing
- Write a personal narrative

THE BIG QUESTION

How are growth and change related? Have you ever felt embarrassed by someone you love? What happened? Did you learn from the experience? Did the experience change you in any way? Discuss with a partner.

Build Background

This reading is a short story called **"Abuela Invents the Zero."** It is about a girl named Connie who is embarrassed by her grandmother. Born in the United States, Connie has lived in New Jersey, U.S.A., all her life. Connie's grandmother was born in Puerto Rico and is visiting the United States for the first time. Because her parents insist, Connie takes her grandmother to church and learns an important lesson as a result.

Vocabulary

Learn Literary Words

Literary Words
characterization
dialogue
sarcasm

Characterization is the creation and development of a character in a story. Writers sometimes show what a character is like by describing what the character thinks and does.

> Felicia usually called her brother, Jason, every Sunday. But this time she didn't feel like getting up to find her cell phone. Felicia knew that her brother would be disappointed, but she was too tired to care.

Writers use **dialogue**, or a conversation between two or more characters, to show through their spoken words how the characters feel. In short stories, dialogue usually appears between quotation marks (" ") to indicate a speaker's exact words.

> "Why didn't you call me last Sunday?" asked Jason.
> "I would have, Jason, but I couldn't find the phone, and then I fell asleep," answered Felicia.

Sarcasm is a form of speech or writing that is used to express criticism or annoyance. It often adds an element of humor, but the attitude behind the humor is usually cutting or bitter. Often the speaker or writer says the opposite of what he or she actually means.

> "Wow, Felicia. That makes me feel good. Thanks for making me such a big priority in your life," said Jason.

Practice

Copy the paragraph below into your notebook. With a partner, write a few lines of dialogue to show what the narrator and her cousin are like. Remember to put each speaker's words in quotation marks. Try to include a sarcastic remark.

> I was on a train to Florida to visit my cousin Maria. I was very excited about the trip. I hadn't seen Maria for five years. Maria was beautiful and popular, and she always wore the coolest clothes. My train arrived a little late. I noticed Maria right away. She was standing in the parking lot next to a shiny new convertible.

Reading 4

Reading 4

Listening and Speaking: Academic Words

Study the purple words and their meanings. You will find these words useful when talking and writing about literature. Write each word and its meaning in your notebook, then say the words aloud with a partner. After you read "Abuela Invents the Zero," try to use these words to respond to the text.

Academic Words
- conduct
- ignore
- instruct
- reluctance

conduct = the way someone behaves	The little girl's good **conduct** made her parents feel proud.
ignore = pay no attention to someone or something	They turned their heads away so as to **ignore** the bully's threat.
instruct = officially tell someone what to do or how to do something	A teacher's job is to **instruct** his or her students.
reluctance = unwillingness to do something	His unhappy face showed his **reluctance** to help his mother.

Practice

WB 64

Work with a partner to answer these questions. Try to include the purple word in your answer. Write the sentences in your notebook.

1. Have you ever been ashamed of your own **conduct**?
2. When is it a good idea to **ignore** a person or a situation?
3. Who will **instruct** you about applying for a job?
4. When have you shown **reluctance** to do something?

▲ I tried this green ice cream with some reluctance, but it turned out to be delicious green-tea ice cream!

Word Study: Idioms

An idiom is a group of words with a special meaning that is different from the ordinary meaning of each separate word. Sometimes you can figure out what an idiom means from the context of the sentence. Other times, you may have to look in a dictionary. When you look up an idiom in the dictionary, look under the first noun found in the idiom. If you can't find it there, or if there is no noun, look under the main word in the idiom. For example, you will find the idiom *come down with* under the verb *come*.

Idiom	Meaning
night and day	"all the time"
come down with	"become ill with"
beat somebody to something	"get to or do something before someone"

Practice

Work with a partner. In the reading, find and underline each of the idioms from the box below. Try to figure out the meaning of the idiom using the context of the sentence. Then look up the idioms in a dictionary. In your notebook, write the idiom and its meaning. Finally, write a sentence for each idiom.

at the top of her voice	end up	I'm out of here	no way
changes his mind	getting myself into	makes a big deal	she means business

Reading Strategy — Make Inferences

Making inferences helps you figure out information that the author hasn't given directly. When you make inferences, or infer, you are "reading between the lines." To make inferences, follow these steps as you read:

- Pay close attention to how the author describes the characters, the events, and the setting. What has the author hinted at but not said?
- Think about your own experiences. Do they help you understand the situation that you are reading about?
- Now use the information in the story and your own experiences to make inferences.

As you read "Abuela Invents the Zero," think about what the author is conveying but not saying directly. What inferences can you make?

Reading 4

Reading 4

**Literature
Short Story**

Set a purpose for reading Read the story to find out how a person can learn an important lesson from someone older and wiser. What lesson does Connie learn?

Abuela Invents the Zero 🎧

JUDITH ORTIZ COFER

"You made me feel like a zero, like a nothing," she says in Spanish, *un cero, nada*. She is trembling, an angry little old woman lost in a heavy winter coat that belongs to my mother. And I end up being sent to my room, like I was a child, to think about my grandmother's idea of math.

It all began with Abuela coming up from the Island for a visit—her first time in the United States. My mother and father paid her way here so that she wouldn't die without seeing snow, though if you asked me, and nobody has, the dirty **slush** in this city is not worth the price of a ticket. But I guess she deserves some kind of award for having had ten kids and survived to tell about it. My mother is the youngest of the bunch. Right up to the time when we're supposed to pick up the old lady at the airport, my mother is telling me stories about how hard times were for *la familia* on *la isla*, and how *la abuela* worked night and day to support them after their father died of a heart attack. I'd die of a heart attack too if I had a troop like that to support. Anyway, I had seen her only three or four times in my entire life, whenever we would go for somebody's funeral. I was born here and I have lived in this building all my life. But when Mami says, "Connie, please be nice to Abuela. She doesn't have too many years left. Do you promise me, Constancia?"—when she uses my full name, I know she means business. So I say, "Sure." Why wouldn't I be nice? I'm not a monster, after all.

So we go to **Kennedy** to get la abuela and she is the last to come out of the airplane, on the arm of the cabin attendant, all wrapped up in a black shawl. He hands her over to my parents like she was a package sent airmail. It is January, two feet of snow on the ground, and she's wearing a shawl over a thin black dress. That's just the start.

> ✓ **LITERARY CHECK**
>
> How does Connie's description of her grandmother in the second sentence serve to **characterize** Connie? What is Connie like?

> ✓ **LITERARY CHECK**
>
> What are some examples of **sarcasm** on this page? What do Connie's sarcastic remarks reveal about her character?

---

slush, partly melted snow
Kennedy, John F. Kennedy International Airport in New York, NY, U.S.A.

Once home, she refuses to let my mother buy her a coat because it's a waste of money for the two weeks she'll be in *el Polo Norte*, as she calls New Jersey, the North Pole. So since she's only four feet eleven inches tall, she walks around in my mother's big black coat looking **ridiculous**. I try to walk far behind them in public so that no one will think we're together. I plan to stay very busy the whole time she's with us so that I won't be asked to take her anywhere, but my plan is ruined when my mother comes down with the flu and Abuela absolutely *has* to attend Sunday mass or her soul will be eternally damned. She's more Catholic than the Pope. My father decides that he should stay home with my mother and that I should **escort** la abuela to church. He tells me this on Saturday night as I'm getting ready to go out to the mall with my friends.

"No way," I say.

I go for the car keys on the kitchen table: he usually leaves them there for me on Friday and Saturday nights. He beats me to them.

"No way," he says, pocketing them and grinning at me.

---

ridiculous, silly
escort, go with

✓ LITERARY CHECK

What examples of **characterization** can you identify in this paragraph?

Before You Go On

1. Why does Connie walk far behind her grandmother?
2. What does Connie's father ask her to do?

On Your Own

How would you feel if you were Connie? Do you think Connie is being unfair to her grandmother? Explain.

Reading 4

Needless to say, we come to a compromise very quickly. I do have a responsibility to Sandra and Anita, who don't drive yet. There is a Harley-Davidson fashion show at Brookline Square that we *cannot* miss.

"The mass in Spanish is at ten sharp tomorrow morning, *entiendes*?" My father is dangling the car keys in front of my nose and pulling them back when I try to reach for them. He's really enjoying himself.

"I understand. Ten o'clock. I'm out of here." I pry his fingers off the key ring. He knows that I'm late, so he makes it just a little difficult. Then he laughs. I run out of our apartment before he changes his mind. I have no idea what I'm getting myself into.

Sunday morning I have to walk two blocks on dirty snow to **retrieve** the car. I warm it up for Abuela as instructed by my parents, and drive it to the front of our building. My father walks her by the hand in baby steps on the slippery snow. The sight of her little head with a bun on top of it sticking out of that huge coat makes me want to run back into my room and get under the covers. I just hope that nobody I know sees us together. I'm dreaming, of course. The mass is packed with people from our block. It's a **holy day of obligation** and everyone I ever met is there.

I have to help her climb the steps, and she stops to take a deep breath after each one, then I lead her down the aisle so that everybody can see me with my **bizarre** grandmother. If I were a good Catholic, I'm sure I'd get some **purgatory** time taken off for my sacrifice. She is walking as slow as Captain Cousteau exploring the bottom of the sea, looking around, taking her sweet time. Finally she chooses a pew, but she wants to sit in the *other* end. It's like she had a spot picked out for some unknown reason, and although it's the most inconvenient seat in the house, that's where she has to sit. So we squeeze by all the people already sitting there, saying, "Excuse me, please, *con permiso*, pardon me," getting annoyed looks the whole way. By the time we settle in, I'm drenched in sweat. I keep my head down like I'm praying so as not to see or be seen. She is praying loud, in Spanish, and singing hymns at the top of her creaky voice.

I ignore her when she gets up with a hundred other people to go take **communion**. I'm actually praying hard now—that this will all be over soon. But the next time I look up, I see a black coat dragging around and around the church, stopping here and there so a little gray head

> ✓ **LITERARY CHECK**
> How does the author use **dialogue** to help develop Connie's character?

---

retrieve, pick up
holy day of obligation, day when Catholics are obliged to, or must, go to church
bizarre, very strange
purgatory, according to the Catholic faith, a place where the souls of dead people go before entering heaven
communion, part of the mass in which people go up to the altar to eat a small piece of bread that is a sign of Jesus Christ's body

can peek out like a **periscope** on a submarine. There are giggles in the church, and even the priest has frozen in the middle of a blessing, his hands above his head like he is about to lead the congregation in a set of jumping jacks.

I realize to my horror that my grandmother is lost. She can't find her way back to the pew. I am so embarrassed that even though the woman next to me is **shooting daggers** at me with her eyes, I just can't move to go get her. I put my hands over my face like I'm praying, but it's really to hide my burning cheeks. I would like for her to disappear. I just know that on Monday my friends, and my enemies, in the **barrio** will have a lot of **senile**-grandmother jokes to tell in front of me. I am frozen to my

---

periscope, tube with mirrors inside it, used to look over the top of something
shooting daggers, shooting fierce looks
barrio, part of an American city where Spanish-speaking people live
senile, mentally confused or behaving strangely because of old age

Before You Go On

1. What happens to Abuela in church?
2. Why doesn't Connie get up to help her grandmother?

On Your Own

Do you feel sympathetic toward Connie? Why or why not?

Reading 4

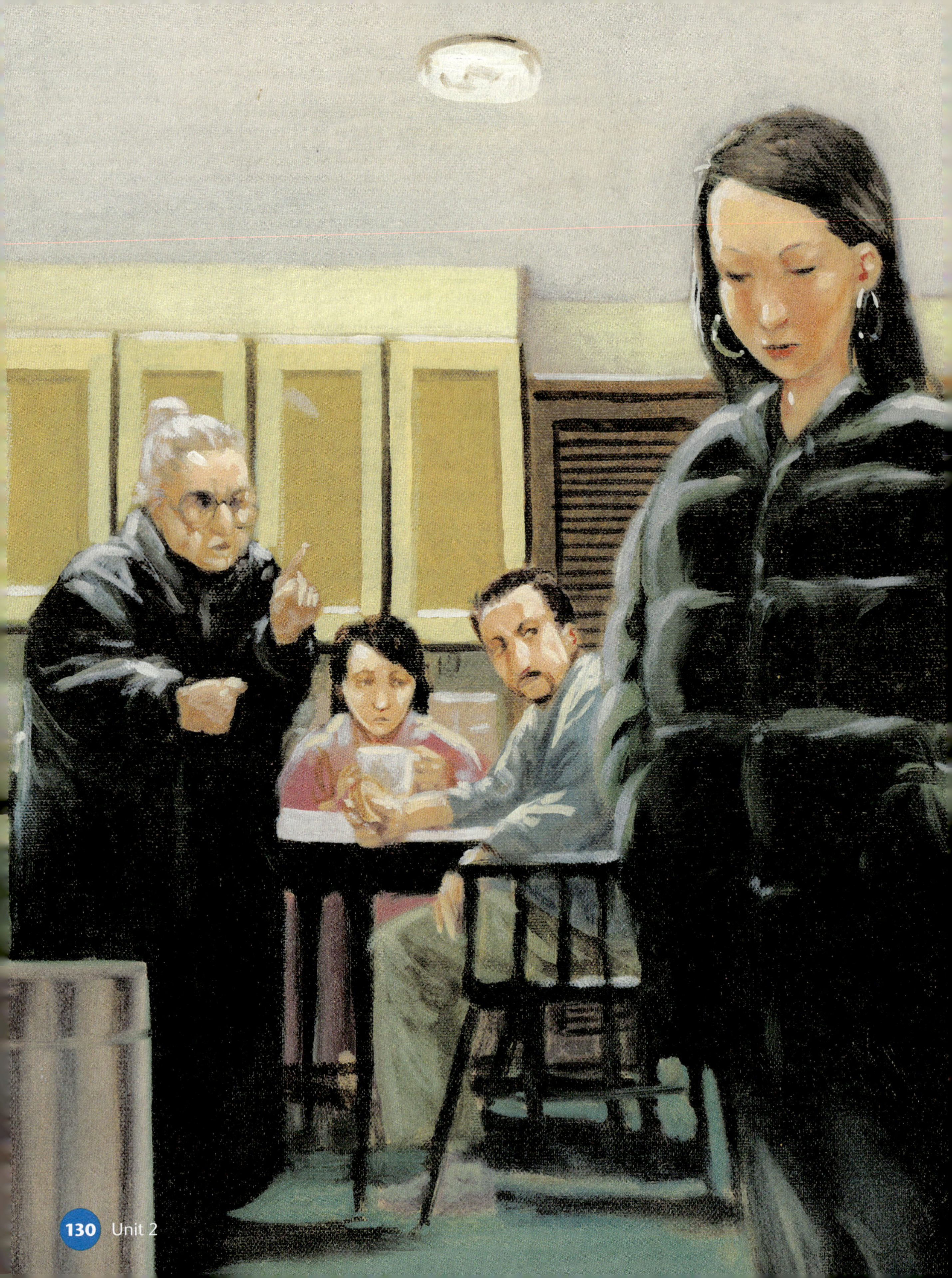

seat. So the same woman who wants me dead on the spot does it for me. She makes a big deal out of getting up and hurrying to get Abuela.

The rest of the mass is a blur. All I know is that my grandmother kneels the whole time with her hands over *her* face. She doesn't speak to me on the way home, and she doesn't let me help her walk, even though she almost falls a couple of times.

When we get to the apartment, my parents are at the kitchen table, where my mother is trying to eat some soup. They can see right away that something is wrong. Then Abuela points her finger at me like a judge passing a sentence on a criminal. She says in Spanish, "You made me feel like a zero, like a nothing." Then she goes to her room.

I try to explain what happened. "I don't understand why she's so upset. She just got lost and wandered around for a while," I tell them. But it sounds lame, even to my own ears. My mother gives me a look that makes me **cringe** and goes in to Abuela's room to get her version of the story. She comes out with tears in her eyes.

"Your grandmother says to tell you that of all the hurtful things you can do to a person, the worst is to make them feel as if they are worth nothing."

I can feel myself shrinking right there in front of her. But I can't bring myself to tell my mother that I think I understand how I made Abuela feel. I might be sent into the old lady's room to apologize, and it's not easy to admit you've been a **jerk**—at least, not right away with everybody watching. So I just sit there not saying anything.

My mother looks at me for a long time, like she feels sorry for me. Then she says, "You should know, Constancia, that if it wasn't for this old woman whose **existence** you don't seem to value, you and I would not be here."

That's when *I'm* sent to *my* room to consider a number I hadn't thought much about—until today.

---

cringe, move back or away from something because it pains you
jerk, person who does things that annoy or hurt other people
existence, state of being alive

About the Author

Judith Ortiz Cofer was an accomplished author of poetry, short stories, and novels for young adults. Born in Puerto Rico in 1952, she and her family moved to New Jersey when she was a girl. Cofer's work has won many awards. *An Island Like You* was named Best Book of the Year by the American Library Association in 1995. *The Meaning of Consuelo* won the America's Award for Children's and Young Adult Literature in 2003. In addition to writing, Cofer taught English and Creative Writing at the University of Georgia.

✓ LITERARY CHECK

How do you think this story would be different if it was told from the grandmother's **point of view**?

Word Skill

Earlier in the story, Connie explains that her full name, *Constancia*, has a special **connotation**, or associated meaning, whenever her mother uses it. What does she say it means? Does her mother's use of *Constancia* have the same connotation here?

Before You Go On

1. Why is Abuela hurt and angry?
2. How does Connie feel about what she did?

On Your Own

Do you think things might change between Abuela and Connie now?

Reading 4 131

Reading 4

Review and Practice

Reader's Theater

Act out the following scene between Connie and her father.

Connie: May I have the keys, Dad? I'm going out.

Father: Not so fast! [*holds the keys above his head*] I'll let you go under one condition.

Connie: [*sighs*] Hurry, Dad, *please*. My friends are waiting for me.

Father: You can go with your friends now, but you must take your grandmother to mass tomorrow. No excuses. Mass begins at 10:00 sharp.

Connie: But Dad!

Father: No "buts," Connie. You will do this for your family.

Connie: Okay, fine. I'll do it. Now please give me the keys. I don't want to miss the fashion show!

> **Speaking Tip**
>
> Be sure to make eye contact with members of your audience.

Comprehension

WB 67

Recall
1. How many times had Connie seen Abuela before this visit?
2. What makes Abuela look ridiculous to Connie?

Comprehend
3. What is Connie afraid will happen on Monday?
4. Why doesn't Abuela speak to Connie on the way home from church?

Analyze
5. How do you think the author feels about Connie's conduct?
6. The barrio is a small community. What effect does that have on Connie?

Connect
7. If Connie were your friend, what would you say to her about the incident and her feelings about Abuela? Explain.
8. Do you think the title of the story is effective? Why? What is it like to feel like a zero? Explain.

Discussion

Discuss with a partner or in a small group.

1. Why do you think Abuela and Connie have different viewpoints about what happened? Explain.
2. If you were Connie, how would you have felt about Abuela? Would you have done anything differently? Explain.
3. What lesson did Abuela teach Connie?

❓ **How are growth and change related?** Do you identify with Connie's embarrassment or do you think she was being selfish? How do you think she will change as a result of her experience with Abuela?

Listening Tip
Give each speaker your attention.

Response to Literature

68

How are senior citizens treated in your home culture? How are they treated in other cultures? Do research at the library or on the internet to find information about how a culture other than your own treats elderly people. Write a paragraph summarizing your findings. You may wish to work with your classmates to publish your paragraphs in a class book.

▲ In many cultures, adults live with and care for their elderly parents.

Reading 4
Grammar

Have to + Verb

Use the phrase *have to* plus the base form of a verb to express necessity or lack of necessity.

Necessity (Positive)	Lack of Necessity (Negative)
I **have to be** polite to my grandmother.	I **don't have to help** her put on her coat.
She **has to go** to church on Sunday.	She **doesn't have to attend** the fashion show.
She **had to go** to her room yesterday.	She **did not have to stay** in her room all day.

Practice A
WB 68

Complete the sentences with the correct form of *have to* and the verb in parentheses. Be sure to use the negative if it is indicated.

1. My father _____ on Saturdays. (work)
2. I _____ homework yesterday. (do)
3. I _____ homework today. (not, do)
4. Last night, my mother _____ dinner. (not, cook)

Grammar Skill

Make sure subjects and verbs agree in number. A singular subject uses a singular verb, (e.g., *He has to get up early*). A plural subject uses a plural verb, (e.g., *We have to get up early*).

Practice B

Copy this chart into your notebook. Complete each sentence with something you have to do (positive) or don't have to do (negative). Then put each sentence in the past using *had to* or *didn't have to*. The first one has been done for you.

Grammar Check

✓ Does **have to** + verb express possibility or necessity?

Positive or Negative	Sentence
1. negative	Example: On Saturdays, I don't have to get up early. Last Saturday, I didn't have to get up early.
2. positive	Every morning,
3. negative	On weekends,
4. positive	After dinner,

Apply

Talk with a partner about things you have to and don't have to do this week.

Conditional Sentences

Conditional sentences are used to talk about events that may or may not occur, depending on other events or conditions. Each conditional sentence has an *if* clause and a result clause. Here is an example:

if clause	result clause
If you get one question wrong,	you fail.

There are different kinds of conditional sentences. Factual conditionals are used to talk about future results of specific events or actions. The verb in the result clause is often preceded by *will*.

If you **get** a good education, more people **will listen** to you.

Unreal conditionals are used to talk about present unreal conditions and their results. Use the simple past in the *if* clause and *could*, *would*, or *might* + verb in the result clause. If the verb is *be* in the *if* clause, use *were* for all persons.

If Mama **went** back to school, she **could have** more opportunities.
If I **were** Lucas, I **would be** angry too.

Grammar Skill
Use a comma when the cause comes first. Do not use a comma if the effect comes first.

Grammar Check
✓ Are unreal **conditional sentences** used to express certainty about something?

Practice A
WB 69

In each sentence, underline the *if* clause once and the result clause twice. Then write *factual conditional* or *unreal conditional*.

1. <u>unreal conditional</u>   <u>I would be happy</u> <u>if my grandparents visited me.</u>
2. _____ Abuela will feel better if Connie apologizes.
3. _____ If I got lost, I would call a family member.
4. _____ If you visit Puerto Rico, you will see some interesting sights.

Practice B

Complete the sentences. Use your own ideas. Write in your notebook.

1. I will feel very happy if . . . *I will feel very happy if it's sunny tomorrow.*
2. If I have free time this weekend, . . .
3. If my relatives visited me, . . .
4. I would take a long trip if . . .

Apply
Talk with a partner and complete these sentences with your ideas: *This class would be very happy if . . . / If I have some time this summer, . . .*

Reading 4

Reading 4
Writing

Write a Personal Narrative

In this lesson, you will write a personal narrative from your own point of view. In a personal narrative, you tell about an experience you have had. Like fictional narratives, personal narratives include dialogue, characterizations, and events related in a sequence; however, the events, dialogue, and people in the personal narrative are real.

> **Writing Prompt**
>
> Write a personal narrative. Then provide some details and descriptions about your experience. Use conditionals and *have to* as appropriate.

1 Prewrite Begin by choosing a memorable experience you had with a family member of an adventure you had with a friend.

- Think about the event. What happened?
- Who are the other characters in your narrative? What did they say?
- List your ideas in a graphic organizer like the one below.

A student named Andrea used this two-column chart to organize her ideas.

who was there	me, my dad, my grandpa, my other relatives
what happened	It rained, but we had fun anyway.
what was said	"We are not going to let an aguasero—a little rainfall—ruin our trip!"

② **Draft** Use your two-column chart to help you write a first draft.

- Remember to keep your purpose for writing in mind.
- Remember to include characters and dialogue.
- Use conditionals and *have to* correctly.

③ **Revise** Read over your draft. Look for places where the writing needs improvement. As you do so, complete (✓) the Writing Checklist. Use the questions in the Writing Checklist to help you revise your story. Then, revise your draft, using the editing and proofreading marks listed on page 467.

④ **Edit and Proofread** Check your work for errors in grammar, usage, mechanics, and spelling. Trade papers with a partner to obtain feedback. Edit your final draft in response to feedback from your partner and your teacher.

⑤ **Publish** Prepare a clean copy of your final draft. Share your personal narrative with the class. Save your work. You'll need to refer to it in the Writing Workshop at the end of the unit.

> **Writing Checklist**
>
> **Organization:**
> ☐ I related my experience in a clear and logical way.
>
> **Sentence Fluency:**
> ☐ My sentences flow smoothly, helping the reader to move from one action to the next.
>
> **Conventions:**
> ☐ I used conditionals and *have to* correctly.

Here is Andrea's personal narrative. Notice that she includes what her parents said.

Andrea Vargas

Rainy River Day

My cousins and I had packed everything we needed for our hike the night before, but when I woke up on Saturday, it was raining. My parents woke everyone up by announcing, "We are not going to let an aguasero—a little rainfall—ruin our trip! We've been preparing for weeks!" While everyone was getting ready, the sun came out. We had to walk down a big mountain to get to the river. We swam, played ball, and slept on the gigantic rocks. For lunch, we made Sancocho de Pollo—chicken stew—in a huge pot. We built a campfire with found wood, and added all the ingredients we had packed for the stew. We cooked and ate, and then put out the fire with sand and water. As we were about to head home, it started raining again. It was a huge aguasero. On the way out, we had to climb up the mountain. But this time, there was a lot of mud, and it was very slippery. I tried and tried to climb up, but I couldn't. Finally, my dad held on to my arm, and I had to walk on the edge of the river. If I had to do it all over again, I would!

Reading 4

Link the Readings

Critical Thinking

What logical connections can you make between the ideas and details in the readings in this unit? Although the readings do not all have the same purpose, they share a common theme and reflect a range of viewpoints. Complete the chart below. Be prepared to support your answers with evidence from each of the texts.

Title of Reading	Purpose	Big Question Link
"How Seeds and Plants Grow" "A Tale of Two Brothers"		
"The Test"		
"Climate Change Puts Nature on the Move"	to inform	
"Abuela Invents the Zero"		Connie learns a lesson about treating her grandmother with respect.

Discussion

Discuss with a partner or in a small group.
- Which unit selection had the biggest impact on you? Which character or situation could you identify with more? Explain.
- **How are growth and change related?** Which unit selection do you think answered the Big Question the best? Explain.

Fluency Check

Work with a partner. Choose a paragraph from one of the readings. Take turns reading it for one minute. Count the total number of words you read. Practice saying the words you had trouble reading. Take turns reading the paragraph three more times. Did you read more words each time? Record your speeds in the chart below.

	1st Reading	2nd Reading	3rd Reading	4th Reading
Number of Words				

Media Literacy & Projects

Work with a partner or in a small group. Choose one of these projects.

1. Do research to learn about changes in one animal's migration route in the last 100 years. Make a graph with the information you find. Display your graph and explain your findings.

2. What do you think will happen when Connie comes out of her room and she and Abuela talk? Write a short dialogue that occurs when they sit down to talk after the incident.

3. Do research at the library or on the internet to learn how to grow a plant. Buy a packet of seeds and follow the instructions on the packet. As the plant grows, create a photo-essay of the different stages. Display your work for the class.

4. Choose one of these topics related to the unit, or create your own topic related to the unit: how plants use photosynthesis; stories about right and wrong; discrimination; the impact of climate change; how the elderly are treated. Research the topic online and take notes. Report your findings to your group.

Further Reading

Choose from these reading suggestions. Practice reading silently for longer and longer periods.

Martin Luther King, Coleen Degnan-Veness
This book tells the amazing story of Dr. King's nonviolent struggle for racial equality and its powerful impact.

The Boy Who Harnessed the Wind, William Kamkwamba
As a teenager living in Malawi, William experiences poverty and a lack of electricity and running water. When his family runs out of money for school, William finds solutions to his country's energy problems.

Where the Red Fern Grows, Wilson Rawls
Billy and his coonhound pups win the coveted gold cup in the annual coon-hunt contest. But when triumph turns to tragedy, Billy learns the beautiful Native American legend of the sacred red fern.

Generation Green: The Ultimate Teen Guide to Living an Eco-Friendly Life, Linda Sivertsen and Tosh Sivertsen
This book is a guide for teens who are curious about making a positive impact on the environment. You'll learn tips for living even greener!

Put It All Together

Listening & Speaking Workshop

Skit

You will write and perform a skit that tells a story.

1 Think About It

Work in small groups. Review the elements of a story by listing the people, places, and events described in "Abuela Invents the Zero." Who are the characters? What is the setting? What events make up the plot?

Think of a story that your group could present as a skit, or short play. You may create your own story, choose one from this book, or use a familiar fairy tale or fable.

2 Gather and Organize Information

Discuss your story. Make a list of the characters, and write down key details about the characters, setting, and plot.

Order Your Notes Make a story map to help you organize your ideas.

Characters Who?	Setting Where and when?	Mood What is the mood?
Problem What conflict does the plot grow out of?	Solution How does the conflict get resolved?	Tone What is the tone?

Prepare a Script Decide who will play each character. Then use your notes and story map to write a script. The dialogue should look like this:

  Nolbu: Where did all these gemstones come from?
  Heungbu: From a melon seed! You won't believe what happened.
  Nolbu: Impossible! Melon seeds grow melons, not gemstones.

Include important details about the setting, props, and action:

Heungbu carefully binds the swallow's leg and carries the bird into the house. Time passes as the bird's leg heals. Then Heungbu sets the bird free.

Use Visuals Make or find the costumes and props you need for your skit.

3 Practice and Present

As a group, practice your skit until you can perform it without looking at the script. If possible, ask a friend or family member to serve as *prompter* while you practice. (A prompter watches the skit and follows along in the script. If someone forgets what to say or do, the prompter quietly reminds him or her.) Practice using your props and wearing your costumes. To make the presentation of your skit richer and more interesting, use a variety of grammatical structures, sentence lengths, sentence types, and connecting words.

Perform Your Skit Face the audience and speak loudly and clearly, even when your body is pointing in another direction. Pay attention to the other actors, and be ready when it's your turn to speak or move!

4 Evaluate the Presentation

A good way to improve your speaking and listening skills is to evaluate each presentation you give and hear. When you evaluate yourself, think about what you did well and what you can do better. Complete (✓) this checklist to help you evaluate your group's skit and the skits of your classmates.

- ☐ Could you understand the story?
- ☐ Did the actors know their parts well?
- ☐ Were the costumes and props helpful and appropriate?
- ☐ Could you hear and understand the actors' words?
- ☐ Could the skit be improved?

Speaking Tips

Always face the audience when you speak, even when you are talking to another character. If you turn away from the audience, people may not be able to hear or understand you.

Use gestures and facial expressions to help convey your character's thoughts and feelings to the audience.

Listening Tips

Listen carefully to the other actors so that you know when to say your lines. Learn your *cues*—words or actions that signal it is your turn to speak.

When you watch a skit, look for actions and gestures to help you understand what people are saying.

Strengthen Your Social Language

Performing a skit helps you learn vocabulary and structures used in conversational situations. Go to your *Digital Resources* and do the activity for this unit. This activity will require you to use language that will help you in conversation.

Put It All Together

Writing Workshop

Fictional Narrative

A fictional narrative is a story invented by the writer. Both novels and short stories are fictional narratives. The events that make up the plot of a fictional narrative are usually told in sequence and focus on a conflict or problem. In the beginning of the story, the problem is introduced. The problem is developed in the middle of the story and is resolved by the end. Fictional narratives also occur in a specific time and place, called the *setting*. Another element is dialogue, or the words characters say to one another. Dialogue helps bring the characters to life.

Writing Prompt
Write a fictional narrative that includes two or more characters, a plot, a setting, and dialogue. Be sure to use conditional sentences correctly.

① Prewrite Think about stories you have read and liked. What did you most enjoy? Were the characters amusing? Was the plot mysterious? Was the setting vivid? Then brainstorm a list of characters for your story in your notebook. Also, think about the point of view from which your narrative will be told. From whose perspective will readers see events?

WB 71

List and Organize Ideas and Details Use a story chart to organize ideas for your fictional narrative. A student named Micah decided to write a story about a musical squirrel named Sammy. Here is his story chart:

Characters	Setting
Who?	Where and when?
Sammy Squirrel	Forest in Spring
Robins and forest friends	
Problem	**Solution**
What conflict does the plot grow out of?	How does the conflict get resolved?
Nobody will let Sammy sing!	Sammy finds a new way to make music.

② Draft Use the model on page 146 and your story chart to help you write a first draft. Remember to tell events in chronological order. Include dialogue to help reveal what your characters are thinking and feeling.

3 Revise

Read over your draft. As you do so, complete (✓) the writing checklist. Use the questions to help you revise your fictional narrative.

Six Traits of Writing Checklist

- ☐ **Ideas:** Is my plot original and interesting?
- ☐ **Organization:** Are events presented in sequence?
- ☐ **Voice:** Does my writing express my personality?
- ☐ **Word Choice:** Does the dialogue suit my characters?
- ☐ **Sentence Fluency:** Do my sentences vary in length and type?
- ☐ **Conventions:** Does my writing follow the rules of grammar, usage, and mechanics?

Here are the changes Micah plans to make when he revises his first draft:

The Squeaky Squirrel Sings

Hi there! The name's Sammy— ~~My name is~~ Sammy Squirrel. I live in the forest, and there's always plenty to do here. My favorit*e* activity use*d* to be listening to the Robins sing. Whenever they sang, every body gathered around to listen. One day, I decided to sing along. Unfortunately, I have a *squeaky* voice that isn't so pleasing to the ear. As I sang along, the crowd turned toward me in disgust.

You have to stop! "Hey!" shouted one of the Robins. "This concert is for animals with fine singing voices, not squeaky screeches!"

The crowd began to laugh. I *wiped away a tear and* quickly ran away. For a while I

Revised to engage reader with a greeting.

Revised to correct spelling and mechanics and to add a descriptive adjective.

Revised for clarity of plot.

Revised to add detail.

Unit 2 143

Put It All Together

    w**a**ndered around the forest alone. **Finally,** I met some new friends—Wilson Woodpecker, Tommy Turtle, and Ricky Rattler. Wilson's large beak prevents him from singing; Tommy is too slow and lazy to sing; and Ricky can only hiss. ~~They can't sing either.~~

Revised to correct spelling and for clarity of flow and pronoun reference.

    One afternoon, as I was climbing down a tree, I accidentally dropped an acorn ~~and~~ **that** hit Tommy's shell. Shocked by the impact, Tommy ~~shouted~~ **yelped**. Shocked by Tommy's ~~shout~~ **yelp**, Ricky rattled his tail, while Wilson tapped his beak against a branch.

Revised to add descriptive language.

    "Hold on! I shouted, "Did you here what we just did?"

    "What? All we did was drop acorns, rattle tails, and peck trees," said Wilson.

    "Exactly!" I declared. "If we come up with the right arrangement, these thumps and pecks **will** turn into a fabulous rhythm!" Excited about this new discovery, we began to work. We created a great beat!

Revised for mechanics and clarity of sequence.

    Before long, All the animals of the forest began to stop by to listen to us. Soon, the Robins invited us to join them in a concert. Combined with the Robin's singing, our strong beat **has** ~~could~~ led to a new kind of music that involve**s** the whole forest, whether good singers or not. And that's how this squeaky squirrel helped bring music into ~~the~~ **our forest** world!

Revised for mechanics and to add descriptive detail.

④ Edit and Proofread Check your work for errors in grammar, usage, mechanics, and spelling. Then trade essays with a partner and complete (✓) the Peer Review Checklist below to give each other constructive feedback. Edit your final draft in response to feedback from your partner and your teacher.

WB 71

Peer Review Checklist

- ☐ Does the first paragraph introduce the story?
- ☐ Is the problem introduced, developed, and resolved?
- ☐ Are the ideas presented in an order that makes sense?
- ☐ Does the description include sensory details where appropriate?
- ☐ Does the dialogue help to bring the characters to life?
- ☐ Is it clear why this story is important to the writer?
- ☐ Could changes be made to improve the fictional narrative?

Put It All Together

Based on the peer review, Micah decided to make these changes to his final draft.

Micah Cowher

The Squeaky Squirrel Sings

Hi, there! The name's Sammy—Sammy Squirrel. I live in the forest, and there's always plenty to do here. My favorite activity used to be listening to the Robins sing. Whenever they sang, everybody gathered around to listen. One day, I decided to sing along. Unfortunately, I have a squeaky voice that isn't so pleasing to the ear. As I sang along, the crowd turned toward me in disgust.

"Hey! You have to stop!" shouted one of the Robins. "This concert is for animals with fine singing voices, not squeaky screeches!"

The crowd began to laugh. I wiped away a tear and quickly ran away. For a while, I wandered around the forest alone. Finally, I met some new friends—Wilson Woodpecker, Tommy Turtle, and Ricky Rattler. They can't sing either. Wilson's large beak prevents him from singing; Tommy is too slow and lazy to sing; and Ricky can only hiss.

One afternoon, as I was climbing down a tree, I accidentally dropped an acorn that hit Tommy's shell. Shocked by the impact, Tommy yelped. Shocked by Tommy's yelp, Ricky rattled his tail, while Wilson tapped his beak against a branch.

"Hold on!" I shouted, "Did you hear what we just did?"

"What? All we did was drop acorns, rattle tails, and peck trees," said Wilson.

"Exactly!" I declared. "If we come up with the right arrangement, these thumps and pecks will turn into a fabulous rhythm!" Excited about this new discovery, we began to work. We created a great beat!

Before long, all the animals of the forest began to stop by to listen to us. Soon, the Robins invited us to join them in a concert. Combined with the Robin's singing, our strong beat has led to a new kind of music that involves the whole forest, whether good singers or not. And that's how this squeaky squirrel helped bring music into our forest world!

Revised to correct spelling of compound word.

Revised to add comma.

Revised to correct punctuation and spelling.

Revised to correct possessive.

5 **Publish** Obtain feedback from your teacher and classmates; then prepare your final draft. Share your fictional narrative with the class.

Test Preparation

Practice

Read the following test sample. Study the tips in the boxes. Work with a partner to answer the questions.

Smithville Needs a Community Garden

1   At the end of West Main Street, there is a vast overgrown and trash-strewn lot where a mall once stood. This vacant lot has become a nuisance to our city. It invites car races, vandalism, and loitering. It is a refuge for all kinds of vermin that live in the tall weeds and trash piles. The city board is currently weighing options for the rehabilitation of that lot. Some want an apartment complex or a new shopping center with businesses. However, I suggest we turn that acre of dirt to good use for the city and grow a community garden.

2   A community garden is an area of public land on which a group of volunteers cultivate crops. There are no fewer than six gardening clubs in Smithville, all of which would be excited for the opportunity to help with such a project. A community garden can provide healthy vegetables and fruits for low-income families. It preserves open space, builds community, and reduces the pollution caused by car exhaust. There are even grants available to fund a new community garden. The loss of potential tax revenue on the lot is nothing compared to the problems a retailer could bring.

3   I encourage the citizens of Smithville to come to the next board meeting and press the council to consider this excellent alternative use of that empty eyesore.

1 This passage is an example of what type of genre?
- **A** A science article
- **B** A newspaper editorial
- **C** An autobiography
- **D** An instruction manual

2 What possible objection to the community garden plan does the author NOT address in the passage?
- **A** The cost of starting and maintaining a community garden
- **B** Whether there will be enough volunteers for the garden
- **C** The loss of tax revenue from possible businesses on the lot
- **D** How the city will provide security against garden vandalism

Taking Tests
You will often take tests to show what you know. Study the tips below to help you improve your test-taking skills.

Tip
Some test questions are written in the negative by using the word *not*. The correct answer will include information that isn't mentioned in the passage.

Tip
Sometimes answer choices are phrased differently than the information in the passage. Don't eliminate an answer just because the exact same words are not in the passage.

WB 72–73

Unit 2

Visual Literacy

Smithsonian American Art Museum

Cycles of Nature

Artists regularly explore our place in the natural world and the life cycles that we all experience before we die. No one goes through life without facing change and undergoing personal and physical growth on some level.

Thomas Hart Benton, *Wheat* (1967)

In Thomas Hart Benton's painting *Wheat*, neat rows of wheat fill the canvas. Ripe stalks of grain crowd the top part of the painting. The first two rows have been cut, but the artist paints green shoots on the bottom to show that the next crop is already on its way.

Benton often dealt with political issues in his work. He may have felt that the neat rows of grain symbolized the democratic masses of America. He chose an angle and a close-up view that brings the viewer in among the rows or "masses." The painting celebrates the natural cycle of crops and the bounty of the harvest in a very fertile land, the United States.

One broken stalk strays across the center of the painting. Benton managed to capture all three vital stages of life in one frame: infancy, mature adulthood, and death.

▶ Thomas Hart Benton, *Wheat*, 1967, oil, 20 x 21 in., Smithsonian American Art Museum

Mary Vaux Walcott, *Untitled (Mixed Flowers)* (1876)

Mary Vaux Walcott, who specialized in painting wildflowers, spent as much time as possible outdoors. She often hiked deep into the wilderness so she could capture the fleeting beauty of various blossoms. She understood that flowers "withered quickly." She wanted to represent what they really looked like rather than paint them as fancier or more colorful than they really were. The Smithsonian American Art Museum has almost 800 of her detailed watercolors in its collection. Her art forms a permanent record of passing beauty.

▲ Mary Vaux Walcott, *Untitled (Mixed Flowers)*, 1876, watercolor, 5⅛ × 2⅜ in., Smithsonian American Art Museum

Heikki Seppä, *Lupin Wedding Crown* (1982)

In *Lupin Wedding Crown*, Heikki Seppä uses a very different medium—silver and gold—to celebrate the natural world. The gold tip of the crown represents a sprig of lupine (alternate spelling), a plant that has tiny honeycomb-like flowers that symbolize abundance and fertility.

The shape and name of the crown reflect Seppä's own roots in Finland, where he was born. There they have a wedding tradition called the Dance of Crowns. Unmarried bridesmaids circle the blindfolded bride, who then tries to place a gold crown on one of their heads. Whoever gets the crown is supposed to be the next one to marry.

All three artists tapped into natural imagery to capture or celebrate a stage of life. Every living thing on Earth is born, grows, and dies. In between these cycles lies many other layers of growth and change. Some are good and some are difficult. It's all part of the natural world.

▲ Heikki Seppä, *Lupin Wedding Crown*, 1982, gold, silver, and diamond, 4 × 8 × 8 in., Smithsonian American Art Museum

Discuss What You Learned

1. Which of these artworks do you think best captures the cycles of nature? Explain your answer.
2. If you were to create an artwork that shows the cycles of nature, what would it look like?

BIG QUESTION
In what way does each of these artworks reflect a different aspect of cycles in nature? Explain your answer.

75–76

Unit 2

Unit 3

How can we tell what's right?

THE BIG QUESTION

This unit is about right and wrong. You'll read about lessons that teach right from wrong. You'll learn about a young woman who supports going to Mars. You'll also learn about athletes who made difficult choices. Reading, writing, and talking about these topics will give you practice using academic language and help you become a better student.

Reading 1
Folktale

"The Beggar King"

Reading Strategy
Identify problems and solutions

Reading 2
Science

"Mars: Pro and Con"

Reading Strategy
Distinguish fact from opinion

Reading 3
Fable

"The Golden Serpent"
retold by Walter Dean Myers

Reading Strategy
Identify the purpose of a fable

Listening and Speaking—Radio Commercial

At the end of this unit, you will choose a topic and create and perform a **radio commercial**.

Writing—Speech

At the end of this unit, you will write and give a **speech**. To help you do this, you will write a review, a letter to the editor, a persuasive paragraph, and an advertisement.

Quick Write

Write the words *Right* and *Wrong* at the top of a sheet of paper. List ideas and actions you believe to be right or wrong under the appropriate word.

Reading 4
Social Studies

"When Is a Winner a Hero?"

Reading Strategy
Summarize

View and Respond

Go to your Digital Resources. Watch the video and answer the questions.

Reading 1

Prepare to Read

What You Will Learn

Reading
- Vocabulary building: *Literary terms, word study*
- Reading strategy: *Identify problems and solutions*
- Text type: *Literature (folktale)*

Grammar
- The modal *must*
- The modal *would* for repeated actions in the past

Writing
- Write a review

THE BIG QUESTION

How can we tell what's right? Every culture has stories that teach a lesson. Sometimes, that lesson teaches how to tell right from wrong. For example, you may know this story, "The Fox and the Crow":

> A fox once saw a crow fly off with a piece of cheese in its beak and settle on the branch of a tree. "That's for me," said the fox, and walked up to the foot of the tree. "Good day, Mistress Crow," he cried. "How well you are looking today. How glossy your feathers are. If your voice is half as beautiful as those feathers, it would please my ears to hear you sing!" The crow lifted up her head and began to caw her best. But the moment she opened her mouth, the piece of cheese fell to the ground, only to be snapped up by the fox. "That was all I wanted," said he. "In exchange for your cheese, I will give you this piece of advice: Do not trust flatterers."

Which stories from your own culture teach a lesson? In small groups, discuss the stories and the lessons they teach. Compare stories from your own culture with those from other cultures. In what ways are the lessons similar?

Build Background

"The Beggar King" is a folktale, or an old traditional story from a specific culture. This folktale from Eastern Europe is about a rich king who enjoys fine clothes and fine foods every day. One day, someone plays a trick on him and leaves him without his fine clothes. People do not recognize him and think he is a beggar. Have you ever mistaken someone for another person? How did you discover you weren't right?

▲ A beggar is poor, while a king is rich. What do you think a beggar king is?

Vocabulary

Learn Literary Words

A **moral** is a lesson taught in a literary work, especially a fable or folktale. It is a practical lesson about right and wrong ways to behave. Many fables have a stated moral that comes at the end of the story. In "The Fox and the Crow," the moral is the last sentence: *Do not trust flatterers*. Readers often have to infer the moral in a folktale.

Motivation is the reason for a character's actions. Motivation results from a combination of the character's personality and the situation in which the character finds him- or herself. For example, in "The Fox and the Crow," the fox is motivated by hunger. The crow is motivated by her need for compliments.

Literary Words
- moral
- motivation

Practice

Work with a partner. Read the fable below. What is the crow's motivation? What is the moral of the fable? Is the moral stated directly or left for the reader to figure out? Explain your answer.

> A crow, near dead with thirst, came upon a pitcher of water. But when the crow tried to drink from the pitcher, he found that there was only a little bit of water in it. He could not reach his head down into the pitcher to get to the water, however hard he tried. At last, the poor crow gave up in despair. Then, suddenly, he had an idea. He dropped a pebble into the pitcher. Then he dropped another pebble into the pitcher. Again and again he dropped pebble after pebble into the pitcher. At long last, he saw the water mount up near him, and with a few more pebbles, he was able to quench his thirst and save his life. And so the crow learned a valuable lesson: Little by little does the trick.

▲ *Aesop's Fable*, a painting by Lizzie Riches

Reading 1

Listening and Speaking: Academic Words

Study the **purple** words and their meanings. You will find these words useful when talking and writing about literature. Write each word and its meaning in your notebook, then say the words aloud with a partner. After you read "The Beggar King," try to use these words to respond to the text.

Academic Words
- adviser
- collection
- recognize
- wisdom

adviser = a person whose job it is to give advice about a specific topic	➡	King Hagag's **adviser** gave him advice from *The Great Book of Kings*.
collection = a group of similar things that you get and keep together	➡	King Hagag had a **collection** of many colorful robes made of expensive materials.
recognize = to realize that you know a person when you see him or her	➡	The palace guards did not **recognize** King Hagag.
wisdom = knowledge gained over a long period of time	➡	*The Great Book of Kings* contains a lot of great **wisdom**.

Practice WB 78

Work with a partner to answer these questions. Try to include the **purple** word in your answer. Write the sentences in your notebook.

1. What people or groups do you think need an **adviser**?
2. Do you know anyone who owns a **collection**? What kind of collection is it?
3. What TV or movie stars do you know about whose appearance in a show or movie changed so much that you did not **recognize** them?
4. Do you know someone who has a lot of **wisdom**? If so, who and why?

Word Study: Irregular Plurals

Most nouns in English can be made plural by adding -s or -es. There are also nouns that are irregular in the plural form. Nouns with irregular plural spellings must be memorized. Study the rules below:

Add -es to nouns that end with -s, -z, -x, -sh, and -ch. Add -es to some nouns that end with -o.

> King Hagag drank from a **glass** that was the finest of all his **glasses**. The farmer showed Hagag a **potato**. He wanted to sell his **potatoes** to the king.

For nouns that end with a consonant + -y, change -y to -i and add -es.

> The king's **belly** was full of good food, but his people's **bellies** were empty.

For nouns that end in -f or -fe, change -f to -v and add -es.

> The farmer's **wife** works hard. The rich men's **wives** do not.

Some nouns don't change in the plural form: *deer*, *series*, and *sheep*.

Practice
WB 79

In your notebook, write the plural forms of these nouns: *search*, *mystery*, *loaf*, *hero*, and *cry*. Check your spellings in a dictionary. Then write a sentence with each word.

Reading Strategy | Identify Problems and Solutions

Identifying problems and solutions helps you understand a story better. To identify problems and solutions, ask yourself these questions:

- What problem does the main character have?
- What would you do about the problem?
- There may be more than one solution to the problem. What do you think the main character will do?
- How is the problem solved? Would you have done the same things as the kind strangers in the story? Explain.

As you read "The Beggar King," ask yourself what problem the king has. How is the problem solved?

WB 80

Reading 1

**Literature
Fable**

Set a purpose for reading Read the folktale to find out how a very rich king changes his way of life. Why does he change his ways?

The Beggar King

An Eastern European Folktale

Once upon a time in a faraway land, there lived a proud and regal king named King Hagag, who was known for his **exquisite** taste in clothing and food.

King Hagag had a collection of robes in every color imaginable, all handmade especially for him by the finest tailors in the land, who journeyed many miles to serve their king. The robes were **exceedingly** soft to the touch, for they were made from the finest silks and the softest velvets in the world. And they were beautiful to look at, as they were colored with special dyes mixed in shades created just for his Highness.

King Hagag's royal kitchen was constantly **aflutter** with the greatest chefs in the land. Each day, the chefs gathered rare and **precious** ingredients that came by ship for the king. And each day, the chefs cooked new and interesting creations, sending tempting **aromas** throughout the castle. At mealtime, the king sat alone at his long table, which was laid out with the finest of china and silver and glasses, and he feasted on dish after **exotic** dish until his belly was **bulging** underneath his fine robes.

After breakfast each morning, King Hagag sat on his throne and listened as his trusted adviser read to him from *The Great Book of Kings*. The book had been written by Hagag's great-great-great-great-grandfather.

One morning, the trusted adviser read these words: "Riches are not forever, and the crown does not **endure** every generation."

---

exquisite, beautiful and delicate
exceedingly, extremely
aflutter, full of excitement
precious, valuable or important
aromas, strong, pleasant smells
exotic, unusual and exciting
bulging, sticking out; swollen
endure, to continue or last for a long time

> **Listening Skill**
>
> As you listen to the audio, listen carefully for patterns of intonation. Pay attention to the rhythm of the words and the way the voice rises and falls. Different sentence types, such as statements, questions, or commands, have different intonation patterns.

King Hagag grew red in the face. "What nonsense is this?" he exclaimed. "Certainly, my riches will be with me forever! And my future son will become king, just as I am king, my father was king, and his father before him."

The trusted adviser said, "Your Majesty, *The Great Book of Kings* contains great wisdom."

"Rip out the page and burn it," roared King Hagag.

"But Your Highness, a page from this book must never be destroyed. The Great Genie is very powerful, and he will—"

"Rip it out, I say!" the king roared, and so the trusted adviser did as he was told.

Before You Go On

1. What did the king do at mealtime?
2. What did the king think of the words, "Riches are not forever, and the crown does not endure every generation"?

On Your Own

Who do you think is right: the king or the adviser? What do you think will happen? Why?

Reading 1   157

Later, King Hagag mounted his royal horse and rode with his trusted adviser to the royal lake for his afternoon swim. When they got to the lake, King Hagag, dressed in his swimming **costume**, jumped into the water and swam clear across the lake, leaving his trusted adviser to watch the horses. When he got to the other side of the lake, seemingly out of nowhere, a young man appeared before him.

"Who are you, and what are you doing inside the royal gates?" the king asked.

"I am the Great Genie, and I have come to teach you a lesson," said the young man. He quickly disappeared and then reappeared on the other side of the lake and began to dress in King Hagag's robes.

King Hagag quickly swam across the lake. By the time he arrived, the Great Genie was atop King Hagag's horse and was riding away with the king's trusted adviser.

"Wait, wait! I am King Hagag! He is an **imposter**," King Hagag shouted, running behind them, but the wise and trusted adviser was under the Great Genie's spell and didn't recognize his true master. The king quickly called the guards to get rid of the **trespasser** who was claiming to be the king.

> ✓ **LITERARY CHECK**
> What is the Great Genie's **motivation**? How is it different from the king's **motivation**?

---

costume, outfit
imposter, someone who pretends to be someone else in order to trick people
trespasser, a person who goes onto someone else's land without permission

"I am King Hagag. I truly am," Hagag insisted to the guards, but they, too, were under the Great Genie's spell and did not recognize him. They deposited Hagag outside of the castle gates, dressed only in his swimming costume.

That night, King Hagag slept with his head against the hard earth. In the morning, he was hungry and wondered what he would eat. On the street, there were no chefs to **summon**, no tantalizing aromas, and no tasty foods set out for him.

Sitting on the ground in his swimming costume, King Hagag appeared to be a beggar, so people began giving him food. A kind baker offered him a slice of simple bread, and a dairy farmer gave him a bit of cheese.

"Thank you, thank you," said Hagag to each generous person as he hungrily ate the simple food. He was surprised by how delicious it tasted. And so it went: Day after day, Hagag relied on the kind strangers who passed him on the sidewalk.

The seasons changed, and the weather became chilly. "If only I had my royal robes," Hagag moaned.

Soon, a woman stopped. "I saw you shivering, so I have sewn you this," she said. She gave him a dull brown robe made of **coarse**, inexpensive fabric. Hagag put on the robe and found that he loved it better than his fine royal robes, for this robe stopped his shivering and made him feel cared for.

---

summon, to order someone to come to a particular place
coarse, rough or thick

Before You Go On

1. How was the Great Genie able to look like the king?
2. What was the king wearing when the guards left him outside the castle gates?

On Your Own

What lesson do you think the Great Genie wants to teach the king?

In the spring, Hagag awoke one day to see crowds on the street. He joined the crowds in time to see the royal **procession** pass. In the royal carriage, he saw the Great Genie, who gave him a little wink. When the procession had passed, Hagag saw a blind farmer who looked lost.

"Are you well, my friend?" asked Hagag.

"No, kind sir, I am not," the farmer said. "Since I have lost my sight, I can no longer work on my farm. And I cannot hire a worker unless I can sell some fruits and vegetables. I came here to see if the king would buy some potatoes for his royal table. But I couldn't talk to the king because of the crowds. Now, I have lost my wife in the crowd. I cannot get back to the farm without her."

"I will take you home," offered Hagag, and he walked the farmer all the way home. When they arrived at the farm, the farmer and his wife offered Hagag a job working in the field. In return, they let him sleep on the haystack in the barn and fed him three small meals each day.

Hagag enjoyed his life on the farm. Even though he was hungry enough to eat all of his food, at each meal, he set some aside some to share with people who were hungry.

At the year's end, the king called a big party in his castle. He invited all of the kingdom, but Hagag did not want to go.

"Please take me to the party," begged the farmer. "I want to talk to the king about buying my fruits and vegetables for his royal table."

---

procession, a line of people moving slowly as part of a ceremony

> ### Reading Skill
> A word **analogy** shows how words are related. Look at these pairs of words: *life/death* and *questions/answers*. How are the words in each pair related? They are antonyms and are useful in descriptions. Find words in this story that complete these pairs.
>
> king / _____
>
> beggar / _____
>
> hungry / _____

Hagag could not refuse the farmer's request. When they got to the party, Hagag tried to hide from the king's eyes, but it was no use. They seemed to follow him wherever he went. Finally, the trusted adviser pulled Hagag aside. "Sir, the king would like a word with you."

"But I am a poor and unimportant man. What could the king want with me?" said Hagag. Still, he followed the trusted adviser to the king's private meeting room.

The king—who was really the Great Genie—looked long and hard at Hagag. Finally, he took off his crown.

"You have learned your lesson well, oh King Hagag. The crown is yours again."

"No, Great Genie, I cannot accept the crown. I work for the farmer now. I must take him home tonight and work in his field in the morning."

The Great Genie laughed as he placed the crown on Hagag's head. "Your Majesty, you may do anything you wish."

King Hagag called the farmer into his private meeting room and told him everything. Then he chose a new worker for the farm and sent the worker and the farmer home in a chariot.

From that day on, King Hagag ruled with the greatest of kindness to all of his subjects. He wore nothing but simple robes made for him by the tailor woman, to whom he paid a handsome wage. And each day, his table was laid out with a colorful array of fruits and vegetables from his friend's farm, and all who were hungry in the kingdom were invited to eat with him.

✓ LITERARY CHECK
What do you think the **moral** of the story is?

Before You Go On
1. At first, the king refuses to put on his crown and take back his throne. Why?
2. How did the king help the farmer?

On Your Own
Why do you think the king changed?

Reading 1 161

> Reading 1

Review and Practice

Reader's Theater 🎧

Act out the following scene.

Adviser: You look very regal and proud this morning, your majesty.
King: *[admiring himself]* Yes, I know!
Adviser: And your red robe looks exquisite. What kind of material is it?
King: It is red velvet and silk, trimmed with gold.
Adviser: The material is very high quality. Is it imported?
King: Yes, of course, like the fine materials for all my other robes.
Adviser: Did you have a good breakfast?
King: *[patting his stomach]* Oh, yes, I had the most wonderful fish dish, followed by chicken, beef, and several desserts.
Adviser: I can guess you're not hungry! So are you ready for me to read to you from *The Great Book of Kings*?
King: Oh, sure. I always want to see if there is anything I can add to my great knowledge.
Adviser: Well, your great-great-great-great-grandfather did have a lot of wisdom. *[taking out and opening book]* Let's see what he had to say on this page. . . .

> **Speaking Tip**
>
> Practice your lines a few times before acting out the scene.

Comprehension 📖 81

Recall

1. What kind of collection does King Hagag have?
2. What does the king's adviser do every morning after breakfast?

Comprehend

3. Why doesn't the adviser want to rip out and burn the page from *The Great Book of Kings*?
4. Why don't the guards recognize the king?

Analyze

5. Why does the adviser say *The Great Book of Kings* contains great wisdom? Is the adviser right?

6. Why do you think this folktale kept being retold? Is it a lesson only for kings? Explain.

Connect

7. Were you surprised by the king's actions? Did you think there would be a different outcome? Explain.

8. Is it okay to trick a person in order to teach a lesson? Explain.

Discussion

Discuss with a partner or in a small group.

Do you think the genie did the right thing by changing King Hagag's situation? If yes, tell why. If no, what else could the genie have done to teach the king a lesson?

How can we tell what's right? Were these characters right or wrong? Give reasons.
- the king asking the adviser to tear the page from the book
- the Great Genie teaching the king a lesson
- the strangers giving the king food and clothes

> **Listening Skill**
>
> Listen carefully to your classmates. Identify the important ideas. Retell or summarize these ideas in your own words in order to confirm that you have understood them correctly.

Response to Literature

WB 81

Write a fable or folktale in comic strip form. You may rewrite an existing story or write an original one. First, decide which scenes from the story you wish to illustrate. Then draw a picture to illustrate each scene. You can use speech bubbles to show dialogue and captions to show narration. Below is an example. Include a moral for your story.

The Lion and the Mouse

Panel 1: You have dared to wake me up? Now, I will eat you. / Please let me go! Who knows? Maybe someday I can help you!

Panel 2: You help me? That is a laugh!

Panel 3: Later, while mouse is freeing lion... / Was I not right?

Moral: Little friends may prove to be great friends.

Reading 1

Grammar

The Modal *must*

Use the modal *must* to express necessity and obligation or to talk about something you have to do. Use *must* + the base form of the verb.

> The adviser **must obey** the king's commands.

Also use the modal *must* to speculate, or make guesses. Use *must* + the base form of the verb to speculate about the present.

> The Great Genie **must be** very smart.

Use *must have* + past participle to speculate about the past.

> The strangers **must have felt** sorry for the beggar king.

Grammar Skill

We use *must* to speculate about the present or past when we are almost 100 percent sure of something. We use *might*, *may*, or *could* when we are only about 50 percent sure.

Practice A WB 82

Work with a partner. For each situation, write a sentence describing it using must. Write your sentences in your notebook. The first is done for you.

1. The king orders the adviser to tear out the page.
   The adviser must obey the king's order.
2. The genie decides the king needs to learn a lesson.
3. The king wakes up hungry.
4. The farmer wants to go to the party and talk to the king.

Grammar Check

✓ When do we use ***must*** + the base form of the verb? When do we use ***must have*** + the past participle?

Practice B

Complete each sentence with *must* and the correct form of the verb in parentheses.

1. All students _____must pass_____ (pass) an exam to graduate.
2. Peter isn't in class today. He _____ (be) sick.
3. Paul wasn't in class yesterday. He _____ (be) sick.
4. You _____ (have) a driver's license in order to drive.
5. My textbook isn't in my book bag! I _____ (leave) it at home.

Apply

Work with a partner. Make a list of things you have to do in order to do well in this class. Use *must* and the base form of the verb.
Example: You must do your homework.

The Modal *would* for Repeated Actions in the Past

There are several different ways to express past actions. One way to express repeated action in the past is to use *would* and the base form of the verb. Look at these ways to express events from the reading.

Simple Past	Past with *would*
Every day, the chefs **prepared** new and interesting dishes for the king.	Every day, the chefs **would prepare** new and interesting dishes for the king.
After breakfast, the king **listened** to his adviser read from *The Great Book of Kings*.	After breakfast, the king **would listen** to his adviser read from *The Great Book of Kings*.

Using *would* and the base form emphasizes that something has happened regularly; the action did not happen just once. This simple past sentence cannot be rewritten with *would* and the base form of the verb because it only happened once: *The Great Genie* **played** *a trick on the king*.

Grammar Skill
Would and the base form of the verb is used to describe repeated actions in the past. *Used to* and the base form of the verb is used to describe a situation that existed in the past but does not exist now.

Practice A

Can these simple past sentences be rewritten as sentences with *would* and the base form of the verb? Write *yes* or *no*. If *yes*, rewrite the sentences in your notebook.

1. The king chose a different robe to wear every morning.
   <u>yes</u>
   The king would choose a different robe to wear every morning.
2. One day, the king chose a red velvet robe. _____
3. The adviser tore a page from the book. _____
4. The chefs put dishes of food on the king's table at every meal.
   _____

Grammar Check
✓ When do we use *would* and the base form of the verb?

Practice B

In your notebook, rewrite the sentences using *would* and the base form of the verb.

1. Last summer, my sister and I played tennis every weekend.
   Last summer, my sister and I would play tennis every weekend.
2. Then we went out for ice cream.
3. Often, we ate our ice cream at the park.
4. Sometimes our friends joined us.

Apply
Work with a partner. Talk about things you and your family have done regularly in the past. Use *would* and the base form of the verb.

Reading 1
Writing

Write a Review

At the end of this unit, you will write a persuasive speech. To do this, you will need to learn skills that writers use to give opinions about a work such as a story, book, movie, or TV show. In this lesson, you will write a review. The purpose of a review is to persuade the reader to either read the work or avoid it.

When you write a review, begin with a brief summary or description of the work. Then give your opinion of it by telling whether you liked it or not. Provide reasons for your opinion, and support it with examples, such as quotations or descriptions.

> **Writing Prompt**
> Write a review of a story, book, movie, or TV show. State your opinion clearly and support it with examples from the work. Be sure to use the modal *must* correctly.

1 Prewrite Begin by choosing a story or work to review.

WB 84

- Write your opinion of the work at the top of a graphic organizer.
- Next, write a reason for your opinion.
- Find at least two examples from the work that support this reason, and add them to the graphic organizer.

Here's a graphic organizer created by a student named Dylan. He wrote his opinion of "The Beggar King," gave a reason, and supported it with examples from the story.

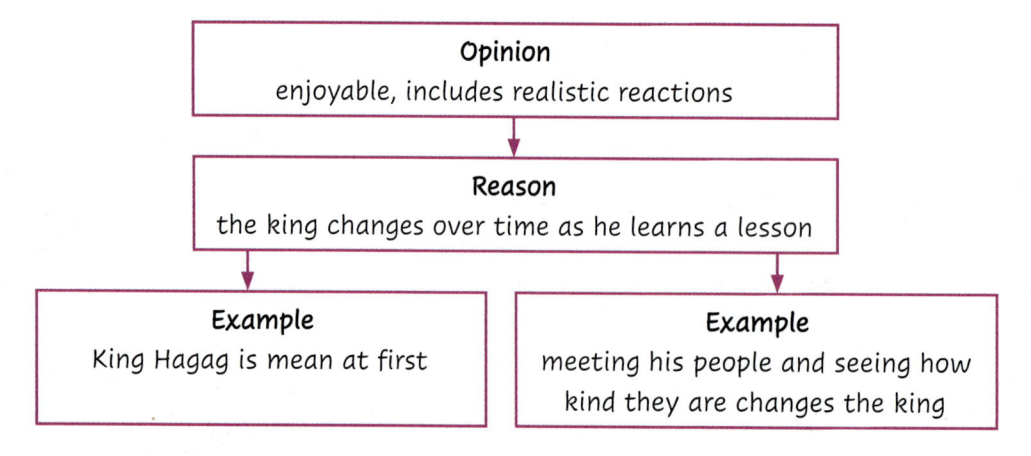

```
                    Opinion
         enjoyable, includes realistic reactions
                       ↓
                     Reason
      the king changes over time as he learns a lesson
                  ↓              ↓
          Example                    Example
   King Hagag is mean at first    meeting his people and seeing how
                                  kind they are changes the king
```

166 Unit 3

2 Draft Use your graphic organizer to help you write a first draft.

- Remember to include a brief summary of the work you are reviewing.
- State your opinion, your reason, and examples for it.
- Be sure to use the modal *must* correctly.

3 Revise Read over your draft. Look for places where the writing is unclear or needs improvement. Complete (✓) the Writing Checklist to help you identify problems. Then, revise your draft, using the editing and proofreading marks listed on page 467.

4 Edit and Proofread Check your work for errors in grammar, usage, mechanics, and spelling. Trade papers with a partner to obtain feedback. Complete (✓) the Peer Review Checklist on Workbook page 84. Edit your final draft in response to feedback from your partner and your teacher.

5 Publish Prepare a clean copy of your final draft. Share your review with the class. Save your work. You'll need to refer to it in the Writing Workshop at the end of the unit.

> **Writing Checklist**
>
> **Ideas:**
> ☐ I stated my opinion and supported it with examples.
>
> **Sentence Fluency:**
> ☐ I used a variety of sentence lengths and patterns.
>
> **Conventions:**
> ☐ I gave my opinion and used *would*, *must*, and appropriate phrases.

Dylan Bishop

Review of "The Beggar King"

I think "The Beggar King" is an enjoyable story that includes realistic reactions in a fairytale-style tale. The main character, King Hagag, is mean and impatient at the beginning of the story. After he orders a page torn from <u>The Great Book of Kings</u> because he does not like what it says, he is transformed into a beggar by a genie. As he meets the poor people of his kingdom and finds out how kind they are, the king discovers that fine clothes and riches do not make a person good. He learns to appreciate the simple things in life. I enjoyed the story because the king's change happens bit by bit as he meets people and has new experiences, which I think is how everyone changes. I wish there could have been one more scene, though, because I would have liked to see how the farmer reacted when he learned that his friend was really the king—it must have been quite a surprise!

Reading 2

Prepare to Read

What You Will Learn

Reading
- Vocabulary building: *Context, dictionary skills, word study*
- Reading strategy: *Distinguish fact from opinion*
- Text type: *Informational Text (science)*

Grammar
- Transition words, phrases, and clauses (for opinions)
- Uses of the modal *could*

Writing
- Write a letter to the editor

THE BIG QUESTION

How can we tell what's right? Work with a partner. Discuss what you know about travel to the planet Mars. How do you know about it—from a science article or from a science-fiction movie? When you listen to people talk about whether humans should visit Mars, how do you decide if they are right or wrong?

Build Background

"Mars: Pro and Con" is a debate about a science topic. In a debate, someone states a viewpoint and gives facts and reasons to support that opinion. Then another person expresses a different opinion. Both people are trying to persuade the audience to agree with their position. You may have seen a debate at school where two teams argue against each other. The more facts they have, the more convincing they will be. Have you ever seen or heard about a debate? Tell what you learned from the debate.

▲ An illustration of our solar system. Mars is the fourth planet from the sun.

Vocabulary

Listening and Speaking: Key Words

Read these sentences aloud with a partner. Use the context to figure out the meaning of the highlighted words. Use a dictionary, the glossary, or a thesaurus to determine or confirm your answers. Then write each word and its meaning in your notebook.

Key Words
- celestial
- extinction
- organisms
- revolution
- rover
- terrestrial

1. Stars, planets, moons, and other objects in the sky are often called celestial bodies.
2. Animals threatened by extinction are often protected so that they don't completely disappear from the planet.
3. All living organisms need water and nourishment to survive.
4. Earth takes one year, or 365 days, to make a complete revolution around the sun.
5. The scientists sent a rover to Mars to drive over the surface, collect samples, and send data back to Earth.
6. Mercury, Venus, and Mars are terrestrial planets because, like Earth, they are made mostly of rock.

Practice

Choose a word from the box above to complete each sentence. Write your sentences in your notebook. Then take turns reading the sentences aloud with a partner.

1. _____ is a risk for snow leopards in the wild because of loss of habitat.
2. In our solar system, the _____ planets are much smaller than the gas giants.
3. _____ that live along the ocean floor have different needs than those that live closer to the surface.
4. One _____ was useful on Mars until its wheels got stuck in the sand.
5. Earth and its moon are two examples of _____ objects.
6. The moon completes one _____ around Earth in about twenty-nine days.

▲ A rover collects data on Mars.

Reading 2

Reading 2

Listening and Speaking: Academic Words

Study the **purple** words and their meanings. You will find these words useful when talking and writing about informational texts. Write each word and its meaning in your notebook, then say the words aloud with a partner. After you read "Mars: Pro and Con" try to use these words to respond to the text.

Academic Words
- biased
- debate
- define
- objectively

Word & Meaning	Example
biased = unfair because of a preference for or dislike of something	As someone who had been fascinated with Mars for years, the woman was **biased** about Mars's importance.
debate = formal discussion of a subject in which people express differing opinions	When I take part in a **debate**, I always make sure I am prepared to argue my point.
define = clearly show what something is or means	Astronomers worked together to **define** what a planet is.
objectively = in a way that is not influenced by a person's feelings, beliefs, or ideas	She had a strong opinion about the decision, so it was not easy for her to listen to both sides **objectively**.

Practice

Work with a partner to answer these questions. Try to include the **purple** word in your answer. Write the answers in your notebook.

1. Have you read something that you thought was **biased**? Explain.
2. Do you or would you enjoy being in a **debate**? Why or why not?
3. How would you **define** what makes a good friend?
4. Is it difficult to listen to your friends' opinions **objectively**? Explain.

▲ High-school students from different countries take part in a debate.

Word Study: Prefixes

A **prefix** is a group of letters added to the beginning of a word. When you add a prefix to a word, you change its meaning and make a new word. Look at the examples below.

Prefix	Meaning	Examples
trans-	across, beyond, or through to the other side	**trans**plant, **trans**port
un-	shows an opposite action; shows an opposite state or negative	**un**learn, **un**qualified
mis-	the opposite of; wrongly or badly	**mis**trust, **mis**lead, **mis**take

Practice

Work with a partner. Complete the sentences by adding the prefix *trans-*, *un-*, or *mis-* to the word in parentheses. Use a dictionary if necessary.

1. Scientists are trying to _____ (lock) the mysteries of the solar system.
2. The rocket launch failed and ended with a _____. (fire)
3. Some people are _____ (happy) about the idea of going to Mars.
4. The _____ (atlantic) flight went from Boston to London.
5. Technology has _____ space exploration since the 1960s. (formed)

▲ The first rocket launches were accomplished without the use of computers.

Reading Strategy — Distinguish Fact from Opinion

Distinguishing facts from opinions will help you draw conclusions about what you read. A fact is something that can be proven, or is true. An opinion is what someone believes or thinks. It's not necessarily true. To distinguish between facts and opinions, follow these steps:

- Ask yourself whether what you are reading can be proven.
- Look for phrases that signal opinions; for example, *I think, I believe, I suppose, personally*.
- Make a note of the facts and opinions you are reading about. Ask yourself how you know which are facts and which are opinions.

As you read "Mars: Pro and Con," look for facts and opinions. How can you tell the difference between them?

Reading 2

Informational Text
Science

Set a purpose for reading Read this debate between two students about whether humans should travel to Mars and build a colony there. Which facts help you decide who is right?

Mars: Pro and Con

▲ An artist imagined what an human explorer on Mars might look like.

Mr. Henniker's class recently debated the question, "Should we go to Mars?" The text of each side's statements appears below.

Explore Mars Now

We need to colonize Mars now. Earth is at a **tipping point** as population pressures and environmental emergencies make it impossible to guarantee a safe future for human beings. Continuing and expanding the exploration of the planet Mars—with the long-term goal of colonizing it—is the next logical step for humankind. I believe that by doing so, we could solve many of the long-term problems we face here on Earth. Here are a few ways that the exploration and settlement of Mars would help our species.

---

tipping point, the moment at which change begins to happen rapidly

1. **We need a backup for Earth.** Every 62 million years, a mass **extinction wipes out** a large portion of life on Earth. Unlike the **organisms** that were wiped out by previous mass extinctions, we humans can plan ahead for such an event—unlikely though it may be in our lifetime. A logical starting point is to find other planets to inhabit. And Mars is a perfect candidate to be a backup for Earth.

2. **We can find new resources.** Earth's resources are limited, and we are using them as fast as we can dig them up. Scientists believe that Mars holds rich deposits of nickel, copper, platinum, and other important minerals. These minerals could not only be used to build a **self-sufficient** human settlement on Mars, but they could also be transported back to Earth. In addition, Mars holds tremendous amounts of water in the form of ice. As clean, fresh water becomes ever scarcer here on Earth, these vast water resources make Mars even more attractive—and urgent. Going to Mars and using its water resources would help the human species survive now and into the future.

3. **We can do this now.** We do not have to invent the technology we need to explore and colonize Mars, as we did for the space programs of the 1960s; we have it right now, in the palm of our hands. In fact, a modern cell phone has more computing power than did the *Apollo* spacecraft that carried astronauts to the moon. Some experts believe that we can "terraform" Mars, providing it with an earthlike atmosphere and enabling people to plant trees and food crops. Key players in the fast-growing space industry, including eccentric billionaires who want to build their own spaceships, are already beginning to propose missions to visit and colonize Mars.

The state of our planet is **tenuous**. Now is the ideal time to look beyond our own horizon, step out into the solar system, and plant our feet firmly on the surface of Mars.

---

wipes out, completely destroys
self-sufficient, able to do things without help

tenuous, very weak

▼ The Mars rovers have found evidence of water on the red planet.

Before You Go On

1. What does the speaker think humans can do to prevent a mass extinction?
2. What resources does Mars have that humans need?

On Your Own

Do you find this position convincing? Why or why not?

▲ Private space exploration companies now exist.

Keep Our Focus on Earth

Since the first NASA rover to Mars began streaming data from the Red Planet back to Earth, excitement has been growing about the possibility of colonizing Mars. Even private companies have begun sending rockets into space. However, our desire to seek celestial answers to our terrestrial problems is misguided. Here is why:

1. **It's too cold.** The average temperature on Mars *at its equator* is similar to that of Antarctica. It is actually too cold for liquid water to exist. Instead, ice turns directly into water vapor and floats off toward the poles. As a result, Mars is not only brutally cold but is also as dry as a desert. Additionally, it takes Mars the equivalent of 687 Earth days to make a full revolution around the sun. That is a long year—and a long winter.

2. **It's too dangerous.** Mars's atmosphere is basically a vacuum, and the little gas it contains is mainly carbon dioxide. People would have to live in spacesuits that deliver a constant

supply of oxygen. The atmospheric pressure is also far too low. Without the protection of a spacesuit, saliva would boil in a person's mouth. A torn spacesuit would lead to a painful death.

3. **It's too expensive.** The technology required to reach and then colonize Mars would cost billions. Even if we develop mining machinery that could operate on Mars, the planet's relatively flat surface makes the possibility of finding rich **deposits** of minerals unlikely; as a result, building materials would have to be transported from Earth at a staggering cost. In addition, there is no guarantee that crops would grow, so Mars colonists would need a constant supply of food. In fact, every single item required for human life would have to come from Earth. Rather than providing new resources to the people of Earth, a Mars colony would steal from the limited resources we have.

Colonizing Mars is too risky and far too expensive, both in dollars and in the potential loss of human life. We could use the billions that would be spent on exploring Mars to solve **pressing** problems that we face every day here on Earth. Perhaps going to Mars is a possibility for the distant future, but for right now, let's keep our feet planted firmly on Earth.

deposits, layers of minerals found in rocks

pressing, urgent

▲ Building even a small facility on Mars would be extremely expensive.

Reading Skill

Take turns rereading the two sides of the debate aloud with a partner. As you read along in the text, listen closely to the way your partner reads. Listen for pauses, stressed words, and rhythm. This will help you understand the each position better.

Before You Go On

1. Why does the speaker suggest it doesn't matter much that Mars has water?
2. What does the speaker suggest we do instead of traveling to Mars?

On Your Own

Do you find this position about the issue convincing? Why or why not?

Reading 2

Reading 2

Review and Practice

Comprehension

Recall
1. According to the first speaker, what benefit do minerals on Mars offer to humans?
2. According to the second speaker, what is the temperature on Mars like?

Comprehend
3. Why does the first speaker think colonizing Mars is a good idea?
4. Why does the second speaker think colonizing Mars is not a good idea?

Analyze
5. What points from each speaker would you disagree with? Why?
6. What is the strongest point each speaker makes about going or not going to Mars?

Connect
7. Do you think we should explore Mars? Why or why not?
8. Do you think we should colonize Mars? Why or why not?

In Your Own Words

Review both viewpoints from the debate "Mars: Pro and Con." Then write the most important facts you learned from each speaker in your notebook. Finally, use your own words to tell a partner the facts you learned.

Discussion

Discuss with a partner or in a small group.

Which reasons do you find most compelling for each viewpoint? Explain.

How can we tell what's right? Which position do you agree with? Why? What facts or reasons helped convince you?

Read for Fluency

It is often easier to read a text if you understand the difficult words and phrases. Work with a partner. Choose a paragraph from the reading. Identify the words and phrases you do not know or have trouble pronouncing. Look up the difficult words in a dictionary.

Take turns pronouncing the words and phrases with your partner. If necessary, ask your teacher to model the correct pronunciation. Then take turns reading the paragraph aloud. Give each other feedback on your reading.

Extension

WB 89

What are the pros and cons of colonizing Mars? Use information from "Mars: Pro and Con" to fill out the chart below. Then use a university or government website to conduct research and find additional ideas. Add them to the chart. Share your ideas in small groups.

Pros	Cons

Reading 2

Grammar

Transition Words, Phrases, and Clauses (for Opinions)

When authors write articles and speakers debate, they use facts to support their ideas or opinions. They also use certain phrases to signal when they give opinions: **I believe** that we can solve many of Earth's problems by colonizing Mars. **In my opinion,** it's too expensive to go to Mars.

The word *that* is optional with some phrases. A comma is used after other phrases.

Phrase with or without *that*	Phrase with comma	Sentence
I think (that) . . . I believe (that) . . . I feel (that) . . .	In my opinion, . . . As far as I'm concerned, . . . If you ask me, . . .	. . . This is why I think so. . . . I'd like to explain why. This is my view. . . .

Practice A

Underline the phrases that signal opinions.

1. <u>I feel that</u> space exploration is a waste of money.
2. As far as I'm concerned, moving water from Mars to Earth is not practical.
3. I believe that space camps are an excellent way for children to learn about space.
4. I think people could not survive on Mars.
5. If you ask me, getting resources from other planets is an excellent idea.

Practice B

In your notebook, rewrite the sentences. Use one of the boldfaced words or phrases and the phrases or statement in parentheses.

1. Mars **is/is not** too cold for people to colonize. (I think that)
 I think that Mars is too cold for people to colonize.
2. Mars's atmosphere **would/would not** kill us. (In my opinion)
3. Martian dust storms **would/would not** be a big problem. (This is my view.)
4. We **should/should not** develop more space exploration technology. (I believe that)
5. We **should/should not** only focus on solving problems right here on Earth. (In my opinion)

Grammar Skill

In academic writing, it is preferable to include the word *that* after *I believe*, *I think*, and *I feel*.

Grammar Check

✓ What **words**, **phrases**, and **clauses** do speakers and writers use to signal that they are stating their **opinions**?

Apply

Write three questions asking for an opinion about space travel and exploration. Then work with a partner. Take turns asking and answering the questions.
Example:
A: Do you think we will ever live on Mars?
B: If you ask me, . . .

The Uses of the Modal *could*

The modal *could* has many purposes. Writers often use it before the main verb to talk about future ability or possibility. It has the same meaning as *may* and *might*: Mars **could have** all the water we need. Humans **could survive** in Mars's cold climate. The words *could*, *may*, and *might* make a statement less certain or probable than *will* or *won't*.

Use *couldn't* to form negative statements. With questions, begin the sentence with *could*: Humans **couldn't** stay on Mars. **Could** you live in a spacesuit?

Practice A

Complete the sentences with *could* and a word from the box.

| have | live | provide | result | ~~take~~ |

1. With continued financial support, I think we ___could take___ the next step.
2. We should look into other places where we _____.
3. It's worth looking into whether Mars _____ additional resources.
4. Imagine what new advancements _____ from a space station on Mars!
5. We _____ very few resources in ten or twenty years.

Practice B

In your notebook, rewrite the sentences with *could* to sound less certain.

1. Astronauts will return to the Moon.
   Astronauts could return to the Moon.
2. The National Aeronautics and Space Administration (NASA) will land on Mars within the next decade.
3. Space programs from several countries will compete to colonize Mars.
4. Private companies will sell flights to Mars to the wealthy.
5. Robots will colonize Mars.

> **Grammar Skill**
> Do not use *could* to state strong predictions. Use *will* instead.

> **Grammar Check**
> ✓ Why do speakers and writers use **the modal *could*** instead of *will* to talk about the future?

> **Apply**
> Work with a partner. Write three predictions about things that might be possible in ten years. Use *could* and the base form of the verb.
> **Example:** In ten years, people could take vacations to the Moon.

Reading 2

Reading 2
Writing

Write a Letter to the Editor

At the end of this unit, you will write a persuasive speech. To do this, you will need to learn skills that writers use to state opinions about a problem, such as pollution, traffic, or crime. In this lesson, you will write a letter to the editor. Begin your letter by explaining the issue that concerns you. Then provide a possible solution. Provide facts and examples to support your position. Conclude by restating your opinion in a strong and persuasive way.

> **Writing Prompt**
> Write a letter to the editor of your school or local newspaper about an issue you fell strongly about in your school or community. Explain the problem, and your proposed solution. Express your opinion clearly. Support your viewpoint with facts and/or examples. Use the modal *could* to suggest possible solutions.

1 Prewrite Begin by identifying a problem that affects your school or community.

WB 92

- Write the problem at the top of a page in your notebook.
- Think about why you feel strongly about the problem. Why do you think the problem needs a solution?
- Think of reasons to support your viewpoint about the problem.
- Write your ideas in a graphic organizer like the one below.

Here's a word web created by a student named Ruth about light pollution. She wrote the problem in the center bubble and the details or reasons for it in the outer ones.

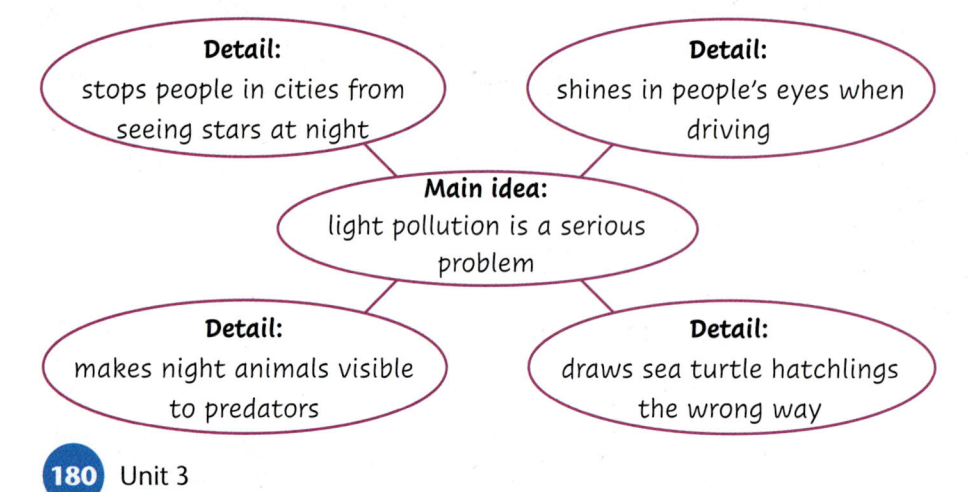

Detail: stops people in cities from seeing stars at night

Detail: shines in people's eyes when driving

Main idea: light pollution is a serious problem

Detail: makes night animals visible to predators

Detail: draws sea turtle hatchlings the wrong way

Unit 3

② Draft Use your word web to help you write a first draft.
- Explain the problem.
- Suggest a solution or solutions.
- Use appropriate phrases to signal your opinion and end with a call to action.
- Be sure to use the modal *could* correctly.

③ Revise Read over your draft. Look for places where the writing is unclear or needs improvement. Complete (✓) the Writing Checklist to help you identify problems. Then, revise your draft, using the editing and proofreading marks listed on page 467.

④ Edit and Proofread Check your work for errors in grammar, usage, mechanics, and spelling. Trade papers with a partner to obtain feedback. Edit your final draft in response to feedback from your partner and your teacher.

⑤ Publish Prepare a clean copy of your final draft. Share your letter to the editor with the class. Save your work. You'll need to refer to it in the Writing Workshop at the end of the unit.

> **Writing Checklist**
>
> **Ideas:**
> ☐ I described a problem in my school or community, reasons it is a problem, and a proposed solution or solutions.
>
> **Conventions:**
> ☐ I used appropriate phrases to give my opinion.
> ☐ I used *could* to talk about possible solutions.

Here is Ruth's letter to the editor. Notice how she presents the problem, suggests solutions, and ends with a call for action.

April 23, 2019

To the Editor,

    I believe that light pollution is a serious problem in our city. You may know that it prevents people in urban areas from seeing stars at night. But you may not know that it harms people and animals. Lights can shine into people's eyes as they are driving, preventing them from seeing where they are going. Streetlights can also harm nocturnal animals. These animals are active in the dark, and the constant light makes them visible to predators. In my opinion, there are many ways we could reduce light pollution. If we turn off lights when they aren't needed and switch to environmentally friendly lighting methods, we could greatly lessen this problem. I strongly urge everyone to take part in fighting this problem.

Sincerely,

Ruth Kace

Reading 3

Prepare to Read

What You Will Learn

Reading
- Vocabulary building: *Literary terms, word study*
- Reading strategy: *Identify author's purpose*
- Text type: *Literature (fable)*

Grammar
- Other uses of *would* in the past
- Subjunctive

Writing
- Write a persuasive paragraph

THE BIG QUESTION

How can we tell what's right? Do you often think about what is the right or wrong thing to do? What kinds of things do you consider when making a decision about right and wrong? Discuss with a partner.

Build Background

"The Golden Serpent" is a fable, or a brief story that teaches a lesson. From India, it is about a wise man who solves problems for the people in his village. Fables have been told in India for thousands of years. The oldest Indian fables have been gathered in a collection called *Panchatantra*. In "The Beggar King," you read about a king who learned a lesson. While this fable is also about a king and about greed, the outcome is quite different. The aim of the *Pachatantra* is to help people live successfully. These tales have been retold in many languages and cultures.

▼ "The Rabbit and the Elephant" is another story from *The Pachatantra*. It tells of the struggle between rabbits and elephants for water, which the humans greedily have used up.

Vocabulary

Learn Literary Words

Literary Words
theme
moral
irony

The **theme** of a fable is the overarching topic. Some common themes addressed by fables are "right and wrong" and "justice and injustice." All fables tell a story to teach a lesson. The story in fables with a theme of "right versus wrong" shows how doing the right thing is always better no matter who you are, the risk involved, or what you may be giving up. The lesson the fable teaches is the **moral**.

Another common feature of fables is an element of **irony**. In the case of "The Golden Serpent," it is ironic that although the king tries to trick the wise man, the wise man ends up tricking him, and the king doesn't even realize it.

Practice
WB 93

Work with a partner. Think of a movie or story you are both familiar with and re-cast it as a fable. Make sure your fable includes a theme and a moral. You might also include irony. Follow this framework: Once upon a time in a faraway land there lived . . . . One day . . . .

▲ What kind of questions do you ask yourself when you are making a difficult decision?

Reading 3 183

Reading 3

Listening and Speaking: Academic Words

Study the **purple** words and their meanings. You will find these words useful when talking and writing about literature. Write each word and its meaning in your notebook, then say the words aloud with a partner. After you read "The Golden Serpent," try to use these words to respond to the fable.

Academic Words

analyze
ethical
justify
principle

analyze = examine or think about something carefully in order to understand it	The man had to **analyze** the ingredients listed on the package to make sure he could eat the bread.
ethical = having to do with right and wrong	Whether or not to keep something that you found is an **ethical** question.
justify = give a reasonable or acceptable explanation for something	He was able to **justify** his absence from school by explaining that he had been ill.
principle = a moral or set of ideas that makes you behave in a certain way	One **principle** that most people live by is that stealing is wrong.

Practice

Choose a **purple** word from the box above to complete each sentence. Then take turns reading the sentences aloud with a partner.

1. My father taught me one _____ I have always lived by: Be kind to others.
2. Sarah tried to _____ her behavior even though she knew what she had done was wrong.
3. We have to _____ the situation before we can make a decision.
4. Deciding whether someone did the right thing may be a(n) _____ issue.

◀ These icons, or figures, illustrate the principle of helping others. What does each action show?

184 Unit 3

Word Study: Long and Short Vowels

Learning about vowel patterns and their different pronunciations will help you read and understand new words. The letters *ea* often stand for long *e* as in *season*. Sometimes these letters stand for long *a* as in *great* or short *e* as in *head*.

Long *e*	Long *a*	Short *e*
reach	great	bread
steal	break	instead

Practice
95

Work with a partner. Read aloud the words in the box below. All of the words contain the letters *ea*, but the vowel sound that these letters stand for varies. In your notebook, make a chart like the one above. Sort the words and write them in your chart under the appropriate headings. Then choose five words and write a sentence using each.

ahead	dead	heaps	reach	stream
beans	heat	meadow	steak	wealth

Reading Strategy: Identify the Purpose of a Fable

Fables started with someone telling a story. The reason people kept telling these stories was probably that the stories were engaging and had universal morals. As is true of most literature, it can be helpful to know the purpose of a work: in this case, why a fable was created and then told over and over again. To identify a fable's purpose, ask yourself these questions:

- Is this entertaining? Am I enjoying reading it? Why?
- Is there an overarching idea or theme that's being developed?
- Are there clues about a moral or a lesson or is one stated in the fable?

As you read the fable, think about the purpose of the story. Why did people keep telling it through the years?

96

Reading 3
Literature
Fable

Set a purpose for reading Read the fable to find out if Pundabi is as wise as the villagers believe he is. Who does what is right?

The Golden Serpent

An Indian fable retold by Walter Dean Myers

There was once a very wise man. He lived on a high mountain and was called Pundabi. With him lived a young boy. The boy's name was Ali.

Each morning Ali would come down the mountain. He would sit in the shade of a fig tree. Many people would come to him. They brought him loaves of bread. In the bread were pieces of fine linen. There would be questions on the linen for the wise Pundabi to answer. They would be questions of life and death, or about the search for happiness.

Each evening Ali would climb the mountain and give the loaves of bread to Pundabi. Pundabi would answer all the questions. Then they would eat the bread.

Ali would take the answers down the mountain. He would give them to the waiting people. Pundabi and Ali lived well this way, and the people loved them dearly.

One day a tall shadow fell across Ali. It was the shadow of the king himself.

"Are you Ali?" the king asked.

"I am he," Ali answered.

"And you live with the wise man Pundabi?"

"That is so," Ali replied.

"And it is true that he is very wise?"

"Yes, it is true," said Ali.

"Then you must bring him to me," the king said.

So Ali went up the mountain. He told Pundabi of the king's request. Pundabi and Ali came down the mountain. They set out for the palace. They went past the river and through the marketplace. They went through the village. Finally they reached another high mountain.

Listening Skill

Follow along in your book as you listen to the audio. Notice the words in bold type. To understand them, read the definitions at the bottom of the page. Knowing the meanings of these words will enhance and confirm your comprehension of the story.

On top of this mountain was the palace.

"I want you to solve a mystery for me." The king spoke from his high throne. "But first we must have lunch." He clapped his hands twice.

Five men brought in five trays of food. There was a tray for Pundabi. There was a tray for Ali. And three trays for the king.

"I am very rich," the king said. "I have much gold and many rubies. And you, Pundabi, are very wise. I can pay you very well."

"What is the mystery?" asked Pundabi.

"I do not know," said the king. "That is for you to discover!"

"But how can Pundabi solve a mystery"—Ali **wrung** his hands—"if there is none to solve?"

"If you are truly wise, Pundabi, it will be done. If you do not solve it, then you are a fraud. I will put you in jail where you belong."

---

wrung, rubbed or pressed together nervously

Before You Go On

1. What does the king want Pundabi to do?
2. Why is Ali worried?

On Your Own

What do you think will happen to Pundabi? Why?

Reading 3

Ali was very afraid. He began to shake.

But Pundabi said, "Let us take a walk. Perhaps our eyes will speak to us."

So they began to walk. They walked by the river. They walked through the village. They stopped by the home of an old woman. They walked around the marketplace. Pundabi's eyes spoke to him.

Then Pundabi began to walk up the mountain toward the palace.

"We will surely go to jail," Ali said. "We cannot solve the mystery. We do not know what it is."

"But we do know what the mystery is." Pundabi spoke, a smile upon his face. "And perhaps we can solve it. Let us go and see the king."

"Have you solved the mystery yet?" the king asked.

"No," said Pundabi. "But we know what the mystery is! It is the mystery of the Golden Serpent."

"The Golden Serpent?" said the king.

"Yes," Pundabi said. "Where is your Golden Serpent?"

"I didn't know I had one," the king said.

"The thief must be very clever," Pundabi said.

"You must find it for me," said the king.

"Let us see," Pundabi said. "Someone must have taken it to sell. Let us go to the market."

So the king called his guards. And off they went to the market.

> ### Word Skill
> The **denotation** (literal meaning) of the word *serpent* is "snake." For many, the **connotation** (associated meaning) of *serpent* is "evil." Why do you think the fable uses a serpent as the mystery as opposed to another animal or object?

> ### ✓ LITERARY CHECK
> Why do you think Pundabi chose the mystery he did? What does it represent? What clues does it give you about the **theme**?

In the market they came upon a young boy. The boy was **turning wood**.

"Perhaps he has stolen the Golden Serpent." The king seized the boy by the arm.

"I have no Golden Serpent," the boy said. "I could not run away with it. My leg is bent from turning."

But the guards searched him well. They searched his blouse and the hay upon which he slept. They even looked at his bent leg.

"It is true," the guards said. "He has nothing. He can hardly walk."

Next they went to the village. They stopped at the house of a widow.

"We are searching for the Golden Serpent," said Pundabi, "which was stolen from the king."

"I do not have it," said the widow. "I have only this small cup of grain."

But the king did not trust her. So the guards searched her hut. They looked in the corners. They looked in the cupboard.

"It is true," said the guards. "She has nothing but this cup of grain."

"Let us go from this **dismal** place," the king said.

Outside they heard a strange cry. Three men walked together. They sang a sad song. The first had a stick. He swung it before him as he walked. The second walked behind the first. The third walked behind the second. Each had a hand on the other's shoulder.

"Perhaps," said Pundabi, "these are your thieves."

"These?" said the king. "Why, they cannot see!"

"How clever of them," said Pundabi.

So they stopped the three blind men and asked of the king's Golden Serpent.

"No," said the first. "I have only this stick for comfort."

"No," said the second. "I have only the few coins I am given."

"No," said the third. "I have but these two friends."

---

turning wood, spinning wood against a tool in order to shape it or carve designs in it
dismal, making you feel unhappy and hopeless

Before You Go On

1. Why do the king's guards search the young boy?
2. Why does the king want to leave the widow's hut?

On Your Own

What do you think the mystery of the Golden Serpent is?

Reading 3

But the king did not trust them. So the guards searched the three blind men.

"They have nothing," said the guards, "except a worm-eaten stick and a few coins. Nothing more."

"Let us return to the palace," the king said.

"But we have not found the Golden Serpent," Pundabi said.

"I no longer want it," the king said bitterly. "I will pay you and you can leave."

At the palace, the king had his counters pay Pundabi in gold coins.

"And what about your people?" Pundabi asked.

"My people?" asked the king.

"Yes. The crippled boy, the poor widow, and the blind beggars," said Ali.

"What about them, indeed!" said the king. "They did not find my Golden Serpent."

"Ah," said Pundabi, "I see. But I have solved your mystery. I know where the Golden Serpent is."

"You do?" said the king. "How splendid!"

"You must close your eyes and count slowly until you reach a hundred. But make sure you are alone so that no one can steal the Golden Serpent again. Then open your eyes. The Golden Serpent will be in your room."

The king closed his eyes and began to count slowly as Pundabi picked up his bag of gold and left the palace.

He went down the steep hill.

He gave some of the gold to the crippled boy.

He gave some to the widow.

He gave some to the blind beggars.

"Pundabi," said Ali. "You are both wise and generous. But there is still one problem."

"And what is that?" asked Pundabi.

"When the king opens his eyes," said Ali, "he will still not find the Golden Serpent."

"No," said Pundabi. "Some people never do. But that is another mystery."

✓ LITERARY CHECK

What do you think the **moral** of the story is?

About the Author

Walter Dean Myers was the author of more than fifty young adult novels and picture books. Born in West Virginia, he grew up in Harlem after moving there at a young age. Myers held a variety of jobs before he won a picture-book writing contest and decided to become a full-time author. Two of his books, *Scorpions* and *Somewhere in the Darkness*, are Newbery Honor books.

Before You Go On

1. The king doesn't find the Golden Serpent, but he pays Pundabi anyway. Why?
2. What does Pundabi do with the gold?

On Your Own

Do you think Pundabi was truly wise? Why or why not?

Reading 3

Review and Practice

Reader's Theater

Act out the following scene.

King: I want you to solve a mystery for me.
Pundabi: Very well. What is the mystery?
King: I do not know. That is for you to figure out!
Ali: [*wrings his hands*] How can Pundabi solve a mystery if there is no mystery to solve?
King: [*to Pundabi*] If you are really a wise man, Pundabi, it will be done. If you do not solve it, then you are a fraud. I will put you in jail where you belong.
Pundabi: [*calmly, to Ali*] Let us take a walk. Perhaps our eyes will tell us the mystery.
  [*later*]
King: [*to Pundabi*] Have you solved the mystery yet?
Pundabi: No, but we know what the mystery is! It is the mystery of the Golden Serpent.
King: The Golden Serpent?
Pundabi: Yes, your Golden Serpent is missing.
King: I didn't know I had a Golden Serpent.
Pundabi: The thief must be very clever.

Speaking Tip

Pay attention to the "stage directions" in brackets so you know who to be looking at, how to speak, and what to do while reading your lines.

Comprehension

Recall

1. How do the villagers get their questions to Pundabi? What does Pundabi do with the questions?
2. What does Pundabi say has happened to the king's Golden Serpent?

Comprehend

3. What problem does Pundabi have? How does he solve it?
4. What do the king's reactions and actions show about him?

Analyze

5. Why do you think the king decides he no longer wants to find the Golden Serpent?
6. Does the king learn anything from Pundabi's lesson? Explain.

Connect

7. Why do you think people keep telling and retelling this fable?
8. Would you recommend that others read this fable? Why or why not?

Discussion

Discuss with a partner or in a small group.

- What do you think? Is being deceitful ever justified? Why or why not?
- **How can we tell what's right?** Who in the story did the right thing? Explain.

Response to Literature

97

Work with a partner. Take notes about the Beginning/Middle/End of the fable and then retell it to each other. Think about how your retellings were the same and different. Underline details that both you and your partner included.

Use your chart to discuss the characters. Answer these questions:

- Which character might benefit from the life lesson revealed in the fable?
- Who was the wise character? Why?

Beginning	Middle	End

Listening Skill

Listen carefully to your classmates. Identify the important ideas. Retell or summarize these ideas in your own words in order to confirm that you have understood them correctly.

Reading 3

Grammar

Other Uses of *would* in the Past

On page 165, you learned about using *would* + the base form of the verb to talk about repeated actions in the past. To talk about the future, we usually use *will*. In "The Golden Serpent," the author uses *would* + the base form of a verb to express the future in the past. *Would* is the past form of *will*.

Future	Future in the Past
The king knows that Ali **will obey** his wishes.	The king knew that Ali **would obey** his wishes.

Would can also be used in implied conditionals. A conditional sentence has two parts: the if *clause* and the result clause. In an implied conditional, the *if* clause is not included. Use *would* + (*not*) + *have* + past participle to express a condition in the past.

Conditional Sentence	Implied Conditional
If he had been here, he **would not have minded**.	He **would not have minded**.

Grammar Skill

We use *would* + the base form of the verb to talk about the future in the past. We use *would have* + past participle to talk about implied conditions.

Practice A

Rewrite the sentences in your notebook so that they are about yesterday.

1. She doesn't know what time he will be coming home.
2. She thinks he will be late.
3. She wonders if he'll be tired.

Grammar Check

✓ When do we use *would* + the base form of the verb? When do we use *would have* + past participle?

Practice B

Circle the correct verb form to complete each sentence.

1. Where is she? She said she **would be** / **would have been** here by now.
2. I didn't know you walked here. My dad **would give** / **would have given** you a ride.
3. Moira is crying. I didn't think she **would feel** / **would have felt** so upset.

Apply

Work with a partner. Make a list of things you think will happen in the next five years. Then imagine it is five years from now. Discuss the things you thought would happen. Use *would* + the base form of the verb.
Example: Five years ago, I thought everyone in this class would . . . .

Subjunctive

Conditionals with *were*

Verbs in the **subjunctive** express conditions that do not currently exist. The subjunctive is used to express wishes, doubts, and possibilities. It is also used to talk about situations that are unlikely or untrue.

Example	Meaning
If he were here now, and **heard** you tell of waiting a little longer before speaking, what do you think he **would say** or **do**?	He is not here now.

Subjunctive Verbs Followed by Base Verb

Sentences with subjunctive verbs are often used to emphasize importance or urgency. In these cases, they are used in *that* clauses, and the subjunctive verb is in the base form.

Example	Meaning
The king **asked** that Ali **bring** him the wise man, Pundabi.	The king said to Ali: "You must bring him to me." (This request was important.)
The king **demanded** that Pundabi **help** him solve a mystery.	The king said to Pundabi, "I want you to solve a mystery for me." (This demand was urgent.)

Grammar Skill

For the subjunctive mood, use a noun or pronoun and the base form of the verb after *that*.

Practice A

For each sentence, write C if the subjunctive mood is used correctly and I if it is used incorrectly.

1. My teacher advised that we should study for the test. _____
2. My parents insist that I be home by 8:00. _____
3. The librarian recommended that we read this book. _____

Grammar Check

✓ What is an example of a situation in which you might use the **subjunctive**?

Practice B

In your notebook, rewrite the quotes as sentences with subjunctive verbs. Use the verb in parentheses.

1. My teacher said: "Hand in your assignment tomorrow." (ask)
2. My grandparents said: "You must stay for dinner." (insist)
3. My cousin said: "You should see that movie." (recommend)

Apply

Work with a partner. Find sentences that characters in the story said when they were discussing something urgent or important. Rewrite them using the subjunctive.

Reading 3

Reading 3

Writing

Write a Persuasive Paragraph

At the end of this unit, you will write a persuasive speech. To do this, you will need to learn skills that writers use to write persuasively.

When you write a persuasive paragraph, begin by introducing a topic you feel strongly about. Clearly state your opinion and give reasons for your viewpoint.

Writing Prompt

Write a persuasive paragraph on a topic or issue you feel strongly about. You might state your opinion of reality shows or your opinion about some aspect of a book or story you have read. Be sure to use *would* correctly.

1 Prewrite Begin by choosing a topic or an issue you feel strongly about.

- Think about why you feel strongly about the topic or issue.
- What reasons can you give to support your opinion?
- List your ideas in a graphic organizer like the one below.

Here's a word web created by a student named Chelsea about "The Golden Serpent." She wrote her opinion of what Pundabi did in the center bubble. Then she wrote reasons in the bubbles below it.

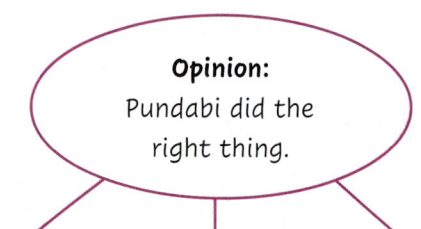

Opinion: Pundabi did the right thing.

Reason 1: The king gave him an impossible command. Pundabi struck back by making up a clever mystery.

Reason 2: The king's command was a waste of Pundabi's time. Pundabi wasted the king's time.

Reason 3: The king paid Pundabi for work he didn't do. Pundabi gave the money to poor people.

② **Draft** Use your word web to help you write a first draft.
- First, state your opinion about the topic or issue.
- State reasons for your opinion.
- Use the modal *would* correctly.

③ **Revise** Read over your draft. Look for places where the writing is unclear or needs improvement. Complete (✓) the Writing Checklist to help you identify problems. Then, revise your draft, using the editing and proofreading marks listed on page 467.

④ **Edit and Proofread** Check your work for errors in grammar, usage, mechanics, and spelling. Trade papers with a partner to obtain feedback. Edit your final draft in response to feedback from your partner and your teacher.

⑤ **Publish** Prepare a clean copy of your final draft. Share your paragragh with the class. Save your work. You'll need to refer to it in the Writing Workshop at the end of the unit.

> **Writing Checklist**
>
> **Ideas:**
> ☐ I stated my opinion and supported it with examples.
>
> **Conventions:**
> ☐ I used the modal *would* correctly.

Here is Chelsea's paragraph. Notice how she states her opinion and gives reasons to support it.

Chelsea Dayton

Pundabi's Actions Were Justified

In my opinion, Pundabi's actions in the story "The Golden Serpent" were justified. If you look at his choices, he did the right thing. First, Pundabi convinces the king that the mystery is the location of a Golden Serpent. The king wants him to find the Golden Serpent, but finding it would be impossible, as the king has never had a Golden Serpent. Pundabi strikes back by using the same approach as the king. He makes up the mystery, and then tells the king that someone must have stolen his Golden Serpent. He appeals to the king's foolishness and sense of greed, and takes him to really poor people who cannot help him. Also, the king pays Pundabi for his services even though he has not found the Golden Serpent. However, Pundabi does not keep the money. Other people would keep the money, but Pundabi generously gives the money to the poor people. I think Pundabi did the right thing in his situation. He struck back against the king's unfair command, wasted the king's time after the king wasted his time, and used the money the king paid him to help poor people.

Reading 4

Prepare to Read

What You Will Learn

Reading
- Vocabulary building: *Context, dictionary skills, word study*
- Reading strategy: *Summarize*
- Text type: *Informational text (social studies)*

Grammar
- Superlative adjectives
- Reciprocal and reflexive pronouns

Writing
- Write an advertisement

THE BIG QUESTION

How can we tell what's right? People like to win, but some things are more important than winning. They include standing up for your beliefs, calling attention to injustice, and being honest. Have you ever had to choose between winning and doing the right thing? What did you do? Work with a partner to discuss your experiences.

Build Background

"When Is a Winner a Hero?" is about three athletes who became famous not just because they were great athletes but also because they did something extraordinary in the face of opposition. Kathrine Switzer was an avid runner who wanted to run in the Boston Marathon, but she wasn't allowed to compete in the all-male race. Cameroonian soccer star Sam Eto'o faced racism both on and off the field and chose to speak out about it. Ivan Fernández Anaya was a runner who could have won an important race, but he chose to help a competitor instead. All of these athletes faced opposition and criticism for who they were or what they did, but they stood up for their beliefs. Do you know of other athletes or celebrities who stand up for something they believe in?

Learning Strategy

Use your prior knowledge. Relating what you already know to a new topic will make it easier to understand new meanings in English.

Athlete	Country	Sport	Challenge
Kathrine Switzer	The United States	running	opposition because she was a woman
Sam Eto'o	Cameroon	soccer	racism
Ivan Fernández Anaya	Spain	running	choosing between winning or helping a competitor

198 Unit 3

Vocabulary

Listening and Speaking: Key Words

> **Key Words**
> athletes
> capability
> gender
> marathon
> racism
> referee

Read these sentences aloud with a partner. Use the context to figure out the meaning of the highlighted words. Use a dictionary, the glossary, or a thesaurus to determine or confirm your answers. Then write each word and its meaning in your notebook.

1. The **athletes** from my country marched proudly in the Parade of Nations in the Olympics.
2. Anna has the **capability** to win a gold medal.
3. Your birth certificate includes information such as name, date of birth, place of birth, and **gender**.
4. People in the **marathon** have to run about 42 kilometers.
5. Before 1954 in the United States, African Americans were not allowed to go to some schools because of **racism**.
6. The **referee** called a penalty with only ten seconds left in the soccer game.

Practice

WB 101

Choose a word from the box above to complete each sentence. Then take turns reading the sentences aloud with a partner.

1. The city streets are closed on Sunday for the annual _____.
2. My cousins run, swim, and ski. They are excellent _____.
3. Martin Luther King, Jr. spoke out against the problem of _____ in society.
4. Some parents want to know the _____ of their baby before it is born, but some prefer to wait.
5. During the basketball game, the _____ called out, "Foul!"
6. Dunking a basketball is beyond my _____.

Reading 4

Reading 4

Listening and Speaking: Academic Words

Study the **purple** words and their meanings. You will find these words useful when talking and writing about informational texts. Write each word and its meaning in your notebook, then say the words aloud with a partner. After you read "When Is a Winner a Hero?" try to use these words to respond to the text.

Academic Words
- address
- controversial
- determined
- witness

address = to speak directly to a person or group	The principal will **address** the students in the auditorium.
controversial = causing disagreement because people have strong opinions	Universal healthcare is a **controversial** issue in the United States.
determined = having a strong desire to succeed at something difficult	Although math is a difficult subject for me, I am **determined** to get a good grade.
witness = to see something happen, especially an accident or crime	If you **witness** a crime, you should provide a report to the police.

Practice

Work with a partner to answer these questions. Try to include the **purple** word in your answer. Write the answers in your notebook.

1. How would you prepare if you had to **address** a large audience?
2. Do you think it is better to discuss or avoid discussing **controversial** topics? Give reasons.
3. What is one thing you are **determined** to experience in your lifetime? Why?
4. Have you ever had the opportunity to **witness** an exciting sports game or musical performance? What happened?

Word Study: Synonyms

Synonyms are words that have the same or nearly the same meaning. For example, *cheerful* is a synonym for *happy*, and *simple* is a synonym for *plain*. As you read, you can use synonyms as context clues to help you figure out the meaning of unfamiliar words.

> Kathrine Switzer trained for the **tough** race that people thought was too **difficult** for women.

Suppose you knew the word *difficult* but not *tough*. The context of the sentence lets you know that *tough* is similar in meaning to *difficult*.

Speaking Skill

Sometimes you can't think of the exact English word or phrase to express your idea. In those instances, you can explain or describe the idea using synonyms you know.

Practice

Work with a partner. Write the words *excellent*, *unusual*, and *barriers* in your notebook. Write a synonym for each word, using a dictionary if necessary. Then write a sentence for each synonym pair.

Reading Strategy: Summarize

Summarizing helps you check your understanding of a text. When you summarize, you identify the main ideas in a text and rewrite them in a few short sentences. To summarize, follow these steps:

- Read the text. Then reread each paragraph or section. What is it mainly about?
- Identify the main idea in each paragraph or section.
- Leave out details. Just focus on the most important points.
- Write a few sentences that convey the main ideas in the text. Use your own words.

As you read "When Is a Winner a Hero?," list the main ideas. Then summarize the text in two or three sentences.

Reading 4

**Informational Text
Social Studies**

Set a purpose for reading Read this article to find out how three athletes showed strength of character, as well as athletic ability. How did each athlete go against the rules to do what's right?

When Is a Winner a Hero?

Athletes strive to win. They push themselves as hard as possible in their quest to be strongest and fastest. Sometimes, however, athletes win in ways that have nothing to do with physical ability and everything to do with character. Here are three notable examples.

Kathrine Switzer, Marathon Maverick

In 1967, Kathrine Switzer was a 19-year-old **journalism** student at Syracuse University in New York. An avid runner, she practiced with the men's cross-country team because the university had no women's team. During months of tough training sessions, Switzer had listened to Coach Arnie Briggs's tales of running in the Boston Marathon, the oldest annual marathon in the world, which was open only to men. Finally, Switzer demanded to know: Why couldn't she run the race herself?

After an animated discussion, Briggs finally shouted, "No **dame** ever ran the Boston Marathon!" He said the race—at 26.2 miles (42.2 kilometers) long—was too difficult for a "fragile" female to run. But having witnessed Switzer's determination, he struck a bargain with the young athlete: If she could complete the distance in practice, he would take her to Boston. Three weeks before the race, Switzer, Briggs, and two friends successfully finished

▲ Boston Marathon, 1967: A race official attempts to physically remove Kathrine Switzer from the marathon.

a practice run. The marathon entry form did not ask athletes to specify gender, so Kathrine Switzer signed up under her journalism **byline**—K.V. Switzer. She was given the official bib number 261. At the beginning of the marathon, Switzer's greatest concern was having the courage to push through the pain and fatigue to finish the race. That would change.

---

journalism, the profession of writing news articles for newspapers, magazines, television, and so on
dame, woman (informal and somewhat rude in modern language)

byline, the writer's name at the beginning of an article

▲ Kathrine Switzer, holding her marathon number, 25 years after she ran the Boston Marathon

At about the fourth mile of the race, Switzer heard the pounding of street shoes behind her. "When a runner hears that kind of noise, it's usually danger—like hearing a dog's paws on the pavement," she recalled. Her **pursuer** was race official Jock Semple, and he screamed at Switzer to get out of his race. As Semple tried to grab Switzer's bib, her friend Tom flung the man to the ground. Switzer kept running, but not before the moment was captured on film for the world to see. As she continued running, Switzer's shock turned to anger. She vowed to prove that women were strong enough to compete at the marathon level.

"I knew if I quit, nobody would ever believe that women had the capability to run 26-plus miles," Switzer recalled. She knew there would be other **repercussions**: People would call her a publicity hound. Her humiliation would become a humiliation for all women in sports. Worst of all, **chauvinists** like Jock Semple would win.

The consequences of failure were so great that Switzer's pain and fatigue became minor concerns. With renewed determination, she powered through the final miles. She finished the race in four hours and twenty minutes, but it would be another five years before the Boston Athletic Association allowed women to run in the Boston Marathon. Now, whenever Switzer attends the Boston Marathon, female racers thank her for leading the way.

---

pursuer, a person who is chasing someone or something
repercussions, consequences that are usually bad
chauvinists, people who don't value the other gender as equals

Before You Go

1. Why did Kathrine Switzer practice with the men's cross-country team?
2. Why did she use the name K.V. Switzer to sign up for the Boston Marathon?

On Your Own

What sports are still available to only one gender? Do you think the rules should change?

Reading 4

Sam Eto'o: Soccer Star and "Racism Hunter"

Cameroonian soccer star Samuel Eto'o is the most decorated African player of all time, having won the African Player of the Year award a record four times. However, it is another type of award that stands out in his mind: the one he won for standing up to racism. In March 2015, Eto'o was awarded the Medal of Tolerance from the European Council on Tolerance and Reconciliation (ECTR) at Kensington Palace in London. The award was given by an organization of former European presidents and prime ministers to fight **xenophobia** in Europe.

Eto'o had long been an accomplished soccer player. But he gained worldwide recognition in 2006 for trying to walk off the field in Spain due to the racist abuse he was suffering. Eto'o had been playing for Barcelona against Real Zaragoza in Spain. Every time he touched the ball, Zaragoza fans would shout racial **slurs** and throw objects onto the field. His teammates convinced Eto'o to continue playing.

But in 2010, when the same thing happened as he played for Inter Milan at Cagliari, the referees called a three-minute delay of the game. The referee addressed both captains, as well as fans, saying the match would stop if the chanting continued. Although these efforts failed, Eto'o himself went on to score the only goal of the match. From that moment on, Eto'o resolved never to back down in the face of racism. "The only path is to stand up and shout," he told the audience after receiving his award.

Eto'o had experienced racism off the field as well. He was trying to buy an expensive watch in London, for example, when the salesperson

▲ Sam Eto'o prepares to walk off the field to decry racism.

pretended his credit card was **declined**. She assumed he was part of a Nigerian credit card scam. Eto'o later spoke to journalists about the event to show that racism is not just a problem in soccer but in society as a whole. "If one of my own makes a mistake, they judge us all," Eto'o said. Had the credit card scammers been white, he observed, the clerk would not have treated the next white customer as Eto'o himself had been treated.

Along with the Medal of Tolerance, ECTR president Moshe Kantor gave Samuel Eto'o a new title. It reflects the soccer star's fierce stand against discrimination: "a hunter against racism."

---

xenophobia, fear of people who come from another country
slurs, harsh insults meant to show dislike for someone

declined, rejected

Iván Fernández Anaya: When Losing Meant Winning

Iván Fernández Anaya is an international running champion. His proudest moment, however, may be the time he gave up an easy win to take second place instead. In December 2012, the Spanish runner was trailing behind Kenyan Olympic bronze medalist Abel Mutai during a cross-country race in Burlada, Spain. First-place Mutai had a big lead until, thinking the race was over, he stopped 10 to 20 meters short of the finish line. It was a **blunder** that could cost him the race.

Behind Mutai, Fernández Anaya, 24, was confused by what he saw. Why had Mutai stopped short of the finish line? He quickly realized that Mutai, who could not speak Spanish, had misidentified the finish line, and he could not understand the spectators who were urging him on to finish.

Fernández Anaya had a decision to make: Should he forge ahead to snatch victory away from Mutai, or should he acknowledge the true winner? He followed his conscience. Fernández Anaya caught up to Mutai and encouraged the Kenyan athlete to continue running and cross the finish line. Without a common language, the Basque runner resorted to gesturing frantically at Mutai, who then went on to win the race.

Due to their language differences, Mutai didn't say much to Fernández Anaya after the race except to thank him. But that didn't matter to Fernández Anaya. He believes athletes should strive to do their best. On that day in December, doing his best meant recognizing that Mutai was the stronger competitor.

"He was the rightful winner," Fernández Anaya said. "As soon as I saw he was stopping, I knew I wasn't going to pass him."

Anaya's coach, Martín Fiz, wasn't pleased with his decision; he would have preferred a win. Fernández Anaya, however, would rather be remembered for his kind act than for coming in first. Though he may have lost a controversial race, he won the hearts of countless fans.

blunder, mistake

▼ Elite runners, like these beginning a race in Barcelona, Spain, are extremely competitive.

Before You Go

1. Why did Eto'o try to walk off the soccer field in 2006?
2. Why did Fernández Anaya gesture frantically to Mutai?

On Your Own

From what you read, how can one person make a difference?

Reading 4

Review and Practice

Comprehension

Recall

1. On what condition did her coach say he would let Switzer run in the marathon?
2. At the 2010 soccer match in Cagliari, how did the referee address the racist chanting?

Comprehend

3. What happened during the race Kathrine Switzer ran that helped change things for women?
4. Why did Mutai not win the December 2012 cross-country race in Spain?

Analyze

5. How could the outcome of each story you read have been different? Did each athlete do what was right?
6. How is each athlete you read about a hero? Explain.

Connect

7. Is winning what's most important in competitive sports? Explain.
8. Which athlete's story affected you the most? Why?

In Your Own Words

Review the steps for summarizing on page 201. Use the chart to summarize the main idea of each athlete's story. Write just a few sentences for each one, using your own words. If you need more space, write the summaries in your notebook. When you have finished, compare charts with a partner.

Section	Summary
Kathrine Switzer, Marathon Maverick	
Sam Eto'o: Soccer Star and "Racism Hunter"	
Ivan Fernández Anaya: When Losing Meant Winning	

Speaking Tip

Remember to use words and phrases that compare and contrast. (For example, *and*, *also*, *but*, and *however*)

Discussion

Discuss with a partner or in a small group.

1. In what ways did Kathrine Switzer's actions help female athletes in general?
2. Why was Ivan Fernández Anaya's decision controversial?

❓ How can we tell what's right? How did each athlete demonstrate that they knew what was right?

Read for Fluency

Reading with feeling helps make what you read more interesting. Work with a partner. Choose a paragraph from the reading. Read the paragraph. Ask each other how you felt after reading the paragraph.

Take turns reading the paragraph aloud to each other with a tone of voice that represents how you felt when you read it the first time. Give each other feedback.

Extension

WB 105

Now that you have read about how three athletes chose to do the right thing when they faced challenges, choose one to write a letter to. In your letter, explain why you think that individual did the right thing.

Listening Skill

Listen to your classmates for implicit ideas, or ideas that they do not directly. Pay attention to the examples the speakers give, their word choice, and their intonation. These things are clues to the speakers' implicit ideas.

Reading 4
Grammar

Superlative Adjectives

In the reading about the three athletes, the author uses superlative adjectives. These adjectives compare three or more things. A superlative adjective usually precedes the noun it modifies, along with the word *the*.

Rule	Adjective	Superlative
For most one-syllable superlative adjectives, add -*est* (or -*st* if the adjective ends in an *e*).	old wise strong	the oldest (woman) the wisest the strongest
For two-syllable superlative adjectives that end in *y*, change the *y* to an *i* and add -*est*.	busy funny crazy	the busiest (evening) the funniest the craziest
For most other two-syllable superlative adjectives, use *most*.	famous pleasant	the most famous (singer) the most pleasant
For superlative adjectives with three syllables or more, use *most*.	important fascinating	the most important (concert) the most fascinating
Some adjectives have irregular superlative forms.	good bad	the best (performance) the worst

Practice A
WB 106

In your notebook, rewrite the sentences using superlative adjectives correctly.

1. The faster runner won the race.
   The *fastest* runner won the race.
2. The more decorated African player of all time is Eto'o.
3. Athletes try to be more successful at their sport.
4. The stronger weightlifter won the competition.

Practice B

Complete the sentences with the correct superlative forms of the adjectives in parentheses.

1. The Olympics is ___the biggest___ sports competition. (big)
2. I am _____ runner in the class. (bad)
3. The city is _____ during the marathon. (busy)
4. Of all qualities, honesty is _____. (important)

Grammar Skill
Use superlatives to talk about the #1 person or thing in the world.

Grammar Check
✓ What word is used before superlative adjectives?

Apply
Work with a partner. Ask and answer questions about different athletes. Use superlatives.
Example: Who is the most famous gymnast in the world?

208 Unit 3

Reciprocal and Reflexive Pronouns

Reciprocal pronouns are used to show a mutual, or two-way, action or feeling. There are two main reciprocal pronouns: *each other* and *one another*. Use *each other* when talking or writing about two people or animals: *Lila and Miranda kicked the soccer ball to* **each other** *for practice.* Use *one another* when talking or writing about more than two people or animals: *At school, my friends and I help* **one another** *understand the homework.*

Reflexive pronouns are used when the subject and the object are the same person: **John** *hurt* **himself***.* (*John* and *himself* are the same person.) Reflexive pronouns are also used for emphasis. In these cases, the reflexive pronoun follows a noun or pronoun: *Why couldn't Switzer enter the race* **herself***? Eto'o* **himself** *scored the only goal of the match.*

> **Grammar Skill**
> Use *-self* for singular reflexive pronouns and *-selves* for plural reflexive pronouns.

Practice A

Circle the correct phrase to complete each sentence.

1. Jerry and Debbie have been friends with (**each other**) / one another for years.
2. The three athletes would have a lot in common with **each other** / **one another**.
3. The two referees tend to make the same calls and talk them over with **each other** / **one another**.
4. The two teammates always support **each other** / **one another**.
5. The neighbors on our street respect **each other** / **one another**.

> **Grammar Check**
> ✓ When do we use the **reciprocal pronouns** *each other*? When do we use *one another*?

Practice B

Complete the sentences with the correct reflexive pronoun.

1. You can see ____yourself____ doing the right thing.
2. My brother wants to work for _____.
3. Elizabeth taught _____ to knit.
4. You and your friends can help _____ to food.
5. The athletes stood up for _____.

> **Apply**
> Work with a partner. Write four sentences about the students in your class. Use reciprocal pronouns and reflexive pronouns. **Example:** We usually do our homework **ourselves**. However, sometimes we help **one another**.

Reading 4

Reading 4
Writing

Write an Advertisement

At the end of this unit, you will write a persuasive speech. To help do this, you are learning how to write persuasively. In this lesson, you will write an advertisement. When you write an advertisement for a product or service, it is important to identify your intended audience. Tailor your ad to this audience. Begin with an attention-getting question or phrase. Then include facts and details that describe the product or service, its function, and how it will benefit the buyer.

> **Writing Prompt**
>
> Create a print ad. Choose a product or a service to advertise, and think about the target audience for it. You can also make up a product or event. Be sure to use superlative adjectives correctly.

1 Prewrite Identify a product or service for your advertisment.

WB 108

- Write the name of the product or service in your notebook.
- Ask yourself what the benefits of this product or service are.
- Think of some facts to support your claims.
- Then arrange your ideas on a word web.

Here's a word web created by a student named Rebecca about a product she wants to promote.

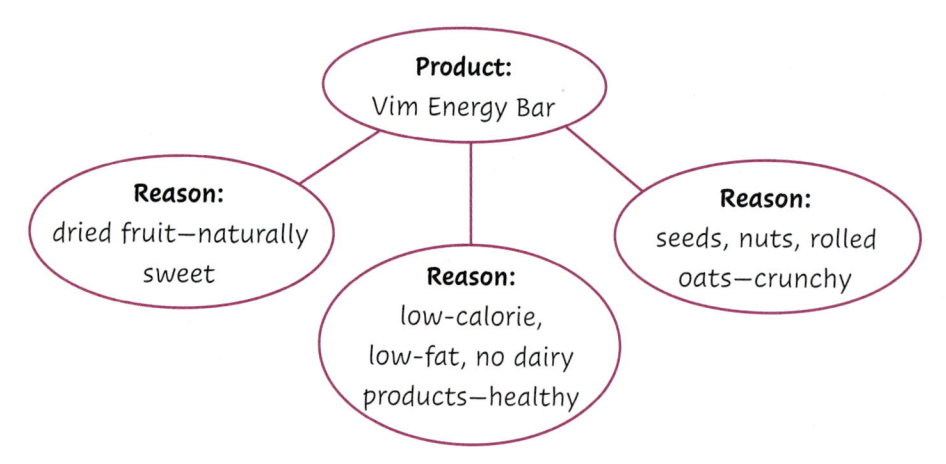

Product: Vim Energy Bar

- **Reason:** dried fruit—naturally sweet
- **Reason:** low-calorie, low-fat, no dairy products—healthy
- **Reason:** seeds, nuts, rolled oats—crunchy

210 Unit 3

② Draft Use your word web to help you write a first draft.

- Use a question or other technique to get your audience's attention.
- Describe the product. Use details from your word web to convince your audience that they need it.
- Use superlative adjectives to convince people that your product or service is the best.
- End by encouraging people to buy your product or use your service.

③ Revise Read over your draft. Look for places where the writing is unclear or needs improvement. Complete (✓) the Writing Checklist to help you identify problems. Then revise your draft, using the editing and proofreading marks listed on page 467.

④ Edit and Proofread Check your work for errors in grammar, usage, mechanics, and spelling. Trade papers with a partner to obtain feedback. Edit your final draft in response to feedback from your partner and your teacher.

⑤ Publish Prepare a clean copy of your final draft. Share your advertisement with the class. Save your work. You'll need to refer to it in the Writing Workshop at the end of the unit.

> **Writing Checklist**
>
> **Ideas:**
> ☐ I described a product or service that will appeal to a target audience.
>
> **Word Choice:**
> ☐ I used details, including adjectives, to describe the service or product.
>
> **Organization:**
> ☐ I began with an attention-getting question and ended by urging people to buy the product.
>
> **Conventions:**
> ☐ I used superlative adjectives correctly.

Here is Rebecca's advertisement. Notice how she opens with a question and ends with an appeal to her audience to try her product.

Rebecca Miles

Vim Energy Bars

Do you need a healthy mid-morning snack? Do you get hungry in the late afternoon? Then try the new Vim Energy Bar! Unlike other snacks, Vim Energy Bars are low calorie and low fat, and they contain no dairy products. But they are packed full of protein and vitamins, making them the most nutritious energy bars you can buy! Vim Energy Bars are full of dried fruit, such as raisins, mangoes, and apricots. They have added chia seeds, almonds, and rolled oats, making them the crunchiest bars you can find. Everything in the bars is organic and natural, and there are no preservatives. Treat yourself to a new Vim Energy Bar today! You will find it is the most delicious and the healthiest energy bar you have ever had.

Link the Readings

Critical Thinking

What logical connections can you make between the ideas and details in the readings in this unit? Although the readings do not all have the same purpose, they share a common theme and reflect a range of viewpoints. Complete the chart. Be prepared to support your answers with evidence from each of the texts.

Title of Reading	Purpose	Big Question Link
"The Beggar King"		
"Mars: Pro and Con"		
"The Golden Serpent"		Pundabi did the right thing by leading the king on.
"When Is a Winner a Hero?"	to inform	

Discussion

Discuss with a partner or in a small group.

- Which selection had the biggest impact on you? Why?
- **How can we tell what's right?** In your opinion, which unit selection best answers the Big Question? Explain why it does this best.

Fluency Check

Work with a partner. Choose a paragraph from one of the readings. Take turns reading it for one minute. Count the total number of words you read. Practice saying the words you had trouble reading. Take turns reading the paragraph three more times. Did you read more words each time? Record the number of words you read each time.

	1st Reading	2nd Reading	3rd Reading	4th Reading
Number of Words				

Media Literacy & Projects

Work with a partner or in a small group. Choose one of these projects.

1. Do research to learn about an athlete who has struggled to achieve his or her goals. Gather information about his or her life and summarize it in a brief essay. Present the essay to the class. Provide an image of the athlete.

2. Do research to learn about sports that women had to struggle to be a part of "professionally." Gather information about the sport, how and why women were not allowed to participate, and how they overcame this obstacle.

3. Find a fable or folktale that is important in your culture. Read the fable aloud to the class. Have the class guess the moral.

4. What kinds of missions to Mars are being planned right now? Describe the mission, including the plan, the dates, and the challenges. Present your findings to the class. Do you think the mission will happen? Explain your opinion.

Further Reading

Choose from these reading selections. Practice reading silently for longer and longer periods.

The Interpreter, Charles Randolph
Silva, an interpreter at the United Nations, overhears a dangerous plot. Can the plot be stopped in time?

The House on Mango Street, Sandra Cisneros
Esperanza Cordero's neighborhood is full of harsh realities and harsh beauty. She is all too aware of the low expectations people have of her. So she must invent for herself what she will become.

Walk Two Moons, Sharon Creech
On a car trip from Ohio to Idaho, U.S.A., with her grandparents, Salamanca Tree Hiddle traces her missing mother's steps. Drawing strength from her Native American ancestry, Salamanca is able to face the truth.

When You Reach Me, Rebecca Stead
Miranda has often noticed a homeless man near her home in New York City. When she finds four mysterious notes addressed to her, a race to save someone's life begins.

Listening & Speaking Workshop: Radio Commercial

Put It All Together

You and a partner will create and present a radio commercial.

1 Think about It

Think about the speakers in "Mars: Pro and Con" What words do they use to make a case for colonizing or not colonizing Mars? How do those words make you feel about their positions?

With a partner, discuss how persuasive words can make you believe something or change your mind about it. Think about persuasive words you have heard used in TV and radio commercials. Make a list of these words.

Work together to list ideas for a radio commercial. Write down your ideas. Here are some examples:

- To generate support for a high-school fundraiser
- To advertise a new product that cleans everything
- To advertise a class that teaches you how to take tests
- To advertise a concert featuring your favorite singer

2 Gather and Organize Information

With your partner, choose a topic from your list. Then write down the information you want to include in your radio commercial. What words will you use to persuade a listener to buy your product or support your cause? You might want to brainstorm ideas.

Research Go to the library or search on the internet to get information about your product or event. Use a dictionary or thesaurus to find persuasive language for your commercial. Take notes on what you find.

Order Your Notes Make a list of arguments, examples, and supporting details you will use to persuade your listener. Then organize your ideas in an outline or another graphic organizer.

3 Practice and Present

Use your outline or other graphic organizer to prepare your presentation. With your partner, choose which parts you will each present. Practice presenting the commercial together. Develop oral, visual, or written cues to help you know when it is your turn to speak. Since your radio audience can't see you, work to convey your message with your words and tone of voice. To make the presentation of your radio commercial richer and more interesting, use a variety of grammatical structures, sentence lengths, sentence types, and connecting words.

Deliver Your Radio Commercial Give your presentation from the back of the room so that your classmates can hear but not see you—as if you were radio announcers. Emphasize certain words by changing the volume or tone of your voice. Slow down when you come to the most important points. At the end of the presentation, ask listeners if your radio commercial was effective. Give audience members a chance to "call in" and tell whether they plan to try your product or event.

> **Speaking Tips**
>
> Be sure to speak clearly and to repeat important details so that your listeners will understand and remember them.
>
> Use sound effects and your voice to get the listener's attention. Work with your partner to improve your timing when you speak.

4 Evaluate the Presentation

You will improve your skills as a speaker and a listener by evaluating each presentation you give and hear. Complete (✓) this checklist to help you evaluate your commercial and the commercials of your classmates.

- ☐ Was the radio commercial persuasive? Why or why not?
- ☐ Was the purpose of the radio commercial clear?
- ☐ Did the speakers give important details in a way that was easy to understand and remember?
- ☐ Did the presenters speak clearly and loudly enough to be heard?
- ☐ Could the radio commercial be improved?

> **Strengthen Your Social Language**
>
> Presenting a radio commercial means communicating well. Go to your Digital Resources and do the activity for this unit. This activity will help you expand your vocabulary using high-frequency English words necessary for fluently presenting a radio commercial.

Put It All Together

Writing Workshop

Speech

In persuasive writing, the writer tries to persuade readers to change their ideas, beliefs, or behavior. An effective speech begins with a clear statement of the writer's opinion. The speech goes on to provide reasons, facts, and examples that support the writer's position. Skilled speechwriters also present both sides of an argument in order to anticipate and counter opposing opinions. A speech concludes with a paragraph that restates the writer's opinion in a new way.

Writing Prompt

Write a five-paragraph speech that expresses your opinion about something you believe needs to be changed in your school or community. Be sure to use modals of necessity and signal words for opinions.

1 Prewrite Brainstorm a list of possible topics for your speech in your notebook. What do you think needs to change in your school or community? How can you persuade others to agree with your opinion? Select one item on your list to write about.

List and Organize Ideas and Details After you choose a topic, make a T-chart. In the Pros column, give arguments that support your opinion. In the Cons column, give arguments that oppose your opinion so that you can counter these in your speech. A student named Leah decided to write a speech in favor of wearing school uniforms. Here is the T-chart she prepared.

Pros	Cons
Uniforms promote equality. They would reduce economic tension. It would be easier to get dressed in the morning.	Uniforms suppress individuality. Uniforms cost money.

2 Draft Use the model on page 220 and your T-chart to help you write a first draft. Make sure that the tone of your speech suits your audience. Include reasons, facts, and examples to support your opinion.

3 Revise

Read over your draft. As you do so, ask yourself the questions in the Writing Checklist. Use the questions to help you revise your speech.

Six Traits of Writing Checklist

- ☐ **Ideas:** Is my opinion clear?
- ☐ **Organization:** Are my ideas presented in an order that makes sense?
- ☐ **Voice:** Does my tone suit my audience?
- ☐ **Word Choice:** Do I use persuasive words that will appeal to listeners?
- ☐ **Sentence Fluency:** Do my sentences flow well when read aloud?
- ☐ **Conventions:** Does my writing follow the rules of grammar, usage, and mechanics?

Here are the changes Leah plans to make when she revises her draft:

School Uniforms—A Very Good Idea!

Do you think that ^most school uniforms are a good idea? In some schools, students are not required to wear them. Though there is a dress code, students ^are generally allowed to wear whatever they want. If ~~people~~ ^anyone asked a student at my school, "Would you like school uniforms?" I can guarantee that the majority would say no. But if we really ~~take a moment to~~ think about the advantages of uniforms, the idea seems a lot more appealing.

Revised for accuracy and to correct spelling and mechanics.

The most important reason that school uniforms would be a good idea is that they would reduce tension between students There would be less focus on who's wearing ~~nicer~~ ^the nicest clothes and how much money someone's clothes cost. As a result, student would be able to focus more on learning and making friends, which is what school is really about.

Revised for emphasis by changing comparative to superlative.

Unit 3 **217**

Put It All Together

School uniforms would ~~also~~ make life a lot easier for other reasons, too. There would be less stress every morning about clothes. Students come to school late, complaining that they've had a bad morning because they didn't know what to wear, ~~or couldn't find a certain shirt.~~ They would have more time for ~~to get a better night's~~ sleep and be less likely to come to school late.

Shouldn't we, as students, try to express ourselves, not through clothes, but through actions? Whether or not we are wearing uniforms, we can still do what makes us happy. A frequent argument against school uniforms is that they suppress individuality. A musician can still play an instrument. An athlete can still play a sport. What makes each of us an individual should be shown through what we do, not what we wear.

Revised to remove redundancy and for clarity of flow and reference.

Revised for clarity of flow.

When we assess the pros and cons of school uniforms, school uniforms don't seem bad. They would teach students that clothes aren't everything and that school shouldn't feel like a contest. I believe that uniforms can help simplify our lives ~~reduce the barriers between students,~~ while enhancing our focus on learning. I urge you to consider enforcing a new rule requiring students to wear uniforms.

Revised for meaning.

4 **Edit and Proofread** Check your work for errors in grammar, usage, mechanics, and spelling. Then trade essays with a partner and complete (✓) the Peer Review Checklist below to give each other constructive feedback. Edit your final draft in response to feedback from your partner and your teacher.

WB 109

Peer Review Checklist

- ☐ Does the first paragraph introduce the topic and the speaker's argument?
- ☐ Are different reasons presented in paragraphs 2, 3, and 4?
- ☐ Is the reason in each paragraph developed with examples and details?
- ☐ Are the reasons presented in an order that makes sense?
- ☐ Does the last paragraph provide a conclusion?
- ☐ Does the last paragraph include the speaker's opinion?
- ☐ Could changes be made to improve the speech?

Put It All Together

Here are the changes Leah decided to make to her final draft as a result of her peer review.

Leah Morales

School Uniforms—A Very Good Idea!

Do you think that most school uniforms are a good idea? In some schools, students are not required to wear them. Though there is a dress code, students are generally allowed to wear whatever they want. If anyone asked a student at my school, "Would you like school uniforms?" I can guarantee that the majority would say no. But if we really think about the advantages of uniforms, the idea seems a lot more appealing.

The most important reason that school uniforms would be a good idea is that they would reduce tension between students. There would be less focus on who's wearing the nicest clothes and how much money someone's clothes cost. As a result, students would be able to focus more on learning and making friends, which is what school is really about. *(Revised to correct errors in mechanics.)*

School uniforms would make life a lot easier for other reasons, too. There would be less stress every morning about clothes. Some students come to school late, complaining that they've had a bad morning because they didn't know what to wear. They would have more time for sleep and be less likely to come to school late. *(Revised for clarity.)*

A frequent argument against school uniforms is that they suppress individuality. Shouldn't we, as students, try to express ourselves, not through clothes, but through actions? Whether or not we are wearing uniforms, we can still do what makes us happy. A musician can still play an instrument. An athlete can still play a sport. What makes each of us an individual should be shown through what we do, not what we wear.

When we assess the pros and cons of school uniforms, school uniforms don't seem bad. They would teach students that clothes aren't everything and that school shouldn't feel like a contest. I believe that uniforms can help simplify our lives, allowing us to focus on learning. I urge you to consider enforcing a new rule requiring students to wear uniforms. *(Revised for clarity.)*

⑤ Publish Obtain feedback from your teacher and classmates; then prepare your final draft. Share your speech with the class.

Test Preparation

Practice

Read the following test sample. Study the tips in the boxes. Work with a partner to answer the questions.

Do We Still Tell Fables?

All cultures have fictional tales that highlight both the requirements of their society and the consequences of breaking the rules. Aesop's fables are among the best-known examples of the genre. Fables teach the listener how a culture operates and how to live in the best way possible with other people. Do we still tell fables in modern times? Some might say we do, but they go by a different name: urban legends.

An urban legend is a story about something that didn't really happen (though it may have some basis in fact), teaches a lesson about danger or justice, and is told as an absolutely true story. Often, the legend is given credibility not by being repeated by an elder (like a fable) but because we hear them from friends who claim to know someone who knows the legend is true. Urban legends have common themes, but two seem predominant: fear of the unknown in the modern world and justice is always done, often in an ironic way.

Sometimes a legend is humorous, as in the man who thought his computer disk drive was a coffee cup holder. Sometimes they are more sinister, like the foreigner who warns of an impending disaster because of some kindness a person has done to him or her. Like a fable, every legend teaches a common lesson: society as we know it is weird and frightening. Be on your guard!

1 According to the passage, how are urban legends like fables?
   A They are both told as though they were true events.
   B They both teach their lessons with humor.
   C Both criticize the society in which they originate.
   D Both teach a lesson about the culture that created them.

2 Based on the information in the passage, what prompts people to tell and believe urban legends?
   A A desire to participate in the community
   B An ignorance of one's own culture
   C A fear of the unknown in the world
   D A desire to pass on a moral

Taking Tests
You will often take tests to show what you know. Study the tips below to help you improve your test-taking skills.

Tip
When you see an answer choice that is an exact phrasing of a sentence in the passage, read it carefully to make sure the information has not been twisted.

Tip
When you have to make an inference or figure out information that is not directly stated in the passage, it helps to paraphrase the main idea of the passage.

WB 111–112

Visual Literacy

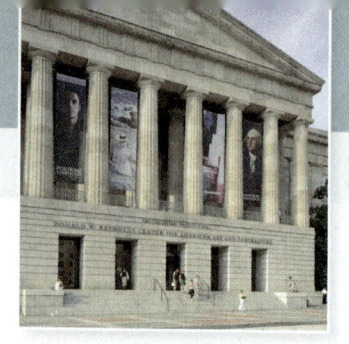

Smithsonian American Art Museum

That's Art?

For centuries when people looked at art, they expected to see traditional paintings or sculptures of recognizable subjects, such as the human body. But over time, artists began to ask the question, "What is art?" Their answers have pushed the definition way beyond framed paintings on a wall.

Deborah Butterfield, *Monekana* (2001)

In *Monekana*, Deborah Butterfield finds a way to create a full-sized image of a horse from what appears to be random pieces of wood. In fact, it's a bronze sculpture based on pieces of Hawaiian Okea wood. The artist brought the wood together into a horse shape and then cast the work in bronze. The special patina, or coating, on the bronze gives it the color of driftwood. *Monekana* is the Hawaiian word for Montana, the state where Butterfield lives and teaches at a university.

◀ Deborah Butterfield, *Monekana*, 2001, bronze, 96 x 129½ x 63½ in., Smithsonian American Art Museum

Sam Gilliam, *Swing* (1969)

In *Swing*, Sam Gilliam cuts his painting loose from any kind of frame. He lets it hang by a few strands of rawhide. Gilliam may have been the first painter to introduce the idea of an unsupported canvas. Traditionally, artists would always stretch a canvas and attach it to a wooden frame before painting it. Inspired in part by the sight of laundry hanging on a clothesline, Gilliam folded and squeezed a huge piece of paint-stained wet canvas and then hung it up before it dried. Even the title of the final work, *Swing*, suggests a movement not normally associated with a finished painting. Gilliam believed that good artists "just work and let things go."

▲ Sam Gilliam, *Swing*, 1969, acrylic and aluminum, 119⅝ × 283½ in., Smithsonian American Art Museum

Man Ray, *Cadeau (Serie II)* (1970)

Man Ray's iron has sharp tacks glued to its bottom. It hardly seems like a *cadeau*, which means "gift" in French. Man Ray once said he took the "greatest pleasure" in changing actual objects. He would remove them from their everyday locations, sometimes alter them, and then exhibit them as art. In the early 1920s, Man Ray was a leader among American and European artists who pushed to redefine what could be officially considered "art." He was one of the first to say that art is just about anything that serves an artist's creative purposes.

All three of these artists had to think about what it means to be an artist and what materials they felt they could use and still call their work "art." In each case, the viewer understands that the object they are looking at is not simply wood, canvas, or an iron, but part of some bigger story shaped by the artist's hand.

◀ Man Ray, *Cadeau (Serie II)*, 1970, iron, 6⅛ × 4 × 3½ in., Smithsonian American Art Museum

Discuss What You Learned

1. How do the three artists use everyday objects in their artworks?
2. In what way does each artist push the boundaries as to what can be considered art?

BIG QUESTION
Do you think all of these objects could be considered art, or would you look at one or more of them and exclaim, *That's art?!* Explain your answer.

113–114

Unit 3　223

Unit 4

Can we think with the heart?

THE BIG QUESTION

This unit is about love, friendship, and the human heart. You will read about different kinds of love. You will also read about the connection between the heart and the mind. Reading, writing, and talking about these topics will give you practice using academic language and help you become a better student.

Reading 1
Social Studies

from *The Story of My Life* by Helen Keller

Reading Strategy
Identify main idea and details

Reading 2
Play

To Capture the Wild Horse

Reading Strategy
Analyze text structure

Reading 3
Social Studies

- The Heart's Wisdom
- "Nourishing Your Heart and Your Brain"

Reading Strategy
Monitor comprehension

Listening and Speaking—How-to
Demonstration
At the end of this unit, you will prepare and give a **how-to demonstration**.

Writing—Expository Essay
At the end of this unit, you will write an **expository essay**. To help you do this, you will write four paragraphs that will help you with an expository essay: a critique, a summary, instructions, and a critical analysis.

Quick Write
Talk with a partner about what you associate with the phrase "having a heart." List your ideas.

Reading 4
Short Story

"Ginger for the Heart" by Paul Yee

Reading Strategy
Recognize and analyze cultural content

View and Respond
Go to your Digital Resources. Watch the video and answer the questions.

Reading 1

Prepare to Read

What You Will Learn

Reading
- Vocabulary building: *Context, dictionary skills, word study*
- Reading strategy: *Identify main idea and details*
- Text type: *Informational text (social studies)*

Grammar
- Possessive adjectives
- Adjectives and adjectival phrases

Writing
- Write a critique

❓ THE BIG QUESTION

Can we think with the heart? What emotional difficulties do you think a person who could not see or hear would have? What kind of emotional help might he or she need? Discuss with a partner.

Build Background

You are about to read excerpts from **The Story of My Life**, Helen Keller's autobiography. An autobiography is a story that a person writes about his or her own life.

Helen Keller was born on June 27, 1880, a perfectly healthy baby. When she was just nineteen months old, she became gravely ill. Although she recovered, her illness left her hearing impaired (unable to hear) and sight impaired (unable to see). When Helen was almost seven years old, a teacher named Anne Sullivan came to live with her and her family. These excerpts tell what happened when Anne Sullivan first came into Helen's life.

▲ People who cannot see can read books in Braille. Look at the Braille text. How do you think it is used?

▲ Helen Keller standing in her study, reading a Braille book

Vocabulary

Listening and Speaking: Key Words

Read these sentences aloud with a partner. Use the context to figure out the meaning of the highlighted words. Use a dictionary, the glossary, or a thesaurus to determine or confirm your answers. Then write each word and its meaning in your notebook.

Key Words
bitterness
defects
eventful
imitate
sensation
tangible

1. Before Helen Keller met Anne Sullivan, she was filled with an intense anger, or bitterness.
2. The diamond was a perfect gem; it had no flaws or defects.
3. That day in 1887 was eventful for Helen because it was when Anne Sullivan entered her life and changed it forever.
4. Some birds, such as parrots, can imitate people by repeating words they hear people say.
5. She had the sensation, or feeling, that something interesting was about to happen.
6. Helen was surrounded by a darkness so tangible, she could almost feel it.

Practice

Choose a word from the box above to complete each sentence. Then take turns reading the sentences aloud with a partner.

1. In dance class, you need to watch the teacher closely and _____ his moves.
2. The day my mother came home with my baby sister was a(n) _____ day for my family.
3. Helen paused for a moment, enjoying the _____ of sun and a gentle breeze on her face.
4. Before she understood the concept of language, Helen got her information from _____ things that she could touch.
5. Because she was filled with _____ and frustration, Helen often misbehaved.
6. Before you buy something, you should examine it to make sure it has no _____.

Reading 1

Listening and Speaking: Academic Words

Study the **purple** words and their meanings. You will find these words useful when talking and writing about informational texts. Write each word and its meaning in your notebook, then say the words aloud with a partner. After you read the excerpts from *The Story of My Life*, try to use these words to respond to the text.

Academic Words

communicate
concept
persistence
transformation

communicate = express your thoughts and feelings so that other people understand them	People **communicate** by using language, facial expressions, and physical gestures, or movements.
concept = idea	Anne Sullivan had to teach Helen the **concept** of language as well as the language itself.
persistence = the act of continuing firmly in some state, purpose, or course of action	Helen's **persistence** and determination helped her achieve her goals.
transformation = a complete change in something or someone	Miss Sullivan's arrival was the beginning of a **transformation** for Helen.

Practice
WB 116

Work with a partner to answer these questions. Try to include the **purple** word in your answer. Write sentences with your answers in your notebook.

1. What are some ways we **communicate** without using words?
2. In what ways is the **concept** of language both simple and complex at the same time?
3. Do you think **persistence** is a quality to be admired or not? Why?
4. What are some things in nature that go through a **transformation**?

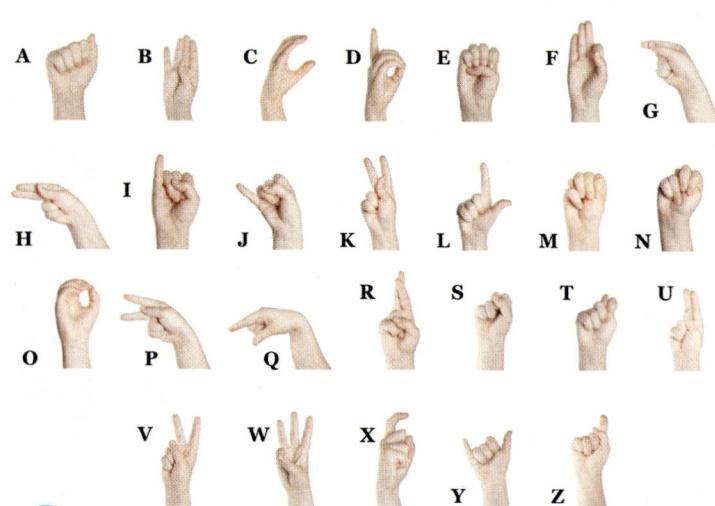

◀ Hands demonstrate the letters of sign language, used to communicate without speaking.

228 Unit 4

Word Study: The Suffix *-ful*

A suffix is a group of letters added to the end of a word to form a new word. The suffix *-ful* means "full of." Adding the suffix *-ful* to a noun, or a base word, changes the word to an adjective. When adding *-ful* to a word of two or more syllables that ends in *y*, change the *y* to *i* before the suffix.

> color + **-ful** = color**ful** (meaning "full of color")
> beauty + **-ful** = beauti**ful** (meaning "full of beauty")

Practice

Work with a partner. Complete the chart by adding *-ful* to each word. Then write a sentence with each new word and read the sentences aloud to your partner. If you need help understanding the meaning of a word, use a dictionary.

Base word	+ -ful	Sentence
event		
bounty		
care		
pity		
wonder		

Reading Strategy — Identify Main Idea and Details

When you read a selection like this autobiography, first notice that it is organized in chapters. Finding the main ideas in each will help you better understand the author's life. Use these steps to help you identify the main ideas:

- Read the first paragraph. Ask: What is the selection mainly about? Write a main idea sentence in your own words.
- Find the chapters and skim them. Ask: What is each chapter mainly about? Skim for a few key words and details and jot them down.
- Read the first chapter and list the main idea. Did you use any of the key words that you listed before? Did you list any details that support the main idea?

As you read, work with a partner to summarize the excerpt from the autobiography of Helen Keller. Did you and your partner choose the same main ideas?

Reading 1

Informational Text
Social Studies

Set a purpose for reading Read this excerpt from Helen Keller's autobiography to find out how meeting Anne Sullivan changed Helen's world. How did Miss Sullivan affect Helen's life?

from
The Story of My Life
HELEN KELLER

◀ Helen Keller explores a blooming tree with her hands.

Listening Skill

As you listen to the audio, look at the photos on pages 232–237. Use these images to help you understand the people and places described in the reading.

Chapter 1

One brief spring, musical with the song of robin and mockingbird, one summer rich in fruit and roses, one autumn of gold and crimson sped by and left their gifts at the feet of an eager, delighted child. Then, in the dreary month of February, came the illness which closed my eyes and ears and plunged me into the **unconsciousness** of a newborn baby. They called it acute congestion of the stomach and brain. The doctor thought I could not live. Early one morning, however, the fever left me as suddenly and mysteriously as it had come. There was great **rejoicing** in the family that morning, but no one, not even the doctor, knew that I should never see or hear again.

Reading Skill

In an autobiography, the writer may use imagery and figurative language. It helps to notice this use of language. In the first paragraph, how does the author use contrasting images for the seasons? What is the effect? Discuss with a partner.

unconsciousness, lack of awareness
rejoicing, celebrating

230 Unit 4

Gradually I got used to the silence and darkness that surrounded me and forgot that it had ever been different, until she came—my teacher—who was to set my spirit free. But during the first nineteen months of my life I had caught glimpses of broad, green fields, a luminous sky, trees, and flowers which the darkness that followed could not wholly **blot out**. If we have once seen, "the day is ours, and what the day has shown."

Chapter 3

My aunt made me a big doll out of towels. It was the most comical, shapeless thing, this **improvised** doll, with no nose, mouth, ears or eyes—nothing that even the imagination of a child could convert into a face. Curiously enough, the absence of eyes struck me more than all the other defects put together. I pointed this out to everybody with **provoking** persistency, but no one seemed equal to the task of providing the doll with eyes. A bright idea, however, shot into my mind, and the problem was solved. I tumbled off the seat and searched under it until I found my aunt's cape, which was trimmed with large beads. I pulled two beads off and indicated to her that I wanted her to sew them on my doll. She raised my hand to her eyes in a questioning way, and I nodded energetically. The beads were sewed in the right place and I could not contain myself for joy. . . .

---

blot out, wipe out completely
improvised, made without preparation, using materials at hand
provoking, making others angry or annoyed

◀ Anne Sullivan

Before You Go On

1. What happened when Helen was nineteen months old?
2. What bothered Helen about her doll? How did she solve the problem?

On Your Own

How would you describe young Helen's outlook on life? Explain.

▲ Anne spelling words into Helen's hand in 1893

Chapter 4

The most important day I remember in all my life is the one on which my teacher, Anne Mansfield Sullivan, came to me. I am filled with wonder when I consider the **immeasurable** contrasts between the two lives which it connects. It was the third of March, 1887, three months before I was seven years old.

On the afternoon of that eventful day, I stood on the porch, dumb, expectant. I guessed vaguely from my mother's signs and from the hurrying to and fro in the house that something unusual was about to happen, so I went to the door and waited on the steps. The afternoon sun penetrated the mass of honeysuckle that covered the porch and fell on my upturned face. My fingers lingered almost unconsciously on the familiar leaves and blossoms which had just come forth to greet the sweet southern spring. I did not know what the future held of marvel or surprise for me. Anger and bitterness had preyed upon me continually for weeks and a deep **languor** had succeeded this **passionate** struggle.

---

immeasurable, enormous
languor, feeling of tiredness
passionate, involving intense feelings

Unit 4

Have you ever been at sea in a dense fog, when it seemed as if a **tangible** white darkness shut you in, and the great ship, tense and anxious, **groped** her way toward the shore with plummet and sounding-line, and you waited with beating heart for something to happen? I was like that ship before my education began, only I was without compass or sounding-line and had no way of knowing how near the harbor was. "Light! Give me light!" was the wordless cry of my soul, and the light of love shone on me in that very hour.

I felt approaching footsteps. I stretched out my hand as I supposed to my mother. Someone took it, and I was caught up and held close in the arms of her who had come to reveal all things to me, and, more than all things else, to love me.

The morning after my teacher came she led me into her room and gave me a doll. The little blind children at the **Perkins Institution** had sent it and **Laura Bridgman** had dressed it; but I didn't know this until afterward. When I had played with it a little while, Miss Sullivan slowly spelled into my hand the word "d-o-l-l." I was at once interested in this play and tried to **imitate** it. When I finally succeeded in making the letters correctly I was flushed with childish pleasure and pride. Running downstairs to my mother, I held up my hand and made the letters for doll. I did not know that I was spelling a word or even that words existed; I was simply making my fingers go in monkey-like imitation. In the days that followed, I learned to spell in this uncomprehending way a great many words, among them *pin, hat, cup,* and a few verbs like *sit, stand,* and *walk*. But my teacher had been with me several weeks before I understood that everything has a name.

---

groped, felt around for something to hold on to
Perkins Institution, school for sight-impaired students founded in 1832
Laura Bridgman, hearing- and sight-impaired woman who had learned to read and write at the Perkins Institution in the 1830s

▲ Helen sitting with her dog and reading a book in 1904

Before You Go On

1. What does Helen say she was like before Anne Sullivan came?
2. Why does Helen call finger-spelling "play"?

On Your Own

To what does Helen compare herself before her education began? Does this help you understand her world? Explain.

One day, while I was playing with my new doll, Miss Sullivan put my big rag doll into my lap also, spelled "d-o-l-l" and tried to make me understand that "d-o-l-l" applied to both. Earlier in the day we had had a tussle over the words "m-u-g" and "w-a-t-e-r." Miss Sullivan had tried to impress it upon me that "m-u-g" is *mug* and that "w-a-t-e-r" is *water*, but I persisted in confounding the two. In despair, she had dropped the subject for the time, only to renew it at the first opportunity. I became impatient at her repeated attempts and, seizing the new doll, I dashed it upon the floor. I was keenly delighted when I felt the fragments of the broken doll at my feet. Neither sorrow nor regret followed my passionate outburst. I had not loved the doll. In the still, dark world in which I lived there was no strong **sentiment** of tenderness. I felt my teacher sweep the fragments to one side of the hearth, and I had a sense of satisfaction that the cause of my discomfort was removed. She brought me my hat, and I knew I was going out into the warm sunshine. This thought, if a wordless sensation may be called a thought, made me hop and skip with pleasure.

▼ The water pump at Helen's home in Tuscumbia, Alabama

---

sentiment, feeling or emotion

We walked down the path to the well-house, attracted by the fragrance of the honeysuckle with which it was covered. Someone was **drawing water** and my teacher placed my hand under the spout. As the cool stream gushed over one hand she spelled into the other the word *water*, first slowly, then rapidly. I stood still, my whole attention fixed upon the motions of her fingers. Suddenly I felt a misty consciousness as of something forgotten—a thrill of returning thought; and somehow the mystery of language was revealed to me. I knew then that "w-a-t-e-r" meant the wonderful cool something that was flowing over my hand. That living word awakened my soul, gave it light, hope, joy, set it free! There were barriers still, it is true, but barriers that could in time be swept away.

I left the well-house eager to learn. Everything had a name, and each name gave birth to a new thought. As we returned to the house every object which I touched seemed to quiver with life. That was because I saw everything with the strange, new sight that had come to me. On entering the door I remembered the doll I had broken. I felt my way to the hearth and picked up the pieces. I tried **vainly** to put them together. Then my eyes filled with tears; for I realized what I had done, and for the first time I felt **repentance** and sorrow.

I learned a great many new words that day. I do not remember what they all were; but I do know that *mother, father, sister,* and *teacher* were among them—words that were to make the world blossom for me, "like **Aaron's rod**, with flowers." It would have been difficult to find a happier child than I was as I lay in my crib at the close of that eventful day and lived over the joys it had brought me, and for the first time longed for a new day to come.

▲ Helen, age 31, working at her desk

---

drawing water, pumping water from a well
vainly, without success
repentance, regret; remorse
Aaron's rod, the staff carried by Moses's brother Aaron, believed to have miraculous power

Before You Go On

1. How does Helen react to what she has done with the doll? Explain.
2. What word does Helen finally understand? How does this happen?

On Your Own

How can you explain the change in Helen? How does this make you feel? Explain.

Reading 1 | 235

Reading 1

Review and Practice

Comprehension

Recall

1. For how much of her life did Helen have the abilities to see and hear?
2. What two feelings does Helen say she did not have after her outburst with the new doll?

Comprehend

3. Why does Helen describe the time before and after Anne Sullivan came into her life as two lives of "immeasurable contrasts"?
4. How did Helen come to understand the mystery of language? What effect did it have on her? Explain.

Analyze

5. Why do you think Helen was suddenly able to feel repentance?
6. Do you think the fact that Helen could once see and hear helped her understand that words are names for things? Explain.

Connect

7. Considering the excerpts from Helen Keller's life, how important are others to our lives? Explain.
8. Considering the excerpts, when you know a certain course of action is right, why is persistence important in life? Explain.

In Your Own Words

Look back at the main ideas and details you listed before and as you read the selection. Were you right? Are there any you'd like to change? Reread the excerpts, look at your list, and revise any main ideas you need to. List each main idea and the details that support it on a graphic organizer like the one below. When you have finished, review your ideas with a partner. Then, revise your organizers to include any new ideas. Finally, use your organizers to tell a friend or family member about the reading.

> **Speaking Tip**
>
> Refer to your notes when you need to, and self-correct as necessary. Remember to look at your audience as much as possible.

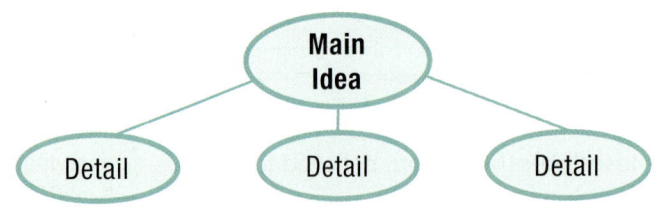

Discussion

Discuss with a partner or in a small group.

1. If Anne Sullivan had not come into Helen Keller's life, how do you think it might have been different? Are there other people or factors that you think contributed to her transformation? Explain.
2. In your view, what is the most important quality Anne Sullivan had that made Helen's progress possible? Explain.

Can we think with the heart? What does Helen Keller's experience say about the power of love? Explain.

Listening Tip

Listen carefully to your classmates. Think about their viewpoints. Do you agree? When you contribute to the discussion, summarize the points you've listened to and tell why you agree or disagree. Be respectful of others' viewpoints in your responses.

Read for Fluency

Work with a partner. Choose a paragraph from the reading. Read the paragraph silently, and think about the feelings it creates for you.

Then take turns reading the paragraph aloud to each other, using a tone of voice that shows the feelings it created for you. Give each other feedback on the reading. Could you tell how each of you felt about what you read?

Extension

WB 119

The story is written from Helen Keller's point of view. What would the story be like if Anne Sullivan told it instead of Helen? Imagine that you are Anne Sullivan, and write a journal entry in your notebook. Tell what happened when you were working with Helen and how you felt about it. When you are finished, read your journal entry to a partner.

▲ Helen Keller and Anne Sullivan play chess in 1900.

Reading 1

Grammar

Possessive Adjectives

A possessive adjective shows possession, or ownership. It is always followed by a noun. Look at the chart to find the correct possessive adjective to use.

	Possessive Adjective	Modifies a Singular Noun	Modifies a Plural Noun
1st Person Singular	my	my teacher	my teachers
2nd Person Singular	your	your key	your keys
3rd Person Singular	her (Helen's) his (the father's) its (the doll's)	her hand his hat its eye	her hands his hats its eyes
1st Person Plural	our	our dog	our dogs
2nd Person Plural	your	your book	your books
3rd Person Plural	their (Helen's and Anne's)	their story	their stories

Practice A   120

Circle the correct possessive adjectives to complete the sentences.

1. The reading is called "The Story of I / Me / (My) Life."
2. She / Her / Hers doll was made of towels.
3. It / Its / It's eyes were made of beads.
4. Our / Ours / We teacher gave us an assignment.
5. You / Your / Yours backpack is over there.
6. They / Their / They're backpacks are over there.

Practice B

Replace the words in parentheses with the correct possessive adjective.

1. I pulled two beads off __her__ cape. (Aunt Jane's)
2. The seasons sped by and left _____ gifts at my feet. (the seasons')
3. Mr. Keller hired Anne Sullivan to teach _____ daughter. (Mr. Keller's)
4. I held the doll and stroked _____ hair. (the doll's)
5. Anne Sullivan said, "She's _____ pupil!" (Anne Sullivan's)
6. Much changed for Helen when Anne came into _____ life. (Helen's)

Grammar Skill

In a direct quote, be sure to use the correct possessive adjective. Example: Pip said, "That's **my** car."

Grammar Check

✓ With what does a **possessive adjective** agree?

Apply

Write three sentences using possessive adjectives about what your classmates are wearing. Then work with a partner. Guess the classmate.

Example:
A: His T-shirt is green.
B: Is it Luis?

Adjectives and Adjectival Phrases

An adjective is a modifier that can describe nouns, noun phrases, or pronouns. An adjectival phrase is a phrase that functions as an adjective. It can consist of a series of adjectives or it can consist of any other elements that modify nouns, noun phrases, or pronouns. An adjectival phrase helps makes up a noun phrase, but it may come before or after the noun itself.

Look at these examples from the reading.

Examples	Meaning
One brief spring, **musical** with the song of robin and mockingbird, . . .	The adjective *musical* modifies the noun phrase *one brief spring*.
I stood on the porch, **dumb, expectant**.	The series of adjectives *dumb, expectant* modifies the pronoun *I*.

> **Grammar Skill**
> Common structures for sentences with adjectives are Noun + *be* + adjective or Noun + *be* + *a/an* + adjective + noun.

> **Grammar Check**
> ✓ What do **adjectives** describe or modify?

Practice A

Underline the noun, noun phrase, or pronoun that the boldfaced word or phrase modifies.

1. I left the well-house **eager to learn**.
2. I became **impatient at her repeated attempts**.
3. . . . one summer **rich in fruit and roses** . . .

Practice B

Complete the sentences with adjective or adjectival phrases from the box.

1. They left their gifts at the feet of a(n) _____ child.	a. cold, clear, and wet
2. I felt no tenderness in the _____ world in which I lived.	b. dark, still
3. I watched the water running over my hand, _____.	c. eager, delighted

> **Apply**
> Write five sentences using adjectival phrases about things you notice with your senses. Then read your sentences to a partner.
> **Example:** We hiked through the snow—white, cold, and deep.

Reading 1 **239**

Reading 1
Writing

Write a Critique

At the end of this unit, you will write an expository essay. To do this, you will need to review skills that writers use in expository writing. One type of expository writing is a critique. When you write a critique, you judge a work based on standards. You tell what the standards are and explain how the work did or didn't meet them.

> **Writing Prompt**
> Write a critique of a story, book, play, or movie. List two or three standards you will use to judge the work. Then explain how the story, book, play, or movie meets them or not. Be sure to use possessive adjectives correctly.

① Prewrite Begin by choosing the work you will critique.

- List the standards your work should meet.
- Think about each standard. If the work meets the standard, how does it do so? If it does not, why not?
- List your ideas in a chart like the one below.

Here's a chart created by a student named Santos for a critique of the movie about Helen Keller and Anne Sullivan called *The Miracle Worker*. He outlines the standard, checks if it was met, and gives an example or detail.

Standard	Standard Met?	Example or Detail
exciting	✓	scene where Anne teaches Helen "w-a-t-e-r"
inspiring	✓	lesson that anything is possible
true story	✓	about real experiences

② Draft Use your chart to help you write a first draft.

- Use a sentence introducing the work at the beginning of the critique.
- Explain what standards you used to judge the work and how the work met them.

- Keep your purpose in mind.
- Use examples or details to support your viewpoint.
- Use possessive adjectives correctly.

3 Revise Read over your draft. Look for places where the writing is unclear or needs improvement. Complete (✓) the Writing Checklist to help you identify problems. Then, revise your draft, using the editing and proofreading marks listed on page 467.

4 Edit and Proofread Check your work for errors in grammar, usage, mechanics, and spelling. Trade papers with a partner to obtain feedback. Use the Peer Review Checklist on Workbook page 122. Edit your final draft in response to feedback from your partner and your teacher.

5 Publish Prepare a clean copy of your final draft. Share your critique with the class. Save your work. You'll need to refer to it in the Writing Workshop at the end of the unit. Here is Santos' critique of *The Miracle Worker*. Notice the examples he gives to show how the film met his standards.

> **Writing Checklist**
>
> **Ideas:**
> ☐ I critiqued a work using two or three specific standards.
>
> **Word Choice:**
> ☐ I used descriptive details, including adjectives and adjectival phrases, to give details and examples.
>
> **Conventions:**
> ☐ I used possessive adjectives correctly.

Here is Santos's critique. Notice how he lists his standards for evaluating films early in the paragraph.

Santos Rivera

<u>The Miracle Worker</u>

Recently I saw a movie called <u>The Miracle Worker</u>—now, it is my favorite film. It has every quality that I look for in a movie: It is exciting, inspiring, and based on a true story. It realistically portrays the difficulties Helen Keller experienced growing up. It shows how Anne Sullivan helped Helen understand what language is by using her fingers to spell words into Helen's hand. My favorite scene in the movie is also the most exciting one. Sullivan puts one of Helen's hands under running water and spells the word <u>water</u> into the other hand. Helen suddenly understands that "w-a-t-e-r" means the liquid gushing over her hand. Anne Sullivan was an amazing teacher, truly deserving of the title "miracle worker." The film definitely lived up to my expectations. It was uplifting and inspirational. It teaches a valuable lesson—that no matter how great certain obstacles may seem, anything is possible.

Reading 2

Prepare to Read

What You Will Learn

Reading
- Vocabulary building: *Literary terms, word study*
- Reading strategy: *Analyze text structure*
- Text type: *Literature (play)*

Grammar
- Simple and compound sentences
- Complex and compound-complex sentences

Writing
- Write a summary

THE BIG QUESTION

Can we think with the heart? You are going to read a short play about a family that learns something about the value of kindness. To help you relate the play to the Big Question, ask yourself these questions and then discuss with a partner:

- Do we think differently with our hearts than we do with our minds?
- Can you think of a time when you did something kind for another person?

Build Background

Plays are stories that are performed by actors who bring the characters and their problems to life. Like movies, plays can be funny or sad, long or short. An act of a play is like a chapter in a book. It tells one part of the story. A scene is part of an act. The scene changes whenever the place or time of the play changes.

To Capture the Wild Horse is a short play in one act. It takes place in a rural area of Wyoming. The action occurs in four scenes: in the kitchen, at a rodeo, out on the plains, and back at the rodeo.

▲ One of the scenes in this one-act play takes place at a rodeo, a horse show traditional in the western U.S.A.

Vocabulary

Learn Literary Words

Literary Words
narrator
soliloquy
stage directions

Some plays have a **narrator**. A narrator is a character who talks directly to the audience and tells about the characters on the stage. He or she may tell what happened before the play or what happens between scenes. At times, the narrator walks in and out of the action as in this example.

> **Narrator:** [*Speaks to audience*] That's my neighbor, Tom. He looks old, doesn't he?

Sometimes, a character talks alone on the stage. This is called a **soliloquy**. A soliloquy reveals a character's thoughts. Read the soliloquy below to find out Artie's thoughts.

> **Scene 3**
> Artie is alone, out in the countryside.
> **Artie:** Lightning's gone lame. He can't get back on his feet. Ray needs a horse. He can't ride Lightning. He needs a horse. I better find Ray a horse.

A play is written to be performed on stage. **Stage directions** are instructions that tell the actors what they should do and how they should do it. Stage directions also describe sets, lighting, and sound effects. They appear in italic type, set off by brackets or parentheses, and are not spoken. It is important to read the stage directions when you read a play because they help you visualize the actions. Read the example below from Scene 2 where Ray is thinking more about an idea he has. What do the stage directions tell you about how Ray feels about his idea now?

> **Ray:** [*Looking nervous*] I hope I can do this, Pa.

Practice

Match each literary word to its purpose. Some literary words have more than one match possible. Discuss your answers with a partner.

1. a narrator _____
2. stage directions _____
3. a soliloquy _____

a. provides information for the actors
b. provides information for the audience
c. can provide insight into a character

Reading 2

Reading 2

Listening and Speaking: Academic Words

Study the **purple** words and their meanings. You will find these words useful when talking and writing about literature. Write each word and its meaning in your notebook, then say the words aloud with a partner. After you read *To Capture the Wild Horse*, try to use these words to respond to the text.

Academic Words
- abandon
- alternative
- circumstances
- conflict
- convince

abandon = to stop doing or planning to do something because of a problem	I decided to **abandon** the idea of entering the competition as I did not think I was ready.
alternative = something that you choose instead of another thing	The road was closed, so we took an **alternative** route.
circumstances = the conditions or facts that affect a situation	Peter's **circumstances** changed after he lost his job. He could not afford to spend much money anymore.
conflict = a feeling of nervousness or unhappiness because you want to do two things at the same time	Choosing between moving to a new home and staying in our old home caused a feeling of **conflict**.
convince = to persuade someone to do something	Mandy is really afraid of horses. No one can **convince** her to ride one.

Practice

WB 124

Work with a partner to answer these questions. Try to include the **purple** word in your answer. Write the sentences in your notebook.

1. Have you ever had to **abandon** a plan? Explain.
2. What is a good **alternative** to junk food?
3. Were your **circumstances** different one year ago? Explain.
4. Have you ever had a feeling of **conflict** about doing something? Explain.
5. What are some ways that someone can **convince** you to do something you don't really want to do?

▲ Dried fruit and nuts are a good alternative to candy when you want a snack.

244 Unit 4

Word Study: Synonyms

Synonyms are words that have the same or nearly the same meaning. The words *wild* and *untamed*, *sure* and *confident*, and *sad* and *depressing* are synonyms. Writers often choose one synonym over another to express a specific idea or emotion. Look at the chart below for examples.

Synonym	Meaning	Sentence
wild (adjective)	(of an animal) living in natural conditions and not raised by humans	There are many **wild** tigers in the jungle.
untamed (adjective)	(of an animal) not trained by people to stay calm when people are near it	The tiger at the circus was **untamed** before it was trained to jump through hoops.

Learning Strategy

If you can't remember a specific word you want to use, try to define it, use other words to describe it, or use a synonym.

Practice
WB 125

Use a dictionary or thesaurus to find the meaning of each synonym. Then write the meaning and a sentence for each one in your notebooks.

1a. gentle (adjective)   1b. soft (adjective)
2a. worried (adjective)   2b. concerned (adjective)
3a. bare (adjective)   3b. empty (adjective)

Reading Strategy | Analyze Text Structure

Plays are meant to be listened to. You'll listen and read along with the text. Plays are presented in acts and scenes, like chapters in a book. This play is a one-act play with four scenes. Plays have dialogue. The characters' names are given, followed by a colon (:) and the words the characters say.

Before you read this one-act play:
- Preview the title and the play. Look for the characters, scenes, and stage directions. With a partner, predict what you think it will be about.

As you listen and read along:
- Read each character's part and any stage directions. Ask yourself how the stage directions help you understand the play.

After you listen to and read the play, try acting it out and reading it aloud in small groups. Use what you know about plays to help you do this.

WB 126

Reading 2

**Literature
Play**

Set a purpose for reading Think about the people in the play. Why does the family need the prize money? What skills do the people in the play value? What skill turns out to be most important in the story?

To Capture the Wild Horse

Scene 1

A man and two boys sit at a kitchen table in a farmhouse on the plains of Wyoming. The kitchen is a bare and shabby room. The Narrator walks in from the side of the stage.

Narrator: [*Speaks to audience*] That's my neighbor, Tom. He looks old, doesn't he? But he's just old before his time from working so hard every day of his life. His boys, Artie and Ray, are on the same path. But Ray has a plan to help make their lives a little easier.

Tom: There's no point in trying, Ray.

Ray: [*Eagerly*] Please, Pa.

> ✓ **LITERARY CHECK**
> Who is the **narrator**? What information does the narrator give you about the story and the characters?

246 Unit 4

Tom: I'm sure that horse they plan to capture is as wild as the Wyoming wind. No one's going to capture him. And I'm not sure anyone should. It's a stupid idea, anyway, making it part of the rodeo. Who wants to watch a whole bunch of cowboys out trying to catch one horse on one day?

Ray: I could do it, with Lightning.

[*Tom gets up and moves to the stove, where he lifts an old enamel coffee pot and pours himself another cup.*]

Tom: Lightning's a good horse, and you're good on him. But are you good enough to catch a wild horse?

Ray: The prize is $10,000, Pa. You know what we could do with $10,000!

Tom: Yeah. I know.

Ray: We could put this farm back on its feet.

Artie: [*Quietly*] Farms don't have feet, Ray.

Tom: Artie, for Pete's sake . . .

Ray: Pa, it's OK. I'll explain it to him. Look here, Artie. Getting back on your feet is a manner of speaking. It means doing well again.

Artie: Oh.

Ray: You know when you're sick and you have to stay in bed? When you're all well, you're back on your feet.

Artie: Sure. I see, Ray.

Ray: Now Pa, listen. It can't hurt. I mean, what do we have to lose? A day or two of working this sad earth?

Tom: And several gallons of gas.

Ray: It's $10,000, Pa!

Tom: You're not going to back down on this, are you, boy?

Ray: Pa, I can do it.

Tom: I guess we'd better make it an early night then. We've got a way to go tomorrow to get to the rodeo.

Before You Go On

1. What are Ray and Tom discussing?
2. Why does the family need money?

On Your Own

Do you think winning the prize money can help this family? Explain.

Scene 2

The rodeo grounds. Cowboys are milling around. Tom and Ray enter, followed by the Narrator.

Narrator: Our young Ray was pretty confident back at the ranch. But now that he's at the rodeo, waiting for Artie to bring Lightning over from the horse trailer, he's feeling a little less sure of himself.

Ray: [*Looking nervous*] I hope I can do this, Pa.

Tom: You're the best rider I've seen since I was a boy. If anybody can lasso that wild horse, you can.

Ray: Thanks, Pa. I just wish Artie would hurry up and get here with Lightning.

Tom: Don't worry, Ray. He'll be along soon. He's probably trying to calm the horse down, just like I'm trying to calm you down!

Scene 3

Artie is alone, out in the countryside.

Artie: Lightning's gone lame. He can't get back on his feet. Ray needs a horse. He can't ride Lightning. He needs a horse. I better find Ray a horse.

> ✓ **LITERARY CHECK**
> What information do you learn from the **soliloquy** in this scene?

Scene 4

Tom and Ray are still at the rodeo grounds, looking worried. Two cowboys are leaning against a fence, and talking.

Cowboy 1: I got it worked out. I'm going to catch that wild horse. I've got a plan.

Cowboy 2: Oh, sure. Are you going to **put salt on its tail**?

Cowboy 1: If you think I'm telling you my plan, you're crazy.

Artie enters. He is leading a horse. Everyone turns and stares.

Artie: Hi, Ray. I got you a horse. Lightning's gone lame, but I got you a horse.

Ray: [*Moving slowly and quietly up to Artie and the horse*] Yes, you did, Artie. You got a good horse. Where did you find him?

Artie: He was by the bluff, Ray. I had to talk to him a long time. He's not Lightning, but he's a good horse. Can you catch the wild horse with him, Ray?

Ray: Well, Artie, I don't think I have to. I think somebody else did.

Artie: I'm too late, Ray? I'm sorry. He didn't want to come with me. I talked and talked. Soft, you know. Gentle. It took a long time.

Ray: [*Smiling*] That's okay, Artie. That's the mustang. You're the one who caught him. You're the one who won the prize.

Narrator: On the long ride home, $10,000 richer, Tom and his boys talked and laughed and imagined life a little easier. And Tom and Ray were reminded that Artie's kindness was a gift to them all.

The end

---

put salt on its tail, get so close that you can easily catch it with your hands

✓ LITERARY CHECK

How do the **stage directions** help you understand what is happening in Scene 4?

Before You Go On

1. What is ironic about how the family wins the prize?
2. What will the family do with the money?

On Your Own

Did the ending surprise you? Explain.

Reading 2

Reading 2

Review and Practice

Dramatic Reading

Reading a play aloud can help to make the characters and their relationships with each other seem more real. Before reading aloud, use information from the play to discuss the characters in small groups. How old are they? What are their personalities like? Consider what you know about the narrator and the characters:

Narrator	person who tells the story, neighbor of family, speaks to audience
Tom	father of the family, old before his time, works hard
Ray	one of Tom's sons, works hard, good horseback rider
Artie	Tom's other son, works hard

In groups of four, read Scene 1 of the play on pages 246–247. Decide which on roles and how to say your lines. Use the stage directions, such as *eagerly* and *quietly*, to help you. Ask your teacher for help with pronunciation, if necessary. Practice reading the scene in groups, and then take turns reading it aloud for the whole class.

> **Speaking Tip**
>
> Rehearse your lines in your group a few times before performing in front of an audience. Pay attention to the stage directions, and vary your voice and actions accordingly.

Comprehension

WB 127

Recall
1. Why does Ray's plan to ride Lightning have to be abandoned?
2. Who finds an alternative horse? Where?

Comprehend
3. What are Tom, Artie, and Ray's circumstances at the beginning of the play?
4. How does Artie convince the horse to come with him?

Analyze
5. How do you know that Ray is experiencing a conflict in Scene 2?
6. Did you predict the outcome or were you surprised? If you predicted it, what details helped you? At what point in the play did you know?

250   Unit 4

Connect

7. The play *To Capture the Wild Horse* is short, only one act. Did you find it effective or would you have liked it to be longer? What would you add to it? Explain.

8. What did you think about the family members? Did your feelings change? Explain.

Discussion

Discuss with a partner or in a small group.

1. Would you recommend the play to others? Would you suggest they listen to it or read it? Why? What can people learn from it?
2. From reading the play, how do you think families can help each other? Can each member of a family learn from another? Explain.

Can we think with the heart? How do you think Ray and Tom would answer the Big Question? Explain.

Response to Literature

WB 127

Work with a partner. Write a newspaper article about the family's winning the prize money and about what they are going to do with the money. To help you do this, role-play a reporter interviewing Artie, with the reporter asking him about how he managed to win the prize for his family and about what the family is going to do with the prize winnings. Use details from the interview to write your article. Share it with the class.

▲ Assorted prizes from a rodeo: trophies and cups

> **Reading 2**
>
> # Grammar

Simple and Compound Sentences

A simple sentence includes a subject and a verb. Simple sentences may follow one of the patterns below.

Lightning <u>became</u> lame. (1 subject + 1 verb)
Tom and Ray <u>felt</u> worried. (2 subjects + 1 verb)
Artie <u>talked</u> to the horse and <u>convinced</u> him to come. (1 subject + 2 verbs)
Tom and his boys <u>talked</u> and <u>laughed</u>. (2 subjects + 2 verbs)

A compound sentence has at least two simple sentences (independent clauses) that are joined with a comma and a coordinating conjunction (such as *and*, *but*, *or*, and *so*). Writers use compound sentences to connect related ideas.

Compound Sentence	Purpose of Conjunction
<u>Lightning's a good horse</u>, **and** <u>you're good on him</u>.	connect similar ideas with *and*
<u>He's not Lightning</u>, **but** <u>he's a good horse</u>.	connect contrasting ideas with *but*
<u>Ray could ride a different horse at the rodeo</u>, **or** <u>he could abandon the idea</u>.	connect choices with *or*
<u>Lightning became lame</u>, **so** <u>they had to find another horse</u>.	connect a cause and effect with *so*

> **Grammar Skill**
>
> Writers use both simple and compound sentences to add variety to their writing.

> **Grammar Check**
>
> ✓ How is a **simple** sentence different from a **compound** sentence?

Practice A

Read the sentences below. Write *S* or *C* to identify them as simple or compound.

1. A man and two boys sat at a kitchen table. _____
2. Roy felt confident at home, but at the rodeo he felt nervous. _____
3. Two cowboys are leaning against a fence and talking. _____

Practice B

In your notebook, connect the two simple sentences with a comma and *and*, *but*, *or*, or *so*. Make one compound sentence.

1. Ray is a good rider. He can use a lasso.
2. Tom works really hard. His boys also work hard.
3. Lightning is lame. The horse from the bluff can walk.

> **Apply**
>
> Write three pairs of simple sentences with related ideas. Then work with a partner. Swap pairs of sentences and connect them to make compound sentences.
>
> **Example:** Today it is raining. It is cold. Today it is raining, and it is cold.

Complex and Compound-Complex Sentences

A complex sentence consists of an independent clause and a dependent clause. An independent clause can stand by itself as a simple sentence. A dependent clause needs to be connected to an independent clause with a subordinator.

Notice the boldfaced dependent clauses, and the different subordinators (subordinating conjunctions) and their purpose.

Example	Subordinators	Purpose
When you're all well, you'll be back on your feet.	when, before, after, as soon as, until, while	to show a time relationship
Ray was nervous **because he was waiting for a long time.**	as, because, since	to show a reason
If anybody can lasso that wild horse, you can.	if, unless	to show a condition

Grammar Skill

If the dependent clause appears at the beginning of the sentence, add a comma. If it is at the end of a sentence, do not add a comma.

Grammar Check

✓ What does a **complex sentence** consist of?

A compound-complex sentence has at least three clauses, including two independent clauses and one dependent clause. In the sentence below, the independent clauses are underlined and the dependent clause is boldfaced. Notice the coordinating conjunction *and*.

> **Because Ray had a plan,** the family decided to act on it, and they ended up winning the prize.

Practice A

Underline the dependent clause in each complex or compound-complex sentence.

1. You have to drink fluids and you must stay in bed <u>when you're sick</u>.
2. Since the main characters are poor, their kitchen is bare and shabby.
3. Artie looked for another horse because Lightning had gone lame.

Practice B

What is the purpose of the dependent clause in each Practice A sentence? Write *time*, *reason*, or *condition*.

1. _____time_____
2. _____
3. _____

Apply

Work with a partner. Write four complex or compound-complex sentences. Use a dependent clause for each of these purposes in the sentences: time, reason, result, or condition.

Example: After this class is over, we will have lunch.

Reading 2

> **Reading 2**
> **Writing**

Write a Summary

At the end of this unit, you will write an expository essay. To do this, you will learn to evaluate, examine, and discuss an idea in detail.

A summary of a story or play, focuses on key details, such as the setting, characters, plot, and main events. When you write a summary, use your own words to tell what happened. Do not include your opinion of the story.

> **Writing Prompt**
> Write a paragraph summarizing a work such as a story, play, book, movie, or television show. Write notes about the setting, main characters, plot, and main ideas in a chart. Be sure to use a combination of simple, compound, complex, and compound-complex sentences for variety.

1 Prewrite Begin by choosing a story, play, book, movie, or television show to summarize.

WB 130

- Describe the setting and list the main characters.
- Describe the plot in one or two sentences.
- Summarize each scene or section, using one or two sentences.

A student named Bradford used a T-chart to begin writing a summary of *To Capture the Wild Horse*:

Play:	To Capture the Wild Horse
Setting:	Rural Wyoming—farmhouse kitchen, plains, rodeo
Characters:	Tom (father), Ray (son #1), Artie (son #2)
Plot:	A family needs money to save their farm. One thinks winning prize money at the rodeo is the answer.
Scene 1:	Ray tells his father and brother that he wants to ride his horse, Lightning, and capture a wild horse at the rodeo. He thinks he can win the $10,000 prize and use the money to save the farm.

2 **Draft** Use your chart to help you write a first draft.
- Use a summary starter, such as *"[Title]" is a [type of work] that is set in [place]. It is about [plot].*
- Write one or two sentences about the main events.
- Use a variety of simple, compound, complex, and compound-complex sentences.

3 **Revise** Read over your draft. Look for places where the writing is unclear or needs improvement. Complete (✓) the Writing Checklist to help you identify problems. Then, revise your draft, using the editing and proofreading marks listed on page 467.

4 **Edit and proofread** Check your work for errors in grammar, usage, mechanics, and spelling. Trade papers with a partner to obtain feedback. Use the Peer Review Checklist on Workbook page 130. Edit your final draft in response to feedback from your partner and your teacher.

5 **Publish** Prepare a clean copy of your final draft. Share your summary with the class. Save your work. You'll need to refer to it in the Writing Workshop at the end of the unit.

Here is Bradford's summary of *To Capture the Wild Horse*. Notice the variety of sentence types he uses.

> **Writing Checklist**
>
> **Ideas:**
> ☐ I summarized the main events of the work I chose. I did not include my opinions.
>
> **Word Choice:**
> ☐ I used my own words to describe the setting, characters, and plot.
>
> **Conventions:**
> ☐ I used a variety of sentences, including simple, compound, complex, and compound-complex sentences.

Bradford Li

Summary of <u>To Capture a Wild Horse</u>

<u>To Capture the Wild Horse</u> is a play set in rural Wyoming. It is about a poor hardworking farm family—Tom, the father, and his two sons, Ray and Artie. At the beginning of the play, Ray tells his father and brother that he wants to ride his horse, Lightning, and capture a wild horse at the rodeo. He thinks he can win the $10,000 prize, which they need to save the farm. At first, his father disagrees, but then he agrees. The next day, at the rodeo, Ray starts to lose confidence while he is waiting for Artie to bring his horse, Lightning. His father encourages him by telling him he is a great rider. In the meantime, Artie learns that Lightning has gone lame, so he decides to look for another horse. At the end of the play, Artie returns with a different horse. He explains that Lightning went lame and he persuaded another horse to follow him. Ray tells Artie the horse that followed him is the wild horse and Artie has won the prize money. The family goes home happier and $10,000 richer.

Reading 3

Prepare to Read

What You Will Learn

Reading
- Vocabulary building: Context, dictionary skills, word study
- Reading strategy: Monitor comprehension
- Text type: Informational text (social studies)

Grammar
- Imperatives
- Adverb phrases and clauses to describe a process

Writing
- Write instructions

THE BIG QUESTION

Can we think with the heart? People often say that thoughts and ideas come from the brain. They also say that feelings and emotions come from the heart. But how are the two connected? Can we feel with the brain and think with the heart? Discuss with a partner.

Build Background

"The Heart's Wisdom" is an article about the heart's role and functions. It explores how people in ancient civilizations thought the heart functioned. It also includes quotes and idioms about how different people view the heart. It explains what scientists have learned about the heart and brain. In addition, the article discusses ways we use the brain and heart, ways to keep them healthy, and strategies for tapping into the heart's wisdom—intuition.

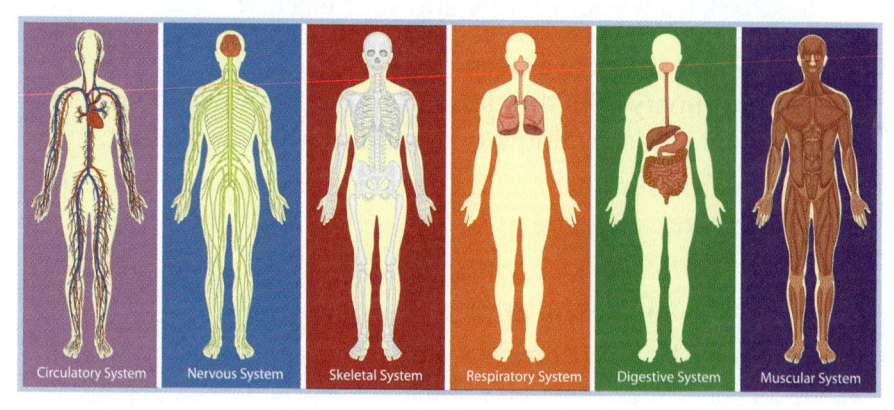

▲ What do the circulatory and nervous systems do? How are they related?

Vocabulary

Listening and Speaking: Key Words

Read aloud and listen to these sentences with a partner. Use the context to figure out the meaning of the highlighted words. Use a dictionary or a thesaurus to determine or confirm your answers. Then write each word and its meaning in your notebook.

Key Words
- arteries
- cholesterol
- circulation
- nutrients
- organs
- sensations

1. It's important for **arteries** to be healthy because they carry blood from the heart.
2. Many doctors say you should eat less butter, cheese, and eggs to reduce **cholesterol**.
3. If your shoes are too tight, they may cut off the blood **circulation** in your feet.
4. Vitamins, minerals, protein, and starch are important **nutrients**.
5. The heart, lungs, and liver are important **organs**.
6. Jumping into a cold pool after a hot shower causes **sensations** of cold and heat at the same time.

Practice

WB 131

Choose a word from the box above to complete each sentence. Then take turns reading the sentences aloud with a partner.

1. One reason to watch your diet is to keep your blood vessels and _____ healthy.
2. Exercising regularly will improve your _____.
3. Skilled doctors can perform surgery on people's _____ and save their lives.
4. High _____ can lead to serious health problems, such as heart disease.
5. There are more _____ in fruits and vegetables than in junk food.
6. We use our brains to process _____ such as smells, sights, and sounds.

▲ Exercise helps with blood circulation and is good for the heart. It is also good for the mind.

Reading 3   257

Reading 3

Listening and Speaking: Academic Words

Study the **purple** words and their meanings. You will find these words useful when talking and writing about informational texts. Write each word and its meaning in your notebook, then say the words aloud with a partner. After you read "The Heart's Wisdom," try to use these words to respond to the text.

Academic Words
- contribute
- evaluate
- function
- source
- struggle

contribute = help make something happen	➡	The right diet and exercise can **contribute** to good health.
evaluate = judge how good or successful something is	➡	You can use both your thoughts and your feelings to **evaluate** a situation.
function = what something, such as a part of your body, does	➡	People in ancient times believed the heart had different **functions** than what we know today.
source = the thing, place, or person that you get something from	➡	People in ancient times thought the heart was the **source** of love, wisdom, and emotions.
struggle = something that takes a lot of effort over a long period of time	➡	For people with long-term illnesses, it can be a **struggle** to do everyday activities, such as walking to the store.

Practice
WB 132

Work with a partner to answer these questions. Try to include the **purple** word in your answer. Write the sentences in your notebook.

1. What can **contribute** to getting good grades?
2. How does your teacher **evaluate** your progress in this class?
3. What **functions** does your cell phone have?
4. What are good **sources** of information to use for a research report?
5. Are any homework assignments a **struggle** for you? If so, what do you do?

Word Study: Related Words

Related words are words that belong to the same word family. They share the same base word and have related meanings. Look at similarities and differences among the related words below:

> **circulate** (*verb*) to move around within a system, or to make something do this
> **circulation** (*noun*) the movement of blood around your body
> **circulatory** (*adjective*) relating to the movement of blood through the body

Once you know the meaning of a base word, you can make a guess about the meaning of other words in that word family. Try to memorize the meanings of as many suffixes as possible. This will help when you are trying to understand the meanings of related words.

Practice

Work with a partner. Copy the words below into your notebook. Write the part of speech and the meaning of each word. Check your work in a dictionary. Finally, use each word in a sentence.

disappoint	intelligent	mind	power
disappointment	intelligence	mindful	powerful

Reading Strategy: Monitor Comprehension

Monitoring comprehension helps you to understand informational texts like this one. To monitor comprehension, follow these steps:

- Read the text. Stop from time to time and ask yourself how much of it you have understood.
- Reread the text. Make a list of ideas that are important and any words that are difficult. Use the words at the bottom of the pages to help you. You can also try to figure out meanings from context and visuals or use a dictionary.
- Try to put the information you read into your own words.

As you read this informational text about the heart, stop from time to time. Ask yourself whether you understand main points and ideas.

Reading 3

**Informational Text
Social Studies**

Set a purpose for reading Read this article to find out how the heart and brain are connected. How can the mind affect the heart? And how can the heart affect the mind?

The Heart's Wisdom

Your heart keeps you alive! This powerful muscle, which is only about the size of a fist, beats 60-100 times each minute to deliver oxygen and nutrient-rich blood to every cell in your body. The health of your heart affects your overall well-being. Some people believe it even contributes to your intelligence and **intuition**. But that can work both ways. How you think and feel can impact this vital organ, too.

▲ When we feel affection and love for others, we often say they are close to our heart.

The Expansive Heart

The idea that the heart and the mind are connected is not a new one. Many ancient civilizations including the Mesopotamians, the Babylonians, the Greeks, and the Chinese believed that the heart played a bigger role in human life than simply pumping blood. They thought of the heart as the source of love, wisdom, emotion, and **insight**. The Egyptians even believed that peoples' goodness could be evaluated by the weight of their heart and are said to have weighed the hearts of people after they died to measure the good and evil they contained.

According to 4th century B.C.E., Greek philosopher Aristotle, the heart was the most important organ in the body. He believed it was the center of human **vitality**, in charge of motion, intelligence, and sensation. He also believed that the sole function of both the brain and the lungs was to keep the heart from overheating.

Across the ages, poets, philosophers, psychologists, authors, and songwriters have contemplated the connection between the heart and the mind. Here are but a few of their thoughts on the heart's **expansive** role in our lives:

"*The heart wants what it wants.*" Emily Dickinson, poet (1830–1886)

"*. . . your vision will become clear only when you can look into your own heart.*" Carl Jung, psychologist (1875–1961)

"*And now here is my secret, a very simple secret: It is only with the heart that one can see rightly; what is essential is invisible to the eye.*" Antoine de Saint-Exupery, *The Little Prince* (1943)

---

intuition, the ability to understand or know something is true based on feelings rather than facts
insight, the ability to understand something clearly

vitality, life and energy
expansive, including a lot of information

260 Unit 4

Heart Idioms	Messages
What is your heart's desire?	The heart wants. (emotions)
My heart aches.	The heart hurts. (emotions)
I know it by heart.	The heart learns. (intelligence)
I have had a change of heart.	The heart decides. (intelligence)
In your heart of hearts, you know it.	The heart knows. (intuition)
Search your heart for the reason.	The heart reveals. (intuition)

▲ In casual speech, we often refer to the heart. Consider these common expressions and their meanings.

What Does Science Say?

Many other poets, writers, and thinkers have cited the heart, and they are not alone: The heart is part of everyday speech. The chart lists common expressions. What do they **imply** about the importance of the heart?

Of course, philosophers, poets, and ancient civilizations were not completely correct. The weight of our hearts cannot reveal our goodness as the Egyptians thought; and contrary to Aristotle's theory, the brain—not the heart—is the organ where most of our thinking happens.

Over time, scientists have made important discoveries about the actual link between the heart and the mind.

The heart, of course, contributes to the function of the brain. Keeping your heart healthy reduces the risk of serious conditions that affect the brain, such as dementia and stroke. However, the reverse can also be true. Recent studies have shown that individuals who practice **mindfulness** tend to keep their hearts healthy and strong.

---

imply, to suggest something is true without saying it directly

mindfulness, a state of awareness that involves being present in the moment

Before You Go On

1. What did ancient civilizations believe about the heart?
2. What did Aristotle believe about the heart?

👤 On Your Own

Which theory about the heart do you find most interesting? Why?

Reading 3

Mindfulness at Work

What is mindfulness exactly? It's a heightened state of awareness. When you're mindful, you're focused on what's happening in the present moment. This focus can help you pay close attention to your body, including your thoughts, feelings, and behavior. There are different ways to tap into this state, such as practicing mediation or doing yoga.

How does mindfulness affect your heart? Picture this: You're reading a book while having lunch. You're not paying attention to your food or how your body feels in the moment. So, it's easy to eat too much. But if you're mindful, you'll stop when your body feels full. People who practice mindfulness are more likely to exercise and eat right. They're also less likely to engage in harmful behavior. All of this can help your heart.

▼ In what ways does technology make it harder for people to be mindful? In what ways can technology help people be mindful?

Heart Sensations

The connection between the heart and the mind not only relates to how we behave in the moment, but also how we feel. Our hearts send **emotional** signals all day long. Imagine being on a roller coaster ride as it's making a steep, slow climb up the track. Finally, it reaches its highest point and pauses at the top—about to make the big drop. How does your heart feel in that moment? No doubt it's beating fast, communicating fear or anticipation.

Now imagine you have tried out for the starring role in your school play and, after a couple of days, a cast list is posted on a bulletin board. Your heart beats wildly with excitement as you walk over to the list because you are pretty sure you are about to be a star. You scan the list, and your name is not there at the top, which means you did not get the starring role. In fact, as you look further, you realize you did not get any role at all. Your heart feels like it is sinking from your chest down into your belly as disappointment floods your body.

emotional, relating to feelings and how they are controlled

Practice Listening to Your Wise Heart

The heart and mind do not always work together, however. Sometimes, they battle each other. But which one should we pay the most attention to?

We are used to listening to our **logical** brains. Have you ever had a decision that was difficult to make? For example, imagine a friend invites you to go out with a group of people you don't know well, but you are not sure if you should go. Your logical brain tells you to weigh the pros and cons. So, you write them down, and the pros outweigh the cons. The answer is clear, and yet, you don't *feel* like you want to go.

That feeling is probably your intuition talking to you. We may not always pay attention, but our intuitions often know what's right for us. Think of it as another way to be mindful. Your intuition may suggest the exact opposite of what your logical mind tells you to do. But sometimes, it may be better to "listen to your heart," as the saying goes.

Should I go to the party?	
Pros	**Cons**
I will see my friend. We will have fun.	I won't know anyone else but my friend.

logical, seeming reasonable and sensible

The Heart Knows

People often relate the heart to other kinds of signals, which have to do with intuition. Intuition involves picking up subtle clues that may not immediately register in your conscious mind but do tap into your emotions. Think about this example.

At the library, Pilar saw her friend Lucas, whom she hadn't seen in a while. "How's everything?" she asked. Lucas smiled broadly, stretching his mouth wide. "Oh, everything's fine!" he answered a bit loudly.

Although Lucas had said everything was fine, Pilar could feel that something was wrong. But Pilar felt silly saying anything because she didn't trust the feeling. After all, Lucas was smiling. So, Pilar ignored her intuition and told him about the book she was about to check out from the library.

The next day, Pilar learned that Lucas's family home had caught fire. "I knew something was wrong!" Pilar thought, and she wondered where that knowledge had come from.

▼ Have you ever felt, deep in your heart, that something is troubling a friend?

Before You Go On

1. What are some reasons someone's heart might start to beat faster?
2. What is the difference between logic and intuition?

On Your Own

Do you usually pay more attention to what your logical mind says or your intuition? Explain.

Reading 3

Asking Your Heart for Answers

To listen to your heart and tap into your intuition, try this practice when you are struggling with a question or decision.

- ✓ Sit somewhere quiet.
- ✓ Place one hand on your heart. Feel it beating.
- ✓ Slow down your breathing.
- ✓ Close your eyes, then ask yourself a question.
- ✓ Be still and quiet. Does an answer come to you?
- ✓ If an answer doesn't come, don't be discouraged. Keep practicing and an answer may come in time.

▼ Mindfulness practices, such as meditation, can benefit both the heart and the mind.

Nourishing Your Heart and Your Brain

Guacamole

Remember that being mindful also means taking care of your body and eating right. Avocados can help you get on the right track to better health. This funny-looking, green fruit contains a wealth of nutrients, so it is no surprise that it's a great choice for both brain and heart health!

Among other benefits, eating avocados can improve the blood supply to the brain, protect the brain's network of connections, promote blood circulation, and keep your heart clear of artery-clogging cholesterol. In addition, avocados taste great! Try this recipe for guacamole.

This recipe makes about 2 cups.
Ingredients:

- 2 large avocados
- 1/4 red onion, chopped
- ½ tomato, chopped (optional)
- 1/8 tsp salt (or to taste)
- 1-2 tsp fresh-squeezed lemon (optional, to taste)
- ½-1 tsp chopped jalapeno pepper (optional)*

1. Carefully cut the avocado in half, scoop out the flesh, and mash
2. Add the remaining ingredients and mix together.
3. Serve with multi-grain chips or spread on a corn tortilla.

*Note: Jalapeno peppers are spicy!

Before You Go On

1. What other foods have you heard of that are especially good for your brain?
2. How is eating avocados good for you?

On Your Own

Have you ever tried listening to your heart to make a decision? Was it helpful?

Reading 3

Review and Practice

Comprehension 📖 135

Recall

1. According to the article, what do some people believe our hearts contribute to?
2. What did Aristotle think the only function of the brain and lungs was?

Comprehend

3. How does heart health contribute to overall health?
4. What are some examples of mindfulness?

Analyze

5. From ancient civilizations to today, how have ideas about the heart and mind changed? Why do you think this is so?
6. How does mindfulness affect the brain and heart?

Connect

7. Why do you think there are so many idioms, or expressions, about the heart?
8. Reread the guacamole recipe on page 267. Are the instructions easy to follow? Explain why or why not.

In Your Own Words

Work with a partner. Review "The Heart's Wisdom." Take turns summarizing the most important ideas in each section. Write one sentence summarizing each section in the chart below.

The Expansive Heart	
What Does Science Say?	
Mindfulness at Work	
Heart Sensations	
Practice Listening to Your Wise Heart	
The Heart Knows	
Asking Your Heart for Answers	

Speaking Tip

Use the images and charts in this reading to help you explain to a partner how the heart can think. Ask your partner for feedback. Can he or she hear and understand what you are saying?

Discussion

Discuss with a partner or in a small group.

1. What information in the article was most surprising to you? Most interesting? Most helpful? Least helpful?
2. Have you ever tried or would you like to try the recommendations given in the article for dealing with a problem or question? Do you think they can be useful?

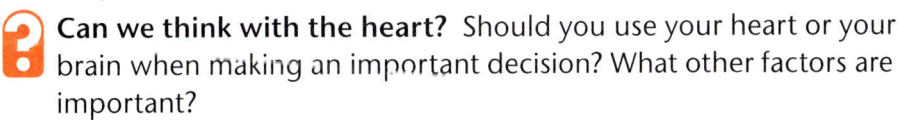

? **Can we think with the heart?** Should you use your heart or your brain when making an important decision? What other factors are important?

> **Listening Skill**
>
> Listen for implicit ideas in a speaker's comments, and ask questions to find out more.

Read for Fluency

It is often easier to read a text if you understand the difficult words and phrases. Work with a partner. Choose a paragraph from the reading. Identify the words and phrases you do not know or have trouble pronouncing. Look up the difficult words in a dictionary.

Take turns pronouncing the words and phrases with your partner. If necessary, ask your teacher to model the correct pronunciation. Then take turns reading the paragraph aloud. Give each other feedback on your reading.

Extension WB 135

Find four more expressions about the heart. Use your dictionary or search online. Then complete the chart below with the quotes or idioms and their messages or meanings. Share in small groups.

Heart Idioms, or Expressions	Messages or Meanings

Reading 3

Grammar

Imperatives

Use an imperative to give directions or instructions, orders, advice, or warnings. The implied subject of an imperative statement is always *you*. In imperatives, do not say or write *you*. The negative form is usually expressed with *don't*.

Instructions	**Cut** the avocado in half.
Orders	**Evacuate** immediately.
Advice	**Remember** that being mindful takes practice.
Warnings	**Slow** down!

You can add to an imperative statement.

<u>Carefully</u> **cut** the avocado in half. **Cut** the avocado in half <u>carefully</u>.	Add an adverb at the beginning or end to describe how to do something.
<u>If an answer doesn't come</u>, **don't be** discouraged.	Add an *if* clause at the beginning or end to show a specific, limiting condition.

▲ Many signs use imperatives.

Practice A

Complete the instructions with the words and phrases in the box.

ask	be	feel	~~sit~~

1. _____Sit_____ somewhere quiet.
2. _____ still and quiet.
3. _____ your heart beating.
4. _____ your heart a question.

Practice B

Complete the chart with *Dos* and *Don'ts* for a healthy heart. Use the phrases in the box and the word *don't* when needed.

~~be optimistic~~   ~~drink soda~~   drink green tea   eat sugary food
exercise regularly   add salt to your food

Dos	Don'ts
1. Be optimistic.	1. Don't drink soda.
2.	2.
3.	3.

Grammar Check
✓ What are different reasons for using the **imperative**?

Grammar Skill
Add *please* at the beginning or the end of an imperative statement to be more polite.

Apply
Write instructions for a recipe that is good for your heart. Use imperatives. Then share with a partner.

Example: Get one fresh apple. Peel it, core it, and slice it . . . .

Adverb Phrases and Clauses to Describe a Process

Adverb phrases and clauses can be used to show relationships between ideas. Adverb phrases and clauses of time can be used to describe steps in a process.

An adverb clause of time is a dependent clause that must be used with an independent clause. It begins with a time word such as *after, as, as soon as, before, once, until, when,* and *while*. If it is placed at the beginning of a sentence, it is followed by a comma.

> **When the roller coaster reaches its highest point**, it slows down.
>
> Your heart sinks **as disappointment floods through your body**.

An adverb phrase is a reduced form of an adverb clause. Like an adverb clause, it must be used with an independent clause. Unlike an adverb clause, it often does not include a verb. Compare these sentences.

Adverb Clauses	Adverb Phrases
Try this practice **when you are struggling with a question or decision**.	Try this practice **when struggling with a question or decision**.
When the roller coaster reaches its highest point, it slows down.	**When reaching its highest point**, it slows down.

Grammar Skill
In academic writing, the adverb clause is often at the beginning of the sentence.

Grammar Check
✓ What must **adverb clauses and phrases** be used with to make a complete sentence or thought?

Practice A

Underline the adverb clause in each sentence.

1. After you cut the avocado in half, scoop out the pulp and mash it.
2. Mix the ingredients together until it has a chunky texture.
3. As soon as the guacamole is ready, serve it with multi-grain chips.

Practice B

Are the boldfaced words adverb clauses or adverb phrases? Write *AC* (adverb clause) or *AP* (adverb phrase).

1. Carbon dioxide gets breathed out **when it reaches the lungs**. __AC__
2. Wear a helmet **when playing certain sports**. _____
3. **Before making a decision**, list the pros and cons. _____
4. Ask your heart for answers **before you make a decision**. _____

Apply
Work with a partner. Write instructions about how to prepare for a test. Use adverb phrases and clauses.

Example: Before you start reviewing your notes, find a quiet place to study . . . .

Reading 3

Reading 3

Writing

Write Instructions

At the end of this unit, you will write an expository essay. To do this, you will need to learn skills that writers use for expository writing. When you write instructions, use a clear sequence of steps. This will make the instructions easy to follow.

> **Writing Prompt**
>
> Write an expository paragraph giving step-by-step instructions that explain how to do something. Be sure to use imperatives, adverb phrases, and adverb clauses correctly.

1 Prewrite Choose something you know how to make or do.

- Think about the steps needed to make or do it.
- Write the steps on sticky notes or slips of paper. You don't have to think about the order now.
- Arrange the steps in a sequence of events chart in an order that makes sense. Is the order correct? Have you missed any steps?

Here's a sequence of events chart created by a student named Alana for a paragraph with instructions to make a fruit smoothie drink.

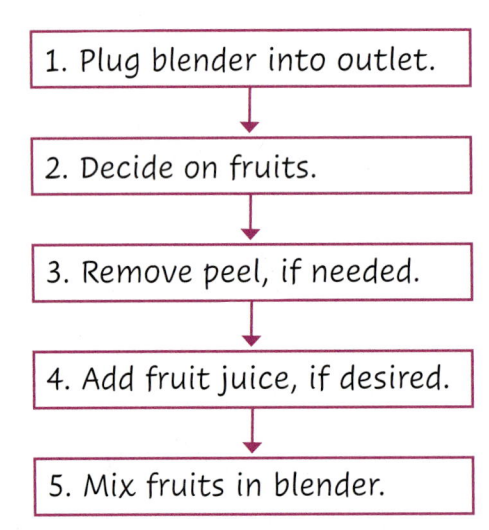

1. Plug blender into outlet.
   ↓
2. Decide on fruits.
   ↓
3. Remove peel, if needed.
   ↓
4. Add fruit juice, if desired.
   ↓
5. Mix fruits in blender.

② Draft Use your sequence of events chart to help you write a first draft.

- Keep in mind your purpose for writing.
- Remember to explain the steps in the correct order.
- Remember to use imperatives.
- Use adverbs (phrases and clauses) and sequence words correctly.

③ Revise Read over your draft. Look for places where the writing is unclear or needs improvement. Complete (✓) the Writing Checklist to help you identify problems. Then, revise your draft, using the editing and proofreading marks listed on page 467.

④ Edit and Proofread Check your work for errors in grammar, usage, mechanics, and spelling. Trade papers with a partner to obtain feedback. Use the Peer Review Checklist on Workbook page 138. Edit your final draft in response to feedback from your partner and your teacher.

⑤ Publish Prepare a clean copy of your final draft. Share your paragraph with the class. Save your work. You'll need to refer to it in the Writing Workshop at the end of the unit.

Here is Alana's paragraph with step-by-step instructions.

> **Writing Checklist**
>
> **Ideas:**
> ☐ I described the steps in order.
>
> **Sentence Fluency:**
> ☐ My sentences flow smoothly, with transitions between steps.
>
> **Conventions:**
> ☐ I used imperatives correctly.
> ☐ I used adverb phrases or clauses correctly.

Alana Marquez

How to Make a Fruit Smoothie

With all of the tasty yet unhealthy food that exists in the world today, it is easy to eat too much of it! This is why it is important to have a healthy, balanced diet. However, just because something is healthy doesn't mean it has to taste bad! Fruit smoothies are delicious, healthy drinks that keep you energized. Here are some simple steps for making this healthy treat. First, get a blender and plug it into an outlet. Next, decide which types of fruits you are going to have in your smoothie. If you are using fruits that have a peel, like a banana, take the peel off before adding it to the blender. Keep in mind that using more types of fruit means a more unique flavor. You may want to add some fruit juice as well. Next, mix all of the fruits in the blender. After the fruits are blended into a smooth liquid, drink and enjoy your smoothie!

Reading 4

Prepare to Read

What You Will Learn

Reading
- Vocabulary building: *Literary terms, word study*
- Reading strategy: *Recognize and analyze cultural context*
- Text type: *Literature (short story)*

Grammar
- Present and past perfect
- Adjective phrases (*-ing, -ed*)

Writing
- Write a critical analysis

THE BIG QUESTION

Can we think with the heart? In small groups, brainstorm expressions with the word "heart," such as *have a heart, take heart, it takes heart, don't you have a heart?, follow your heart, from the bottom of my heart*. In your group, discuss: What does it mean to "have a heart"?

Build Background

The next reading is a short story from the book *Tales from Gold Mountain: Stories of the Chinese in the New World*. This book tells about the struggles that some of the first Chinese Americans faced. **"Ginger for the Heart"** takes place during the gold rush in North America, during the nineteenth century. Many people moved to northwestern North America during this time to try to find gold and become rich. Hundreds of thousands of Chinese immigrants took part in the gold rush.

This story is about a young Chinese-American woman named Yenna. In this story, Yenna has to make a choice between her family and her true love. What do you think *ginger for the heart* might mean or refer to?

▲ Chinese immigrants panning for gold in California

Vocabulary

Learn Literary Words

Literary Words
characterization
figurative language
symbol

Characterization refers to an author's development of a character. Readers learn about a character from what the character says, thinks, and does, from descriptions of the character, and from ways other characters react to the character.

> His shoulders were broad and strong, yet his eyes were soft and caring.

Writing that is not meant to be taken literally is called **figurative language**. Authors often use it to help readers visualize characters and understand their feelings. Figurative language may include comparisons, such as similes. It may also include imagery, which appeals to the senses.

> She had ivory skin, sparkling eyes, and her hair hung long and silken, shining like polished ebony.

A **symbol** is anything that stands for or represents something else. Authors use symbols to create an added level of meaning. Read the excerpt from "Ginger for the Heart" below.

> I will wait for you, but, like this piece of ginger, I, too, will age and grow dry.

Practice

WB 139

Work with a partner. Look at the ideas. In the second column, write what you would choose as a symbol to represent each idea. Explain your choices.

Idea	Symbol
love	
evil	
balance	
luck	
peace	

Reading 4

Reading 4

Listening and Speaking: Academic Words

Study the purple words and their meanings. You will find these words useful when talking and writing about literature. Write each word and its meaning in your notebook, then say the words aloud with a partner. After you read "Ginger for the Heart," try to use these words to respond to the text.

Academic Words
- bond
- devoted
- mutual
- significance

bond = something that connects two people or animals with a shared interest or emotion	As Ayisha was training her horse, she developed a strong **bond** with the animal.
devoted = giving someone or something a lot of love, concern, or attention	The woman was very **devoted** to her parents and spent a lot of time taking care of them.
mutual = felt by two or more people toward one another	The two men had a **mutual** respect for each other.
significance = importance or meaning of something	We could not understand the **significance** of our father's watch until he told us the story of how he received it.

Practice (WB 140)

Work with a partner to answer these questions. Try to include the purple word in your answer. Write the sentences in your notebook.

1. What symbol shows the **bond** between the two people in the photograph?
2. Is there a field of study, such as biology, technology, or music, that you can imagine yourself being **devoted** to? Explain.
3. What **mutual** interests or feelings do you and your friends share?
4. What things do you own that have a lot of **significance** to you?

Word Study: The /z/ Sound

The /z/ sound is found in words that have the letters *z*, *x*, or *s*. The /z/ sound may be at the beginning or end of syllables.

The letter *s* often stands for the /z/ sound. The letter *s* is often pronounced /z/ when it is after a voiced consonant. The third-person singular (-*s*) and plurals (-*s*, -*es*) are usually pronounced with the /z/ sound.

Beginning of a Syllable	End of a Syllable
mu**s**ic	other**s**
vi**s**ible	storie**s**
zoo	ja**zz**
ha**z**y	ama**z**ement

Practice 141

With a partner, write a sentence for each word in the box below in your notebooks. Practice saying the /z/ sound by reading your sentences aloud to your partner. Use a dictionary to find the definition of any new words.

balconies	crazy	miners	refuse
because	invisible	railings	wiser

Reading Strategy — Recognize and analyze cultural context

Recognizing and then analyzing the cultural context of a story helps you understand it better. Cultural context includes the beliefs, art, ideas, and values of a particular group. Follow these steps:

- Think about the characters' native culture and what you already know. Notice any details about the culture that you did not know before. How do these affect your understanding of the story?
- Think about the characters. What beliefs and traditions affect, or could affect, the bond that two characters have? Does it change their bond? Why?

As you read "Ginger for the Heart," think about what Chinese immigrants who came to North America in the 1800s experienced.

142

Reading 4 275

Reading 4
Literature
Short Story

Set a purpose for reading Read this story to find out how a gift of ginger helps keep a couple's love alive. What do you think the ginger represents?

Ginger for the Heart

PAUL YEE

The buildings of Chinatown are stoutly constructed of brick, and while some are broad and others thin, they rise no higher than four solid storeys. Many contain stained-glass windows decorated with flower and diamond patterns, and others boast balconies with fancy wrought-iron railings.

Only one building stands above the rest. Its turret-like tower is visible even from the harbor, because the cone-shaped roof is made of copper.

In the early days, Chang the merchant tailor owned this building. He used the main floor for his store and rented out the others. But he kept the tower room for his own use, for the sun filled it with light. This was the room where his wife and daughter worked.

His daughter's name was Yenna, and her beauty was beyond compare. She had ivory skin, sparkling eyes, and her hair hung long and silken, shining like polished **ebony**. All day long she and her mother sat by the tower window and sewed with silver needles and silken threads. They sang songs while they worked, and their voices rose in wondrous harmonies.

---

ebony, hard black wood

In all Chinatown, the craftsmanship of Yenna and her mother was considered the finest. Search as they might, customers could not **discern** where holes had once pierced their shirts. Buttonholes never stretched out of shape, and seams were all but invisible.

One day, a young man came into the store laden with garments for mending. His shoulders were broad and strong, yet his eyes were soft and caring. Many times he came and many times he saw Yenna. For hours he would sit and watch her work. They fell deeply in love, though few words were spoken between them.

Spring came and boats bound for the northern gold fields began to sail again. It was time for the young man to go. He had borrowed money to pay his way over to the **New World**, and now he had to repay his debts. Onto his back he threw his blankets and tools, food and warm jackets. Then he set off with miners from around the world, clutching gold pans and shovels.

Yenna had little to give him in farewell. All she found in the kitchen was a ginger root as large as her hand. As she stroked its brown knobs and bumpy eyes, she whispered to him, "This will warm you in the cold weather. I will wait for you, but, like this piece of ginger, I, too, will age and grow dry." Then she pressed her lips to the ginger, and turned away.

"I will come back," the young man said. "The fire burning for you in my heart can never be **extinguished**."

Thereafter, Yenna lit a lamp at every nightfall and set it in the tower window. Rains lashed against the glass, snow piled low along the ledge, and ocean winds rattled the frame. But the flame did not waver, even though the young man never sent letters. Yenna did not weep uselessly, but continued to sew and sing with her mother.

There were few unmarried women in Chinatown, and many men came to seek Yenna's hand in marriage. Rich gold miners and sons of successful merchants bowed before her, but she always looked away. They gave her grand gifts, but still she shook her head, until the men grew weary and called her crazy. In China, parents arranged all marriages, and daughters became the property of their husbands. But Chang the merchant tailor treasured his daughter's happiness and let her be.

One winter, an **epidemic** ravaged the city. When it was over, Chang had lost his wife and his eyesight. Yenna led him up to the tower where he could feel the sun and drifting clouds move across his face. She began to sew again, and while she sewed, she sang for her father. The lamp continued to burn steadily at the tower window as she worked.

---

discern, see
New World, America
extinguished, put out
epidemic, a large number of cases of a particular infectious disease happening at the same time

✓ LITERARY CHECK
What is the fire a **symbol** of here?

✓ LITERARY CHECK
How is **figurative language** used to show how strongly devoted Yenna is?

Before You Go On
1. Where does the young man go?
2. What does Yenna give the young man as a farewell present?

On Your Own
As time passes, do you think Yenna feels the same about the young man? How do you know? What will happen?

With twice the amount of work to do, she labored long after dusk. She fed the flame more oil and sent her needle skimming through the heavy fabrics. **Nimbly** her fingers braided shiny cords and coiled them into butterfly buttons. And when the wick sputtered into light each evening, Yenna's heart soared momentarily into her love's memories. Nights passed into weeks, months turned into years, and four years quickly flew by.

One day a dusty traveler came into the store and flung a bundle of ragged clothes onto the counter. Yenna shook out the first shirt, and out rolled a ginger root. Taking it into her hand, she saw that pieces had been nibbled off, but the core of the root was still firm and fragrant.

She looked up. There stood the man she had promised to wait for. His eyes appeared older and wiser.

"Your gift saved my life several times," he said. "The fire of the ginger is powerful indeed."

"Why is the ginger root still firm and heavy?" she wondered. "Should it not have dried and withered?"

"I kept it close to my heart and my sweat coated it. In lonely moments, my tears soaked it." His **calloused** hands reached out for her. "Your face has not changed."

"Nor has my heart," she replied. "I have kept a lamp burning all these years."

"So I have heard," he smiled. "Will you come away with me now? It has taken many years to gather enough gold to buy a farm. I have built you a house on my land."

For the first time since his departure, tears cascaded down Yenna's face. She shook her head. "I cannot leave. My father needs me."

---

nimbly, quickly; skillfully
calloused, covered in thick, hard skin

"Please come with me," the young man pleaded. "You will be very happy, I promise."

Yenna swept the wetness from her cheeks. "Stay with me and work this store instead," she implored.

The young man stiffened and stated proudly, "A man does not live in his wife's house." And the eyes that she remembered so well gleamed with determination.

"But this is a new land," she cried. "Must we forever follow the old ways?"

She reached out for him, but he brushed her away. With a curse, he hurled the ginger root into the fireplace. As the flames leapt up, Yenna's eyes blurred. The young man clenched and unclenched his fists in anger. They stood like stone.

At last the man turned to leave, but suddenly he knelt at the fireplace. Yenna saw him reach in with the tongs and pull something out of the flames.

"Look!" he whispered in amazement. "The ginger refuses to be burnt! The flames cannot touch it!"

Yenna looked and saw black burn marks charring the root, but when she took it in her hand, she found it still firm and moist. She held it to her nose, and found the fragrant sharpness still there.

The couple embraced and swore to stay together. They were married at a lavish banquet attended by all of Chinatown. There, the father passed his fingers over his son-in-law's face and nodded in satisfaction.

Shortly after, the merchant Chang died, and the young couple moved away. Yenna sold the business and locked up the tower room. But on nights when boats pull in from far away, they say a flicker of light can still be seen in that high window. And Chinese women are reminded that ginger is one of their best friends.

> **✓ LITERARY CHECK**
>
> Think about the **characterization** of the two young people. What is their conflict? What do their reactions show about their character?

> **✓ LITERARY CHECK**
>
> What is the ginger root a **symbol** of?

> **Word Skill**
>
> Words can have denotations and connotations. The denotation of the word *fragrant* is: "having a pleasant odor." The word has a positive connotation. How does the author's use of the word *fragrant* add to the story?

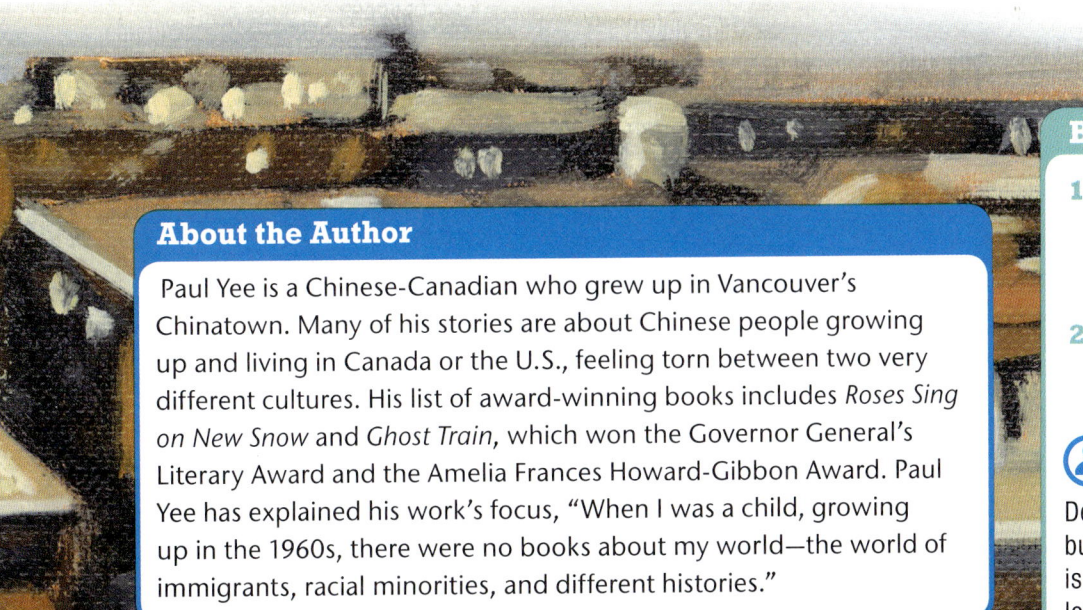

About the Author

Paul Yee is a Chinese-Canadian who grew up in Vancouver's Chinatown. Many of his stories are about Chinese people growing up and living in Canada or the U.S., feeling torn between two very different cultures. His list of award-winning books includes *Roses Sing on New Snow* and *Ghost Train*, which won the Governor General's Literary Award and the Amelia Frances Howard-Gibbon Award. Paul Yee has explained his work's focus, "When I was a child, growing up in the 1960s, there were no books about my world—the world of immigrants, racial minorities, and different histories."

Before You Go On

1. Why does the young man throw the ginger into the fireplace?
2. What happens to the ginger root in the fire?

On Your Own

Do you think "a fire burning in your heart" is a good description of love? Why or why not?

Reading 4

Review and Practice

Reader's theater 🎧

Act out the following scene between Yenna and her father.

Chang: Why do you hang a lamp in the window every night?

Yenna: If the flame goes out, I know the man I love will not come home to me.

Chang: But Yenna, he has been gone for four years. And he has not written you one letter in all that time.

Yenna: Yes, that is true.

Chang: Daughter, you know I treasure your happiness. I am afraid for you. What if he does not come back?

Yenna: I gave him my promise. I will wait for him.

Chang: You are sure of him?

Yenna: I am sure of my own heart. My heart is as steady as that lamp burning in the window.

> **Speaking Tip**
>
> Know your character! Show that character's feelings with the intonation of your voice and facial expressions.

Comprehension WB 143

Recall

1. Why does the young man go to the gold fields?
2. What causes Chang to lose his wife and his eyesight?

Comprehend

3. Why doesn't Yenna leave with the young man when he first asks her?
4. Why doesn't the ginger root burn in the fire?

Analyze

5. How did the ginger root save the young man's life?
6. What is "fire of the ginger"?

Connect

7. Do you think Yenna and the young man will be good for each other? Explain.
8. Do you think that it's important in most cultures for a parent to approve of the people young people choose to be with? Use the story, as well as what you know, to help you explain.

Discussion

Discuss with a partner or in a small group.

1. Chang was a loving father, and Yenna was a devoted daughter. Do you think Yenna did the right thing by not leaving her father? Why or why not?
2. What is the significance of the fact that the ginger didn't burn? Do you think it would have burned if it had dried up? Explain.

Can we think with the heart? Do you think that Yenna and her true love thought with their hearts? Explain.

> **Listening Tip**
>
> Listen for viewpoints you hadn't considered. Listen for the important details that support those viewpoints. How well do the details support the speaker's ideas? Ask questions if you want to know more.

Response to Literature

WB 143

Imagine that the young man had written a letter to Yenna. Use details from the story to help you. Do some research at the library or on the internet to find more details about this period of time and the gold rush. Use details in the letter from him to Yenna to explain what he was doing while away. Be sure to reflect the young man's character and mention the ginger root!

▲ Workers panning for gold in California

Reading 4
Grammar

Present and Past Perfect

Writers use the present perfect to talk about an action that started in the past and has consequences in the present. It is formed with *have/has* and the past participle. Look at these examples from the story.

Example	Meaning
It **has taken** many years to gather enough gold to buy a farm.	The young man started to gather gold to buy a farm years ago. Now he has enough to buy one.
I **have built** you a house on my land.	He started to build a house in the past. Now the house is finished.

> **Grammar Skill**
> You can use the simple past instead of the past perfect if the time frame is specific. The words *before* and *after* help make the time frame specific and clear.

Writers use the past perfect to talk about an action that happened before another action in the past. It is formed with *had* and the past participle. Look at these examples from the story.

Example	Order of Events
When the epidemic was over, Chang **had lost** his wife and his eyesight.	First event: loss of wife and eyesight Later event: epidemic is over
There stood the man she **had promised** to wait for.	First event: she promised to wait Later event: he stood in front of her

> **Grammar Check**
> ✓ When do you use the **present perfect**? When do you use the **past perfect**?

Practice A
WB 144

Complete the sentences with *has*, *have*, or *had*.

1. Your face ____has____ not changed. You look the same.
2. My heart _____ not changed either. I still love you.
3. Since you left, I _____ kept a lamp burning every night.

Practice B

Complete the sentences with *have*, *has*, or *had* and the past participle form of the verb in parentheses.

1. Ben and Perry are old friends. They ____have known____ each other since kindergarten. (know)
2. My uncle _____ for the police department before he started selling cars. (work)
3. My aunt _____ in Miami for two years. (live)

> **Apply**
> Write three sentences about something you have accomplished. Then trade with a partner. Now imagine it is five years from now. Write new sentences that tell what your partner had done by his or her age today.
>
> **Example:**
> A: I have traveled to ten states. B: By the time she was ten, Yolanda had traveled to ten states.

Adjective Phrases (*-ing, -ed*)

Adjective clauses (or relative clauses) are used to modify a noun or noun phrase. Like other clauses, they have a subject and a verb. They are dependent clauses that begin with a relative pronoun (such as *that, who, whom,* or *which*).

An adjective phrase is a reduced form of an adjective clause. To make an adjective phrase from an adjective clause with the verb *be*, omit the relative pronoun along with the form of the *be* verb.

Adjective Clause	Adjective Phrase
The fire **that is burning for you in my heart** can never be extinguished.	The fire **burning for you in my heart** can never be extinguished.
Many contain stained-glass windows, **which are decorated with flower and diamond patterns**.	Many contain stained-glass windows **decorated with flower and diamond patterns**.

To make an adjective phrase from an adjective clause with certain verbs other than *be,* omit the relative pronoun and add *-ing* to the base form of the verb.

Adjective Clause	Adjective Phrase
The Chinese immigrants **who lived in Chinatown** worked really hard.	The Chinese immigrants **living in Chinatown** worked really hard.
Rich and successful men **who wanted to marry Yenna** brought her grand gifts.	Rich and successful men **wanting to marry Yenna** brought her grand gifts.

> **Grammar Skill**
> Adjective clauses and phrases usually follow the noun or noun phrase that they modify.

> **Grammar Check**
> ✓ What is an **adjective phrase**?

Practice A

WB 145

Underline the adjective clause in each sentence.

1. The ginger <u>that was thrown in the fire</u> didn't burn.
2. The man who stood before her looked older and wiser.
3. One winter, an epidemic that caused much illness and death ravaged the city.
4. Yenna worked in a room in the tower that was filled with light.

Practice B

In your notebook, rewrite the sentences from Practice A, using adjective phrases.

1. The ginger thrown in the fire didn't burn.

> **Apply**
> Write three sentences about people or places in your city or town. Use adjective clauses. Then trade sentences with a partner. Underline the adjective clauses. If possible, change them to adjective phrases.
> **Example:** The people <u>who work at the library</u> are really nice. The people <u>working at the library</u> are really nice.

Reading 4

Reading 4

Writing

Write a Critical Analysis

A critical analysis is a type of expository writing in which you analyze a literary work, giving your viewpoint of it. To write a critical analysis, begin with a personal response. Then, briefly tell what happens in the story so that your reader can appreciate your reaction to it.

> **Writing Prompt**
>
> Choose a story or piece of literature to write a critical analysis. In your paragraph, write your viewpoint about the work and a brief overview of it. Support your viewpoint with textual evidence. Be sure to use adjective phrases correctly.

1 **Prewrite** Review the story or piece of literature.

WB 146

- Think about your general response to it. How did you feel about it?
- Identify the ideas you want to focus on. List them on a chart.
- On the chart, list evidence from the work to support your ideas.

Here's an ideas and textual evidence T-chart created by a student named Andrea for her critical analysis of "Ginger for the Heart."

Ideas	Textual Evidence
powerful love story	They stay together
title connects ginger root with love	title—"Ginger for the Heart"
their love after many years—still strong and sweet	ginger root core was still firm and fragrant
after throwing ginger root in fire—cannot be destroyed	ginger root core was still firm, moist, and fragrant

② **Draft** Use your T-chart to help you write a first draft.
- Remember to include a sentence with your main response to the work you chose to analyze.
- Include a brief overview of the work as it relates to your response.
- Check that your viewpoint about the work is clear.
- Be sure to use adjective phrases correctly.

③ **Revise** Read over your draft. Look for places where the writing is unclear or needs improvement. Complete (✓) the Writing Checklist to help you identify problems. Then, revise your draft, using the editing and proofreading marks listed on page 467.

④ **Edit and Proofread** Check your work for errors in grammar, usage, mechanics, and spelling. Trade papers with a partner to obtain feedback. Use the Peer Review Checklist on Workbook page 146. Edit your final draft in response to feedback from your partner and your teacher.

⑤ **Publish** Prepare a clean copy of your final draft. Share your critical analysis with the class. Save your work. You'll need to refer to it in the Writing Workshop at the end of the unit.

Here is Andrea's critical analysis of "Ginger for the Heart."

Writing Checklist

Ideas:
☐ I gave my viewpoint of the work, supporting my ideas with textual evidence.

Sentence Fluency:
☐ My sentences flow smoothly, with transitions connecting my ideas.

Conventions:
☐ I used adjective phrases correctly.

Andrea Vargas

"Ginger for the Heart"

"Ginger for the Heart" is a powerful love story. What makes it so remarkable is that the couple is about to leave each other, when the ginger root, a symbol of their unwavering love, brings them back together. Throughout the story, the ginger root connecting them is there. First, Yenna gives the young man a ginger root to remember her by. Four years later, when the young man returns, the ginger root is still "firm and fragrant." This shows that their love is still alive, like the ginger keeping fresh for years. Later in the story, the young man throws the ginger root into the fire, but it doesn't burn. This is a sign that their love will continue and the two vow to stay together forever.

Link the Readings

Critical Thinking

What logical connections can you make between the ideas and details in the readings in this unit? Although the readings do not all have the same purpose, they share a common theme and reflect a range of viewpoints. Complete the chart below. Be prepared to support your responses with evidence from each of the texts.

Title of Reading	Purpose	Big Question Link
from *The Story of My Life*		Anne Sullivan's love changed Helen Keller's life.
To Capture the Wild Horse		
"The Wisdom of the Heart"		
"Ginger for the Heart"	to entertain	

Discussion

Discuss with a partner or in a small group.
- Which reading had the biggest impact on you? Why?
- **Can we think with the heart?** Which guides you more in life: your logic or your heart? Explain.

Fluency Check

Work with a partner. Choose a paragraph from one of the readings. Take turns reading it for one minute. Count the total number of words you read. Practice saying the words you had trouble reading. Take turns reading the paragraph three more times. Did you read more words each time? Record the number of words you read each time.

	1st Reading	2nd Reading	3rd Reading	4th Reading
Number of Words				

Media Literacy & Projects

Work with a partner or in a small group. Choose one of these projects.

1. Create a poster showing the circulatory system and the nervous system and how they interact. Present your poster to the class and discuss the connection between heart and brain.

2. Research an advice column on the internet. Then, create an advice column with letters from Yenna. Ask for advice from her point of view about: not hearing from the young man; losing her mother; helping her father deal with losing his sight; and her feelings about the young man asking her to leave with him. Write letters from the advice columnist with advice for Yenna.

3. Think of a place you know well: your school, home, gym, or somewhere you visit often. Write a short play with several characters. Make sure to include a narrator and stage directions.

4. Do you know what a brain teaser is? Research *brain teasers* online. Find two to present to the class. Create a worksheet for the class to use to solve the two brain teasers.

Further Reading

Choose from these reading selections. Practice reading silently for longer and longer periods.

The Hunchback of Notre-Dame, Victor Hugo
This book tells the classic story of the deformed Quasimodo and his love for the beautiful, doomed Esmeralda.

Our Town, Thornton Wilder
This Pulitzer Prize-winning drama perfectly describes the relationships between the people living in the small village of Grover's Corners.

Bird, Angela Johnson
Determined to find her stepfather, Cecil, and bring him home, Bird runs away from her Cleveland home to Alabama. Along the way, she helps two lonely boys and comes to understand what family really means.

Voices in the Air, Naomi Shihab Nye
This is a collection of over 100 poems about artists, writers, and historical figures of the past that inspired this award-winning poet.

Put It All Together

Listening & Speaking Workshop

How-To Demonstration

You will tell and show the class how to do something.

① Think About It

You will explain and demonstrate to the class how to do an activity of your choice. Think about something that you know how to do well. How would you show someone else how to do it?

With a partner, make a list of words you might use during a demonstration. Review how to use imperatives to give simple commands and instructions.

Work together to make a list of ideas for a how-to demonstration. Think of activities you could demonstrate in class. Here are some examples:

- How to use the Braille alphabet
- How to solve a brain teaser
- How to play the guitar
- How to make a puppet

② Gather and Organize Information

Choose a topic from your list. Write down what you already know about how to do the activity. Try to write step-by-step instructions. Consider what supplies or tools you will need for your demonstration. Which imperatives can you use to describe each step?

Research Go to the library, talk to an adult or a professional, or search on the internet to get information. Take notes on what you find.

Order Your Notes Make a list of the steps needed to do your activity. Check to be sure that your steps are in logical order.

Use Visuals Find or make props you can use as you demonstrate the steps of your activity. You may wish to create posters, pictures, or other visuals to make your presentation more interesting and effective.

3 Practice and Present

Use your list when you begin practicing your demonstration. Then try talking to an audience without looking at your notes. You may want to give your presentation in front of a mirror or to a friend or family member. Keep practicing until you are relaxed and confident.

Deliver Your How-To Presentation A classroom demonstration is formal. Look at your audience as you speak. Be clear as you present your steps. Slow down when you come to the most important points. To make the presentation of your demonstration richer and more interesting, use a variety of grammatical structures, sentence lengths, sentence types, and connecting words. At the end of the presentation, ask listeners if they have any questions about your demonstration.

4 Evaluate the Presentation

You will improve your skills as a speaker and a listener by evaluating each presentation you give and hear. Use this checklist to help you judge the demonstrations of your classmates.

- ☐ Did the speaker present the how-to demonstration in logical steps?
- ☐ Did the demonstration give you enough information to do the activity on your own?
- ☐ Did the speaker use props and pictures or other visuals effectively?
- ☐ Did the speaker answer your questions to your satisfaction?
- ☐ Could the how-to demonstration be improved?

Speaking Skill

Be sure to speak clearly. Ask your listeners for feedback and encourage questions. As you answer the questions, give thoughtful answers to show that you were listening carefully.

Listening Tips

Give each speaker your full attention, and listen carefully.

Think about the presentation. Would you be able to explain the steps to someone else? Take notes so you can ask questions at the end of the demonstration.

Strengthen Your Social Language

In social context as well as in your content-area classes, you need to be able to ask for and give information. Go to your Digital Resources and do the activity for this unit. This activity will help you expand your vocabulary using high-frequency English words necessary for identifying and describing people, places, and objects.

Put It All Together

Writing Workshop

Expository Essay

In this unit, you've written a variety of expository paragraphs and learned some techniques to develop them. Like an expository paragraph, an expository essay gives information about a topic. An expository essay begins with an introductory paragraph that presents the writer's main idea. Three body paragraphs develop and support the main idea with details and examples. The writer ends with a concluding paragraph that restates the main idea in an interesting way.

> **Writing Prompt**
>
> Write a five-paragraph essay that expands on one of the paragraphs you wrote for this unit. Be sure to vary your sentence structure and use simple, compound, and complex sentences correctly.

① Prewrite Review your previous work in this unit. Decide on the paragraph you want to expand on. Think about your reader. In your notebook, answer these questions:

- What do my readers already know about this topic?
- What questions might they have?
- How can I make my essay interesting to my readers?

List your main ideas and the most important supporting details in a graphic organizer. A student named Santos decided to expand on the paragraph he wrote to critique his favorite movie. Here is the main idea chart he prepared.

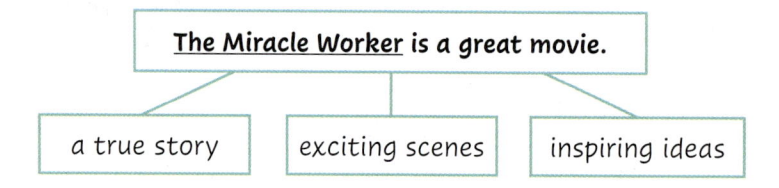

```
        The Miracle Worker is a great movie.
        /              |              \
  a true story    exciting scenes    inspiring ideas
```

② Draft

Use your graphic organizer and the model on page 294 to help you write a first draft.

- Keep your purpose in mind: to expand on a paragraph you wrote for this unit.
- As you expand on your paragraph, choose details to support your main ideas.
- Arrange details in the order that best fits your topic.
- Be sure to vary your sentence structure and use simple, compound, and complex sentences correctly.

③ Revise

Read over your draft. Think about how well you have addressed questions of purpose, audience, and genre. Your purpose is to inform and persuade. Is your essay clearly organized? Is it appropriate in content and tone for the intended audience? Keep these questions in mind as you revise your draft. Complete (✓) the Writing Checklist below to help you identify additional issues that may need revision. Mark your changes on your draft using the editing and proofreading marks listed on page 467.

Six Traits of Writing Checklist

- ☐ **Ideas:** Is my main idea clear?
- ☐ **Organization:** Do I present supporting details in a logical order?
- ☐ **Voice:** Does my writing show my interest in the topic?
- ☐ **Word Choice:** Do I use sequence words to tell when events happen?
- ☐ **Sentence Fluency:** Did I use transition sentences between paragraphs?
- ☐ **Conventions:** Does my writing follow the rules of grammar, usage, and mechanics?

Put It All Together

Here are the changes Santos plans to make when he revises his first draft:

The Miracle Worker

Recently, I ~~thought~~ *was thinking* that ~~a movie called~~ The Miracle Worker is my favorite film. It tells the true story of a remarkabel woman named Helen Keller. When she is only nineteen months old, an illness destroys her sight and hearing. Although she faces huge obstacles, Helen goes on to become the first sight- and hearing-impaired woman to earn a college degree.

[Helen needs a teacher who specializes in helping children with disabilities.] As a young child who can neither see nor hear, Helen is unable to learn basic aspects of everyday life. She does not know what things are, what people want, or how to behave.

When Helen is seven, her family finds a skilled tutor named Anne Sullivan, *(the "miracle worker" of the film's title)*. At first, the teacher makes little progress in helping Helen. She u~~z~~*s*es her fingers to spell words into Helen's hand. Still, Helen doesn't understand that the finger movements ~~are~~ *represent* words. At one point, Sullivan becomes frustrated because Helen is unable to distinguish between the words water and mug.

Revised to correct mechanics.

Revised for clarity of flow.

Revised for clarity and to add detail, to correct spelling, and to add a more descriptive verb.

Then Sullivan has a brilliant idea. She takes Helen to the water pump. This is the most exciting scene in the movie! Sullivan puts one of Helen's hands into the running water and finger-spells the word water into Helen's other hand. Helen suddenly understands that "w-a-t-e-r" means the liquid gushing over her hand. Learning this one word is a break through for Helen. Once she knows that everything has a name, she is eager to learn as many new words as she can.

Although The Miracle Worker is both uplifting and sad, there is a larger idea symbolized by Helen's break through. No matter how great the obstacles may seem, no matter what the setbacks, anything is possible. Take my advice and watch this movie.

Revised to clarify sequence and flow.

Revised for mechanics.

Revised to avoid repetition.

Revised to use an imperative to be more persuasive.

4 **Edit and Proofread** Check your work for errors in grammar, usage, mechanics, and spelling. Then trade essays with a partner and complete (✓) the Peer Review Checklist below to give each other constructive feedback. Edit your final draft in response to feedback from your partner and your teacher.

WB 147

Peer Review Checklist

- ☐ Is the essay clearly organized?
- ☐ Does the first paragraph introduce the writer's opinion about the topic and main ideas?
- ☐ Does each body paragraph focus on a main idea?
- ☐ Do the body paragraphs include details and examples that support the main ideas?
- ☐ Does the concluding paragraph summarize the main ideas and most important details in an interesting way?
- ☐ Can any changes be made to improve the essay?

Santos Rivera

The Miracle Worker

Recently, I was thinking that The Miracle Worker is my favorite film. It tells the true story of a remarkabel woman named Helen Keller. When she is only nineteen months old, an illness destroys her sight and hearing. Although she faces huge obstacles, Helen goes on to become the first sight- and hearing-impaired woman to earn a college degree.

Revised for spelling.

As a young child who can neither see nor hear, Helen is unable to learn basic aspects of everyday life. She does not know what things are, what people want, or how to behave. Helen needs a teacher who specializes in helping children with disabilities.

When Helen is seven, her family finds a skilled tutor named Anne Sullivan (the "miracle worker" of the film's title). At first, ~~the teacher~~ Sullivan makes little progress in helping Helen. She uses her fingers to spell words into Helen's hand. Still, Helen doesn't understand that the finger movements represent words. At one point, Sullivan becomes frustrated because Helen is unable to distinguish between the words water and mug.

Revised for clarity.

Then Sullivan has a brilliant idea. She takes Helen to the water pump. This is the most exciting scene in the movie! Sullivan puts one of Helen's hands into the running water and finger-spells the word water into Helen's other hand. Helen suddenly understands that "w-a-t-e-r" means the liquid gushing over her hand. Learning this one word is a break through for Helen. Once she knows that everything has a name, she is eager to learn as many new words as she can.

Revised for spelling of compound word.

Although The Miracle Worker is both uplifting and sad, there is a larger idea symbolized by Helen's break through. No matter how great the obstacles may seem, no matter what the setbacks, anything is possible. Take my advice and watch this movie!

5 **Publish** Obtain feedback from your teacher and classmates; then prepare your final draft. Share your essay with the class.

WB 148

Test Preparation

Practice

Read the following test sample. Study the tips in the boxes. Work with a partner to answer the questions.

The Pounding Heart

Hector tapped his badly chewed pencil against the edge of his desk. He tried to look as far to the right as he could without appearing to avoid looking to his left. Livia was sitting to his left, and Hector desperately wanted to ask her a question that he was also desperately afraid to ask. He tapped his pencil harder and faster until it fractured along a bite-line and fell to the floor. He bent to his left to grab it quickly, and his head met with a hard object doing the exact same thing.

"Oooh! Ow!" Livia said, rubbing the side of her head. She started to laugh as she squinted through the pain. "Sorry. I thought I dropped something."

Hector, rubbing his head, laughed as well. Hector stared at her, saying in his mind the words he had rehearsed over and over to himself. If only he could say them out loud, he might be in heaven on Friday night. It would be a darkened gymnasium, but he would be in heaven, nonetheless.

"Hector?" Livia whispered.

Hector jumped. He'd been staring at her. "What?" he said.

"What, what? What do you want? You keep saying my name."

Hector had been completely unaware that he had been saying Livia's name out loud. He cleared his throat and a strange calm overcame him. He looked at her and smiled. She smiled back and his whole body relaxed. He leaned in and whispered his question.

"Yes," Livia said as she blushed. "I'd love to."

1 What question did Hector likely want to ask Livia?
- **A** If she would help him study for Friday's test
- **B** If she would watch him play basketball this week
- **C** If she would come to his house for a party
- **D** If she would go with him to a school dance

2 What is the setting of the story?
- **A** A gymnasium at night
- **B** A classroom during the day
- **C** The bleachers of stadium
- **D** A school cafeteria

Taking Tests
You will often take tests to show what you know. Study the tips below to help you improve your test-taking skills.

Tip
Sometimes, important information is given in a simple phrase or word in the story. When reading a fiction passage, make mental notes of information that you may need later.

Tip
When reading fiction, it is extremely helpful to visualize the scene. Put yourself into the action as though you were watching a favorite movie. This helps you remember the information when answering questions.

WB 149–150

Visual Literacy

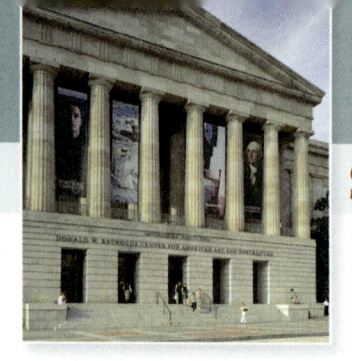

Smithsonian American Art Museum

Bonding or Breaking?

Artists love drama, and matters that involve human emotions often provide plenty of it. The portrayal of friendship, lovers, or family ties in paintings, sculpture, and other media has served as the storyline of some amazing American art.

William T. Wiley, *Love Poem— Poem by Michael Hannon* (1997)

For almost thirty years, painter William T. Wiley created works of art inspired by the poems of Michael Hannon. In *Love Poem*, Wiley uses the following poem by Hannon, which appears at the bottom center of the painting's border:

Fear of death—a kind of desire,
and fear of desire—a kind of death.

Clouds like ships—ships like clouds.

I love you, even if this world
is just a dream—even if it isn't.

Wiley obviously captured the ship, clouds, and water imagery in his watercolor, but he added something of his own to the "poem." Notice the musical clefs which look like fancy *f*s throughout the

William T. Wiley, *Love Poem—Poem by Michael Hannon,* 1997, watercolor, 41 x 27 in., Smithsonian American Art Museum ▶

296 Unit 4

watercolor. There is one on each side of the larger heart floating in the center of the wave, and then two more in the white center of the heart. Wiley loved to work with repeating shapes. He also played music, in particular the fiddle and the mandolin—both instruments have this clef shape on their wooden fronts. The heart is a symbol of love, but some unsettling things are happening in this watercolor. The water swirls, and the ship is so close to the edge of a wave it looks as if it might topple over. But, of course, Hannon's poem is also a bit edgy since it uses words that contrast sharply: fear and desire, love and death.

Washington Allston, *Hermia and Helena* (before 1818)

The two friends pictured in this painting sit so close together that they look like one figure. Each has a hand on the book they share. Washington Allston borrowed the storyline for this cozy scene from the British playwright William Shakespeare's play, *A Midsummer Night's Dream*. The comedy centers on two friends who fall in love with the same man. Can their friendship survive as they compete for his affections? In the play, Shakespeare has Helena (the figure on the right in the painting) describe what her bond with Hermia has felt like as they grew up together.

> So we grew together,
> Like a double cherry . . .
> Two lovely berries moulded on one stem.

In his painting, Allston shows the two women as a "double cherry" sitting on a rock in a splendid landscape. The setting suggests the enchanted wood where most of the comedy's action takes place.

Love is the greatest emotion, but also perhaps the most difficult. Both of these artists make it clear that when it comes to matters of the heart, things can be complicated.

▲ Washington Allston, *Hermia and Helena,* **before 1818, oil, 30⅜ x 25¼ in., Smithsonian American Art Museum**

Discuss What You Learned

1. What does each artwork add to the literature it was based on?
2. If you were to create an artwork based on a piece of literature, what would you choose and how would you illustrate it?

BIG QUESTION

How does each of these artworks show the concepts of bonding or breaking?

151–152

Unit 5

What can we learn from times of war?

THE BIG QUESTION

This unit is about war. You'll read about World War I—often called the "Great War." You'll also read about heroes of World War II. Reading, writing, and talking about this topic will give you practice using academic language and help you become a better student.

Reading 1
Social Studies

"World War I"

Reading Strategy
Identify cause and effect

Reading 2
Poetry, Song, Prose

Poems by John McCrae and Wilfred Owen, a war song, and a letter home

Reading Strategy
Recognize historical context

Reading 3
Social Studies

"In the Name of His Father" by Fred Tasker

Reading Strategy
Draw conclusions

Listening and Speaking—Oral Report

At the end of this unit, you will give an **oral report**.

Writing—Expository Essay: News Article

In this unit, you'll write an **expository essay** in the form of a **news article**. To help you do this, you will write a cause and effect paragraph, a compare and contrast paragraph, a news article, and a paragraph to support a position. At the end of the unit, you'll expand on one of the paragraphs to write an expository essay.

Quick Write

Write *war* in your notebook. Make a list of words and phrases you associate with war.

View and Respond

Go to your Digital Resources. Watch the video and answer the questions.

Reading 4
Poetry

"Sonnet to My Brother, a Soldier" and "He Died at His Post" by J.W. Holman

Reading Strategy
Read aloud

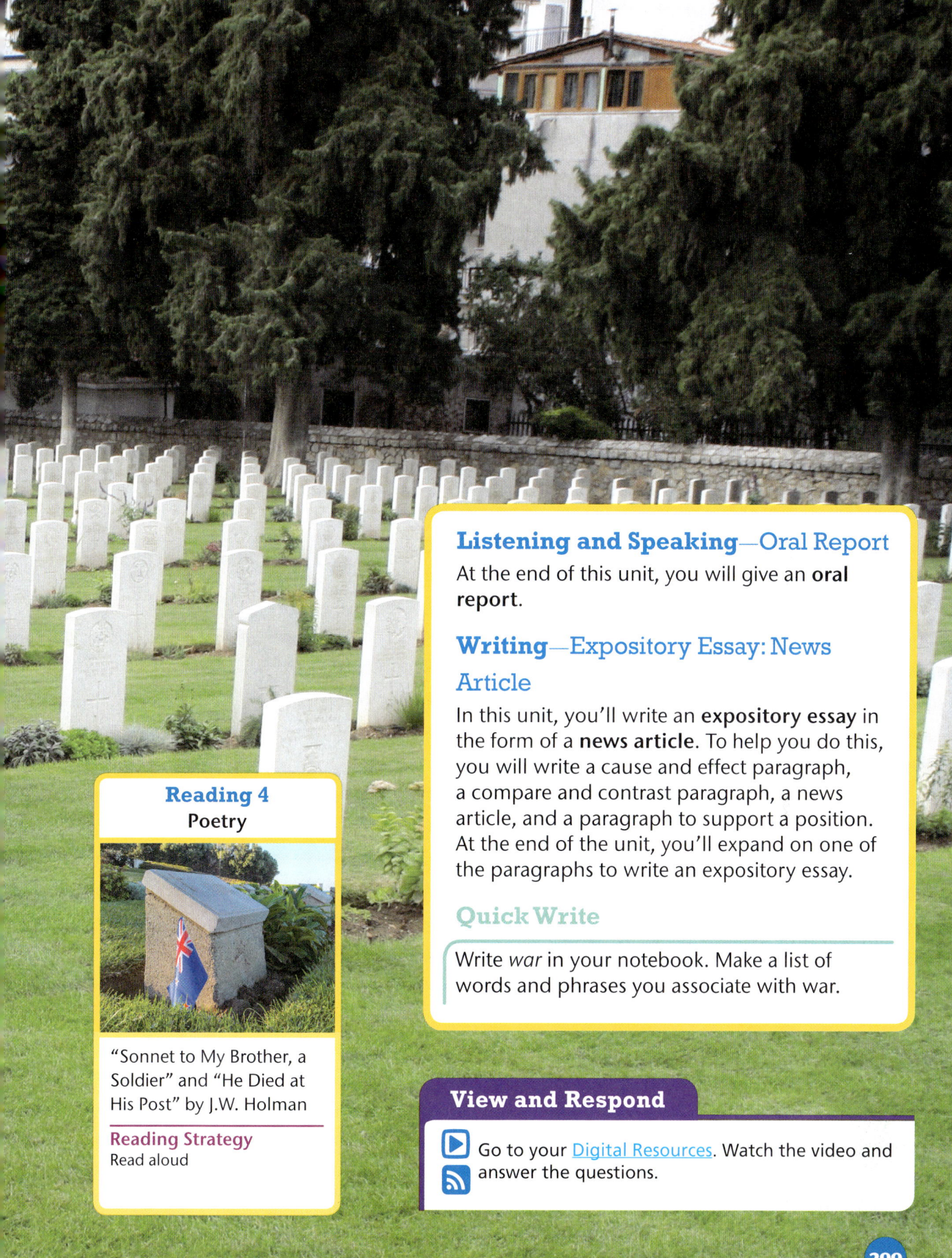

Reading 1

Prepare to Read

What You Will Learn

Reading
- Vocabulary building: Context, dictionary skills, word study
- Reading strategy: Identify cause and effect
- Text type: Informational text (social studies)

Grammar
- Appositives
- Prepositions of time: *in, on, at, by, before,* and *until*

Writing
- Write a cause and effect paragraph

THE BIG QUESTION

What can we learn from times of war? War causes great pain and suffering, but it can also teach us important lessons. We study history to learn these lessons. How does war change people's lives? How does it affect history?

Build Background

"World War I" is an article that tells what caused World War I and explains what made it different from previous wars. The map below shows Europe in 1914, at the beginning of the war. The timeline shows four important events that occurred during the war.

▶ Europe in 1914, at the beginning of World War I

1914 — Austria-Hungary declares war on Serbia. Germany sides with Austria-Hungary. France, Russia, and Britain declare war on Germany.

1917 — The United States declares war on Germany.

1918 — Germany surrenders. The war ends.

1919 — Germany signs a peace treaty.

300 Unit 5

Vocabulary 🎧

Listening and Speaking: Key Words

Read these sentences aloud with a partner. Use the context to figure out the meaning of the highlighted words. Use a dictionary, the glossary, or a thesaurus to determine or confirm your answers. Then write each word and its meaning in your notebook.

> **Key Words**
> alliance
> armistice
> assassination
> civilians
> surrendered
> trenches

1. The United States banded together with other countries, forming an **alliance** to fight Austria-Hungary and Germany.
2. In 1918 Germany signed an **armistice**, an agreement to stop fighting immediately.
3. In 1914 a man killed Archduke Franz Ferdinand, nephew to the emperor of Austria-Hungary. As a result of the archduke's **assassination**, Austria-Hungary declared war on Serbia.
4. Unfortunately, during a war many **civilians**—citizens who are not members of the military forces—are hurt or killed.
5. The Germans **surrendered** because they realized that they could not win the war.
6. The soldiers spent most of their time in deep holes called **trenches**, where they were protected from enemy fire.

Practice

Choose a word from the box above to complete each sentence. Then take turns reading the sentences aloud with a partner.

1. The man was arrested for planning a(n) _____ of the president.
2. The soldiers dug _____ that were 6 to 8 feet deep.
3. It is not easy to reach a(n) _____ when groups of people are at war.
4. The two countries formed a(n) _____ to work together for one cause.
5. Many _____ —while waiting at home, worrying about their loved ones—were injured when a bomb accidentally went off in their neighborhood.
6. The enemy _____ after recognizing that the war could not be won.

▲ An American war photographer sets up a camera in a waterlogged trench.

Reading 1

Listening and Speaking: Academic Words

Study the **purple** words and their meanings. You will find these words useful when talking and writing about informational texts. Write each word and its meaning in your notebook, then say the words aloud with a partner. After you read "World War I," try to use these words to respond to the text.

Academic Words
- neutral
- resources
- technology
- tension
- vehicle

neutral = not supporting either side in an argument, competition, or war	Sweden did not wish to get involved in the war, so it remained **neutral**.
resources = all the money, property, and other goods that are available for use	Germany's desire for land and other **resources** helped to bring about the war.
technology = the combination of all the latest knowledge, equipment, and methods used in scientific or industrial work	The invention of computers and other advances in **technology** have changed how people fight wars.
tension = the emotionally charged relationship between people or groups of people	The mounting **tension** between the two groups suddenly erupted in an act of violence that started a war.
vehicle = writing, a piece of art, or an event used to transmit or express ideas	Poetry is a **vehicle** for the reader to understand a poet's attitudes and emotions.

Practice
WB 154

Choose a **purple** word from the box above to complete each sentence. Then take turns reading the sentences aloud with a partner.

1. There was so much _____ between the two countries that people expected fighting to break out soon.
2. Advances in _____ enabled many countries to build deadlier weapons.
3. Some countries used colorful posters as a _____ to excite interest in the war.
4. The two groups hoped that by sharing their _____, they could find a solution faster.
5. Switzerland is a _____ country; it will not support either side in a war.

▲ WWI soldiers wearing gas masks operate a machine gun.

Word Study: Roots

Many English words come from Greek or Latin and still retain parts of the words from which they came. These word parts are called *roots*. The chart below shows some roots, their meanings, their origins, and some English words that contain them.

Root	Meaning	Origin	English Word
capit	head	Latin	capital
cent	one hundred	Latin	century
civ	citizen	Latin	civilian
fac	do, make	Latin	factories
mar	sea	Latin	submarine
port	carry	Latin	support
scope	see, watch	Greek	periscope
techn	art, skill	Greek	technology
tens	stretch, strain	Latin	tension

Practice WB 155

With a partner, look through "World War I" to find and underline each of the English words in the chart above. In your notebook, copy the context sentence for each word. Then talk about what the word means and write a definition for each one.

Reading Strategy | Identify Cause and Effect

Recognizing cause-and-effect relationships can help you understand a text about a complex topic like war. To recognize cause and effect, follow these steps:

- As you read, look for important events in the war and think about what caused them or happened as a result of them. Use the headings to help you. Ask yourself questions, such as: Why did this happen? What happened as a result of this?
- Look for words and phrases that typically signal causes and effects, such as *one reason*, *because*, and *so*. Also, look for verbs such as *caused*, and for other words, such as *when*, as they may signal cause-and-effect relationships among important events.

As you read "World War I," look for important events and cause-and-effect relationships among them.

WB 156

Reading 1
Informational Text
Social Studies

Set a purpose for reading Read this article to find out the major causes and effects of World War I. How did the war change the world forever?

World War I

Background to the Conflict

At the beginning of the twentieth century, there was tension among countries in Europe. One reason for this tension was the shifting balance of power. Each country worked hard to ensure that no other country had more power than it did. Britain, France, and Germany were competing against one another for overseas trade. The British were alarmed that the Germans were building larger, more modern factories. The Germans were anxious that France was gaining power and wealth in the form of colonies. Germany wanted more land and resources and greater military strength. In addition, Russia and Austria-Hungary were struggling for power in the Balkan states in southeastern Europe. Because of these tensions, six countries formed two powerful alliances:

- Britain, France, Russia
- Germany, Austria-Hungary, Italy

By the middle of 1914, Europe was close to war.

A German factory in 1914 ▲

The Assassination

In 1914, Austria-Hungary ruled Bosnia and Herzegovina, a province in the Balkans in southeastern Europe. Bosnia and Herzegovina and Serbia, a country in the same area, were at one time both part of the **Ottoman Empire**. Serbia won its independence, but Bosnia and Herzegovina was made part of Austria-Hungary. Because many Serbs lived in Bosnia and Herzegovina, Serbia wanted control over the province. This rivalry caused tension between Serbia and Austria-Hungary.

Archduke Franz Ferdinand, the nephew of the emperor of Austria-Hungary and heir to the throne, visited Sarajevo, the capital of Bosnia and Herzegovina. The Serbs living in the province were angered by the archduke's visit. On June 28, 1914, a Bosnian student, supported by a group of Serbian **terrorists**, assassinated him. Austria-Hungary declared war on Serbia on July 28. The war quickly spread as other countries defended their allies. By mid-August 1914, most of Europe was at war.

Within a year, many countries had joined in the war.

Ottoman Empire, empire based in Turkey, which included large parts of Eastern Europe, Asia, and North Africa. It began about 1300 and ended in 1922.

terrorists, people who use violence against ordinary people to obtain political demands

▲ Gavrilo Princip, the man who assassinated Archduke Franz Ferdinand and his wife

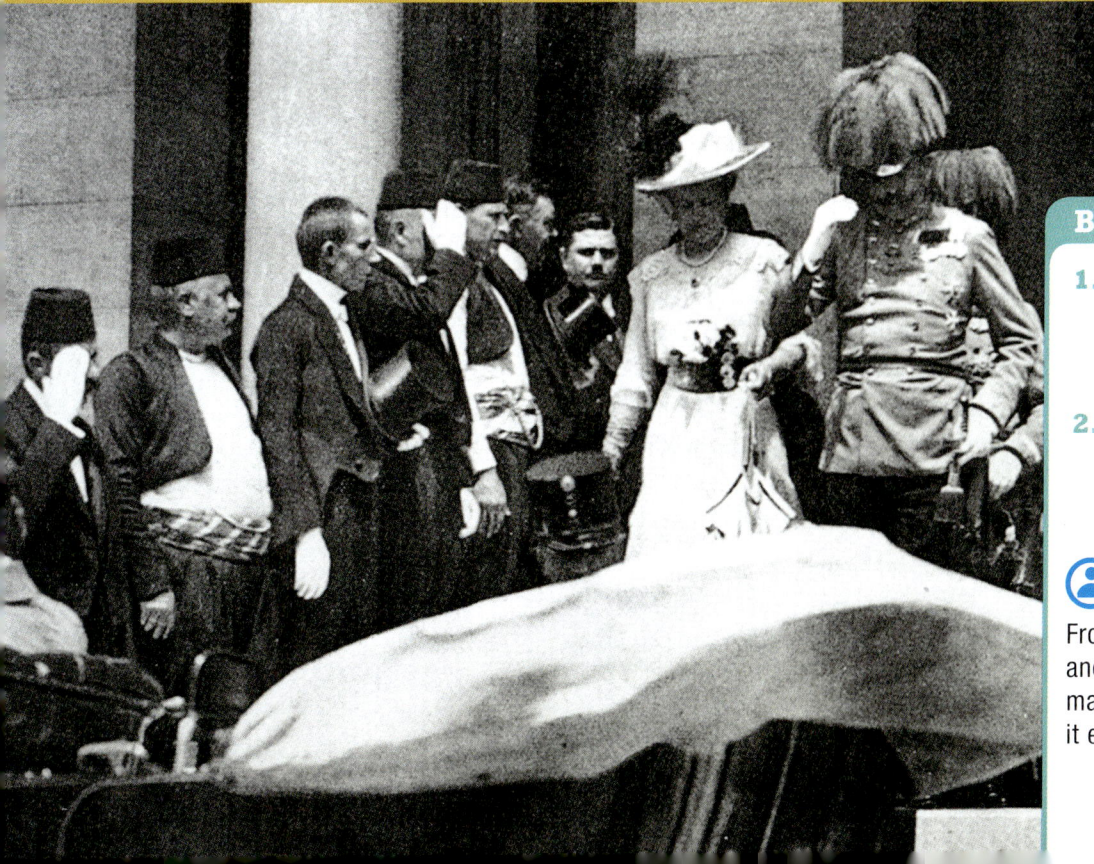

▼ Archduke Franz Ferdinand and his wife, Sophie, before the assassination

Before You Go On

1. Who ruled Bosnia and Herzegovina in 1914? Why did this cause tension?
2. What happened as a result of Archduke Franz Ferdinand's assassination?

On Your Own

From what you've read and know, what are the main causes of war? Is it ever just one event?

Reading 1

This chart shows how the countries were divided.

Allied (Entente) Powers		Central Powers
British Empire	French Republic	German Empire
Newfoundland	Kingdom of Belgium	Grand Duchy of Baden
India	Russian Empire (1914–17)	Kingdom of Bavaria
Australia	Kingdom of Italy (1915–18)	Kingdom of Prussia
New Zealand	United States (1917–18)	Kingdom of Saxony
South Africa	Kingdom of Serbia	Kingdom of Württemberg
United Kingdom	Kingdom of Romania (1916–18)	Austro-Hungarian Monarchy
Canada	Empire of Japan	Ottoman Empire
	Kingdom of Greece (1917–18)	Kingdom of Bulgaria (1915–18)
GREAT WAR 1914-1918	Portugal (1916–18)	Emirate of Jabal Shammar

The First Modern War

World War I is often called the first modern war because new technology made the weapons deadlier than ever. In addition, factories could produce larger quantities of weapons. Here are some of the modern weapons used during the war:

Machine guns These guns, invented by an American, shot many bullets very quickly.

Submarines These underwater ships shot torpedoes—bombs that are fired underwater.

Poison gas and gas masks Poison gas caused choking, blindness, **blisters**, and sometimes death. Gas masks protected soldiers from poison gas.

Tanks These combat vehicles carried two machine guns apiece and had metal belts over their wheels to help them climb over **obstacles** five feet high. They were covered with heavy **armor**, so they were difficult to destroy.

Periscope rifles Two mirrors were attached to a rifle so that when lifted over the top of the trenches, the soldier could see the enemy.

Fighter airplanes These small planes were armed with machine guns.

---

blisters, bumps on the skin containing clear liquid, often caused by a burn

obstacles, objects that block a person's way

armor, a strong metal layer or shell that protects

◀ A gas mask

▼ A fighter airplane

▼ A submarine

▲ A tank

Before You Go On

1. Why is World War I often called the first modern war? Explain.
2. What were tanks able to do? Why were they difficult to destroy? Where in the reading did you find your answer?

On Your Own

Why do you think a world war today would be catastrophic? What has changed about the world since World War I?

Reading 1 307

◀ American troops in the trenches near Verdun, France

▼ The trenches stretched almost 650 kilometers (400 mi.).

Life in the Trenches

Soldiers dug trenches for protection from the enemy. The trenches were muddy after it rained, so soldiers put wooden boards—called duckboards—on the ground to help keep their feet dry. The trenches were **stifling** in the summer and bitterly cold in the winter. Rats and lice spread diseases such as a brand-new illness called trench fever.

Soldiers spent about a week at a time in the trenches. Then they went to a rest area where they could wash and change clothes before returning to their underground posts. Most of the fighting was at night, so soldiers often slept during the day. They wrote letters home or kept diaries. Many soldiers were homesick. They had a hard life in the trenches.

The United States Enters the War

From the beginning of the war, President Woodrow Wilson wanted the United States to stay neutral. People in the United States were divided about the war. Many U.S. citizens were from European countries, so there was support for both sides. In 1915, Germany announced it would attack all neutral ships headed to Britain. In 1917, Germany announced **unrestricted** submarine warfare.

---

stifling, very hot and difficult to breathe in
unrestricted, not limited by anyone or anything

This meant that Germany's submarines would attack all foreign cargo ships to stop supplies from getting to Britain. When Germany sank some U.S. ships, President Wilson declared war on Germany and joined the Allies.

Germany Surrenders

By 1918, the Allies had stopped supplies from going to Germany, where people were starving because there was so little food. By October, the Allies had defeated Bulgaria and Turkey. In November, Germany asked the Allies for an armistice. They signed an armistice on November 11, 1918. After more than four years, the war finally ended. Germany surrendered and a peace treaty was signed on June 28, 1919.

After the War

With the end of World War I, the map of Europe changed. Some countries, such as Germany, had to give up land. Other countries, such as Greece, gained land. Austria-Hungary and the Ottoman Empire were broken up into separate countries.

More than 65 million soldiers fought in the war, of whom more than half were killed or injured—8 million killed, 2 million dead of illness and diseases, 21 million wounded, and nearly 8 million taken prisoner or missing. More than 6 million civilians died, too. People hoped it would be the "war to end all wars," but it wasn't. World War II followed only twenty-one years later.

▲ U.S. president Woodrow Wilson

Country	Soldiers Killed
Germany	1,773,700
Russia	1,700,000
France	1,357,800
Austria-Hungary	1,200,000
British Empire	908,371
United States	116,516
Serbia	45,000

Before You Go On

1. What was hard about life in the trenches?
2. Why did the United States decide to enter the war?

On Your Own

From what you read and know about wars, how do they affect civilians?

Reading 1

> Reading 1

Review and Practice

Comprehension 📖 157

Recall
1. Which six countries formed powerful alliances at the outset of the war?
2. Before the United States joined them in 1917, which countries were part of the Allies? Which countries made up the Central Powers and fought against the Allies?

Comprehend
3. What events led to Germany's surrender?
4. How did Europe change as a result of World War I?

Analyze
5. How do wars affect relationships among countries? Do wars resolve conflicts? Was World War I the "war to end all wars"?
6. Looking back on World War I, what could have been done to prevent it? Explain.

Connect
7. In some parts of the world, young men and women are required to serve in the armed forces for a certain period of time. What's your opinion of this requirement? Do you think it is fair? Why or why not?
8. Do you think warfare should be subject to rules or codes of behavior? Why or why not?

In Your Own Words

Work with a partner. Use a cause and effect chart like the one below to discuss the key events of World War I.

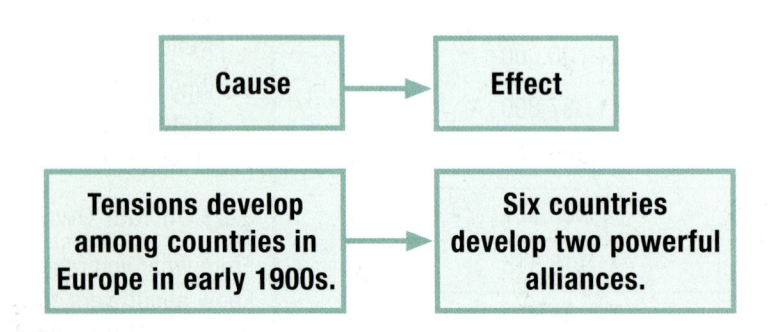

Cause → Effect

Tensions develop among countries in Europe in early 1900s. → Six countries develop two powerful alliances.

> **Speaking Tip**
> Read your charts several times before you begin speaking so that you don't have to refer to them often. Self-correct as necessary.

310 Unit 5

Discussion

Discuss with a partner or in a small group.

- Why do you think the U.S. tried to remain neutral? Do you think the war would have had a different outcome if the U.S. had not entered it? What factors might have prevented the war? Explain.

What can we learn from times of war? World War II was declared just twenty-one years after World War I ended. Why do you think this was so? Why do you think the countries involved did not learn from the mistakes they made in the First World War?

Read for Fluency

It is often easier to read a text if you understand the difficult words and phrases. Work with a partner. Choose a paragraph from the reading. Identify the words and phrases you do not know or have trouble pronouncing. Look up the difficult words in a dictionary.

Take turns pronouncing the words and phrases with your partner. Then, take turns reading the paragraph aloud and giving each other feedback.

Extension

WB 157

Work in small groups. Compare the map with the map on page 300. Which countries gained land as a result of World War I? Which countries lost land? Which countries are new? Share your ideas with other groups.

▶ Europe in 1919, after World War I

Listening Tip

If you don't understand a classmate's comment, ask him or her to clarify it for you.

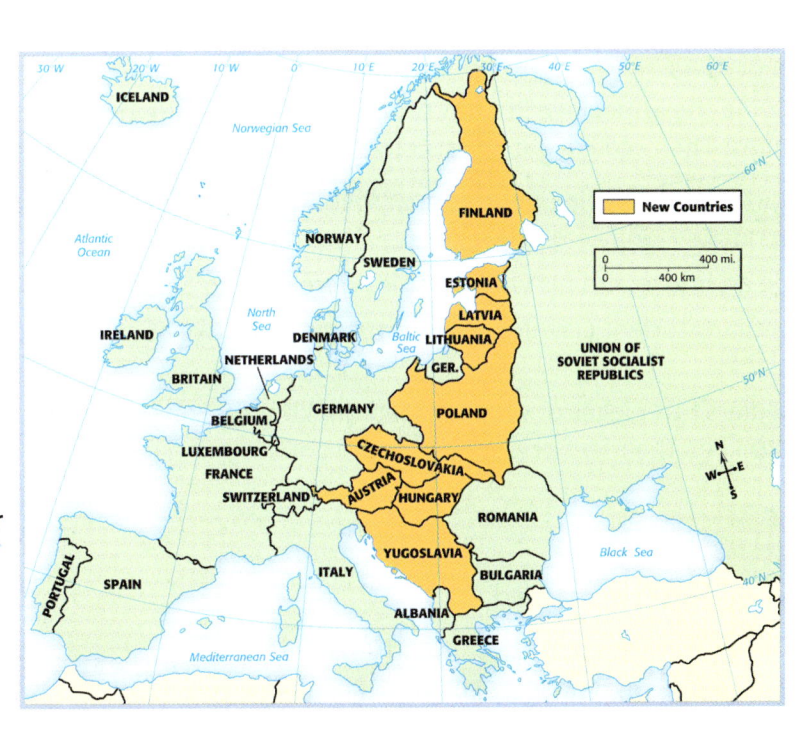

Reading 1 **311**

> Reading 1
># Grammar

Appositives

An appositive is a noun or noun phrase that defines or identifies another noun. An appositive immediately follows the noun it defines.

> Archduke Franz Ferdinand, **the nephew of the emperor of Austria-Hungary and heir to the throne**, visited Sarajevo, **the capital of Bosnia and Herzegovina**.
> [appositives define or identify *Archduke Franz Ferdinand* and *Sarajevo*]

A restrictive appositive is essential to the noun it identifies; a nonrestrictive appositive is not essential information and, when it is omitted, the sentence can still be understood.

Restrictive—do not use commas	The country **Serbia** was with the Allies. [There is more than one country. The information, *Serbia*, is essential.]
Nonrestrictive—use comma(s)	Ferdinand died in the capital of Bosnia and Herzegovina, **Sarajevo**. [There is only one capital of Bosnia and Herzegovina. The information, *Sarajevo*, is not essential.]

Grammar Skill

Restrictive appositives are similar to restrictive adjective clauses. Nonrestrictive appositives are similar to nonrestrictive adjective clauses.

Grammar Check

✓ When are commas used with **appositives**?

Practice A
WB 158

Underline the appositive in each sentence and circle the noun it identifies. Then write *R* if it is restrictive and *N* if it is nonrestrictive.

1. (World War I), the first modern war, began with the assassination of Archduke Franz Ferdinand. __N__
2. The archduke and his wife, Sophie, were visiting Sarajevo. _____
3. Bosnian student Gavrilo Princip shot the archduke at close range. _____
4. Soldiers put pieces of wood, called duckboards, on the ground to help keep their feet dry. _____

Practice B

Add commas where needed.

1. I saw a movie with my best friend Ana.
2. We watched the movie *The Hunger Games* on TV.
3. Jennifer Lawrence the actress who plays Katniss was in that movie.
4. Novelist Suzanne Collins wrote the original novel *The Hunger Games*.

Apply

Work with a partner. Make sentences about the teachers in your school. Use appositives.

Example: *Our math teacher, Ms. Lopez, gives difficult tests.*

Prepositions of Time: *in, on, at, by, before,* and *until*

The prepositions *in*, *on*, and *at* can be used to show a point in time. A preposition is followed by a noun or noun phrase. Together, this group of words makes up a prepositional phrase. A prepositional phrase of time can appear at the beginning or at the end of a sentence. When it begins a sentence, it is followed by a comma.

Grammar Skill

Use *until* to talk about an action that continues up to a point in time. Use *by* to mean at or before that point in time.

We use the prepositions *in*, *on*, and *at* in these ways.

at + specific time or time of day	at noon; at 5:00 p.m., at night
on + specific day or date	on Monday; on June 18, 1919
in + specific month, year, or time of day	in June; in 1919; in the evening

The prepositions *by, before,* and *until* have similar meanings. Notice the differences in these sentences.

Sentence	Meaning
You must be back in class **by 1:00**.	The latest you can return to class is 1:00.
You must be back in class **before 1:00**.	The latest you can return to class is 12:59.
You have a lunch break **until 1:00**.	Your lunch break is over at 1:00.

Grammar Check

✓ Which **preposition of time** do you use to talk about a birth date?

Practice A

WB 159

Circle the correct preposition to complete each sentence.

1. The soccer game is **at** / **in** /**(on)** Sunday.
2. It will probably be over **at** / **in** / **on** 4:00 p.m.
3. I can stay out **by** / **before** / **until** 9:00 p.m. on the weekend.

Practice B

Complete the sentence with a preposition of time from the box.

in	at	~~before~~	until

1. I leave the house _before_ 8:00 a.m. every day.
2. Our classes are in session _____ the end of June.
3. The corner store closes _____ 11:00 p.m.
4. I like to go to the beach _____ the summer.

Apply

Work with a partner. Discuss your usual weekend activities. Use different prepositions of time.

Example: On Saturday, I usually sleep until ten.

Reading 1

Reading 1

Writing

Write a Cause and Effect Paragraph

At the end of this unit, you will write an expository essay. To do this, you'll need to learn some of the skills writers use in expository writing.

There are many ways to organize ideas in an expository paragraph. One of these is by cause and effect. In such a paragraph, you explain the causes and effects of an event or you discuss a topic in terms of cause and effect. For example, a cause and effect paragraph about World War I might list the events that led up to the war. It might also discuss the consequences of the war. The paragraph should clearly show relationships among causes and effects.

> **Writing Prompt**
>
> Write a cause and effect paragraph. You might write about a problem in your community (such as pollution) or a conflict you learned about in social studies. Use signal words such as *because* to show cause-and-effect relationships. Be sure to use appositives and prepositions of time correctly.

① Prewrite Choose a problem or conflict.
WB 160

- Think about the problem or conflict you chose and its causes.
- List three causes in a graphic organizer.
- Arrange the causes in order.

Here is a graphic organizer created by a student named Andrea about the events leading up to World War I and their effect.

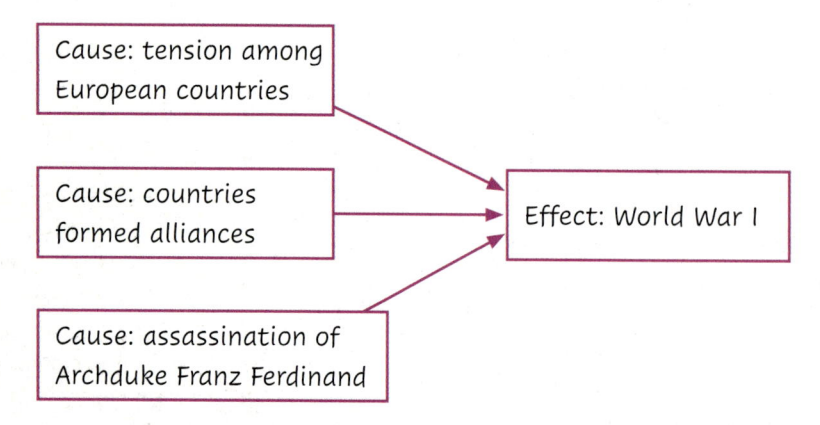

Cause: tension among European countries	→	
Cause: countries formed alliances	→	Effect: World War I
Cause: assassination of Archduke Franz Ferdinand	→	

314 Unit 5

2) Draft Use your organizer to help you write a first draft.

- Remember to state cause and effect relationships clearly.
- Use words and phrases, such as *first, then, finally, because,* and *effect* to signal cause-and-effect relationships.
- Be sure to use appositives and prepositions of time correctly.

3) Revise Read over your draft. Look for places where the writing is unclear or needs improvement. Complete (✓) the Writing Checklist to help you identify problems. Then, revise your draft, using the editing and proofreading marks listed on page 467.

4) Edit and Proofread Check your work for errors in grammar, usage, mechanics, and spelling. Trade papers with a partner to obtain feedback. Use the Peer Review Checklist on Workbook page 160. Edit your final draft in response to feedback from your partner and your teacher.

5) Publish Prepare a clean copy of your final draft. Share your cause and effect paragraphs with the class. Save your work. You'll need to refer to it in the Writing Workshop at the end of the unit.

Here is Andrea's cause and effect paragraph.

> **Writing Checklist**
>
> **Ideas:**
> ☐ I explained the problem or conflict and its causes clearly.
>
> **Sentence Fluency:**
> ☐ I used a variety of sentence lengths and patterns.
>
> **Conventions:**
> ☐ I used prepositions of time and appositives correctly.

Andrea Vargas

World War I

World War I had many causes. First, there was great tension among European countries in the nineteenth century. Each country wanted more power than its neighbor. Countries with similar interests formed alliances. Britain, France, and Russia formed the Allied Powers, while Germany, Austria-Hungary, and Italy formed the Central Powers. This added to the tension. The war finally started after the assassination of Archduke Franz Ferdinand, the nephew of the emperor of Austria-Hungary, on June 28, 1914. The United States was neutral until 1917, when Germany attacked U.S. cargo ships heading to Britain. Then the United States was forced to fight. The war lasted until 1918. About 10 million soldiers and 6 million civilians died. It was more destructive than previous wars because factories could produce deadlier weapons more quickly than ever. The war's effect on Europe was devastating.

Reading 2

Prepare to Read

What You Will Learn

Reading
- Vocabulary building: *Literary terms, word study*
- Reading strategy: *Recognize historical context*
- Text type: *Literature (poetry, song, prose)*

Grammar
- Contrast
- Pronouns and antecedents

Writing
- Write to compare and contrast

THE BIG QUESTION

What can we learn from times of war? The works you are about to read were written during World War I. Times of war are always highly emotional. People have to cope with feelings of anger, sadness, and loss. During wartime, writers and other artists can be especially productive or vocal. Talk with a partner about the kinds of feelings that wars bring out in people. Why might times of war also be times of great artistic achievement?

Build Background

This reading includes two poems, part of a song, and a personal letter. The poems are both about the deaths of World War I soldiers. **"In Flanders Fields"** was written by Lieutenant Colonel John McCrae, a Canadian doctor who worked as a surgeon on the battlefield. He wrote the poem for a friend who died in battle. McCrae himself died of pneumonia while on active duty in 1918.

The English poet Wilfred Owen wrote the second poem, **"Anthem for Doomed Youth."** Owen was one of the most famous World War I poets. He died one week before the war ended. Three musicians recorded the song **"Three Wonderful Letters from Home"** in 1918 in New York City. **"Letter Home"** was written by a young British journalist, Frank Earley, from the front.

▲ American soldiers writing letters in 1918

Vocabulary

Learn Literary Words

> **Literary Words**
> extended metaphor
> figurative language
> personification

Figurative language adds layers of meaning to the literal meanings of words. It is language that the reader isn't supposed to take literally. Authors, like poets, use it to help readers visualize what's happening or identify feelings. One type of figurative language is metaphorical language.

A metaphor is a figure of speech in which one thing is spoken of as though it were something else. Metaphors do not use connecting words, such as *like* or *as*. An **extended metaphor** continues the comparison throughout a poem.

Another form of figurative language is **personification**. This is used to give human qualities to something not human—for effect. Look at these examples from the poem "Arms and the Boy," by Wilfred Owen.

> Let the boy try along this bayonet-blade
> How cold steel is, and keen with hunger of blood;

> Lend him to stroke these blind, blunt bullet-leads,
> Which long to nuzzle in the hearts of lads,

How is the bayonet, personified? In the context of war, what do you think this means? How are the bullets personified? Notice how the poet says they are "blind" and "long to nuzzle in the hearts of" young men. The poet uses this language to show what he feels about war: bullets kill without distinguishing their victims.

Practice

Work with a partner. Circle the examples of figurative language in this excerpt from a poem by Emily Dickinson, "Autumn." Of these examples, which ones are also examples of personification? Explain.

> The morns are meeker than they were,
>   The nuts are getting brown;
> The berry's cheek is plumper,
>   The rose is out of town.
> The maple wears a gayer scarf,
>   The field a scarlet gown.
> Lest I be old-fashioned,
>   I'll put a trinket on.

Reading 2

Listening and Speaking: Academic Words

Study the **purple** words and their meanings. You will find these words useful when talking and writing about literature. Write each word and its meaning in your notebook, then say the words aloud with a partner. After you read the poems, song, and letter, try to use these words to respond to the texts.

Academic Words
- context
- create
- impact
- similar

context = situation and conditions which surround something	The reader must know the **context** of these poems—World War I—in order to appreciate them fully.
create = make	Sometimes, wars **create** new job opportunities for people.
impact = the effect that an event or situation has on someone or something	A war in the Middle East may have an **impact** on gas prices around the world.
similar = almost the same	The two poems express **similar** ideas—they both discuss the terrible experiences soldiers have during war.

Practice

WB 162

Choose a **purple** word from the box above to complete each sentence. Then take turns reading the sentences aloud with a partner.

1. The two countries became allies because they had _____ beliefs and ideas.
2. Writers and other artists sometimes _____ works of art as a way of dealing with pain and loss.
3. After we read about the events, we began to understand them in the _____ of the times.
4. The change in leadership of the small country had an _____ felt throughout the world.

▲ World War I had a huge impact on the United Kingdom.

318 Unit 5

Word Study: Homophones

A homophone is a word that sounds the same as another word, but has a different meaning and usually a different spelling. Words such as *sea* and *see* or *rose* (the flower) and *rose* (the verb) are homophones. To figure out which word is being used, read the word in context or check its spelling. If you still do not know which word is correct, check a dictionary.

Word	Part of speech	Meaning
real	adjective	actually existing and not just imagined
reel	noun	a round object onto which things such as film or special string for fishing can be wound

Practice

Work with a partner. Find at least one word from the homophones below in the poems, song, or letter. Try to figure out the meaning of the words through context. Then use a dictionary to check the meaning and to find the meaning of the other words. Write sentences using the other words.

here/hear	one/won	their/they're/there	weight/wait
hour/our	son/sun	through/threw	write/right

Reading Strategy: Recognize Historical Context

Recognizing the historical context of a work of literature can make it more meaningful and easier to understand. A work's historical context refers to the time period in which it was written and what was happening then. To recognize historical context, follow these steps:

- Use what you already know about the time period in which or about which a work was written.
- Look for references to events or situations from that time period.
- Think about how the time period affected the writer and what the writer writes about.

As you read the poems, the song, and the letter, think about how World War I affected the writers and their work. Think about how knowing what was going on at a particular period of time affects your feelings about what you are reading.

Reading 2

Literature
Poetry, Song, Prose

Set a purpose for reading Read these works written during World War I. How did the writers of each work respond to the horrors of war in their own way?

In Flanders Fields

In Flanders fields the **poppies** blow
Between the crosses row on row,
   That mark our place; and in the sky
   The larks, still bravely singing, fly
Scarce heard amid the guns below.

We are the Dead. Short days ago
We lived, felt dawn, saw sunset glow,
   Loved and were loved, and now we lie
      In Flanders fields.

Take up our **quarrel** with the **foe**:
To you from failing hands we throw
   The torch; be yours to hold it high.
   If ye break faith with us who die
We shall not sleep, though poppies grow
      In Flanders fields.

—*John McCrae, MD (1872–1918)*
Lieutenant Colonel in the Canadian Army

---

poppies, bright red flowers
quarrel, complaint
foe, enemy

> ✓ **LITERARY CHECK**
>
> What is the **figurative** meaning of "we throw the torch"?

About the Poet

John McCrae was born in Canada in 1872. He wrote "In Flanders Fields," perhaps the most famous World War I poem ever written, in 1915 while working as a medical officer in Belgium. Shortly after, he was transferred to France to run a hospital. There he died of pneumonia in 1918.

Anthem for Doomed Youth

What passing-bells for these who die as cattle?
   Only the monstrous anger of the guns.
   Only the **stuttering** rifles' rapid rattle
Can patter out their hasty **orisons**.
No mockeries for them; no prayers nor bells,
Nor any voice of mourning save the choirs,—
The shrill, **demented** choirs of wailing **shells**;
And bugles calling for them from sad shires.

What candles may be held to speed them all?
   Not in the hands of boys, but in their eyes
Shall shine the holy glimmers of goodbyes.
   The **pallor** of girls' brows shall be their **pall**;
Their flowers the tenderness of patient minds,
And each slow dusk a drawing-down of blinds.
        —Wilfred Owen (1893–1918)

---

stuttering, repeating the same sound
orisons, prayers
demented, insane
shells, cartridges fired from a shotgun
pallor, unnatural paleness
pall, burial garment

> ✓ **LITERARY CHECK**
> Identify two examples of **personification** in the poem.

> ✓ **LITERARY CHECK**
> How does the poet use an **extended metaphor**, or comparison, to describe the "services" for the soldiers?

About the Poet

Wilfred Owen was born in 1893. After visiting a military hospital, he decided to join the French Army and fight in World War I. Horrified by what he saw, he began writing poetry. Most of his poems are observations about the tragedy of war. In 1918, he was killed in battle.

Before You Go On

1. Who is the "we" in the poem "In Flanders Fields"?
2. Considering that an anthem can be sung by a choir in a church, what is the irony of the title of the poem "Anthem for Doomed Youth"?

On Your Own

Which poem better expresses your feelings about war? Explain.

Three Wonderful Letters from Home

Words by Joe Goodwin and Ballard MacDonald
Music by James F. Hanley

First Verse

Three letters left a village bound for
   somewhere over there,
Three letters to a lonesome soldier lad.
Each one a loving story told;
Each one was worth its weight in gold—
Three messages that made his poor heart glad:

Chorus (once after each verse)

For the first was just old fashioned,
And it breathed a mother's prayer.
While the next one started "Darling,
God protect you over there."
And the third was filled with kisses,
Sent to Daddy **'cross the foam**—
From his mother, wife and baby,
Three wonderful letters from home.

Second Verse

Each word was like a soft **caress** that
soothed his aching heart,
And drove away the **misery** and the pain.
Then joy returned to take their place
And brought a vision of each face,
As o'er and o'er he read their words again:

'cross the foam, across the sea
caress, gentle touch
misery, sadness

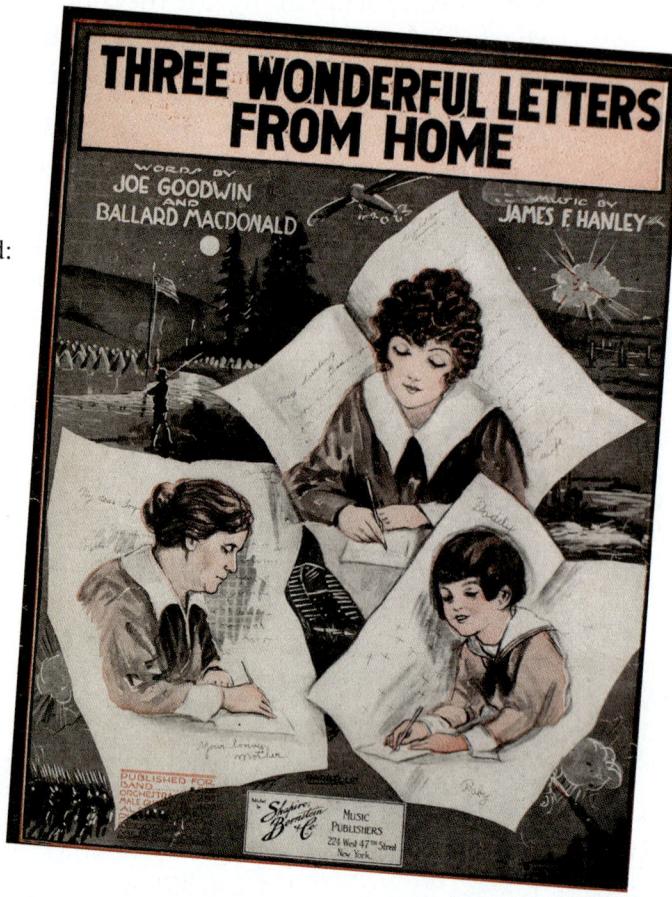

About the Songwriters

Songwriters Joe Goodwin and Ballard MacDonald wrote this song, and James F. Hanley, a lyricist, composed it. The song reached number 13 on the music charts in June 1918.

✓ LITERARY CHECK

How is "each word was like a soft caress" an example of **figurative language**?

Letter Home

**Sunday afternoon,
1st September, 1918**

My dear Father,

It is a strange feeling to me but a very real one, that every letter now that I write home to you or to the little sisters may be the last that I shall write or you read. I do not want you to think that I am **depressed**; indeed on the contrary, I am very cheerful. But out here, in odd moments the realization comes to me of how close death is to us. A week ago I was talking with a man . . . who had been out here for nearly four years, untouched. He was looking forward with certainty to **going on leave** soon. And now he is dead—killed in a moment during our last advance. Well, it was God's will.

I say this to you because I hope that you will realize, as I do, the possibility of the like happening to myself. I feel very glad myself that I can look the fact in the face without fear or **misgiving**. Much as I hope to live through it all for your sakes and my little sisters'! I am quite prepared to give my life as so many have done before me. All I can do is put myself in God's hands for him to decide, and you and the little ones pray for me to the Sacred Heart and Our Lady. . . .

Well, I have not much time left and I must end. With my dear love.
Pray for me.

Your son,
Frank

---

depressed, sad
going on leave, taking time off from active duty
misgiving, doubt or negative feeling about the future

About the Author

Frank Earley was a British journalist. His letters home were usually full of cheer. It is only in this last letter that he sounds thoughtful. The day after Earley wrote this letter, he suffered a wound to the chest and died. He was nineteen years old.

Reading Skill

Listen to the way your teacher reads this text. Listen to the way words are pronounced and think about what they mean. Ask your teacher to explain difficult ideas or words.

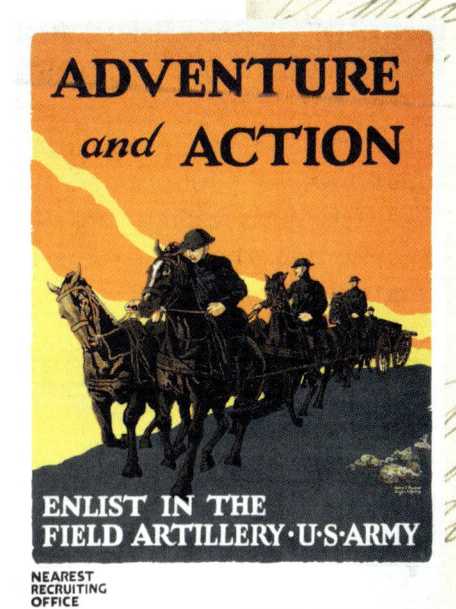

Before You Go On

1. Why do you think the songwriters wrote a song about three kinds of letters soldiers receive from home?
2. From his letter and what you know about the author Frank Earley, what is ironic about his letter home?

On Your Own

Why do you think these works are especially moving messages about war?

Reading 2

Review and Practice

Dramatic Reading

One of the best ways to appreciate a poem is to read it aloud, with feeling. Work in small groups of two or three to read the poems on pages 320–321. For "In Flanders Fields," decide who will read the first, the second, and the third stanzas. For "Anthem for Doomed Youth," decide who will read the first and second stanzas.

Read your stanza to your partner or group and talk about it. What feelings does it create? Underline words you want your listeners to notice. How will you say the words to show feelings? Practice reading your stanza. Ask your partner or group for feedback. When you are ready, take turns reading your stanzas aloud with your partner or in your group. Then, take turns, in your groups, reading the poems aloud to the class.

> **Speaking Tip**
>
> Let the punctuation in the poem guide you as you read aloud. A period, dash, semicolon, or comma is a signal to pause.

Comprehension

Recall

1. What are the choirs in Owen's poem?
2. What is the strange feeling Frank Earley talks about in his letter?

Comprehend

3. What do the rows of crosses in Flanders Fields mark?
4. What is the effect of the two questions Owen asks in his poem? How do they help his comparison?

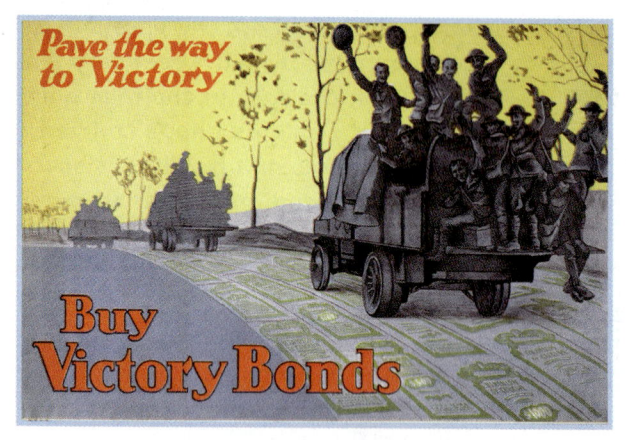

Analyze

5. Which poem expresses a bleaker attitude? Explain.
6. Which letter or description of it in the song affected you the most? Why?

Connect

7. Why do you think the individuals wrote the works they did about the war? Which one do you think would have had the greatest impact on a soldier fighting in the war?
8. Which work do you think is the most effective vehicle to use to convey feelings about the war? Why?

▲ This poster advertises Victory Bonds. How is it connected to the poems you have read?

324 Unit 5

Discussion

Discuss with a partner or in a small group.

1. Why do you think flowers are mentioned in both poems? What other images are effective in the poems? Why?
2. Of the three genres included in this reading, the song is the only one that does not focus on death. Why do you think this is so?
3. How could you use the works to persuade people that war is not the answer? Which one would you focus on? Why?

What can we learn from times of war? Which work do you think had the strongest message about the horrors of war? Which would you recommend if you could only use one for people to read to better understand the effects of World War I? Why?

Listening Tip

Give speakers time to express their ideas. When there is a pause, give your viewpoint.

Response to Literature

WB 165

Choose one of the three kinds of letters mentioned in "Three Wonderful Letters from Home." Imagine you are the mother, wife, or baby (young child) and write a letter to your son, husband, or father. What will you say? How can you comfort your loved one? Use the other works, as well as the article you read about the war, for details to help you. Share your letters by taking turns reading them aloud to the class.

▼ American troops using French tanks during World War I

Reading 2
Grammar

Contrast

Writers often contrast things, or to show how they are different by using signal words. Notice that the conjunctions *but* and *yet* usually follow a comma, and the transitions *however* and *on the contrary* usually follow a period or semicolon.

Coordinating conjunctions (but, yet)	I am very cheerful, **but** sometimes I realize how close death is.
Transitions (however, on the contrary)	I am very cheerful. **However**, sometimes I realize how close death is. I am very cheerful; **however**, sometimes I realize how close death is.

> **Grammar Skill**
>
> Use *on the contrary* to emphasize a distinct difference.
> **Example:** *This soup isn't salty. On the contrary, it's quite sweet.*

Compare things, or show how they are similar, by using the conjunction *and* on its own or with the signal word *both* to link people, places, objects, or ideas that are alike in some way.

Coordinating conjunctions (and; both … and; and … both)	The song **and** the letter are about soldiers. **Both** the song **and** the letter are about soldiers. The song **and** the letter are **both** about soldiers.

> **Grammar Check**
>
> ✓ Which **contrast signal words** follow commas? Which follow periods and semicolons?

Practice A

Circle the correct signal word in each sentence.

1. I am smart, **yet** / **on the contrary** sometimes I make mistakes.
2. The movie and the book are **yet** / **both** really good.
3. Both Ana **but** / **and** Maria are really tall.

Practice B

In your notebook, rewrite the sentences below using the signal word(s) in parentheses. Adjust the punctuation as needed.

1. A poem is spoken, but a song is sung. (however)
2. I may seem shy at first. However, I actually am very outgoing. (but)
3. He studied hard; however, he did not pass the test. (yet)

> **Apply**
>
> Work with a partner. Identify two people in your family. Use different signal words to compare and contrast them.
>
> **Example:** *Both my mother and my father are hardworking. However . . .*

Pronouns and Antecedents

An antecedent is the word, phrase, or clause that a pronoun refers to. All pronouns must agree in number (singular or plural) and gender (masculine, feminine, or neutral) with their antecedents.

Look at these examples from the poems you read. The boldfaced pronouns refer to the antecedents before them.

> Sent to Daddy 'cross the foam—from **his** mother, wife, and baby
> The torch; be yours to hold **it** high.

Grammar Skill
With a singular noun, use a singular pronoun. With a plural noun, use a plural pronoun.

Review the position of different kinds of pronouns and adjectives on this chart. Make sure you use them correctly.

Subject Pronouns	I, we, you, he, she, it, they	**I** have a book.
Object Pronouns	me, us, you, him, her, it, them	Give the book to **me**.
Possessive Adjectives	my, our, your, his, her, its, their	It is **my** book.
Possessive Pronouns	mine, yours, hers, his, ours, yours, theirs	The book is **mine**.

Grammar Check
✓ How do **pronouns** agree with their **antecedents**?

Practice A

Underline the pronoun(s) and possessive adjective(s) and circle their antecedents.

1. The students left their coats in the closet.
2. Dan has his bag, but Jill doesn't have hers.
3. Kate and Jenn came to my concert, but I didn't see them.
4. The children made their teacher very upset with them.

Practice B

Circle the correct pronoun or possessive adjective to complete each sentence. Then, underline the antecedent.

1. I had lunch with my brother. I enjoyed having lunch with **he** / **him** / **his**.
2. My sister bought a new coat. **Her** / **She** / **Hers** coat is too small.
3. I don't need a new coat. **Mine** / **My** / **Me** still fits.
4. I really like **you** / **your** / **yours** coat. It looks great!

Apply
Write four sentences describing someone in your family. Then tell a partner about him or her.
Example: *My father is an accountant. His office is . . .*

Reading 2

Writing

Write to Compare and Contrast

At the end of this unit, you will write an expository essay. To do this, you'll need to learn how writers develop expository writing. When you compare, you tell how two people, places, things, or ideas are alike. When you contrast, you tell how they are different. One way to organize ideas in compare-and-contrast writing is to compare in and then contrast.

> **Writing Prompt**
>
> Write a paragraph that compares and contrasts two books, stories, or other works. Remember to show how the two works are alike and how they are different. Be sure to use words that signal contrast correctly.

1 Prewrite Identify two works to compare and contrast.

- Think of all the ways they are similar and different.
- Which ideas are similar about both? Which ideas show how the works are different?
- List your ideas on a Venn diagram like the one below.

Here's a Venn diagram created by a student named Jessica to contrast the song and the letter.

Three Wonderful Letters Home:
—song
—written in third person
—about an imaginary soldier
—sentimental, hopeful tone

Both:
—about a soldier's loneliness
—written during WWI
—written to cheer people up

Letter Home:
—personal letter
—written in first person
—about a real soldier
—thoughtful, somber tone

② Draft Use your Venn diagram to help you write a first draft.
- Begin by writing about the similarities of the two works.
- Then write about the differences.
- Use signal words to show how the two works are similar and different.

③ Revise Read over your draft. Look for places where the writing is unclear or needs improvement. Complete (✓) the Writing Checklist to help you identify problems. Then, revise your draft, using the editing and proofreading marks listed on page 467.

④ Edit and Proofread Check your work for errors in grammar, usage, mechanics, and spelling. Trade papers with a partner to obtain feedback. Use the Peer Review Checklist on Workbook page 168. Edit your final draft in response to feedback from your partner and your teacher.

⑤ Publish Prepare a clean copy of your final draft. Share your compare and contrast paragraph with the class. Save your work. You'll need to refer to it in the Writing Workshop at the end of the unit. Notice how she first shows how the song and letter are similar and then describes how they are different.

Here is Jessica's compare and contrast paragraph.

> **Writing Checklist**
>
> **Organization:**
> ☐ My paragraph describes the similarities and differences between two works.
>
> **Word Choice:**
> ☐ I used words such as *both* to signal similarities and words such as *however* to signal differences.
>
> **Conventions:**
> ☐ I used words to signal contrast correctly.

Jessica Reider

Letters to and from Home

"Three Wonderful Letters from Home" and "Letter Home" are both about the loneliness soldiers experience during war and the ones they left back home. The song and the letter are both written during the same time period—World War I. They also are similar in purpose: The song was written to lift soldiers' spirits, and the letter was written to cheer up loved ones at home. However, the point of view is different in the two pieces. "Three Wonderful Letters from Home" is written in the third person about an imaginary soldier, while "Letter Home" is written in the first person, by an actual soldier to his family members. The two pieces also have very different tones. The song is sentimental and hopeful, but the letter has a thoughtful, somber tone.

Reading 3

Prepare to Read

What You Will Learn

Reading
- Vocabulary building: *Context, dictionary skills, word study*
- Reading strategy: *Draw conclusions*
- Text type: *Informational text (social studies)*

Grammar
- Passive
- Using quotations

Writing
- Write a news article

THE BIG QUESTION

What can we learn from times of war? Think about heroes you have read about. What did they do that was heroic? What risks did they take? How does war bring out the worst and the best in people? Discuss with a partner.

Complete this KWLH chart about what you know and want to know about World War II. When you have completed Reading 3, fill in what you learned and how you learned it.

K What do I **know**?	W What do I **want** to know?	L What did I **learn**?	H **How** did I learn it?

Build Background

"In the Name of His Father" is a news article about a man named Chiune (chee-YOO-nay) Sugihara. During World War II, Sugihara lived in Lithuania and worked as a diplomat for Japan. At that time, the German dictator, Adolf Hitler, directed a major effort to kill the Jewish people of Europe. Hitler's soldiers forced Jews to live in places called concentration camps, where they were treated cruelly and, in many cases, killed.

Sugihara knew what was happening. He found a way to help Jewish refugees and, in doing so, risked his own life. Sugihara saved the lives of thousands of people and has come to be considered a hero. Hitler was eventually defeated and World War II ended in 1945, but not before more than 6 million innocent Jewish people died.

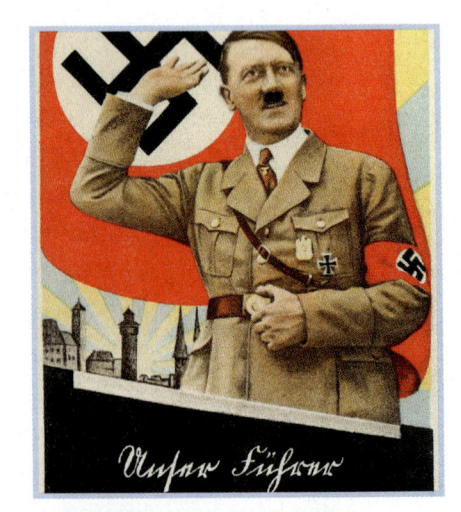

▲ German poster of Adolf Hitler, 1930s

330 Unit 5

Vocabulary

Listening and Speaking: Key Words

Read these sentences aloud with a partner. Use the context to figure out the meaning of the highlighted words. Use a dictionary, the glossary, or a thesaurus to determine or confirm your answers. Then write each word and its meaning in your notebook.

Key Words
consulate
diplomat
heroism
honor
lecture
refugees

1. Some of the government workers who represent the United States in Italy work at the consulate in Milan.
2. The diplomat from the United States represented the views of his country at the meeting with other countries in Germany.
3. The soldiers showed great heroism when they rescued the children in the village.
4. They honor people for brave deeds by awarding them a medal.
5. During the lecture, the professor told his class about great heroes of World War II.
6. The people who live in a country at war often lose their homes and become refugees who must move to a new place.

Practice

Choose a word from the box above to complete each sentence. Then take turns reading the sentences aloud with a partner.

1. My family helped the _____ who arrived here after escaping from the war in their home country.
2. My father is going to work for the government at the _____ in Lyon, France.
3. The soldier gave a very interesting _____ about his experiences.
4. The _____ spoke on behalf of his country at the conference.
5. They are going to _____ a soldier by naming a park after him.
6. The woman showed true _____ when she helped her elderly neighbors escape the fire.

The Old District, Lyon, France

Reading 3

Listening and Speaking: Academic Words

Study the **purple** words and their meanings. You will find these words useful when talking and writing about informational texts. Write each word and its meaning in your notebook, then say the words aloud with a partner. After you read "In the Name of His Father," try to use these words to respond to the text.

Academic Words
- document
- estimate
- exploits
- integrity
- sympathetic

document = a piece of paper that has official information written on it	➡	Your birth certificate is an official **document** that you can use to get a passport.
estimate = guess the value, size, number, etc., of something	➡	They **estimate** that there will be thousands of refugees after the war.
exploits = brave and exciting actions	➡	My grandfather told us all about his **exploits** and adventures as a soldier during the war.
integrity = the quality of being honest and having high moral principles	➡	Her **integrity** was never in question, as she is always honest.
sympathetic = showing that you understand how sad, hurt, lonely, etc., someone feels	➡	We were **sympathetic** to the struggle of the refugees and wanted to help them in any way we could.

Practice
WB 170

Work with a partner to answer these questions.
Try to include the **purple** word in your answer. Write the sentences in your notebook.

1. What official **document** shows that a person is the citizen of a country?
2. What do you **estimate** is the world's population?
3. Name a hero or heroine you read about. What were his or her **exploits**?
4. How important is a friend's **integrity** to you?
5. When have you felt **sympathetic** toward a friend or family member?

▲ Passports, such as these, are needed to travel between countries.

Word Study: The Suffix -ness

A suffix is a letter or group of letters added to the end of a word. When you add a suffix to the end of a word, you often change the meaning and part of speech of the word. The suffix -ness can be added to an adjective to make a noun. Generally, adding the suffix -ness will not change the spelling of a word. However, if the word has two or more syllables and ends in y, such as happy, change the y to an i before adding -ness.

Adjective	+ ness = Noun
awkward	awkwardness
conscious	consciousness
happy	happiness
silly	silliness

Practice

Work with a partner. List the words in the box below in your notebook. Add -ness to the end of each word to make a new word. Then write a sentence with each new word, and read it aloud to your partner.

| empty | kind | lonely | strange | thick |

Reading Strategy: Draw Conclusions

When you draw conclusions, you use details from a text and your own experiences to figure out what is happening in the text or a point that is not stated. To draw a conclusion, follow these steps:

- When you are unsure about something, look for clues about meaning and take notes.
- Think about what you already know from your own or similar experiences.
- Draw a conclusion about what is happening in the text by considering the clues and what you already know.

As you read "In the Name of His Father," think about what life was like for Jewish people living in parts of war-torn Europe during World War II and about the kind of person Sugihara was and how he helped them.

Reading 3
Informational Text
Social Studies

Set a purpose for reading As you read this news article, think about what kind of person Chiune Sugihara was. Why did he risk his life to save thousands of people he didn't know?

In the Name of His Father

Fred Tasker

The Miami Herald
January 24, 2000

It's with a certain awkwardness that Hiroki Sugihara, 63, traveled the world to lecture about the heroic acts of his late father during World War II. It violated a cultural sense of modesty. "For a Japanese, it sounded like you were showing off," he said.

Yet he had to. Too few in the world were aware of that heroism, he believed. Too few knew what his father, Chiune Sugihara, "the Japanese **Schindler**," did in 1940 when, as a mid-ranking **diplomat** in Lithuania, against the orders of his own government, he wrote 6,000 exit visas to get desperate Polish Jews out of the way of the approaching Nazi Holocaust.

"Thanks to him, I'm alive," said George Borenstein, then a 36-year-old Polish Army soldier. Borenstein had fled to Lithuania after the Germans defeated the Polish Army. And he knew the German Army was killing Jews and the Soviet Army was sending such **refugees** to Siberia. "They were starving in Siberia. I lost a brother there. But [Sugihara] got me a visa. I got out."

Ousted from the foreign ministry after the war, Sugihara lived in **obscurity** for decades, selling light bulbs, then importing oil, until an Israeli diplomat in Tokyo, another of the refugees he saved, sought him out and set about making things right.

▲ Chiune Sugihara

Schindler, German man who saved the lives of 1,200 Jews during World War II

obscurity, the state of not being known

334 Unit 5

He was honored by the Israeli government as one of "the righteous among nations"—non-Jews who helped save Jews during the Holocaust. It's the same honor given German businessman Oskar Schindler and Swedish diplomat Raoul Wallenberg, whose efforts to save Jews from death at the hands of the Nazis are far better known.

Sugihara was the subject of an Oscar-winning documentary, and his family was given a heroism award from The Immortal Chaplains' Foundation.

Hiroki Sugihara remembered it well, even though he was not quite 4 when it happened. It was 1940. German troops invading Poland had expelled that country's Jews, and hundreds were huddled in the square in Kaunas, Lithuania, where his father's consulate stood, seeking permission to flee to any safe country that would take them. And the United States and Great Britain were **balking at** accepting new refugees.

"I asked my father why I couldn't go outside to play as usual," Sugihara said. "He told me it might be dangerous. The refugees were very **agitated**. I asked him what would happen to them, and he said they might be killed. I was concerned for the children, because some of them were my age. So I said, 'Why can't you help them?' And he said, 'I might.'"

---

balking at, refusing to
agitated, very nervous and upset

Before You Go On
1. Where did Sugihara work in 1940?
2. How did Sugihara help Polish Jews?

On Your Own
Did it surprise you that Sugihara lived in obscurity for decades? Why do you think that was so?

▲ Yukiko Sugihara

For seven fevered weeks that July and August, the elder Sugihara worked 20 hours a day, writing an estimated 6,000 to 10,000 exit visas for the refugees. Three times he wired his government for permission to write more; three times he was told to stop. He kept writing.

Even as he and his family boarded the train to leave Lithuania for Berlin on his government's orders, Sugihara kept writing visas, throwing them out the window to refugees running alongside. "We will never forget you," one of them called, according to one book on Sugihara's exploits.

With documentation, the refugees were able to travel across Russia, take the Siberian Express railway to Vladivostok and eventually reach Japan or other countries. There they were treated well during the war. Despite its alliance with Nazi Germany, [Japan] had little history of **anti-Semitism**.

"When there were shortages, the [Japanese] people even shared their food with them," said Anne Akabori, the Sacramento librarian who, in 1996, translated into English the book *Visas for 6,000 Lives*, written by Sugihara's wife, Yukiko.

As the war ended, Sugihara, then posted in Romania, was captured by the Soviets and sent to a concentration camp with his wife and son for 18 months. Arriving back in Japan in 1947, he approached the country's postwar foreign ministry, hoping for a sympathetic reception and perhaps even a new assignment. Instead, they demanded his **resignation**.

The world knew little of [Sugihara] until 1968, when Joshua Nisri, economic attaché to the Israeli Embassy in Tokyo, sought him out. Nisri was a Polish teen in 1940, one of the refugees Sugihara saved. Since then, Sugihara's story has been slowly **seeping into the world consciousness**.

In 1985, just a year before Sugihara died, the Israeli government honored him as "A Man of Justice of the Peoples of the World."

His story spread further after the fall of communism freed Lithuania and other Eastern European countries to express their true feelings. It was only in 1991, during a celebration of Lithuanian independence, that a **monument** was erected and a street named after Sugihara in Kaunas.

---

anti-Semitism, hatred of Jewish people
resignation, leaving his job permanently
seeping into the world consciousness, becoming known to the world
monument, large structure built to remind people of an important event or to honor a famous person

In 1996, Boston University religion Professor Hillel Levine published a book, *In Search of Sugihara* (The Free Press, $25), calling Sugihara's exploits braver even than those of Wallenberg and Schindler, both of whom also rescued thousands of Jews during the war.

Wallenberg was sent to Hungary by the Swedish government with its specific backing, Levine argued; Schindler had at least a partial economic motive, using the Jews he saved to work in his factories. Sugihara acted purely on principle, Levine said. Sugihara's story became better known in the United States after 1994, when the movie *Schindler's List* raised the world's interest in those who had helped Jewish refugees during the war. In 1997, a documentary about Sugihara, *Visas and Virtue*, by Chris Tashima and Chris Donahue, won an **Oscar** in the Live Action Short Category.

More recently, Sugihara was honored by the Holocaust Oral History Project and the Wiesenthal Museum of Tolerance in Los Angeles at a ceremony attended by *Schindler's List* filmmaker Steven Spielberg.

One of the first questions the younger Sugihara is asked during his lectures is why an **obedient** Japanese diplomat would take such a risk to himself and his family to help strangers.

Levine's book says survivors remember him as "the angel," a kind man who "treated them with respect, smiled at them and offered a cup of tea."

Said Akabori, the Sacramento librarian: "I believe it was deeply rooted in the Japanese spirit called 'bushido,' which means reaching the highest level of physical, mental, and spiritual **attainment**. When you think something is right you do it, without worrying about yourself." After all, she said, Sugihara's family is descended from Samurai, the ancient warrior **caste** to whom honor came before money or personal safety.

The younger Sugihara credited that explanation, saying, "When he was growing up, he was taught that code. You have to sacrifice yourself to help somebody else."

The elder Sugihara, in a speech in 1985, a year before he died, put it more simply: "It is the kind of sentiment anyone would have when he actually sees the refugees face to face, begging with tears in their eyes.

"He just cannot help but sympathize with them."

Oscar, film awards granted by the Academy of Motion Picture Arts and Sciences

---

obedient, rule-following
attainment, something you have succeeded in getting
caste, group of people who have a particular position in society

Before You Go On

1. What happened to Sugihara when he returned to Japan?
2. Why did Akabori use "bushido" to explain what Sugihara did?

On Your Own

What would you have done if Sugihara were your father? Explain.

Reading 3

Review and Practice

Comprehension

Recall

1. What did Chiune Sugihara do when he was ousted from the foreign ministry after the war?
2. What is the estimated number of Jewish refugees that Sugihara wrote exit visas for?

Comprehend

3. Why was Hiroki Sugihara hesitant about describing his father's heroic acts in his lectures?
4. How was his father finally honored?

Analyze

5. Why do you think the news reporter ended the article with quotes from a speech Chiune Sugihara gave?
6. Why do you think the newspaper ran this story so many years after the war?

Connect

7. Would you recommend this article to others to read? Why?
8. From what you learned in the article, how do you feel about the Sugihara family (mother, father, son) and each of their contributions to history? Explain.

In Your Own Words

The people whose lives Sugihara saved considered him a hero. Many, many years later, others recognized his heroism. Draw conclusions about Sugihara's life and personality based on what you have read or your own prior knowledge. Copy and complete the word web below to help you tell a partner about what Sugihara did and why you think he deserves to be honored.

Speaking Tip

Be sure to convey interest in your topic. Your enthusiasm will help to keep your audience engaged.

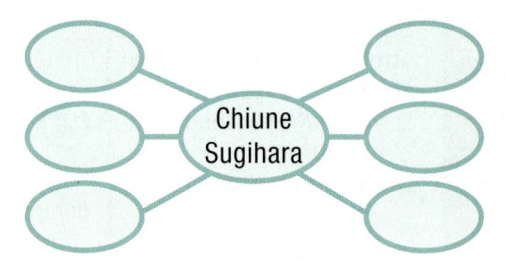

Discussion

Discuss with a partner or in a small group.

1. From what you learned in the article, do you agree with Hillel Levine that Sugihara's actions were "braver even than those of Wallenberg and Schindler"? Why or why not?
2. What is your position about Sugihara's being ousted from the foreign ministry? What would you say or do to try to change that decision? Why?

❓ **What can we learn from times of war?** Sugihara's acts of heroism were on a grand scale and affected many people. What defines an act of heroism? Can people commit "small" acts of heroism in their everyday lives? Explain.

Listening Tip

Be sure to let a speaker know when he or she makes an interesting point. You can say, "That's a good point," "I see what you mean," or "That makes sense."

Read for Fluency

Reading with feeling helps make what you read more interesting. Work with a partner. Choose and read a paragraph from the article silently, and think about the feelings it creates for you. Then take turns reading the paragraph aloud to each other, using a tone of voice that shows the feelings it created for you. Give each other feedback on the reading. Could you tell how each of you felt about what you read?

Extension

WB 173

Imagine you are reading this news article online. Work in small groups to write comments about the news article. Comment on others' ideas. Do research and add information. Input comments on a computer or list them. Here's an example:

What a great article. I had never heard of him before. I'm going to read his wife's book!
—Kim Lee

I hadn't, either. I'm going to find out more information about him and about his wife. Kim, are you reading the translation or his wife's book in Japanese? His wife was pretty amazing, too. —Tim G.

This statue in Nayoga, Aichi, Japan, commemorates the quiet valor of Chiune Sugihara. ▶

Reading 3
Grammar

Passive

Writers use the active form to focus on who or what does the action—the performer. They use the passive form to focus on whom or what the action happens to—the receiver.

> Active: The Soviets **captured** Sugihara at the end of the war.
> Passive: Sugihara **was captured** by the Soviets at the end of the war.

Grammar Skill

Active sentences that do not have a direct object cannot be changed into passive sentences.

In a sentence that uses a passive form, a phrase that begins with *by* identifies the performer of the action. The *by* phrase may be omitted if the performer is unknown or not as important as the receiver.

> A street **was named** after Sugihara in Kaunas, Lithuania.

The passive can be used with different verb forms.

Example	Verb Form	Pattern
Schindler and Wallenberg **are** far better **known**.	simple present	is/are + past participle
Finally, his story **is being told**.	present continuous	is/are + being + past participle
Now he **has been honored** by the Israeli government.	present perfect	have/has + been + past participle
Three times he **was told** to stop.	simple past	was/were + past participle

Grammar Check

✓ When do writers use the **passive**?

Practice A
WB 174

Underline the passive forms in these sentences.
1. "In the Name of His Father" <u>was written</u> by Fred Tasker.
2. *Schindler's List* was directed by Steven Spielberg.
3. The movie has been given awards by the Academy of Motion Picture Arts and Sciences.

Practice B

In your notebook, rewrite these active sentences as passive sentences. Use a *by*-phrase if necessary.
1. Cellin Gluck made a movie about Sugihara in 2015.
2. Film critics have highly praised the movie.
3. The police treated the refugees badly.

Apply

Work with a partner. Write four active sentences that include a direct object and that are about real or fictional heroes. Then change them into passive sentences.
Example: The tiny hero saved the world from the giant. The world was saved from the giant by the tiny hero.

340 Unit 5

Using Quotations

Writers use quotation marks to include another person's exact words in a text. Quotations from reliable sources can make writing more credible and interesting. They also provide strong supporting details for writers' ideas.

Example	Reason
The younger Sugihara credits that explanation: **"You have to sacrifice yourself to help somebody else."**	to show exactly what someone said or wrote
It violated a cultural sense of modesty. **"For a Japanese, it sounds like you are showing off,"** he said.	to support an idea in a previous phrase or statement
". . . people even shared their food with them," says Anne Akabori, . . .	to show the ideas are from a credible source

> **Grammar Skill**
>
> A comma or period at the end of a quotation goes inside the closing quotation marks.

Practice A

175

Match the word or phrase in quotation marks with the reason the writer used this form of punctuation.

1. "Thanks to him, I'm alive," said George Borenstein, . . . _____
2. The elder Sugihara put it more simply: "It is the kind of sentiment anyone would have when he actually sees the refugees face to face." _____
3. He was a kind man who "treated them with respect, smiled at them and offered a cup of tea." _____

a. to show exactly what someone said or wrote

b. to support an idea in a previous phrase

c. to show the ideas are from a credible source

> **Grammar Check**
>
> ✓ When do you use single **quotation marks**?

Practice B

Put quotation marks in the correct places in these sentences.

1. He has been called one of the righteous among nations.
2. I asked my father why I couldn't go outside to play as usual, Sugihara said.
3. We will never forget you, one of them called.

> **Apply**
>
> Work in small groups. Write a statement about someone heroic. Pass it to the student to your right. Then use quotation marks to quote what your classmate wrote. Read it to the group.
>
> **Example:** My grandfather is my hero. Jay wrote, "My grandfather is my hero."

Reading 3

Reading 3
Writing

Write a News Article

One kind of expository writing is a news article. An effective news article gives the reader information in a brief and interesting way. Your paragraph should answer as many of the 5Ws as possible. The 5Ws are the questions *Who?*, *What?*, *When?*, *Where?*, and *Why?*. Try to get the reader's attention with an interesting opening sentence.

> **Writing Prompt**
>
> Write a paragraph for a short news article about a class trip, a visit to a museum, or an issue that affects you at home or in school. Include an opening sentence that answers the 5Ws and gets the readers' attention. Add details that will keep readers interested. Be sure to use the passive correctly.

1 Prewrite Begin by thinking of an event or issue that would make a good news article.

- Ask yourself the 5W questions about the event or issue.
- List your answers in a graphic organizer such as a chart.

Here's a 5Ws chart created by a student named Nicholas. He is writing a news article about a class visit to Washington, DC, highlighting one famous memorial there.

Who	Mrs. Bell's social studies class
What	trip to war memorial
When	last Thursday and Friday
Where	Vietnam Veterans Memorial Washington, D.C
Why	to learn about the Vietnam Veterans Memorial

2 Draft Use your 5Ws chart to help you write a first draft.

- Remember to answer the 5W questions.
- Remember to include an opening sentence that will get the reader's attention.
- Be sure to include both active and passive sentences.

③ **Revise** Read over your draft. Look for places where the writing is unclear or needs improvement. Complete (✓) the Writing Checklist to help you identify problems. Then, revise your draft, using the editing and proofreading marks listed on page 467.

④ **Edit and Proofread** Check your work for errors in grammar, usage, mechanics, and spelling. Trade papers with a partner to obtain feedback. Use the Peer Review Checklist on Workbook page 176. Edit your final draft in response to feedback from your partner and your teacher.

⑤ **Publish** Prepare a clean copy of your final draft. Share your news article with the class. Save your work. You'll need to refer to it in the Writing Workshop at the end of the unit.

> **Writing Checklist**
>
> **Ideas:**
> ☐ I included information about the 5Ws in my opening sentence(s).
>
> **Sentence Fluency:**
> ☐ I used a variety of sentence lengths and patterns.
>
> **Conventions:**
> ☐ I used the passive correctly.

Here is Nicholas's news article. Notice his opening sentence and 5W questions it answers.

Nicholas Kasterine

Students Visit D.C.

April 13, 2019

While most of us finished an uneventful week, Mrs. Bell's social studies class spent last Thursday and Friday sightseeing in Washington, D.C. The class viewed many important sights, such as the Lincoln Memorial and the Washington Monument. By all reports, the trip's highlight was a visit to the Vietnam Veterans Memorial, which was built to honor the soldiers who died or went missing during the Vietnam conflict. The history of the memorial is noteworthy. In 1980, five years after the war ended, a contest was held for the memorial's design. Maya Ying Lin, only 20 years old, won with a simple idea—two huge black walls jutting out of the ground, forming a V shape. The names of the dead or missing men and women have been carved into the walls. The design sparked controversy at first because it was abstract and didn't include statues or other traditional features. But, according to Mrs. Bell's students, the monument is very moving. It honors each soldier individually, yet seeing all the names together makes you think about the total human cost of the war.

Reading 4

Prepare to Read

What You Will Learn

Reading
- Vocabulary building: *Literary terms, word study*
- Reading strategy: *Read aloud*
- Text type: *Literature (poetry)*

Grammar
- Comparison structures
- Inverted word order in poems

Writing
- Write to support a position

THE BIG QUESTION

What can we learn from times of war? You are going to read a poem about two brothers who were on opposite sides during the U.S. Civil War. You will also read a ballad about a soldier who lost his life in the same war. Before you begin, ask yourself these questions:

- What wars have I read about in my history or social studies classes?
- How has war affected people I have read about or know?

Build Background

The poems you will read, **"Sonnet to My Brother, a Soldier"** and **"He Died at His Post,"** are about the Civil War, a war fought between the North (Union states) and the South (Confederate states) from 1861 until 1865. The two sides had different ideas about such issues as slavery. The Union soldiers wore blue uniforms, while the Confederate soldiers wore gray uniforms. Since the uniforms were homemade and became dirty and faded in battle, it was sometimes difficult to recognize which side a soldier was on.

A Union soldier (left) and a Confederate soldier (right) ▶

Vocabulary

Learn Literary Words

There are many different kinds of poems. You will read a sonnet and a ballad.

A **sonnet** is a fourteen-line poem. There are many types of sonnets, but most follow this structure: four lines to present the subject and theme; four lines to develop the theme; four lines to complete the theme; two lines of conclusion.

A **ballad** is a poem that tell stories in rhyme. Sometimes it is also set to music.

A **symbol** is anything that stands for or represents something else. For example, a heart is a symbol for love. Authors and poets use symbols to create an added level of meaning.

Imagery, or descriptions that appeal to the five senses, is one way that poets create vivid descriptions. Look at the examples of imagery in the following chart.

Sense	Example
sight	Rebel gray and Union blue
sound	peaceful his sleep
touch	soft be his pillow

Literary Words
- sonnet
- ballad
- symbol
- imagery

Practice

Work with a partner. Match a word from the first box with what it could symbolize in the second box. Explain your choice to your partner.

Symbol	Symbolizes . . .
flowers	danger
night	freedom
the sky	death
a fox	intelligence
a storm	youth

Reading 4

Reading 4

Listening and Speaking: Academic Words

Study the **purple** words and their meanings. You will find these words useful when talking and writing about literature. Write each word and its meaning in your notebook, then say the words aloud with a partner. After you read the sonnet and the ballad, try to use these words to respond to them.

Academic Words

- bond
- indicate
- tragic
- universal

bond = a shared feeling or interest that unites people or animals	Peter formed a strong **bond** with his dog, Buddy.
indicate = show that something is probably true	The gray clouds in the sky **indicate** that it will probably rain.
tragic = very sad and shocking	The movie about the war was **tragic** because so many soldiers died.
universal = existing everywhere or affecting everyone	Music has **universal** appeal. Almost everyone likes some kind of music.

Practice
WB 178

Work with a partner to complete these sentences. Try to include a **purple** word in your response. Then take turns reading the sentences aloud.

1. Wars often have _____ outcomes.
2. Although the twins live far apart, they have a strong _____ and talk on the phone every day.
3. The change in leadership of the small country had _____ effects felt throughout the world.
4. Spaces between parts of a poem _____ that it is divided into stanzas.

▲ Twins often have a special bond that lasts throughout their lives.

346 Unit 5

Word Study: Spelling Long e

Learning the relationships between sounds and letters will help you read and spell words correctly. The letter *e* stands for different sounds. Short *e* is usually spelled *e*. Long *e* has several *different* spellings: *ee, ea, e,* and *y*. Read aloud the examples of each long *e* sound-spelling in the chart below.

ee	ea	e	y
steel	team	we	country
sleep	peas	he	proudly
free	peaceful	he	history

Practice 📖 179

Work with a partner. Take turns pronouncing the words in the box below. Then write the words in the correct column of the chart.

eat	family	jeans	she	sweet	thee
Eden	glory	me	story	sea	weep

ee	ea	e	y

Reading Strategy | Read Aloud

Reading aloud brings a poem to life. It can make reading a poem more fun and the lines more memorable. To read a poem aloud, follow these steps:

- Make sure you know how to pronounce important words.
- Notice the rhyming words at the end of lines. Practice reading them aloud.
- Notice exclamation marks and question marks. Read sentences that end in exclamation marks with more emphasis. Read lines that end with question marks in a questioning tone.
- Notice where to pause. If there are stanzas, pause longer at the end of each stanza. Pause for a shorter time after commas, dashes, and periods within stanzas.

As you read the poems "Sonnet to My Brother, a Soldier" and "He Died at His Post," pay attention to pronunciation, rhyming words, punctuation, and pauses. When you read with a group, speak clearly and listen carefully.

Reading 4
Literature
Poetry

Set a purpose for reading The sonnet is about two brothers who find themselves on opposite sides in the Civil War in the United States from 1861 to 1865. The ballad is about a soldier who died at his post on the battlefield of the same war. How did the two authors use poetry to their express feelings about war? What is similar and different about their messages?

Sonnet to My Brother, a Soldier

What brothers were ever closer than we?
Both born on the same day, at the same hour.
Inseparable, as close as two peas.
Stronger than steel, the bond that was ours.
We grew farm strong together—we recovered
Father's favorite team of horses when
  they ran away.
As we calmed the horses down, we discovered
That two can do twice the work of one in one day.
But now country calls, and when called we go.
And as men we share a soldier's harsh life.
You left in a different direction, though,
And right you call left, and left I call right.
Do you wonder now what father would say to
See my Rebel gray and your Union blue?

✓ **LITERARY CHECK**
How does the poet use **imagery** to convey the brothers' situation?

✓ **LITERARY CHECK**
Why is a **sonnet** an effective way to convey the message in this poem?

Before You Go On

1. What do you find out about the brothers in the first two lines?
2. What event has separated the brothers?

On Your Own

How about you? Do people in your family or people close to you always agree? Why or why not?

348 Unit 5

He Died at His Post

By J. W. Holman

A soldier had **fallen**! 'Tis well that we weep!
O soft be his pillow, and peaceful his sleep!
Far, far from his home, and the friends he loved most,
He fell in the conflict, and died **at his post**.

When brave ones were **summoned** their country to save,
He hasted war's perils to share with the brave,
And proudly he stood in the van of the host,
And, like his Great Captain, he died at his post.

No more shall earth's conflicts disturb his repose,
He has gone where the weary are free from life's woes;
There covered with glory, on **Eden's** bright coast,
'Twill be sweet to remember he died at his post.

Farewell youthful soldier! we ne'er will forget,
The life thou has offered, the death thou has met!
Of thee may our nation in history **boast**;
And tell the whole world, thou didst die at thy post.

A soldier has fallen; but long shall remain
The star-spangled flag which he died to **sustain**;
For, sooner than let our loved country be lost,
A nation of freemen will die at their post!

---

fallen, died
at his post, doing his job
summoned, called
Eden, paradise; heaven
boast, speak of proudly
sustain, keep alive

> **✓ LITERARY CHECK**
> What **symbols** does the poet use?

> **✓ LITERARY CHECK**
> What makes this **ballad** like a song?

Before You Go On

1. What happened to the soldier?
2. What is the rhyme scheme of the poem?

On Your Own

Do you think the poem is relevant today? Explain.

Reading 4

Review and Practice

Dramatic Reading

One of the best ways to appreciate a poem is to read it aloud, with feeling. Work with a partner or in small groups of five to read the poems on pages 348–349. For "Sonnet to My Brother, a Soldier," decide how you will divide up the poem and which lines each of you will read aloud. For "He Died at His Post," decide who will read each stanza.

Read your lines or stanza to your partner or group and talk about it. What feelings does it create? Underline words you want your listeners to notice. How will you say the words to show feelings?

Practice reading your lines or stanza. Ask your partner or group for feedback. When you are ready, take turns reading your lines or stanzas aloud with your partner or in your group.

Then, take turns, with your partner or in your groups, reading the poems aloud to the class.

> **Speaking Tip**
>
> Face the audience and listen carefully to know when to say your lines.

Comprehension

181

Recall

1. In the sonnet, what does the brother compare his and his brother's bond to?
2. In the ballad, what one word indicates about how old the soldier is?

Comprehend

3. In the sonnet, why does the brother wonder what their father might say?
4. In the ballad, what will last long after the soldier has fallen?

Analyze

5. How has what the brothers share changed?
6. How is the ballad universal in meaning?

Connect

7. Which poem had a greater effect on you? Why?
8. Do you think the sonnet and ballad are more effective than stories would be about what happened to the brothers and the soldier? Why?

Discussion

Discuss with a partner or in a small group.

1. Which poem do you find more tragic? Explain.
2. What qualities do you think it takes to be a soldier and fight for a cause? Explain.
3. A civil war like the one described in the sonnet is one within a country and between its citizens. What makes civil wars so hard? Explain.

What can we learn from times of war? Which unit selection helped you the most to understand the impact of war? Did you choose one of these poems? Why or why not? Explain.

Response to Literature

Work with a partner. Work together to write a news article about the brothers leaving for war and an obituary notice about the soldier who died. Use the information given in the poems. Find examples of news articles and obituary notices in newspapers or online. Share your article and notice with the class.

> **Listening Tip**
>
> If you can't understand your classmate, say, "Excuse me, could you please repeat that?"

▲ A collection of songbooks from the World War I era

Reading 4

Reading 4
Grammar

Comparison Structures

Study the charts below for common ways to compare two things. Notice how the comparative form is followed by the word *than*.

Examples	Use
Our bond **was stronger than** steel. My brother **worked harder than** I.	Add *-er* to adjectives or adverbs of one syllable to show how two things are different.
My sister is **more clever than** I am. She learns things **more quickly than** I do.	Use *more* with adjectives of two or more syllables and adverbs ending in *-ly*.

> **Grammar Skill**
> To make comparative forms of adjectives ending in *-y*, change the *-y* to *-i* and add *-er*.

Another way to make comparisons is to use the structure *as . . . as*. Notice how this comparison is not followed by *than*.

Examples	Use
We were **as happy as** can be. I can run **as quickly as** my brother.	Use *as* + adjective/adverb + *as* to show that two things are equal.
I am **not as old as** my brother. I do**n't** write **as neatly as** he does.	Use *not . . . as* + adjective/adverb to show that two things are not equal.

> **Grammar Check**
> ✓ Which **comparison structure** do you use to show that two things are equal?

Practice A

WB 182

Complete the sentences with the correct comparative form of the adjective or adverb in parentheses.

1. A rock _____ paper. (hard)
2. My brother can eat dinner in five minutes, but I eat _____ my brother. (slow)
3. My father is 38 and my mother is 35. My mother is _____ my father. (old)

Practice B

In your notebook, write sentences comparing the two things, using the adjective or adverb given.

1. a car / expensive / a bike
2. a bus ticket / cheap / a plane ticket
3. sweater / same color / that car
4. a hurricane / worse / thunderstorm

> **Apply**
> Write four sentences comparing another town with where you live now. Then read them to a partner.
>
> **Example:** Siena is not as busy as our city. People move much more slowly . . .

Inverted Word Order in Poems

In poems and songs, writers may invert the usual word order to emphasize ideas, make the lines rhyme, or make the lines have the same meter.

Look at this excerpt from "Sonnet to My Brother, a Soldier." Notice how the writer places the modifying phrase before the noun that it modifies. This emphasizes the strength of the bond.

Inverted Word Order in Poem	Usual Word Order
Stronger than steel, the bond that was ours.	Our bond was stronger than steel.

Look at this excerpt from "He Died at His Post." Notice how the writer inverts the word order to emphasize the words *soft* and *peaceful*.

Inverted Word Order in Poem	Usual Word Order
O soft be his pillow, and peaceful his sleep	O his pillow is soft and his sleep is peaceful . . . .

Grammar Skill
Common ways to invert word order include placing a verb before its subject, a noun before its preposition, or an adjective after the noun it modifies.

Grammar Check
✓ Why do poets and songwriters use **inverted word order**?

Practice A
WB 183

Match the excerpted lines from the poem with the lines in the usual word order.

1. when called we go _____
2. soft be his pillow _____
3. proudly he stood _____

a. he stood proudly
b. we go when called
c. his pillow is soft

Apply
Work with a partner. Find a poem that has inverted word order. Rewrite the inverted lines in the usual word order.

Practice B

In your notebook, rewrite these lines from poems in usual word order.

1. And often is his gold complexion dimmed
2. Sometime too hot the eye of heaven shines.
3. Whose woods these are I think I know.

Reading 4

Writing

Write to Support a Position

At the end of this unit, you'll write an expository essay in the form of a news article. Now, you'll write a paragraph that tells your position on something and support that position with reasons and evidence.

> **Writing Prompt**
> Write a paragraph that supports your position about some aspect of war. Be sure to use comparison structures and quotations correctly.

1 Prewrite Choose a topic about one aspect of war.

WB 184

- Think about your position about the topic.
- List two or three reasons for it.
- List your ideas in a graphic organizer.

Here's a word web created by a student named Larissa. She decided to use her reactions to the sonnet for her paragraph. She describes what happened to the brothers as though it actually did.

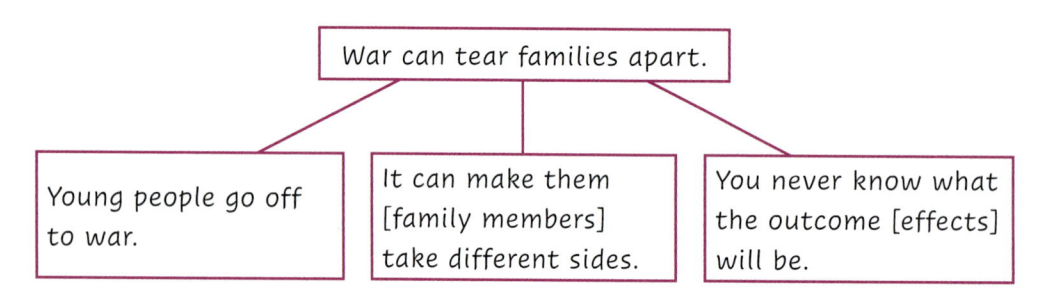

```
                    War can tear families apart.
                   /             |              \
Young people go off    It can make them      You never know what
to war.                [family members]      the outcome [effects]
                       take different sides.  will be.
```

354 Unit 5

2 Draft Use your word web to help you write a first draft.
- Keep your purpose for writing in mind.
- Remember to state your opinion and give two or three reasons that support it.
- Be sure to use comparison structures correctly.

3 Revise Read over your draft. Look for places where the writing is unclear or needs improvement. Complete (✓) the Writing Checklist to help you identify problems. Then, revise your draft, using the editing and proofreading marks listed on page 467.

4 Edit and Proofread Check your work for errors in grammar, usage, mechanics, and spelling. Trade papers with a partner to obtain feedback. Use the Peer Review Checklist on Workbook page 184. Edit your final draft in response to feedback from your partner and your teacher.

5 Publish Prepare a clean copy of your final draft. Share your paragraph with the class. Save your work. You'll need to refer to it in the Writing Workshop at the end of the unit.

> **Writing Checklist**
>
> **Ideas:**
> ☐ I stated my opinion about war and provided two or three reasons for it.
>
> **Sentence Fluency:**
> ☐ My sentences flow smoothly, with transitions from one idea to the next.
>
> **Conventions:**
> ☐ I used comparison structures correctly.

Here is Larissa's position paragraph. Notice how she writes about the situation in the sonnet as if it actually happened and uses details from it to support her position.

Larissa Flores

Effects of War on Families

War can tear families apart. In one case during the Civil War, two twin brothers who had been close all their lives and had done everything together found themselves headed off to war. However, they were fighting on different sides, so they wouldn't be together. As one brother said, their bond was stronger than steel. He explained that they were as close as two peas. Everyone remembered the day they rescued their father's runaway team of horses. They learned that day that two could do twice the work of one. When asked why they joined the war, they replied, "When our country calls, we go." They would share one thing throughout the war—a soldier's difficult life—while they fought on different sides. One would be wearing the gray uniform of the Rebel forces, while the other would wear the Union blue. Everyone hoped they would not have the same bad luck of other young soldiers who died in the war. Not only can war separate families, but it can also have tragic effects on them.

Link the Readings

Critical Thinking

What logical connections can you make between the ideas and details in the readings in this unit? Although the readings do not all have the same purpose, they share a common theme and reflect a range of viewpoints. Complete the chart. Be prepared to support your responses with evidence from each of the texts.

Title of Reading	Purpose	Big Question Link
"World War I"		explains events in World War I
"In Flanders Fields" "Anthem for Doomed Youth" "Three Wonderful Letters from Home" "Letter Home"		
"In the Name of His Father"	to inform	
"Sonnet to My Brother, a Soldier" "He Died at His Post"		

Discussion

Discuss with a partner or in a small group.

- Which reading had the biggest impact on you? Why?
- **What can we learn from times of war?** What lessons do you think people should have learned from World War I and World War II?

Fluency Check

Work with a partner. Choose a paragraph from one of the readings. Take turns reading it for one minute. Count the total number of words you read. Practice saying the words you had trouble reading. Take turns reading the paragraph three more times. Did you read more words each time? Record the number of words you read each time.

	1st Reading	2nd Reading	3rd Reading	4th Reading
Number of Words				

Media Literacy & Projects

Work with a partner or in a small group. Choose one of these projects.

1. In many cultures, flowers, such as the poppies from the poem, are used symbolically. Research some flowers that have symbolic meaning. Find out the origin of this symbolism. Draw or paint, or find and arrange in a collage, pictures of the flowers you chose.

2. Do research at the library or on the internet to find out information about artists who, like the writers in this unit, lived during times of war. Study their artwork. Then create a collage, sculpture, painting, or other work of art that expresses your feelings about war.

3. Do research at the library or on the internet to find photos of war refugees. Make prints or photocopies of the photos and display them for the class. Discuss effects of war on refugees.

4. Find out about a museum or memorial that relates to a war and write a summary about it. Go online and search for war museums. Explore the website and write a summary of what you find. Examples of war museums are: Utah Beach D-Day Museum in France and Hiroshima Peace Memorial Museum in Japan.

Further Reading

Choose from these reading selections. Practice reading silently for longer and longer periods.

A Tale of Two Cities, Charles Dickens
This book tells the story of two men in love with the same woman during the time of the French Revolution. The three of them are faced with the dangers of life in war-torn France.

The Big Lie, Isabella Leitner
When the Nazis took over Europe during World War II, Isabella and her family were taken from their home in Hungary and sent to concentration camps. Isabella's story is one of pain, loss, survival, and hope.

Thura's Diary: My Life in Wartime Iraq, Thura Al-Windawi
In a diary written during the first year of the Iraq war, Thura, the oldest daughter of a Shia family living in Baghdad, shares her experiences and feelings.

Sadako and the Thousand Paper Cranes, Eleanor Coerr
After World War II, Sadako is suffering from the effects of radiation sickness. She embarks on a quest to create 1,000 paper cranes with her classmates.

Put It All Together

Listening & Speaking Workshop

Oral Report

You will give an oral report about any topic related to the subject of war.

① Think About It

In small groups, discuss the texts you have read in this unit. Which ones were most interesting to you? What new information did you learn about times of war? What questions do you still have?

Work together to develop a list of war-related topics for an oral report. Write down your ideas. Here are some examples:

- Civilian life during a war
- The manufacturing of weapons
- The causes of World War I or World War II
- The role of women in World War I or World War II

② Gather and Organize Information

Choose a topic from your group's list. Write down what you already know about the topic. Look at an encyclopedia or a website to find out more about it. Decide what the focus of your oral report will be.

Research Go to the library, talk to an adult, or use the internet to find more information about your topic. Look for facts, examples, and details to support your main ideas. Take notes as you read. Be sure to write down the sources of the information you wish to include.

Order Your Notes Make an outline that lists your main ideas and the facts, examples, and details to support them. Be prepared to tell where you found your information. Think of an interesting way to begin your oral report—perhaps with a question, a quotation, or an anecdote. Plan a conclusion that summarizes your findings. You may wish to copy your outline onto numbered note cards.

Use Visuals To make your report more interesting and effective, find or create pictures, maps, posters, or other visuals that can help convey your ideas. Indicate in your outline or note cards when you will use each visual.

3 Practice and Present

Practice giving your oral report, referring to your outline or note cards to make sure you include all the important ideas and facts. To make the presentation of your oral report richer and more interesting, use a variety of grammatical structures, sentence lengths, sentence types, and connecting words. Keep practicing until you can present your oral report confidently, glancing occasionally at your notes. Make sure you are facing your listeners.

Deliver Your Oral Report Although a report is a formal presentation, you should appear relaxed and comfortable as you deliver it. Pause at the beginning and in between the different parts of your report. Speak in a clear but natural voice and hold up or display your visuals so everyone can see them. Emphasize important points by slowing down and changing the tone of your voice. At the end of your report, ask your classmates if they have any questions.

Speaking Tips

Connect with your audience by making eye contact with as many people as possible.

Pronounce names and numbers correctly. Label your visuals clearly. Write in large enough letters for your audience to read easily.

Listening Tips

Focus on the speaker's main ideas. If you have a question, write it down so you can ask it later. Don't let it distract you as you listen.

Listen for the speaker's sources. Do you think his or her information is reliable? Why or why not?

4 Evaluate the Presentation

You will improve your skills as a speaker and as a listener by evaluating each presentation you give and hear. Use this checklist to help you evaluate your oral report and the reports of your classmates.

- ☐ Were the speaker's main ideas clear, well supported by research, and related to war?
- ☐ Did the speaker support his or her ideas with facts, examples, and details?
- ☐ Could you hear and understand the speaker easily?
- ☐ Did the speaker answer any questions you had about the topic?
- ☐ Are there ways the speaker could improve the oral report?

Strengthen Your Social Language

Giving oral reports will help you become a clear and organized speaker. Go to your Digital Resources for this unit. This activity will help you with strategies for creating and delivering oral reports.

Put It All Together

Writing Workshop

Expository Essay: News Article

In this workshop, you will write an expository essay. As you have learned, an expository essay provides information about a topic. You've also learned that one type of expository writing is a news article. A news article reports on an event or issue of current interest to readers. The first paragraph of a news article introduces the topic and answers the 5Ws: **Who** participated? **What** happened? **When** did it happen? **Where** did it happen? **Why** did it happen? Two or more body paragraphs develop this information with additional details, facts, and examples. A concluding paragraph sums up the information in a way that readers will remember.

Writing Prompt
Write a five-paragraph news article reporting on an event or issue of interest in your school, neighborhood, or community. Be sure to use appositives and prepositional phrases correctly.

1 Prewrite Brainstorm a list of topics in your notebook. Before you choose one, think about your readers. Are you planning to write your article for the school newspaper, a family newsletter, or a local newspaper? Once you have decided on your target audience, review your list of topics. Choose one that your readers will want to know about.

List and Organize Ideas and Details Use a 5Ws chart to organize your ideas. A student named Nicholas decided to write an article for his school newspaper about a class trip to Washington, D. C. Here is his chart:

Who?	Mrs. Bell's social studies class
What?	Class trip
When?	Last Thursday and Friday
Where?	Washington, D.C.
Why?	Sightseeing

2 Draft
Use the model on page 364 and your 5Ws chart to help you write a first draft. Include an introductory paragraph, three body paragraphs, and a concluding paragraph. Be sure to answer the 5Ws in your first paragraph and to develop the information in your body paragraphs.

3 Revise

Read over your draft. As you do so, ask yourself the questions in the writing checklist. Use the questions to help you revise your news article.

> **Six Traits of Writing Checklist**
>
> ☐ **Ideas:** Does my first paragraph introduce my topic in a interesting way?
> ☐ **Organization:** Do I present the events in a logical order?
> ☐ **Voice:** Does my tone fit my topic and audience?
> ☐ **Word Choice:** Do I use words appropriately?
> ☐ **Sentence Fluency:** Do my sentences vary in length and construction?
> ☐ **Conventions:** Does my writing follow the rules of grammar, usage, and mechanics?

Here are the revisions Nicholas plans to make when he revises his first draft:

Students Visit D.C.

While most of us finished an uneventful week, Mrs. Bell's social studies class spent last Thursday and Friday sightseeing in Washington, D.C. By all reports, the trip's highlight was a visit to the Vietnam Veterans Memorial, built ~~for honoring~~ *to honor* the soldiers who died or went missing during the Vietnam war. The memorial covers two a~~ch~~res and consist*s* of ~~4~~ *four* parts: the Wall of Names, the Three Servicemen Statue, the Vietnam Women's Memorial, and the In Memory Plaque. The memorial attracts over three million people every year*,* yet it was once the subject of controversy.

Revised for mechanics and to correct capitalization.

Revised for spelling and mechanics.

Revised for comma.

Unit 5 **361**

Put It All Together

According to tour guide Bill Walsh, in 1980, Congress created a national contest ~~for selecting~~ to select the design of the memorial. The jury choose the winner on May 6, 1981, a young woman named Maya Ying Lin, who had designed the memorial as a project for Yale University.

Revised for comma and mechanics.

Lin's design was ~~very~~ controversial, in part because it was original and didn't include many of the things that traditional memorials do, such as statues. The memorial has ~~now~~ since been enlarged to include the other components. Lin proposed just a simple, plain wall with the names of the ~~deceeesed~~ deceased and missing listed on it. Some people did not like this and wanted a different kind of monument.

Revised for redundancy.

Revised for precision and moved for flow.

Revised for spelling.

Much as students were impressed by all parts of the memorial, some found the wall especially moving. The black granite on which the names are engraved is reflective, so visitors can see their own faces as they walk along. This symbolizes the linking of past and present.

Revised for error with passive and mechanics.

The Vietnam veterans Memorial is visited by many people each year. Some, like Mrs. Bell's students, come on school trips; others travel long distances to see the name of a loved one on the wall. The memorial is powerful. Several students said that it made them feel closer to the men and women who served our country in the Vietnam conflict.

Revised to add detail.

④ Edit and Proofread Check your work for errors in grammar, usage, mechanics, and spelling. Then trade news articles with a partner and complete (✔) the Peer Review Checklist below to give each other constructive feedback. Edit your final draft in response to feedback from your partner and your teacher.

WB 185

Peer Review Checklist

- ☐ Does the news article have an interesting opening?
- ☐ Does the introductory paragraph answer the 5Ws?
- ☐ Do the body paragraphs develop the information in the opening paragraph with details, facts, and examples?
- ☐ Does the concluding paragraph sum up the information in a memorable way?
- ☐ Is the information presented in an order that makes sense?
- ☐ Could changes be made to improve the essay?

Put It All Together

Nicholas Kasterine

April 13, 2019   Students Visit D.C.

Revised to include date.

While most of us finished an uneventful week, Mrs. Bell's social studies class spent last Thursday and Friday sightseeing in Washington, D.C. By all reports, the trip's highlight was a visit to the Vietnam Veterans Memorial, built to honor the soldiers who died or went missing during the Vietnam War. The memorial covers two acres and consists of four parts: the Wall of Names, the Three Servicemen Statue, the Vietnam Women's Memorial, and the In Memory Plaque. The memorial attracts over three million people every year, yet it was once the subject of controversy.

According to tour guide Bill Walsh, in 1980, Congress created a national contest to select the design of the memorial. The jury choose the winner on May 6, 1981, a young woman named Maya Ying Lin, who had designed the memorial as a project for Yale University.

Revised to use the simple past correctly.

Lin's design was controversial, in part because it was original and didn't include many of the things that traditional memorials do, such as statues. Lin proposed just a simple, plain wall with the names of the deceased and missing listed on it. Some people did not like this and wanted a different kind of monument. The memorial has since been enlarged to include the other components.

Much as students were impresed by all parts of the memorial, some found the wall especially moving. The black granite on which the names are engraved is reflective, so visitors can see their own faces as they walk along. This symbolizes the linking of past and present.

Revised for spelling.

The Vietnam veterans Memorial is visited by many people each year. Some, like Mrs. Bell's students, come on school trips; others travel long distances to see the name of a loved one on the wall. The memorial is powerful. Several students said that it made them feel closer to the men and women who served our country in the Vietnam conflict.

Revised to correct an error in capitalization.

⑤ Publish Obtain feedback from your teacher and classmates; then prepare your final draft. Share your news article with the class.

WB 186

Test Preparation

Practice

Read the following test sample. Study the tips in the boxes. Work with a partner to answer the questions.

The Gettysburg Address

1   "Fourscore and seven years ago . . ." It is an introduction that is known to most Americans whether they can identify its source or not. These are the first five words of arguably one of America's greatest speeches, given by President Abraham Lincoln on November 19, 1863, at the dedication of a National Cemetery. While the power of these few words is tremendous on its own, understanding the context in which the speech was given makes their meaning even deeper and more memorable.

2   The Battle of Gettysburg was fought from June 30 to July 3, 1863. The Union Army beat the Confederates, but at a very high cost. After four days of fighting, more than 51,000 soldiers were dead, injured, or missing. On November 19 of that year, a National Cemetery in which the lost soldiers of both sides were buried would be dedicated.

3   Edward Everett, a famous orator of the day, was the keynote speaker. He spoke to the audience for two hours. The president, Abraham Lincoln, was asked to come merely as a formality. He spoke for only two minutes. He spoke simply about the very foundations of American freedom and the sacrifice of the men who lay in the ground. His hope that a "government of the people, by the people, for the people, shall not perish from the earth" is still our greatest hope today.

1 Based on the passage, it can be inferred that the author believes which of the following about the Gettysburg Address?
- **A** It should have been much longer.
- **B** Its context lessened its impact on the audience.
- **C** It is an extremely important part of U.S. history.
- **D** It is not a well-known text in the United States.

2 What was ironic about Lincoln's address at the time it was given?
- **A** It did not refer to the battle that had taken place there.
- **B** It was written by Edward Everett the day before.
- **C** It was given at the dedication of a National Cemetery.
- **D** It was not the featured speech on the occasion.

Taking Tests
You will often take tests to show what you know. Study the tips below to help you improve your test-taking skills.

Tip
If you are able to write on your test sheets, write key words and important information in the margins around the passage to help you quickly locate information later.

Tip
If you think of an answer to the question before looking for it in the answer choices and don't see it as an option, think of another answer to the question and look again.

WB 187–188

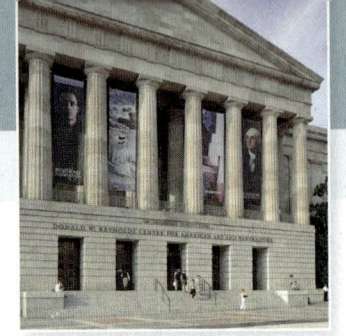

Visual Literacy
Smithsonian American Art Museum

Citizens on the Home Front

Almost every country in the world has experienced times of war. War involves deep emotions and harsh consequences. Artists often use their work to try to make sense of it all.

Norman Rockwell, *Save Freedom of Speech* (1943)

In *Save Freedom of Speech*, Norman Rockwell celebrates the right of the common man to speak his mind. The speaker, shown with rough hands, is wearing an old jacket. Most of the other people are turning to look at him, so that everything focuses on the speaker. The other men in suits and ties look like successful businessmen, but the speaker stands straight, looks firmly ahead, and speaks his mind without fear.

Save Freedom of Speech was one of four paintings that Rockwell created after the United States entered World War II in 1941. President Franklin Delano Roosevelt believed that the country had to do whatever it took to protect what he called the four freedoms: freedom of speech, freedom of worship, freedom from want, and freedom from fear. Rockwell's paintings were eventually made into posters that the U.S. government used to help sell bonds to raise money to support the war.

▲ **Norman Rockwell,** *Save Freedom of Speech,* 1943, lithograph, 56 x 48 in., Smithsonian American Art Museum

Roger Shimomura, *Diary: December 12, 1941* (1980)

In *Diary: December 12, 1941*, Roger Shimomura shows a young Japanese woman wearing a kimono. She is sitting in a traditional Japanese-style room. In contrast, the shadow of Superman, an American comic book character, appears on one of the screens. Normally, this comic image projects strength and security, but the fact that it's a shadow makes it a little scary.

Shimomura captures the mixed feelings many Japanese Americans felt after the Japanese bombed a U.S. naval station in Hawaii called Pearl Harbor in 1941. The U.S. government became suspicious of anyone with Japanese ancestry, even if they were U.S. citizens and their family had lived in this country for generations. Many Japanese Americans were forced from their homes and put into goverment detention camps where they could be watched for any signs of betrayal. Shimomura's grandmother was one of the Japanese Americans put into a camp in Idaho. She kept a daily journal of her experiences, which Shimomura later found and read when he was an adult. He decided to do a series of twenty-five paintings, uniform in size and style, based on parts of her diary. He blended comic art with a style found in more traditional Japanese printmaking to compose his complex scene.

▲ Roger Shimomura, *Diary: December 12, 1941*, 1980, acrylic, 50¼ x 60 in., Smithsonian American Art Museum

Discuss What You Learned

1. Compare and contrast the two artworks. How are their points of view about war both similar and different?
2. Why do you think Roger Shimomura included the comic book character Superman in his painting, and what does this figure stand for?

BIG QUESTION
How did each artist use the subject of citizens on the home front to help them try to make sense of the war?

189–190

Unit 5 367

Unit 6

What makes animals so amazing?

THE BIG QUESTION

This unit is about animals. You'll read a story, a science article, poems, and a novel excerpt about different animals. Reading, writing, and talking about this topic will give you practice using academic language and help you become a better student.

Reading 1
Short Story

"The Talking Bird"

Reading Strategy
Connect ideas

Reading 2
Science

"Getting to Know Real Bats" by Laurence Pringle

Reading Strategy
Evaluate new information

Reading 3
Poetry

Poems by Emily Dickinson, Galway Kinnell, and Joseph Bruchac

Reading Strategy
Read aloud

Listening and Speaking—TV Documentary

At the end of this unit, you'll prepare and present a **TV documentary**.

Writing—Research Report

At the end of this unit, you'll write a **research report** about an idea, issue, or event related to animals. You may decide to write about endangered species or wild animals—even about bats! So pay attention to the topics in this unit: They may give you ideas. To help you write your essay, you'll write an introductory paragraph, classifying paragraphs, a paragraph that supports a main idea, and a paragraph with an interpretive response.

Quick Write

Make a T-chart labeled *Animals* and *Abilities*. List animals and their abilities.

Reading 4
Novel

from *White Fang* by Jack London

Reading Strategy
Sequence

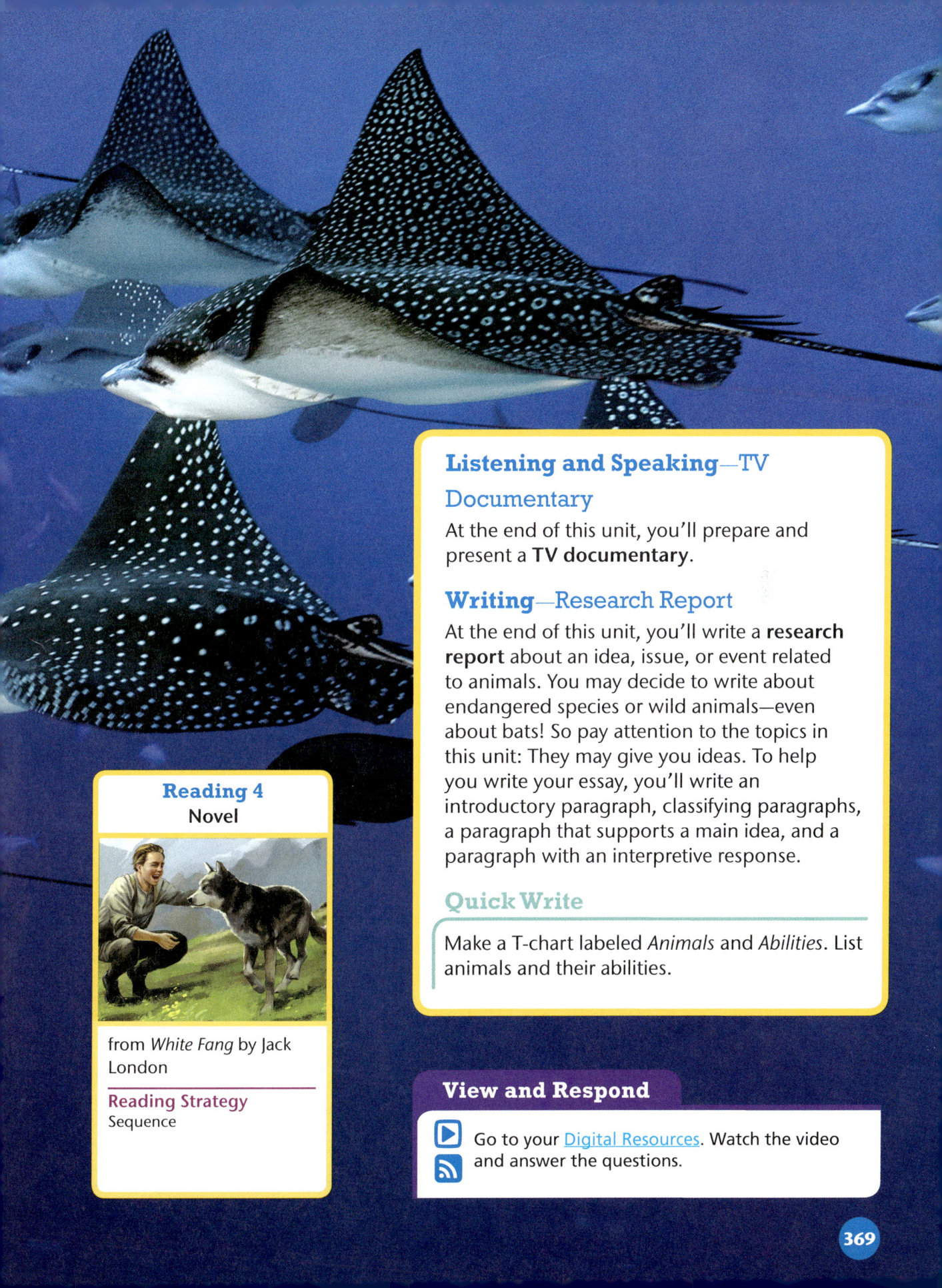

View and Respond

Go to your Digital Resources. Watch the video and answer the questions.

Reading 1

Prepare to Read

What You Will Learn

Reading
- Vocabulary building: *Literary terms, word study*
- Reading strategy: *Connect ideas*
- Text type: *Literature (short story)*

Grammar
- Reduction of adjective clauses to adjective phrases
- Inverted word order in prose

Writing
- Write an introductory paragraph

THE BIG QUESTION

What makes animals so amazing? What special skills do they have naturally? Have you ever tried to teach a pet to do something?

In a small group, talk about the skills that animals are born with and the skills a pet owner or an animal trainer might need to teach them.

Build Background

"The Talking Bird" is a Chinese folktale about an old woman who finds a baby bird and takes care of it. The bird has some very unusual skills. The story takes place many years ago in a rural village in China. Later in the story, the woman travels with the bird to a big city.

▼ Gullin, China, on the Li River

Vocabulary

Learn Literary Words

An **archetype** is a type of character or situation that appears in literature often enough to be considered universal. Many well-known characters in literature are based on archetypes. In the classic book and movie *The Wizard of Oz*, the main character, Dorothy Gale, is an example of an archetype—the **protagonist**. The protagonist is the hero of a story, the character who must overcome obstacles to achieve a goal. The Wicked Witch is an example of another archetype—the **antagonist**. The antagonist is the character who tries to prevent the protagonist from reaching the goal. Such "opposite" character types are called foils. A **foil** is a character who, by contrast, highlights the qualities of another character. The Wicked Witch's wickedness serves as a contrast to Dorothy's goodness. Archetypes can help us better understand the characters and the story.

> **Literary Words**
> archetype
> protagonist
> antagonist
> foil

Practice

Work with a partner. For each of the archetypes in the numbered list below, choose a character from the word box that would serve as a foil. Then choose two pairs and write a sentence about each pair.

fool	beggar
helpless victim	greedy villain
humble underdog	

1. wise man
2. Earth Mother
3. loud-mouthed braggart
4. queen
5. bully

▲ This artwork in Montreal's botanical gardens illustrates the Earth Mother archetype. What character might be a foil for this archetype?

Reading 1

Reading 1

Listening and Speaking: Academic Words

Study the **purple** words and their meanings. You will find these words useful when talking and writing about literature. Write each word and its meaning in your notebook, then say the words aloud with a partner. After you read "The Talking Bird," try to use these words to respond to the text.

Academic Words
attached
complexity
consequence
thrive

attached = strongly connected to someone or something	The young child was **attached** to his mother and never wanted to leave her.
complexity = the complicated nature of something	The **complexity** of the text made it difficult to understand.
consequence = something that happens as a result of a particular action	One **consequence** of the storm was that many people did not have electricity.
thrive = to become very successful, strong, or healthy	The cactus **thrives** in a hot, dry climate.

Practice
WB 192

Work with a partner to answer these questions. Try to include the **purple** word in your answer. Write the sentences in your notebook.

1. What person are you **attached** to? What object are you attached to?
2. Do you find any subject difficult because of its **complexity**? If so, which one?
3. What is a **consequence** of not studying for a test?
4. What kinds of plants and animals **thrive** in your area?

▲ She loves music, and she is especially attached to her guitar—she takes it everywhere!

Word Study: Suffixes

A suffix is a letter or group of letters added to the end of a word. Suffixes show the part of speech of a word—adjective, adverb, noun, or verb. When you add a suffix to a word, you change the meaning of the word. Study the chart of suffixes below, and discuss the meanings of the words in the *Examples* column with a partner. Can you guess the meaning of the word by looking at the meaning of the suffix?

Suffix	Part of Speech	Meaning	Examples
-en	verb	cause to become	thick**en**, strength**en**
-ful	adjective	having	boast**ful**, thank**ful**
-ward	adverb	direction or manner	west**ward**, back**ward**
-ance	noun	action or state	disturb**ance**, griev**ance**

Practice

Work with a partner. As you read "The Talking Bird," look for words with the suffixes *-en, -ful, -ward,* or *-ance*. Make a list of the words you find. Discuss the meaning of each word, using a dictionary if necessary. Write a sentence for each word.

Reading Strategy | Connect Ideas

Connecting ideas in a short story helps you follow what's happening and understand the characters' motivations better. To make connections in a short story, follow these steps:

- Pause to connect ideas, such as how characters are alike and different.
- Underline important ideas and details.
- If one idea reminds you of another, write yourself a note or question to watch for as you read.

As you read "The Talking Bird," connect ideas often.

Reading 1

Reading 1

**Literature
Short Story**

Set a purpose for reading Read this story to find out about an old woman who finds and cares for a baby bird. What makes this bird unusual?

The Talking Bird
A Chinese folktale

Once upon a time—long, long ago in China—an old woman saw a small poof of scraggly feathers in her yard: a baby bird that had fallen from its nest. The woman, who had a big heart, scooped up the tiny, pitiful creature. She brought it inside her house, where she carefully fed and cared for it. The bird thrived.

Even though under the woman's care the bird grew bigger and stronger, it did not become beautiful. Its feathers were still scraggly and thin; its beak, crooked to one side. Nor did the bird sing **melodiously**—its singing voice could break glass. However, the bird could do one thing well—talk. And talk it did! It **screeched** in the morning as the sun came up. It squawked when the old woman was eating her lunch. And it screeched before the old woman went to sleep. But the woman had become attached to the bird, so she didn't mind.

---

melodiously, pleasantly musical
screeched, shouted in a loud, sharp, unpleasant way

> ✓ **LITERARY CHECK**
>
> What kind of person is the old woman? What **archetype** is the old woman an example of? Is this character believable? Do you know someone like her? If so, whom?

374 Unit 6

Now, even though the old woman who rescued the bird was sweet and kind, the bird said mean things to all he saw. To the neighborhood cat, it said, "Scat, **craven** cat!" To the dog, it screeched, "You're too flabby, Fido!" And when **illustrious** people would visit the woman, the bird would announce that they smelled like thousand-year-old eggs. As a consequence, the old woman's friends and family could not understand why she loved the bird, but she did.

One day the woman's sister visited. After being taunted by the bird for hours, the sister asked in frustration, "Why do you let that bird speak like that? You are a nice person. But your bird is annoying and rude. He's such a nuisance!"

As the old woman started to reply, the bird squawked, "Good-bye, you old hag. Please come again when you can't stay so long." The old woman shrugged at her sister and smiled softly.

Not long after, the old woman decided to take a trip to a city far away. Afraid to travel alone, she took the bird with her. After she had gone northward for two days, as the bird accompanied the old woman down an empty narrow street, two scary-looking men blocked their path.

"Hey, you **lunkheads**!" the **brazen** bird loudly cried. "What do you think you are doing, you **thuggish** idiots?" The men, who were robbers, waved away the bird **nonchalantly**. They took advantage of the noise to snatch the old woman's purse right out of her hands. "You cowardly thieves!" screeched the bird. "I'll peck out your eyes! Come back!" But the robbers stole all the old woman's money.

---

craven, completely lacking courage
illustrious, famous and admired because of what a person has achieved
lunkhead, a simpleminded person
brazen, not embarrassed about behaving in an unacceptable way
thuggish, used to describe violent behavior in which people fight and attack others
nonchalantly, in a manner that is calm and unconcerned

> ✓ **LITERARY CHECK**
>
> In what way are the thieves a **foil** for the old woman?

> **Before You Go On**
>
> 1. How did the bird change under the woman's care?
> 2. Why didn't the bird's constant talking bother the woman?
>
> 👤 **On Your Own**
>
> How do you think other people along the way will react to the bird? How will the bird react to them?

Soon a curious crowd of people, **drawn** by the fuss, gathered around. One of the people in the crowd was a very rich man. The man watched the brazen bird with delight.

To the old woman, he said, "I will give you three silver coins for that **cheeky** bird."

"I'm sorry, sir," said the old woman. "I love my bird. I cannot sell him."

The bird angrily **interjected**, "**Stingy** man! I am worth at least five silver coins!"

"Sold!" **bellowed** the rich man. "For five silver coins."

The old man's response saddened the old woman. She did not want to sell her beloved pet; but the bird flew onto the rich man's arm, and the woman continued forward on her path.

The rich man put the bird into a golden cage, smiling brightly.

"Hey! Mister Moneybags! I'm dirty from traveling. I smell as bad as you do, so I'd like to take a bath," the bird said.

The rich man, surprised by the bird's announcement, opened the golden cage. The bird flew to a nearby fountain. The bird splashed and sputtered and splashed in the fountain water for a very long time. Then with a loud flapping of its wings, away it flew. Because that's what birds do.

---

drawn, caused to come to a place by something of interest
cheeky, rude or disrespectful, sometimes in a way that is amusing
interjected, interrupted
stingy, not generous, especially with money
bellowed, shouted very loudly and strongly

Naturally, the bird flew back toward the old woman, who was overjoyed to see her beloved—if **belligerent**—pet. She then used the five coins to hire a cart to take them home.

A few days later, the old woman was at home wrapping five silver coins to send back to the rich man. Her sister again came for a visit.

"Hello there, you stale old mouse!" the bird shrieked. "I see you found the most **repulsive** dress in town to wear today."

The sister, used to such abuse from the bird, **glowered** at it.

"I see you still have that **ghastly** bird," she said, sneering and shaking her head. "I will never understand why you keep such a wretched, beastly creature."

The old woman shrugged at her sister and smiled softly.

---

belligerent, very unfriendly and wanting to argue or fight
repulsive, extremely unpleasant, in a way that almost makes a person feel sick
glowered, looked at someone in an angry way
ghastly, very bad or unpleasant

Before You Go On

1. What was unusual about the things the bird said to other people?
2. What happened after the rich man let the bird out of the cage?

On Your Own

What do you think the bird will do next?

Reading 1

Reading 1

Review and Practice

Dramatic Reading 🎧

Reading a narrative aloud can help to make the characters seem more real. Working in groups of three, read aloud the passage from page 378. Decide who will read the lines for the rich man, the old woman, and the bird. Speak more emphatically for the sentences that end with exclamation points. Pay attention to the words used to describe how each character speaks, such as *interjected* and *bellowed*. Ask your teacher for help with pronunciation, if necessary. Practice reading the passage in your group, and then read it aloud for the whole class.

> **Speaking Tip**
>
> Practice your lines in front of a mirror a few times before your performance.

Comprehension

Recall
1. How did the baby bird look when the old woman found it?
2. What helped the bird grow and thrive?

Comprehend
3. Why did the bird tell the rich man it wanted to take a bath?
4. What kind of person is the old woman? How do you know?

Analyze
5. Why do you think the old woman became attached to the bird?
6. Why do you think the rich man bought the bird?

Connect
7. Why do you think people like the old woman accept bad behavior from a pet or even a person they are attached to? Explain.
8. Would you recommend this story to others to read? Explain.

▲ A blue and gold macaw

Discussion

Discuss with a partner or in a small group.

1. How does the use of imagery and dialogue help you understand the archetypes of the old woman and the thieves?
2. If you were the old woman, what would you have done about the bird's bad behavior? Explain.

What makes animals so amazing? Why do you think people get so attached to their pets? Have you ever been attached to an animal? If so, what was amazing about the animal?

> **Speaking Skill**
>
> When you don't know the exact English word or phrase, explain or describe the idea using words you know.

Response to Literature

195

Choose one of these situations:
- The old woman's sister is treated badly by the bird. Write a letter from the sister to the old woman about the bird. Offer advice about what the old woman should do. Explain your feelings.
- The people in the town have probably noticed the bird's bad behavior. Write a note to post at a local shop about the problems the bird is causing.

Take turns sharing your letters or notes with the class.

Reading 1
Grammar

Reduction of Adjective Clauses to Adjective Phrases

An adjective phrase or clause modifies or describes a noun or pronoun. A clause has a subject and verb, while a phrase does not. An adjective clause may be shortened to a phrase. In the examples below, the clause is shortened to a phrase by omitting the relative pronoun (*who*, *that*, or *which*) and the verb *be*.

> Not long after, the old woman decided to take a trip to a city **that was far away**. *(adjective clause)*
>
> Not long after, the old woman decided to take a trip to a city **far away**. *(adjective phrase)*
>
> Soon a curious crowd of people, **who were drawn by the fuss**, gathered around. *(adjective clause)*
>
> Soon a curious crowd of people, **drawn by the fuss**, gathered around. *(adjective phrase)*

Grammar Skill
Sometimes, you can reduce an adjective clause to an adjective phrase.
Example: *The bird, which was squawking madly, flew into a tree.* can be shortened to *The bird, squawking madly, flew into a tree.*

Practice A
WB 196

Underline the adjective phrase in each sentence.

1. The rich man, <u>surprised by the bird's announcement</u>, opened the golden cage.
2. The sister, used to such abuse from the bird, glowered at it.
3. The old woman, overjoyed to see her beloved pet, took the bird home.
4. The old woman, afraid to travel alone, took the bird with her.

Grammar Check
✓ What is omitted to change an **adjective clause** to an **adjective phrase**?

Practice B

Reduce the adjective clause in each sentence to an adjective phrase. Write the new sentence in your notebook.

1. Did you read about the bird who was known for its bad behavior?
   Did you read about the bird known for its bad behavior?
2. The woman's sister, who was upset by the bird, remained silent.
3. The bird, which was yelling insults, surprised people.
4. A rich man, who was interested in the bird, offered to buy it.

Apply
Complete the sentence starters about a folktale you are familiar with. Use adjective phrases. Then tell a partner about it.
Example: [Name of story] is a folktale popular in [country]. The protagonist . . .

Unit 6

Inverted Word Order in Prose

As in poems and songs, writers of prose may invert the usual word order for special effect or to emphasize certain things. Look at the examples of sentences with inverted word order from the folktale. Compare them with the regular word order.

Inverted Word Order	Regular Word Order
To the neighborhood cat, it said, "Scat, craven cat!"	It said to the neighborhood cat, "Scat, craven cat!"
"Sold!" bellowed the rich man.	The rich man bellowed, "Sold!"
Then with a loud flapping of its wings, away it flew.	It then flew away, flapping its wings loudly.

In the first example, placing the phrase *to the neighborhood cat* first emphasizes who the bird was talking to. In the second example, placing the adverb *away* before *it flew*, emphasizes that the bird leaves, or gets *away*. The writer places the most important words first.

> **Grammar Skill**
>
> To use inverted word order in prose, writers often place the most important words first.

Practice A
📖 197

Identify which sentences use inverted word order and which use regular word order. Write *inverted* or *regular*.

1. On a hillside, a little boy lived with his parents. ___inverted___
2. Peter was his name. _____
3. His parents were shepherds. _____
4. "Wolf!" cried Peter. _____
5. The neighbors ran out of their homes. _____
6. No wolf was there on the hillside. _____

> **Grammar Check**
>
> ✓ Why do prose writers use **inverted word order**?

Practice B

In your notebook, rewrite these lines in regular word order.

1. At the bus driver, the man shouted, "Wait for me!"
   The man shouted at the bus driver, "Wait for me!"
2. And wait the taxi did.
3. To the cat, Eric said, "Come here!"
4. With a bored expression, away walked the cat.

> **Apply**
>
> Write a sentence about an animal using inverted word order. Then trade sentences with a partner. Rewrite your partner's sentence, using regular word order.
> **Example:** "Woof! Woof!" barked the dog.

Reading 1 **381**

Reading 1

Writing

Write an Introductory Paragraph

At the end of this unit, you will write a research report. In this lesson, you'll learn how to narrow a topic and write an introductory paragraph. When you narrow a topic, you're better able to research and present information. After narrowing your topic, you will do research and write an introductory paragraph for your report. Remember that an introductory paragraph gets the reader's attention and introduces the specific question you are trying to answer in your research.

> **Writing Prompt**
>
> Choose a topic related to animals. Use a graphic organizer to narrow your topic and write a question to direct your research. Research your topic, changing the question as you need to. Then write an introductory paragraph for a research report on the topic. Use adjective phrases correctly.

1 Prewrite Begin by choosing a very broad, general topic related to animals.

WB 198

- Narrow your topic to one kind of animal, such as a bird. Then keep narrowing your topic. Decide on a kind of bird and one of its features or abilities, such as its ability to talk.

- What do you want to find out about the narrowed topic? Think of a specific question to guide your research.

- Complete a graphic organizer with a general, or very broad topic, narrowed topic, and research question.

Here's a graphic organizer created by a student named Theo. He listed his general topic idea and then narrowed it until he came up with a specific question to guide his research and to use to introduce his topic.

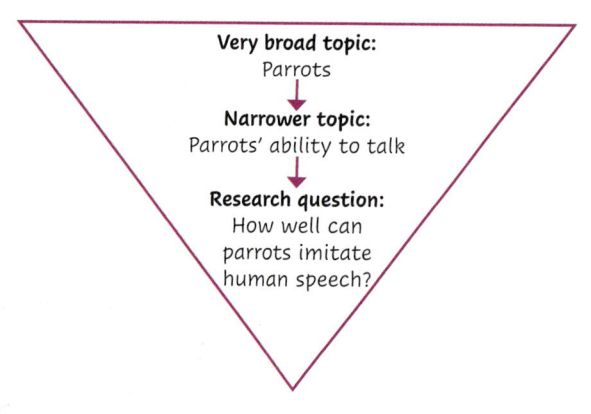

Very broad topic:
Parrots

Narrower topic:
Parrots' ability to talk

Research question:
How well can parrots imitate human speech?

382 Unit 6

② **Draft** Use your graphic organizer to help you write a first draft.

- Begin the introduction with a hook that gets the readers' attention. Consider posing your question.
- Introduce your narrowed topic.
- Explain what research question or questions your research report will answer.
- Use adjective phrases where needed.

③ **Revise** Read over your draft. Look for places where the writing is unclear or needs improvement. Complete (✓) the Writing Checklist to help you identify problems. Then, revise your draft, using the editing and proofreading marks listed on page 467.

④ **Edit and Proofread** Check your work for errors in grammar, usage, mechanics, and spelling. Trade paragraphs with a partner to obtain feedback. Use the Editing and Proofreading Marks on Workbook page 231. Edit your final draft in response to feedback from your partner and your teacher.

⑤ **Publish** Prepare a clean copy of your final draft. Share your introductory paragraph with the class. Save your work. You'll need to refer to it in the Writing Workshop at the end of the unit.

> **Writing Checklist**
>
> **Ideas:**
> ☐ I clearly explained the question my report will answer.
>
> **Word Choice:**
> ☐ I used specific words to explain my ideas.
>
> **Conventions:**
> ☐ I used adjective phrases correctly.

Here is Theo's introductory paragraph for his research report. Notice that he adjusted his research question.

Theo Hidalgo

How Well Can Parrots Communicate?

Everyone knows that parrots can repeat human speech. But can they speak intelligently? Can they understand the meaning of words? Can they answer questions? This research report will show that, indeed, they can. There is proof that parrots can make sentences in response to questions. This phenomenon was proven by Dr. Irene Pepperberg, a psychologist studying avian intelligence. Dr. Pepperberg trained an African grey parrot named Alex to understand vocabulary, name certain things, count to six, and understand some concepts. This report will provide details about what Alex learned and what this shows about parrot intelligence.

Reading 2

Prepare to Read

What You Will Learn

Reading
- Vocabulary building: *Context, dictionary skills, word study*
- Reading strategy: *Evaluate new information*
- Text type: *Informational text (science)*

Grammar
- Relative pronouns as subjects
- Noun clauses with *that*

Writing
- Write classifying paragraphs

THE BIG QUESTION

What makes animals so amazing? What do you know about bats? Copy the K-W-L-H chart into your notebook. Work in small groups to complete the first two columns. As you read "Getting to Know Real Bats," complete the third and fourth columns of the chart.

K What do I **know**?	W What do I **want** to know?	L What did I **learn**?	H **How** did I learn it?

Build Background

This reading is a science article about bats. Bats are flying mammals. Some eat insects, and some eat fruit. Bats live everywhere in the world except Antarctica and certain remote islands.

Some people believe that bats are aggressive and even dangerous. In **"Getting to Know Real Bats,"** you will learn that bats are shy creatures that can be very helpful to human beings.

▶ A swarm of bats emerging from a cave

384 Unit 6

Vocabulary 🎧

Listening and Speaking: Key Words

Read these sentences aloud with a partner. Use the context to figure out the meaning of the highlighted words. Use a dictionary, the glossary, or a thesaurus to determine or confirm your answers. Then write each word and its meaning in your notebook.

> **Key Words**
> echolocation
> mammals
> nocturnal
> prey
> the wild
> wingspan

1. By using echolocation, or by bouncing sounds off objects and listening to the echoes, bats can fly around in the dark without crashing into things.
2. Snakes are not mammals. They do not have hair on their bodies, and they do not nurse their young.
3. Many forest animals are nocturnal. They sleep or hide during the day and hunt for food at night.
4. Many predatory animals hide so they can capture and eat their prey.
5. I have seen tigers in a zoo, but I have never seen them in the wild.
6. The scientist measured the bat's wingspan; it was six feet from one wing tip to the other wing tip.

Practice 📖 199

Work with a partner to complete these sentences in your notebooks. Include the word(s) in your sentence.

1. Bats use a radar-like system . . . (echolocation)
2. Whales are . . . (mammals)
3. The owl is a . . . (nocturnal)
4. Cats that are not pets . . . (prey)
5. In the Amazon rainforest . . . (the wild)
6. The eagle's . . . (wingspan)

▲ A lesser long-nosed bat pollinates a saguaro cactus.

Reading 2

Reading 2

Listening and Speaking: Academic Words

Study the purple words and their meanings. You will find these words useful when talking and writing about informational texts. Write each word and its meaning in your notebook, then say the words aloud with a partner. After you read "Getting to Know Real Bats," try to use these words to respond to the text.

Academic Words

accurate
beneficial
features
ignorance

accurate = exactly correct	The scientists took special care to make sure the information was **accurate**.
beneficial = good or useful	Bats are **beneficial** because they eat insects, keeping insect populations in check, and they pollinate plants, helping the plants reproduce.
features = parts of something that stand out because they seem important, interesting, or typical	The most impressive **features** of the school were a new computer lab, a sports arena, and an art studio.
ignorance = lack of knowledge or information about something	The man showed his **ignorance** of how to treat wild animals when he picked up the baby bird and took it home.

Practice

WB 200

Work with a partner to answer these questions. Try to include the purple word in your answer. Write the sentences in your notebook.

1. How can you get an **accurate** measurement of your height?
2. How is scientific research **beneficial** to human beings?
3. What **features** of dogs make them good choices for pets?
4. How can human **ignorance** endanger the lives of animals?

▲ A Waterhouse's leaf-nosed bat with a katydid it has caught

Word Study: Compound Words

Spelling compound words can be confusing. The best way to see if you have spelled a hyphenated word correctly is to look it up in a dictionary.

Hyphenated words can be used as adjectives to modify nouns. Use a hyphen between two words before the modified word. Study the chart below.

	Hyphenated Words	**Example**
make + believe =	make-believe	These are **make-believe** bats.
high + pitched =	high-pitched	The bat made a **high-pitched** noise.
warm + blooded =	warm-blooded	The bats found their **warm-blooded** prey.
disease + carrying =	disease-carrying	Bats are usually not **disease-carrying** creatures.

Practice
201

Work with a partner to complete these sentences in your notebook, using the compound adjectives in parentheses.

1. Many birds, bats, and frogs are . . . (insect-eating)
2. The police followed . . . (high-speed)
3. The salad was made . . . (cut-up)
4. To kill mosquitoes, we use . . . (all-natural)
5. The ice cream shop had . . . (forty-two)

Reading Strategy   Evaluate New Information

Evaluating new information helps you understand a text as it broadens your knowledge. To evaluate new information, follow these steps:

- Before you read, ask yourself what you already know about the subject.
- As you read, make a note of the new facts and ideas you find.
- Compare the new information to what you already know.
- How does the new information broaden your knowledge of the subject? Do you agree with what you read?

Before you read "Getting to Know Real Bats," think about what you already know about bats. As you read, make a note of new and interesting facts and ideas. Are there any you want to find out more about?

202

Reading 2

**Informational Text
Science**

Set a purpose for reading Read this science article to find out some surprising information about bats. What amazing abilities do bats have?

Getting to Know Real Bats

LAURENCE PRINGLE

Bats. To some people, this word means scary, ugly, disease-carrying creatures that are almost blind and sometimes fly into and become **entangled** in women's hair. These are make-believe bats. Real bats are quite different.

Bats make up nearly a quarter of all mammals on earth and live on all continents except Antarctica. They are the only mammals that fly. "Just as dolphins have mastered the sea," says Merlin Tuttle, "bats have mastered the sky."

There are two main groups of bats. About two hundred species—the megabats—are large, fruit-eating bats called flying foxes. They live in the tropics of Asia and Africa. Some have wingspans of nearly six feet, and others fly about in the daytime, not at night. Flying foxes have big eyes and see very well.

Nearly eight hundred species of small, insect-eating bats make up the second group—the microbats—with forty-two kinds living in Canada and the United States. The smallest mammal on earth is a bat: the bumblebee bat of Thailand. It weighs less than a penny.

Also in this group is a species of bat that catches frogs, one that scoops fish out of the water, others that catch birds and

---

entangled, twisted and caught in

▲ A flying fox in flight

▲ A close-up of a flying fox

▲ A bat with a moth it has caught

rats, and three species that lap blood from little bites they nip in the skin of cattle and other warm-blooded prey. These vampire bats live in the warmest regions of South and Central America.

Microbats have small eyes, but they can probably see as well as mice and other small mammals. Their food is mostly flying insects, which they catch in the air at night. To accomplish this, a bat flies with its mouth open, emitting high-pitched squeaks that humans cannot hear. Some of the sounds echo off flying insects as well as tree branches and other obstacles that lie ahead. The bat listens to the echoes and gets an **instantaneous** picture in its brain of the objects in front of it.

From this echolocation, or sonar, as it is called, a bat can tell a great deal about a mosquito or another flying insect. "With extreme **precision**," Merlin Tuttle says, "bats can perceive motion, distance, speed, **trajectory**, and shape. They can detect and avoid obstacles no thicker than a human hair, and millions of bats sometimes fly at the same time in a large cave without jamming each other's sonar. Their abilities far surpass our present understanding."

Some people still shudder at the thought of being face-to-face with a bat. Most of this fear is a result of ignorance about bats and of seeing only images of bats looking their worst, with mouths open and teeth bared.

instantaneous, immediate

precision, accuracy, exactness
trajectory, curved path of a flying object

Before You Go On

1. What can bats do that no other mammal can do?
2. What are the two main groups of bats?

On Your Own

Do you like bats? Why or why not?

In 1978 Merlin Tuttle began to think about the image that many people have of bats. He was asked to write a chapter about bats for a book on mammals to be published by the National Geographic Society. Then he saw the photographs that were going to illustrate his words.

Merlin recalls, "I had never considered the impact of the bat pictures that were then typical; most showed bats snarling in self-defense. Because of their shy nature and nocturnal habits, bats are exceptionally difficult to portray photographically as they really are in the wild. When first captured, they either try to fly away, bare their teeth in a threat display, or **hunker down**, eyes closed, expecting the worst. Impatient photographers typically held a bat by its wings, blew into its face, and snapped a quick picture when the bat tried to defend itself with a snarl."

Photos like these, enlarged and published in books and magazines, reinforced the **notion** that bats were vicious and fearsome. Merlin wanted his chapter to show bats accurately, and the book editors agreed to try. A *National Geographic* staff photographer, Bates Littlehales, was assigned to take bat photos, under Merlin's direction. After several weeks, however, only a few good photos were taken, despite their best efforts.

Merlin was an **amateur** photographer when he met Bates Littlehales, who generously shared his knowledge. After Littlehales left to return to *National Geographic*, Merlin began to experiment with the high-speed photography needed to capture bats in flight. When an editor tried to arrange for Littlehales and Tuttle to travel to Mexico to take photos of fishing bats, Littlehales said that Merlin had learned enough about photography to try it alone.

From other **mammalogists**, Merlin learned where to look in Mexico for fishing bats. After several nights of great effort, he and his assistants caught seven

---

hunker down, crouch, keep low to the ground
notion, idea

amateur, someone who does something for pleasure or interest, not as a job
mammalogists, scientists who study mammals

▲ A big brown bat baring its teeth in self-defense

▲ A big brown bat with a normal, calm expression

▲ A fisherman bat with a minnow in its feet

of the bats in nets. The bats became **docile** after several hours of gentle care but refused to take food.

After much frustration, Merlin was about to give up and release the bats, but first he tried tucking bits of cut-up minnow under their lips. Eventually one bat ate a piece of minnow. "Then," Merlin recalls, "to our great elation, he grabbed a whole minnow from my hand, eating it with gusto. The others continued to refuse even small pieces, but we perched them on each side of the feeding bat until, one by one, each **succumbed** to the temptation. An hour later, all seven bats were eagerly eating from our hands and allowing themselves to be photographed with their meals, some in flight.

"When I returned from the trip and had the film developed, I was amazed to see the spectacular photographs that resulted. Even more impressive, when I showed the photographs to others, I soon saw that most people's negative attitudes about bats could be changed in minutes. They simply needed an opportunity to see bats as they really are. Bats that are not afraid can be just as curious, **winsome**, and even comical as any household pet."

People who acknowledge that bats are appealing may still fear them because they believe that bats commonly carry the disease **rabies**.

---

docile, quiet, calm, easy to control
succumbed, gave in
winsome, pleasant and attractive
rabies, disease that kills animals, including people

Before You Go On

1. Why are bats difficult to portray accurately?
2. How were the photos of the fishing bats different?

On Your Own

What do you think is the greatest challenge of studying bats? Explain.

Reading 2   **391**

▲ Merlin Tuttle photographing a bat

This idea originated in the early 1960s, when research seemed to show that bats were not harmed by rabies, yet passed the deadly disease on to other animals. Further study showed that this was not true, but most people and health officials heard about only the first, **erroneous** research.

erroneous, incorrect or wrong

Merlin Tuttle notes that "bats can get rabies, the same as dogs and cats can, but when they do get it they die quickly, just as other animals do. Anyway, less than half of one percent of bats contract rabies, and, unlike most mammals, even when bats are **rabid** they rarely become aggressive."

rabid, infected with rabies

A pallid bat perched on a limb ▼

▲ A male great fruit bat guards a female and a baby.

The greatest threat posed by bats is an indirect one: the actions of **unscrupulous** or uninformed pest control companies using poisons to kill bats in attics of homes. One widely used poison, chlorophacinone (Rozel), has been clearly shown to pose a serious health threat to people. At least fifteen states still allow its use, and some pest control operators in other states use it illegally.

There are simple, non-chemical ways to keep bats out of houses. Besides, some people are pleased to have a colony of insect-eating bats in or near their homes. "Just leave bats alone," Merlin concludes, "and the odds of being harmed are infinitesimally small."

---

unscrupulous, behaving in an unfair or dishonest way

About the Author

Laurence Pringle has written over one hundred books for young readers. Although his focus is mainly on animals and nature, he does write an occasional work of fiction or a book about a social studies topic. Before he became a writer, he studied wildlife biology at Cornell University and the University of Massachusetts. He also worked as a teacher and an editor. Pringle grew up in New York, where he still lives with his wife and children.

Before You Go On

1. According to the author, what are the greatest threats posed by bats?
2. What can you infer is beneficial about having bats near your home?

On Your Own

After reading this article, did you change how you feel about bats? Explain.

> **Reading 2**

Review and Practice

Comprehension 📖 203

Recall
1. What are megabats? What are microbats? Describe their features.
2. What is sonar, or echolocation? What do bats use echolocation for?

Comprehend
3. Why are bats usually portrayed as frightening creatures?
4. How are bats different from other mammals?

Analyze
5. How did the author and Merlin Tuttle fight against ignorance?
6. In what ways do you think bats are beneficial to people?

Connect
7. Would you recommend this article to others to read? Why or why not?
8. What two or three things about bats would you like to know more about? Why?

▲ A Peter's dwarf epauletted bat eats a fig.

In Your Own Words

Imagine you are telling a friend or family member about bats. What would you say to help change their attitudes about bats? Choose words from the chart below to describe bats. Explain why, according to the author, bats have been misunderstood and unjustly feared for so long. Say whether you agree and explain.

Types of Bats	megabats, microbats, flying foxes, vampire bats
Features of Bats	echolocation, high-pitched squeak, small eyes, wingspan
Nature of Bats	nocturnal, docile, comical, gentle, timid

> **Speaking Tip**
> Ask listeners if they have any questions.

A Gambian epauletted fruit bat with her young ▶

Discussion

Discuss with a partner or in a small group.

1. Of all the animals in the world, do you think bats are among the most amazing? Explain.
2. What ideas did you have about bats before reading this article? Were your ideas accurate?

What makes animals so amazing? From what you read or know, what makes bats so amazing? Explain.

Listening Skill

Listen carefully to reasons and explanations others give to see if you agree. Paraphrase or summarize their ideas to make sure you have understood.

Read For Fluency

It is often easier to read a text if you understand the difficult words and phrases. Work with a partner. Choose a paragraph from the reading. Identify the words and phrases you do not know or have trouble pronouncing. Look up the difficult words in a dictionary.

Take turns pronouncing the words and phrases with your partner. If necessary, ask your teacher to model the correct pronunciation. Then take turns reading the paragraph aloud. Give each other feedback on your reading.

Extension

WB 203

Bats eat thousands of mosquitoes every night. Many people encourage bats to nest around their homes by building bat boxes. Bat boxes are flat wooden structures where bats roost. Work with a partner to do research at the library or on the internet to find out more information about bat boxes. Share your findings with the class.

Bat boxes give bats safe places to live.

Reading 2 **395**

> **Reading 2**
>
> # Grammar

Relative Pronouns as Subjects

Writers use relative, or adjective, clauses to combine ideas in two sentences. A relative clause always begins with a relative pronoun. The relative pronouns *who, that, which,* and *whose* substitute for a noun, noun phrase, or pronoun. Notice how the two sentences about *the photographs* are combined in the example below.

>   subject
> Then he saw *the photographs*. **They** were going to illustrate his words.
>
>   subject
> Then he saw *the photographs* **that** were going to illustrate his words.

Grammar Skill

Use *who* or *that* to refer to a person. Use *which* or *that* to refer to an animal or a thing. Use *whose* to indicate possession.

Notice how the boldfaced relative pronouns below refer to the nouns and noun phrases in italics.

> Tuttle was grateful to *the people*, **who** generously shared their knowledge.
> *Bats* **that** lap blood from cattle are called vampire bats.
> *The photographer* **whose** pictures we like is Merlin Tuttle.

Grammar Skill

How are **relative pronouns** used?

Practice A

Circle the correct relative pronoun to complete the sentence.

1. Mammologists are scientists (**who**) / whose / which study mammals.
2. Megabats are bats who / whose / that live in the tropics.
3. The idea that / who / whose bats carry rabies started in the 1960s.
4. Littlehales was the photographer who / whose / which photos were used.

Practice B

In your notebook, rewrite each pair of sentences as one sentence. Use a relative pronoun to join them.

1. I read the article by the scientist. He knows about bats.
   I read the article by the scientist who knows about bats.
2. Chlorophacinone is a poison. It kills bats.
3. The photos show bats. The bats seemed frightened.
4. Megabats are large bats. The bats eat fruit.
5. They built the bat box. It was in the tree.

Apply

Write sentences about a pet or an animal you are familiar with. Use relative pronouns. Then tell a partner about it.

Example: Parrots are birds that repeat humans' words. . . .

Noun Clauses with *that*

A noun clause is a dependent clause that acts as a noun. Writers use noun clauses with *that* to report what someone said, observed, thought, or claimed. Specific reporting verbs are used for specific purposes.

Example	Purpose and Reporting Verbs
Littlehales *said* that Merlin had learned enough about photography to try it alone.	to report what someone said *said, explained, stated*
I soon *saw* that most people's negative attitudes about bats could be changed in minutes.	to report what someone observed *saw, observed, noticed*
They *believe* that bats commonly carry the disease rabies.	to report what someone thinks *believe, think, suggest, claim*
Further study *showed* that this was not true.	to report a conclusion *show, conclude, demonstrate*

> **Grammar Skill**
>
> Noun clauses with *that* often replace a person's exact words in reported speech, as in the example in the first row of the chart.

> **Grammar Check**
>
> ✓ Why do writers use **noun clauses with *that*?**

Practice A

Circle the correct reporting verb to complete each sentence.
1. The report **demonstrated** / **saw** that bats can get rabies.
2. While studying bats, Merlin **noticed** / **believed** that most photos of bats show them snarling in self-defense.
3. Many people **think** / **see** that all bats are dangerous.
4. While observing bats at night, Merlin **demonstrated** / **concluded** that they are difficult to photograph.
5. In the 1960s, research **showed** / **thought** that bats were not harmed by rabies.

Practice B

In your notebook, rewrite each sentence, using a noun clause with *that* and the reporting verb in parentheses.
1. Our teacher: "There are two kinds of bats." (explained)
   Our teacher explained that there are two kinds of bats.
2. A scientist: "Animals in the wild seem happier than animals in zoos." (observed)
3. Many people: "Bats are very dangerous." (believe)
4. The study: "Bats are important to people." (concluded)

> **Apply**
>
> Work in small groups. Take turns making statements and reporting them, using noun clauses with *that*.
>
> **Example:**
> Ana: It is hot today.
> Pedro: Ana said that it is hot today . . .

Reading 2

Reading 2

Writing

Write Classifying Paragraphs

One way to organize your ideas in a research report is by categories; this is also called *classifying*. When you classify, you discuss one category at a time, pointing out how the categories are similar and different. For example, suppose you were writing about flying animals. You might discuss birds in one part of the report and bats in another. You might say that birds and bats are similar in that they both can fly. They are different in that bats are mammals but birds are not.

> **Writing Prompt**
> Write two paragraphs that classify a group of animals. Discuss the similarities and differences among the animals. For example, you may choose to classify cats, such as lions and cheetahs. Use a T-chart to organize your ideas. Use relative pronouns correctly.

1 Prewrite Begin by choosing two similar groups of animals or species, such as lions and cheetahs, tuna and salmon, or butterflies and moths.

- Research how the two groups of animals are similar and different.
- Complete a T-chart with information about how the groups are similar and different.
- Decide how to organize the information from your T-chart in two paragraphs. Which animal will you discuss first? Second?

A student named Leah listed her ideas about two kinds of bats in this T-chart.

Megabats	Microbats
—larger —long noses: called flying foxes —large eyes —sense of smell: find fruit and nectar —small ears: hear well —live in tropics of Africa, Asia, and Australia —fewer species	—smaller —small eyes: don't see as well —feed at night —use echolocation to find food (insects) —hunt by sending out high-pitched sounds & listening for echoes —more species

② Draft Use your T-chart to help you write a first draft.

- At the beginning of the first paragraph, state what two groups you will classify. Then describe the first group. Briefly explain how it is different from the second group.
- In the second paragraph, describe the second group. Explain how it is different from the first group. Then add a concluding sentence about how the two groups are similar.
- Use adjective clauses to combine ideas as needed. Be sure to use subject pronouns correctly.

③ Revise Read over your draft. Look for places where the writing is unclear or needs improvement. Complete (✓) the Writing Checklist to help you identify problems. Then, revise your draft, using the editing and proofreading marks listed on page 467.

④ Edit and Proofread Check your work for errors in grammar, usage, mechanics, and spelling. Trade papers with a partner to obtain feedback. Use the Peer Review Checklist on Workbook page 00. Edit your final draft in response to feedback from your partner and your teacher.

⑤ Publish Prepare a clean copy of your final draft. Share your classifying paragraphs with the class. Save your work. You'll need to refer to them in the Writing Workshop at the end of the unit.

Writing Checklist

Ideas:
☐ I described the two groups of animals clearly.

Word Choice:
☐ I used details, including adjective clauses, to make distinctions

Organization:
☐ I wrote about one group in each paragraph.

Conventions:
☐ I used subject pronouns correctly.

Leah Morales

Two Kinds of Bats

There are two major groups of bats: megabats and microbats. In general, megabats are larger than microbats. Because of their long noses, megabats are often called flying foxes. They have large eyes that can see well during the day and at night, and they use their senses of sight and smell to find the fruit and nectar that they eat.

Microbats are generally smaller than megabats. They have small eyes that see well, but not as well as megabats. Because microbats are active at night, they rely on echolocation to find food and to avoid obstacles in the dark. Most microbats eat insects. While flying, they hunt by sending out high-pitched sounds and listening for echoes. There are many more species of microbats than megabats, but both kinds of bats play an important part in keeping nature in balance.

Reading 3

Prepare to Read

What You Will Learn

Reading
- Vocabulary building: *Literary terms, word study*
- Reading strategy: *Read aloud*
- Text type: *Literature (poetry)*

Grammar
- Typical and atypical word order
- Simple past (irregular) and past progressive

Writing
- Support the main idea

THE BIG QUESTION

What makes animals so amazing? Animals have been the subject of paintings and poetry since prehistoric times. Why do you think people are so fascinated by animals? Are you familiar with any art or poems about animals? What are they called? What do the titles tell you about the paintings or poems? Discuss with a partner.

Build Background

You are about to read three poems about animals: **"A Narrow Fellow in the Grass," "Daybreak,"** and **"Birdfoot's Grandpa."** For each poem, think about the speaker's attitude toward the animal being described. Is the animal described in a humorous way? A loving way? A respectful way? Asking these questions will help you understand and appreciate the poems.

▲ A painting of a horse in the Cave of Lascaux, in France

400 Unit 6

Vocabulary

Learn Literary Words

Literary Words
figurative language
imagery
metaphor
simile

Figurative language refers to the use of words in an unusual or imaginative manner. This language goes beyond the literal meanings of the words. Writers use figurative language to make their ideas more effective, persuasive, and powerful. Figurative language such as imagery, metaphors, and similes gives readers a better understanding of the writer's ideas.

Imagery uses figurative language to describe things while appealing to the senses. Read these lines from "Birdfoot's Grandpa" by Joseph Bruchac.

> The rain was falling,/a mist about his white hair. . . .

These lines use imagery to appeal to the reader's sense of sight, creating an image of a cloud of mist above the man's white hair.

Metaphors are implied comparisons in which one thing is spoken about as though it were something else. Read these lines from a "A Narrow Fellow in the Grass" by Emily Dickinson.

> A narrow Fellow in the Grass
> Occasionally rides—
> You may have met Him—did you not,
> His notice sudden is—

In the lines above, a snake is compared to a narrow fellow riding along the grass.

Similes are comparisons that use the words *like* or *as*. Read these lines from the poem "Daybreak" by Galway Kinnell. What similes can you find?

> dozens of starfishes/were creeping. It was/as though the mud were a sky/and enormous, imperfect stars/moved across it slowly. . . .

Practice

With a partner, read the lines below. Tell whether each line is a simile or a metaphor. Underline the two things that are being compared.

1. The skinny cat was like a scarecrow covered with fur.
2. He bounced as he walked, as though he had springs under his feet.
3. The road was a ribbon of moonlight.

Reading 3

Reading 3

Listening and Speaking: Academic Words

Study the purple words and their meanings. You will find these words useful when talking and writing about literature. Write each word and its meaning in your notebook, then say the words aloud with a partner. After you read "A Narrow Fellow in the Grass," "Daybreak," and "Birdfoot's Grandpa," try to use these words to respond to the text.

Academic Words
- appreciation
- attitude
- category
- vehicle

appreciation = an understanding of the meaning or beauty of something	Daniel's visit to the museum gave him a better **appreciation** of the work of Pablo Picasso.
attitude = the opinions and feeling you have about something	The poet's choice of words shows her **attitude** toward the topic.
category = a group of the same kind of things	What **category** is this 14-line poem, sonnet or ballad?
vehicle = something people use as a way to spread ideas	Art is an important **vehicle** for sharing opinions.

Practice
WB 208

Complete these sentences in your notebook. Include the purple word in your sentence.

1. Pam's night at the opera . . . (appreciation)
2. In opinion essays, we include . . . (attitude)
3. The art museum has . . . (category)
4. Music can be . . . (vehicle)

▲ Ancient cave paintings in Thailand provided a vehicle for people to express what their daily lives were like.

Word Study: Words with Double Letters

Knowing spelling rules can help you in your writing. Keep a list of these in your notebook and memorize them.

In a single-syllable word ending in *b, d, g, l, m, n, p, r,* or *t* that has a consonant-vowel-consonant pattern, double the final consonant letter. Here are some examples:

Base Word	Add *-ed, -er, -est,* or *-ing*	Double Letter Spelling
mad	mad + *-er*, mad + *-est*	madder, maddest
big	big + *-er*, big + *-est*	bigger, biggest
pop	pop + *-ed*, pop + *-ing*	popped, popping
wrap	wrap + *-ed*, wrap + *-ing*	wrapped, wrapping

Practice
WB 209

Complete each sentence by adding the correct ending to the base word in parentheses. If the base word follows a consonant-vowel-consonant pattern, use double letters.

1. The young man is _____ at the store on his way home. (stop)
2. I was _____ to catch the bus. (rush)
3. My older sister is the _____ of all the girls. (slim)
4. We _____ our car in the back of the parking lot. (spot)
5. This shirt looks a bit _____ than what I wanted. (red)

Reading Strategy | Read Aloud

Reading aloud brings literature to life. It can make reading more meaningful and enjoyable, especially in the case of poetry. When you read poetry aloud, keep these ideas in mind:

- Pay close attention to the sounds of the words.
- Think about the structure of the poem. Many poets use rhyme, but not all do. Which words in the poem rhyme with one another?
- Notice the rhythm of the language the poet has used.
- Use your voice as expressively as you can while you are reading.

As you read the poems aloud, notice the similarities and differences among them. Which one do you enjoy reading aloud the most?

WB 210

Reading 3

**Literature
Poetry**

Set a purpose for reading Read these poems to discover new ways of thinking about and appreciating three animals. In what ways are they amazing?

A Narrow Fellow in the Grass

A narrow Fellow in the Grass
Occasionally rides—
You may have met Him—did you not,
His **notice** sudden is—

The Grass divides as with a Comb—
A spotted **shaft** is seen—
And then it closes at your feet
And opens further on—

He likes a **Boggy Acre**,
A Floor too cool for Corn—
Yet when a Boy, and Barefoot,
I more than once, at Noon

Have passed, I thought, a Whip lash
Unbraiding in the Sun—
When, stooping to secure it,
It wrinkled, and was gone—

Several of Nature's People
I know, and they know me—
I feel for them a **transport
Of cordiality**—

But never met this Fellow
Attended or alone
Without a tighter breathing,
And Zero at the Bone—
—Emily Dickinson

notice, warning
shaft, long, thin object
Boggy Acre, wet and muddy ground
unbraiding, becoming straight
transport of cordiality, sudden feeling of friendliness

✓ LITERARY CHECK

What **imagery** does the poet create? What **metaphors** do you find in the poem? How does the **figurative language** used in the poem help you visualize the snake?

Word Skill

In Western literature, the word *snake* often has a negative **connotation**. It is associated with trickery or evil, bringing to mind scary images of snakes, their movements, and their potential for deception.

404 Unit 6

Before You Go On

1. What does the poet mean by "And Zero at the Bone"?
2. How does the "narrow fellow" affect the grass as he moves?

On Your Own

How would you feel if you encountered the snake in the poem? Why?

About the Poet

Emily Dickinson (1830–1886) was one of the greatest American poets. She wrote over 1,700 poems, but only ten were published in her lifetime. She says in one of her poems: *This is my letter to the world/That never wrote to me.* Many of her poems explore love, death, and nature.

Reading 3 405

Daybreak

On the **tidal** mud, just before sunset,
dozens of starfishes
were creeping. It was
as though the mud were a sky
and enormous, imperfect stars
moved across it as slowly
as the actual stars cross heaven.
All at once they stopped,
and, as if they had simply
increased their **receptivity**
to gravity, they sank down
into the mud, faded down
into it and lay still, and by the time
pink of sunset broke across them
they were as invisible
as the true stars at daybreak.
—*Galway Kinnell*

tidal, relating to the rise and fall of the ocean
receptivity, readiness to give in to

Reading Skill

Listen to the way your partner reads this text. If you don't understand an idea or word, ask your partner to clarify or explain. This will help you understand the poem.

✓ LITERARY CHECK

What is the mud compared to in the **simile**? How does the **figurative language** help you visualize the setting and the starfishes?

About the Poet

Galway Kinnell (1927–2014) was a well-known American poet. Many of his poems describe connections between human beings and other creatures. Some of his most famous poems, such as "The Bear," "The Porcupine," and "St. Francis and the Sow," use sensory details to describe an animal.

Birdfoot's Grandpa

The old man
must have stopped our car
two dozen times to climb out
and gather into his hands
the small toads blinded
by our lights and leaping,
live drops of rain.

The rain was falling,
a mist about his white hair
and I kept saying
you can't save them all,
accept it, get back in
we've got places to go.

But, leathery hands full
of wet brown life,
knee deep in the summer
roadside grass,
he just smiled and said
they have places to go, too.

—Joseph Bruchac

✓ LITERARY CHECK

What images does the poet create? How does the poet's use of **imagery** help you with meaning?

About the Poet

Joseph Bruchac writes poems, short stories, and novels. Both his writing and his style of storytelling reflect his Native-American heritage. The author of more than seventy books, he has won many awards, including Writer of the Year and Storyteller of the Year in 1998. Bruchac grew up in New York, near the Adirondack Mountains, where he still lives.

Before You Go On

1. In what ways are the starfishes like real stars?
2. How is the old man's attitude toward the toads different from the speaker's?

👤 On Your Own

Have you ever seen beauty or dignity in ordinary creatures? Explain.

Reading 3

Review and Practice

Reading 3

Dramatic Reading

Work in groups to reread, discuss, and interpret "A Narrow Fellow in the Grass," "Daybreak," and "Birdfoot's Grandpa." Read each poem line by line and talk about the images that come to mind. Identify similes, metaphors, and other types of figurative language. Find examples of imagery. Discuss how each poem makes you feel. Try to figure out difficult words or phrasing from context. Consult a dictionary or your teacher for help if necessary.

After you analyze the poems, choose one to memorize. Then recite the poem within your group. Comment on one another's reading and make suggestions for improvements. You may wish to hold a contest with the class in which each group competes to present the best oral reading.

> **Speaking Tip**
>
> Match the tone of your voice to the tone of the poem. Speak slowly and with feeling.

Comprehension

Recall

1. Where and when does "Daybreak" take place?
2. In "Birdfoot's Grandpa," why does the old man stop his car several times?

Comprehend

3. Why is the old man concerned about the toads in the poem "Birdfoot's Grandpa"?
4. Who is the "narrow fellow in the grass"? How does the speaker of the poem feel whenever he meets the fellow in the grass?

Analyze

5. What do you think the poet Kinnell's attitude toward the starfishes was? Why?
6. What attitudes do the poets show about the animals they wrote about?

Connect

7. Which poem did you enjoy the most? Why?
8. Which experience in the poems could you identify with more? Why?

Discussion

Discuss with a partner or in a small group.

1. How could you use the poems to convince someone who doesn't think so, that animals are amazing? Explain.
2. Imagine that there's a poetry contest for the three poems with these categories: best imagery, best picture of one animal, best attitude about an animal, best one for enjoyment. Which would you nominate for each category? Why?

What makes animals so amazing? How do you think the poets whose work you just read would answer this question?

> **Listening Tip**
>
> Give speakers time to express their ideas. Listen carefully. Be open-minded to ideas that are different from yours. When there is a pause, give your viewpoint.

Response to Literature

211

Each of the poems you have read is about an animal. Think about an animal that you find especially interesting and amazing. List everything you know about this animal. Then do research to find out more. Write a paragraph telling what makes the animal amazing. When you are finished writing, read your paragraph to the class.

Reading 3
Grammar

Typical and Atypical Word Order

In English sentences, typical or usual word order is subject + verb (+ object). An adjective usually goes before the noun it modifies or after the verb **be**. A prepositional phrase typically appears after the verb or the object. Look at the examples showing typical word order.

Example	Word order
The old man stopped our car.	subject + verb + object
We saw enormous stars.	adjective + noun
They were invisible.	be + adjective
They sank into the mud.	verb + prepositional phrase

> **Grammar Skill**
> Poets may place important words at the end of a line of poetry to emphasize them.

Poets often use atypical word order in their poetry.

In the following example from "A Narrow Fellow in the Grass," Emily Dickinson uses atypical word order to give the poem a certain rhythm and to create a half, or slant, rhyme between *rides* and *is*.

Atypical Word Order	Typical Word Order
A narrow Fellow in the Grass Occasionally rides— You may have met Him—did you not, His notice sudden is—	A narrow Fellow occasionally Rides in the Grass— You may have met Him—didn't you? His notice is sudden—

> **Grammar Check**
> ✓ What is **typical word order** in a sentence?

Practice A
(WB 212)

Identify which lines in the poem use typical word order and which use atypical word order. Write *typical* or *atypical*.

1. Through the meadow cows roam ___atypical___
2. Eating the grass _____
3. The field, green _____
4. Until with stomachs full _____
5. Home they go _____

> **Apply**
> Work with a partner. Write a poem about an animal. Use atypical word order.
> **Example:** Swimming in the sea, the whale . . .

Practice B

Find and read a poem with atypical word order. In your notebook, rewrite the lines in typical word order.

Simple Past (Irregular) and Past Progressive

Many verbs have an irregular form in the simple past—they do not have an *-ed* ending. You must to memorize them.

be → was/were	have → had	meet → met
break → broke	keep → kept	say → said
give → gave	lie → lay	sink → sank

Notice these examples of irregular past verbs in the poem "Daybreak":

> . . . they **sank** down/into the mud, faded down/into it and **lay** still, and by the time/pink of sunset **broke** across them/they **were** as invisible/as the true stars at daybreak.

The past progressive shows an action that was in progress at a specific time in the past. It continues over a period of time, and it may be interrupted by another action. Form the past progressive with *was* or *were* and the present participle.

> On the tidal mud, just before sunset,/dozens of starfishes **were creeping.** . . . All at once they stopped, . . .

In the example above, the action in progress is *creeping*. The past form verb *stopped* interrupts the action.

Grammar Check
✓ When do you use the **past progressive**?

Grammar Skill
Remember to use *was* with the subjects *I, he, she,* and *it.* Use *were* with the subjects *you* and *they.*

Practice A

Complete each sentence with the irregular past form of a verb from the box.

be	break	keep	~~meet~~

1. I __met__ my cousin at the movie theater.
2. I dropped the glass and _____ it.
3. My grandmother _____ her photographs in a photo album.
4. Many stars _____ in the sky.

Practice B

Complete each with the past progressive form of the verb in parentheses.

1. My brother __was sleeping__ (sleep) when I called.
2. My parents _____ (watch) TV last night.
3. The sun _____ (shine) all day.
4. I wasn't home last night. I _____ (study) in the library.

Apply
Work in small groups. Make a progressive story. Take turns adding sentences in the simple past and past progressive. Be sure to use irregular verbs correctly.

Example:
A: One day, I was walking to school, and a strange thing happened.
B: I met a talking cat. The cat said. . . .

Reading 3 **411**

Reading 3

Writing

Support the Main Idea

At the end of this unit, you will write a research report. One skill you will need to know in order to write a research report is how to support your main idea with details, including facts and examples.

> **Writing Prompt**
>
> Write a paragraph about an animal with a main idea supported by facts and examples. You might choose to write about a pet, or about an animal in the wild. List your ideas in a main idea and details web. Be sure to use typical word order.

① Prewrite Begin by identifying an animal to write about.

- What is your main idea about this animal? What do you find most interesting about it?

- Complete a chart with facts, details, and examples that illustrate or elaborate on your main idea.

- Record your main idea and supporting details in a graphic organizer, such a a word web.

Here's a word web created by a student named Dylan about snakes and their unique senses.

Main Idea: Snakes—unique senses

Detail 1: Sight = not strong

Detail 2: Hearing = not strong (no external ears, sense vibrations)

Detail 3: Smell = very strong (no external nose, use tongue to analyze what is close by)

Detail 4: Touch = very strong (sensitive underbelly, some can sense heat)

② Draft Use your word web to help you write a first draft.
- State your main idea in the first sentence.
- Include supporting details.
- Be sure to use the typical word order.

③ Revise Read over your draft. Look for places where the writing is unclear or needs improvement. Complete (✓) the Writing Checklist to help you identify problems. Then, revise your draft, using the editing and proofreading marks listed on page 467.

④ Edit and Proofread Check your work for errors in grammar, usage, mechanics, and spelling. Trade papers with a partner to obtain feedback. Use the Peer Review Checklist on Workbook page 00. Edit your final draft in response to feedback from your partner and your teacher.

⑤ Publish Prepare a clean copy of your final draft. Share your paragraph with the class. Save your work. You'll need to refer to it in the Writing Workshop at the end of the unit.

Here is Dylan's main idea and supporting details paragraph.

> **Writing Checklist**
>
> **Ideas:**
> ☐ I stated my main idea and supporting details clearly.
>
> **Word Choice:**
> ☐ I used precise words to explain the main ideas and details that support it.
>
> **Conventions:**
> ☐ I used typical word order.

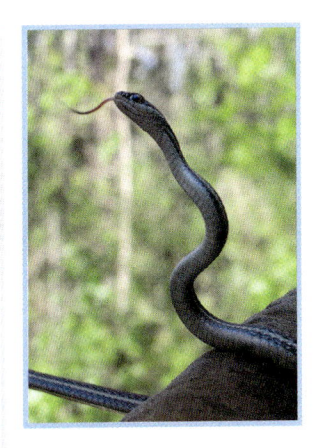

Dylan Bishop

Snakes' Senses

Snakes have unique senses, unlike the senses of most other animals. They do not have a strong sense of sight or hearing, so they rely mostly on their acute senses of smell and touch. Snakes do not have external ears. Instead, they have inner ears inside the head. They can hear by feeling vibrations through the ground. The vibrations pass through the snake's sensitive underbelly and travel through the body to reach a bone connected to the inner ear, which senses the vibrations. This is one way snakes can tell when other animals are moving toward them. Snakes also don't have an external nose. They use their tongue to take in particles from the air and analyze them in their mouth. By doing this, they can tell if a predator or a potential meal is nearby. Some snakes can sense body heat in other animals, an ability which helps them detect warm-blooded prey such as mammals and birds.

Reading 4

Prepare to Read

What You Will Learn

Reading
- Vocabulary building: *Literary terms, word study*
- Reading strategy: *Sequence*
- Text type: *Literature (novel excerpt)*

Grammar
- Gerunds
- Infinitives
- Using quotation marks for exact words
- Quotation marks: Terms, expressions, and titles

Writing
- Write an interpretive response

❓ THE BIG QUESTION

What makes animals so amazing? Look at the image below. What is the setting? What are the people doing? What animals appear in the image and what role do you think they play? Discuss with a partner.

Build Background

This reading is an excerpt from Jack London's novel *White Fang*. *White Fang* has been translated into 89 languages and has been adapted into many films, cartoons, artworks, and other written texts. *White Fang* takes place in Canada and later in California, during the 1890s gold rush. The excerpt you are going to read takes place in California—the Southland. Most of the story is told from the point of view of the wolf-dog White Fang. The excerpt follows White Fang as he interacts with Weedon, his master, and as he manages to find his "voice" at a critical point.

▲ Gold rush prospectors cross a river in this 1898 engraving

Vocabulary

Learn Literary Words

Literary Words
setting
point of view
flashback
foreshadowing

The **setting** of a story is the time and place of a story's action. The setting of a story can change, as it does in the excerpt from *White Fang* that you are going to read. The setting changes from an area where White Fang's master, Weedon, is out riding a horse to Weedon's home.

A story may be told from the third-person **point of view** to reveal the thoughts and feelings of one of the characters. In this excerpt, the novel's narrator gives readers insights into White Fang and his thoughts and feelings.

A **flashback** is a part of a story in which the action jumps back to events that happened earlier in the story or in a character's past. Flasbacks interrupt the current action and reveal something about the past. As you read, notice how flashbacks help you follow the events of the story and better understand characters.

Foreshadowing is language that suggests something that is about to happen. For example, read this passage from the story:

> It was in connection with the riding, that White Fang achieved one other mode of expression—remarkable in that he did it but twice in all his life. The first time occurred when the master was trying to teach a spirited thoroughbred the method of opening and closing gates without the rider's dismounting.

This passage raises questions for the reader: *What is the mode of expression? When will White Fang use it next?* The author might answer these questions in the following sentences, or later. Foreshadowing keeps the reader wondering what comes next.

Practice

WB 215

Work with a partner. Take turns reading the quotes and answering the question(s).

1. "What he didn't know is that he would never set foot in that house again." Is this an example of foreshadowing or a flashback? Explain.
2. "The snow lay in drifts across the front porch and the hard winter light threw long shadows against the side of the house." What is the setting? How do you know?

Reading 4   **415**

Reading 4

Listening and Speaking: Academic Words

Study the purple words and their meanings. You will find these words useful when talking and writing about informational texts. Write each word and its meaning in your notebook, then say the words aloud with a partner. After you read the excerpt from *White Fang*, try to use these words to respond to the text.

Academic Words
- abandon
- committed
- resist
- reveal

abandon = to leave something behing permanently	As the fire approached, many famillies had to **abandon** their homes.
committed = used all the time and energy that you could to achieve something	The woman **committed** all of her time to studying wolves. She read many articles, and observed them in the wild as much as she could.
resist = to stop yourself from doing something you really want to do	The woman couldn't **resist** calling out to the wolf, but this was a mistake.
reveal = to uncover and show something	When he growled, he **revealed** his sharp teeth.

Practice
WB 216

Work with a partner to answer these questions. Try to include the purple word in your answer. Write the sentences in your notebook.

1. Have you ever had to **abandon** a project you started? Explain.
2. What is something you are very **committed** to learning?
3. What kind of food is hard for you to **resist**?
4. In what situation might you **reveal** someone's secret?

▲ Scientists are committed to finding ways to preserve wolf populations.

Word Study: Frequently Misspelled Words

Spelling can be difficult in English. Some words are particularly tricky. Learning how to spell these words correctly can save you time looking up words in a dictionary. Look at the examples below.

Frequently Misspelled Words	Spelling Errors
believe	Mixing up letters, such as *beleive*
existence	Confusing endings, such as *existance*
vicious	Mixing up sound-spellings, such as *viscious*
disappearing	Missing double letters, such as *disapearing*
until	Adding double letters, such as *untill*
grateful	Confusing spellings of what sounds like the word but isn't, such as *greatful*

Practice
WB 217

Work with a partner. Correct the spelling errors in the following words. Write the words in your notebook. Check your work in a dictionary. Then write a sentence with each word.

| diffrent | disipline | inteligent | intimmidate | labratories |

Reading Strategy — Sequence

The story you are going to read is an excerpt from a novel. The author of a novel may not present each event in sequence. In an excerpt from a novel, there may be references to other parts of the novel. To help you follow the events in this excerpt, ask yourself:

- When did this event happen? Why is it important to the events I am reading about?
- Is this a flashback to an event that happened earlier? A foreshadowing of what is going to happen? Why is the author bringing it up now?
- Which event happened first?

As you read the excerpt from *White Fang*, create a sequence chart that includes the main events.

WB 218

Reading 4

Fiction Novel

Set a purpose for reading Read this excerpt to find out what White Fang learns and manages to do at a critical point in the story. Why is it important?

from White Fang
by Jack London

The months came and went. There was plenty of food and no work in the Southland, and White Fang lived fat and prosperous and happy. Not alone was he in the geographical Southland, for he was in the Southland of life. Human kindness was like a sun shining upon him, and he flourished like a flower planted in good soil.

And yet he remained somehow different from other dogs. He knew the law even better than did the dogs that had known no other life, and he observed the law more **punctiliously**; but still there was about him a suggestion of lurking **ferocity**, as though the Wild still lingered in him and the wolf in him merely slept.

. . . .

He missed the snow without being aware of it. "An unduly long summer," would have been his thought had he thought about it; as it was, he merely missed the snow in a vague, subconscious way. In the same fashion, especially in the heat of summer when he suffered from the sun, he experienced faint longings for the Northland. Their only effect upon him, however, was to make him uneasy and restless without his knowing what was the matter.

White Fang had never been very demonstrative. Beyond his snuggling and the throwing of a **crooning** note into his love-growl, he had no way of expressing his love. Yet it was given him to discover a third way. He had always been susceptible to the laughter of the gods. Laughter had affected him with madness, made him frantic with **rage**. But he did not have it in him to be angry with the love-master, and when that god elected to laugh at him in a good-natured, bantering way, he was nonplussed. He could feel the pricking and stinging of the old anger as it strove to rise up in him,

---

punctiliously, carefully, with attention to detail
ferocity, a state of being extremely violent
crooning, singing or speaking in a soft voice
rage, a strong feeling of anger

but it strove against love. He could not be angry; yet he had to do something. At first he was **dignified**, and the master laughed the harder. Then he tried to be more dignified, and the master laughed harder than before. In the end, the master laughed him out of his dignity. His jaws slightly parted, his lips lifted a little, and a quizzical expression that was more love than humour came into his eyes. He had learned to laugh.

Likewise he learned to **romp** with the master, to be tumbled down and rolled over, and be the victim of innumerable rough tricks. In return he feigned anger, bristling and growling ferociously, and clipping his teeth together in snaps that had all the seeming of deadly intention. But he never forgot himself. Those snaps were always delivered on the empty air. At the end of such a romp, when blow and cuff and snap and snarl were fast and furious, they would break off suddenly and stand several feet apart, glaring at each other. And then, just as suddenly, like the sun rising on a stormy sea, they would begin to laugh. This would always culminate with the master's arms going around White Fang's neck and shoulders while the latter crooned and growled his love-song.

---

dignified, behaving in a serious, calm way
romp, to play in a noisy way

Before You Go On

1. Where did White Fang live before? How is White Fang adjusting to life in the Southland? Explain.

2. How would you describe the relationship between White Fang and his master?

On Your Own

What do you think it means that White Fang had learned to laugh? Explain.

Reading 4

But nobody else ever romped with White Fang. He did not **permit** it. He stood on his dignity, and when they attempted it, his warning **snarl** and bristling mane were anything but playful. That he allowed the master these liberties was no reason that he should be a common dog, loving here and loving there, everybody's property for a romp and good time. He loved with single heart. . . .

The master went out on horseback a great deal, and to accompany him was one of White Fang's chief duties in life. In the Northland he had evidenced his **fealty** by **toiling** in the **harness**; but there were no **sleds** in the Southland, nor did dogs pack burdens on their backs. So he rendered fealty in the new way, by running with the master's horse. The

---

permit, to allow
snarl, a low, angry noise
toiling, working hard
harness, leather or fabric bands that fit on an animal
sleds, small vehicles that slide over snow
fealty, loyalty to a master

longest day never played White Fang out. His was the gait of the wolf, smooth, tireless and effortless, and at the end of fifty miles he would come in jauntily ahead of the horse.

It was in connection with the riding, that White Fang achieved one other mode of expression—remarkable in that he did it but twice in all his life. The first time occurred when the master was trying to teach a spirited thoroughbred the method of opening and closing gates without the rider's dismounting. Time and again and many times he ranged the horse up to the gate in the effort to close it and each time the horse became frightened and backed and plunged away. It grew more nervous and excited every moment. When it **reared**, the master put the **spurs** to it and made it drop its fore-legs back to earth, whereupon it would begin kicking with its hind-legs. White Fang watched the performance with increasing **anxiety** until he could contain himself no longer, when he sprang in front of the horse and barked **savagely** and warningly.

Though he often tried to bark thereafter, and the master encouraged him, he succeeded only once, and then it was not in the master's presence. A scamper across the pasture, a jackrabbit rising suddenly under the horse's feet, a violent sheer, a stumble, a fall to earth, and a broken leg for the master, was the cause of it. White Fang **sprang** in a rage at the throat of the offending horse but was checked by the master's voice.

"Home! Go home!" the master commanded when he had ascertained his injury.

White Fang was disinclined to desert him. The master thought of writing a note, but searched his pockets vainly for pencil and paper. Again he commanded White Fang to go home.

The latter regarded him wistfully, started away, then returned and **whined** softly. The master talked to him gently but seriously, and he cocked his ears, and listened with painful intentness.

"That's all right, old fellow, you just run along home," ran the talk. "Go on home and tell them what's happened to me. Home with you, you wolf. Get along home!"

White Fang knew the meaning of "home," and though he did not understand the remainder of the master's language, he knew it was his will that he should go home. He turned and trotted reluctantly away. Then he stopped, undecided, and looked back over his shoulder.

"Go home!" came the sharp command, and this time he obeyed.

---

reared, stood up on the back legs
spurs, sharp objects on a rider's boot
anxiety, fear of what might happen
savagely, in a violent manner
sprang, jumped up quickly
whined, made a high sound because of pain or unhappiness

Before You Go On

1. What was the other mode of expression that White Fang learned? When did he first use it and why?
2. Does White Fang express himself this way again? Does the reader know when or why? Explain.

On Your Own

What do you think will happen next?

The family was on the porch, taking the cool of the afternoon, when White Fang arrived. He came in among them, panting, covered with dust.

"Weedon's back," Weedon's mother announced.

The children welcomed White Fang with glad cries and ran to meet him. He avoided them and passed down the porch, but they cornered him against a rocking-chair and the railing. He **growled** and tried to push by them. Their mother looked apprehensively in their direction.

"I confess, he makes me nervous around the children," she said. "I have a dread that he will turn upon them unexpectedly some day."

---

growled, made a low, angry sound

Growling savagely, White Fang sprang out of the corner, overturning the boy and the girl. The mother called them to her and comforted them, telling them not to bother White Fang.

"A wolf is a wolf!" commented Judge Scott. "There is no trusting one."

"But he is not all wolf," interposed Beth, standing for her brother in his **absence**. "You have only Weedon's opinion for that," rejoined the judge. "He merely surmises that there is some strain of dog in White Fang; but as he will tell you himself, he knows nothing about it. As for his appearance—"

He did not finish his sentence. White Fang stood before him, growling fiercely.

"Go away! Lie down, sir!" Judge Scott commanded.

White Fang turned to the love-master's wife. She screamed with fright as he seized her dress in his teeth and dragged on it till the frail fabric tore away. By this time he had become the centre of interest.

He had **ceased** from his growling and stood, head up, looking into their faces. His throat worked spasmodically, but made no sound, while he struggled with all his body, convulsed with the effort to rid himself of the incommunicable something that strained for utterance.

"I hope he is not going mad," said Weedon's mother. "I told Weedon that I was afraid the warm climate would not agree with an Arctic animal."

"He's trying to speak, I do believe," Beth announced.

At this moment speech came to White Fang, rushing up in a great burst of barking.

"Something has happened to Weedon," his wife said decisively.

They were all on their feet now, and White Fang ran down the steps, looking back for them to follow. For the second and last time in his life he had barked and made himself understood.

---

absence, not present; not in the place where expected
ceased, stopped

About the Author

Jack London (1878–1916) was a journalist and author best known for his novels *The Call of the Wild* and *White Fang*. London grew up in California, taking odd jobs and reading travel books and novels at the library. He won his first writing award at age 17 with only an 8th grade education, and went on to write over 50 novels in his lifetime.

Before You Go On

1. What does the family think when they first see White Fang? How do you know?
2. What does White Fang manage to do that changes their minds?

On Your Own

What do you think will happen next in the story?

Reading 4

Review and Practice

Reader's Theater 🎧

Act out the following scene just after White Fang has barked for the second time in his life.

Weedon's Wife: [*decisively*] Oh no! Something's happened to Weedon.
The boy and girl: That's why White Fang ran by us. He usually comes right up to us.
Judge Scott: [*softening about the wolf*] Well, he sure did get our attention!
Beth: And he barked! I've never heard him bark before. He was trying to tell us something!
Weedon's Wife: And that's why he tugged at my dress. He never does that! Let's all hurry up. White Fang wants us to follow him! He'll take us to Weedon. Hurry now. [*She grabs the children's hands and motions for everyone to follow White Fang.*]

> **Speaking Tip**
>
> Read any words in brackets to help you know how to say your lines. Practice in your group before you present to the class.

Comprehension

WB 219

Recall
1. When was the first time White Fang barked?
2. When was the second time?

Comprehend
3. What happened to Weedon? How does White Fang help him?
4. How does the family react to White Fang? What are they going to do?

Analyze
5. How does Jack London, the author, reveal that he thinks animals are amazing? Explain.
6. How do Weedon and White Fang show they are committed to each other? Give examples.

Connect
7. Do you agree more with Judge Scott or with Weedon's sister, Beth, about White Fang? Explain.
8. Would you recommend this story to a friend to read? Explain.

Discussion

Discuss with a partner or small group.

1. White Fang was a wild animal who would naturally resist contact with humans. How do you think he developed a relationship with humans?
2. How do you think the relationship between White Fang and his master will continue to evolve?

What makes animals so amazing? To you, what makes White Fang so amazing? Explain.

Listening Skill

Think about what you are hearing. Try to relate it to what you already know.

Response to Literature

Work with a partner to write how you think the story ends. Begin by discussing this question: *What happens after the family goes off in search of Weedon?* When you are ready and have decided on an ending, write it in your notebook or enter it on a computer. Use a narrator and include dialogue. Describe how the characters feel about what has happened. Explain how the family feels about White Fang now. Remember that the narrator also reveals White Fang's feelings, so include them, too. Consider how you think White Fang felt when he hesitated to obey: Do you think he felt like he was abandoning his master? Also, consider that this is the only other time White Fang barks in his life. When you are satisfied with your ending, share it with the class.

◀ The moment the family realizes something is wrong happens when White Fang manages to bark.

Reading 4

Grammar

Gerunds

A gerund is the base form of the verb, followed by *-ing*. It can be the subject of a sentence, the object of certain verbs, or the object of a preposition.

> **Grammar Skill**
> Gerunds are usually singular.

Example of Gerund	Role in Sentence
Growling and snarling are natural for White Fang.	subject of a sentence
He had ceased **growling** . . .	object of certain verbs
The master thought about **writing** a note . . .	object of a preposition

The following verbs are almost always followed by gerunds.

avoid consider	enjoy finish	postpone practice	quit recommend	risk stop

Practice A

Underline the gerund in each sentence. Then write *S* if it is the subject of a sentence, *OV* if it is the object of a verb, or *OP* if it is the object of a preposition.

1. The park rangers stopped <u>looking</u> for the wolves. __OV__
2. White Fang started following his master around. _____
3. Barking did not come easily to White Fang. _____
4. Weedon's wife talked about feeling nervous around White Fang. _____

> **Grammar Check**
> ✓ How can a **gerund** be used in a sentence?

Practice B

Complete each sentence with the gerund form of a verb from the box.

eat	read	take	~~write~~

1. Have you finished __writing__ your essay?
2. Do you recommend _____ this book?
3. I considered _____ a course in photography.
4. I haven't finished _____ my lunch.

> **Apply**
> Use these sentence starters and gerunds to write sentences.
> I enjoy . . . / I avoid . . . / I recommend . . .
> Then share them with a partner.
> **Example:** I enjoy playing tennis.

Infinitives

An infinitive is formed by the word *to* followed by the base form of the verb. It can be used after certain verbs and in the construction *it + be +* adjective *+* infinitive.

> **Grammar Skill**
> Infinitives often express the purpose of something.

Example of Infinitive	Role in Sentence
Again he commanded White Fang **to go** home.	after certain verbs
Beth understood that White Fang's aim was **to bark**.	after a form of the verb *be*
It is difficult **to work** with wild horses.	after *it + be +* adjective

The following verbs are often followed by infinitives.

agree	decide	need	refuse	want
ask	hope	plan	seem	

Practice A

Complete each sentence with the infinitive form of a verb from the box.

become	~~buy~~	eat	make	predict	research

> **Grammar Check**
> ✓ What is the **infinitive** form?

1. I need <u>to buy</u> a new pair of jeans.
2. My goal is _____ a chemist.
3. It is important _____ your topic carefully.
4. My brother refused _____ his dinner.
5. The reason I joined the club was _____ friends.
6. It is impossible _____ what will happen to the oceans.

Practice B

Complete each sentence with an infinitive and your own ideas.

1. After high school, I hope <u>to go to college</u>.
2. This weekend, I want _____.
3. This evening, I need _____.
4. Last weekend, I decided _____.
5. It is easy for me _____.
6. It is difficult for me _____.

> **Apply**
> Write five interview questions using an infinitive form. Then work with a partner. Take turns asking and answering the questions.
> **Example:**
> A: What do you like to do on weekends?
> B: I like to watch movies.

Reading 4

Using Quotation Marks for Exact Words

Writers use quotation marks to quote exact words, or direct speech, in research reports. Be sure to enclose the exact words in quotation marks and use commas correctly. Study this quote from *White Fang*.

> London shows how White Fang finally manages to communicate an emergency with his second bark, "At this moment speech came to White Fang, rushing up in a great burst of barking."

For a long quotation, use a block quotation. A block quotation is indented, single-spaced, and not included in quotation marks.

> London describes how White Fang and the master play:
>   Those snaps were always delivered on the empty air. At the end of such a romp, when blow and cuff and snap and snarl were fast and furious, they would break off suddenly and stand several feet apart, glaring at each other. And then, just as suddenly, like the sun rising on a stormy sea, they would begin to laugh.

Grammar Skill

You can also use the phrase *According to [person/source]*, before a quotation. For example, you can write: *According to Jack London, "You can't wait for inspiration. You have to go after it with a club."*

Practice A

Add the missing quotation marks and commas to these sentences.

1. The professor stated Your results are not conclusive.

   The professor stated, "Your results are not conclusive."

2. Wolves are wild animals, but they can be tamed she said.

3. He explained The novel *White Fang* is about nature and humans in the Yukon in the late 1800s.

4. The researchers concluded There is much to learn about how to protect wolves.

Grammar Check

✓ When you use **quotation marks** for a quote, can you change the speaker's or writer's words?

Practice B

Read each person's statement. In your notebook, rewrite each sentence using a reporting verb. Use commas and quotation marks correctly.

1. Emma: Wolves are found all over the world.

   Emma said, "Wolves are found all over the world."

2. Beto: Wolves live and hunt in packs.

3. Francesca: Jack London was a journalist and novelist.

4. Luis: *White Fang* is a novel about explorers and nature.

Apply

Work with a partner. Find five quotes from other readings in this unit and highlight them.
Example: From "Getting to Know Real Bats": "Just leave the bats alone," Merlin concludes.

Quotation Marks: Terms, Expressions, and Titles

Writers use quotation marks for different reasons. The writer can use them to call attention to special or unfamiliar terms or to names.

Sentence	Reason for Quotation Marks
I set an alert on my phone for articles with the word "wolf" published during the day.	Set off the term "wolf"
We named our new cat "White Fang" because she growls.	Set off nicknames unusual names for pets

Quotations can also be used for other purposes. For example, they can be used to set off a term that will be defined or to set off the title of an article, a poem, or a short story.

The *Canis lupus* is known as the "gray wolf."	Set off the definition of a term
Angela Carter is the author of the short story, "The Company of Wolves."	Set off the title of a short story, a song, or a poem

> **Grammar Skill**
>
> Titles of longer written works, such as novels, are italicized or underlined, not set off with quotation marks.

Practice A

📖 223

Why are the words in each sentence set in quotation marks? Write *T* for title of work, *SP* for special term, and *D* for term to be defined.

1. The "buffer zone" is the area between two different wolf pack territories. <u>D</u>
2. I really like the poem "Daybreak." _____
3. Our nickname for my uncle is "Big Bird." _____
4. "Coydog" is used to describe a hybrid of a dog and a coyote. _____

> **Grammar Check**
>
> ✓ What should you set off with **quotation marks**?

Practice B

Add quotation marks in the correct places in each sentence.

1. My favorite song is Imagine by John Lennon.

    My favorite song is "Imagine" by John Lennon.
2. Getting to Know Real Bats is an informative article.
3. Acidification is the name for the process of becoming acid.
4. We named our cat Pashmina because she is very soft.

> **Apply**
>
> Work with a partner. Think of an example for each use of quotation marks described in the chart. Write them in your notebook.

Reading 4

Reading 4
Writing

Write an Interpretive Response

At the end of this unit, you will write a research report about an idea, issue, or event related to animals. To help you do this, you wrote an introductory paragraph, classifying paragraphs, and a paragraph with details to support a main idea. In this lesson, you will write a paragraph with an interpretive response. You will explore an author's purpose and evaluate whether you believe the author achieved that purpose.

> **Writing Prompt**
>
> Choose a favorite book, story, or article about an animal you find amazing. You can choose an article, a story, or a poem from this unit. Identify the author's purpose and tell how well the author met that purpose. Be sure to include the title of the work. Also, include any quotes from the work that support your evaluation and punctuate them correctly. When appropriate, use gerunds and infinitives in your writing.

1 Prewrite Begin by choosing a book, a story, or an article for your paragraph.

WB 224

- Write what you believe is the author's purpose.
- List ways that the author achieved that purpose.
- Include quotations that support your ideas.
- Use a graphic organizer to list your ideas and support for them.

Here's an idea web created by a student named Hudson for an interpretive response about the excerpt from *White Fang*.

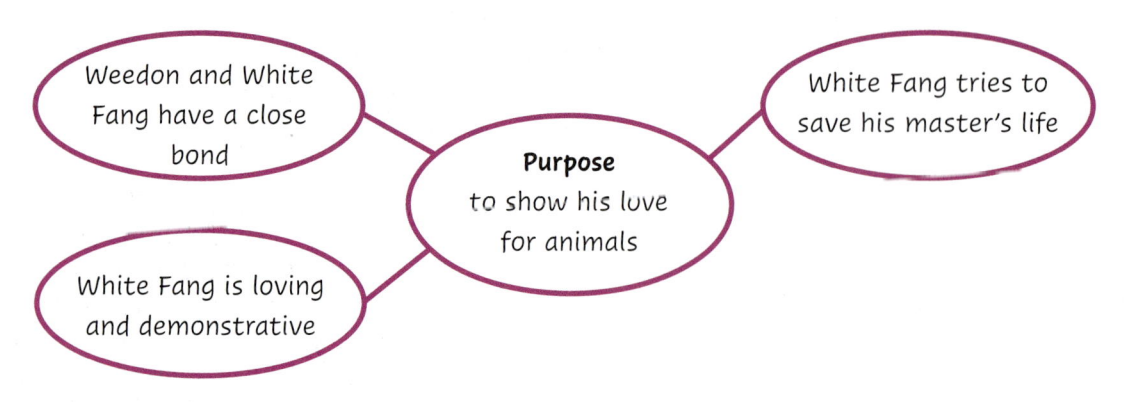

- Weedon and White Fang have a close bond
- White Fang tries to save his master's life
- White Fang is loving and demonstrative

Purpose to show his love for animals

430 Unit 6

② Draft Use your idea web to help you write a first draft.
- Identify the author's purpose.
- Include ways the author achieved the purpose.
- Include quotations to support your ideas.
- Be sure to write titles and punctuate quotes correctly.
- Use gerunds and infinitives correctly.

③ Revise Read over your draft. Look for places where the writing is unclear or needs improvement. Complete (✓) the Editing and Proofreading Marks on WB page 231 to help you identify problems. Then, revise your draft, using the editing and proofreading marks listed on page 467.

④ Edit and Proofread Check your work for errors in grammar, usage, mechanics, and spelling. Trade papers with a partner to obtain feedback. Use the Peer Review Checklist on Workbook page 00. Edit your final draft in response to feedback from your partner and your teacher.

⑤ Publish Prepare a clean copy of your final draft. Share you paragraph with the class. Save your work. You'll need to refer to it in the Writing Workshop at the end of the unit.

> **Writing Checklist**
>
> **Ideas:**
> ☐ I included at least one direct quote from the source.
>
> **Word Choice:**
> ☐ I used words correctly to explain my ideas.
>
> **Conventions:**
> ☐ When I used quotation marks, I used them correctly.

Here is Hudson's paragraph. Notice that he punctuates the quote correctly.

Hudson Hirano

My Response to White Fang

In my opinion, the author Jack London wrote White Fang to show his love for animals: especially ones that come from the wild. London sees the wolf as very demonstrative to people. In the excerpt, White Fang learns three ways to show his love: snuggling, growling in a loving way, and laughter. Then, he learns another way to express himself: barking. The author shows how White Fang actually instinctively knows what to do when his master breaks his leg in a horseback-riding accident. When his master commands him several times to "go home," White Fang does just that. When he reaches the family, he gets their attention and manages to bark. As Beth said, "He's trying to speak, I do believe." The whole scene in the end with the family following White Fang to find and help Weedon is so touching. How could you not feel the author's love for an animal that tries to save his master's life?

Link the Readings

Critical Thinking

What logical connections can you make between the ideas and details in the readings in this unit? Although the readings do not all have the same purpose, they share a common theme and reflect a range of viewpoints. Complete the chart below. Be prepared to support your answers with evidence from each of the texts.

Title of Reading	Purpose	Big Question Link
"The Talking Bird"		
"Getting to Know Real Bats"	to inform	
"A Narrow Fellow in the Grass" "Daybreak" "Birdfoot's Grandpa"		Each animal is amazing in its own way.
from *White Fang*		

Discussion

Discuss with a partner or in a small group.
- Which reading had the biggest impact on you? Why?
- Which animal from the unit do you think is the most amazing? Why?
- **What makes animals so amazing?** What do you think is amazing about the animals you studied in this unit? Explain.

Fluency Check

Work with a partner. Choose a paragraph from one of the readings. Take turns reading it for one minute. Count the total number of words you read. Practice saying the words you had trouble reading. Take turns reading the paragraph three more times. Did you read more words each time? Record the number of words you read each time.

	1st Reading	2nd Reading	3rd Reading	4th Reading
Number of Words				

432 Unit 6

Media Literacy & Projects

Work with a partner or in a small group. Choose one of these projects.

1. Many poets have written about animals. For example, T. S. Eliot wrote a book of poetry about cats called *Old Possum's Book of Practical Cats*. Write a poem about a pet or an animal you have seen at the zoo. Read your poem to the class.

2. Find out how you can become a volunteer at your local animal shelter or sanctuary. Make a poster to recruit volunteers. Then share your poster with the class.

3. Changes to an animal's habitat can have a great impact on the animal. Do research to find out how changes to a particular animal's habitat are affecting the animal. Present your findings on a poster.

4. Now that you have read about animals, do some research online to find videos that will give you more information about an animal that interests you from the unit. For example, you may choose to research videos on a species of talking bird or a species of frog. Make a list of the videos that you watched and write a summary of what you learned about the animal.

Further Reading

Choose from these reading selections. Practice reading silently for longer and longer periods.

Jim Smiley and His Jumping Frog and Other Stories, Mark Twain
This collection includes Twain's humorous story of a jumping-frog contest during California's gold rush days.

Never Cry Wolf, Farley Mowat
The author, an animal behaviorist, lived alone on the frozen tundra, learning about the Arctic wolves and caribou.

The Compassion of Animals: True Stories of Animal Courage and Kindness, Kristin Von Kreisler
This collection of true stories tells about animals who risked their lives to keep the humans they love out of danger.

Life of Pi, Yann Martel
A young man has to survive on a lifeboat in the middle of the ocean with one companion: a tiger.

Put It All Together

Listening & Speaking Workshop

TV Documentary

A TV documentary is a show that provides information about something in the real world. It is longer and more detailed than a TV news report. Documentaries usually include narration, interviews, film clips, photos, and other visuals. With a group, you will present a documentary about an animal, animal species, or organization that works with animals.

① Think About It

Work in small groups. Discuss what you have learned about animals in this unit. Which animals did you find most interesting? What animals would you like to learn more about? Make a list of possible topics for your documentary. Here are some examples:

- How elephants communicate
- The importance of bees
- Manatees: what they are and why they're endangered

Work with your group members to choose a topic for your documentary.

② Gather and Organize Information

As a group, list facts you already know about your topic and questions you want to have answered. You can look at an encyclopedia or a government or university website for ideas. Remember to ask *Who, What, When, Where,* and *Why* questions.

Research Research your topic at the library or on the internet. Coordinate your efforts with other group members to avoid duplicating work. Take notes and look for useful visuals as you read.

Order Your Notes Share your notes with group members. Together, decide which information to include in your documentary, and arrange it in an order that makes sense. Make an outline for your presentation, and work with your group members to assign tasks. Prepare questions to ask in real or role-played interviews. Make note cards to use during your part of the documentary.

Use Visuals List the visuals you'll need. Decide who will find or make each one. Use a variety of images, including photos and maps. If a video recorder is available, you can film interviews with people. You can also role-play an interview during your presentation, letting one student play an expert.

③ Practice and Present

Practice your part until you know it well. Use your note cards only as a memory aid. Then practice your documentary with your group members. To make the presentation of your documentary richer and more interesting, use a variety of grammatical structures, sentence lengths, sentence types, and connecting words. Listen carefully to each other, and give suggestions to help make the presentation clearer and more interesting. If you plan to show video clips, make sure you have the necessary equipment and know how to use it. Practice as a group until the whole presentation runs smoothly.

Deliver Your TV Documentary Present your documentary to the class. Remember that TV documentaries are usually formal. When it's your turn to speak, face the audience (or imaginary TV camera) and speak loudly and clearly. Hold up your visuals and/or pass them around the class at appropriate times.

④ Evaluate the Presentation

You will improve your skills as a speaker and a listener by evaluating each presentation you give and hear. Complete (✓) the checklist to help you judge your documentary and the documentaries of your classmates.

- ☐ Was the topic of the documentary interesting? Was it well researched?
- ☐ Did the visuals illustrate the most important points clearly?
- ☐ Did the documentary answer the 5Ws: *who*, *what*, *when*, *where*, and *why*?
- ☐ Was the group well prepared?
- ☐ Could the documentary be improved?

Speaking Tips

Write just a few words on each note card, in big letters, to remind you of your main ideas.

Focus on presenting facts, not your own opinions. Identify the sources of your information.

Listening Tips

Listen for answers to the 5Ws: *who*, *what*, *when*, *where*, and *why*.

Focus on the speaker's main points. Write down anything you find especially interesting or surprising so you can ask questions or do your own research later.

Strengthen Your Social Language

In school, you will often need to present information to an audience, often in collaboration with others. Go to your Digital Resources and do the activity for this unit. This activity will help you acquire skills and experience in giving an oral presentation.

Put It All Together

Writing Workshop

Research Report

In a research report, writers explain a topic they have studied in detail. They include information gathered from different sources. A good research report begins with a paragraph that introduces the writer's topic and main ideas. Each body paragraph focuses on a main idea. Facts, details, and examples support each main idea. A concluding paragraph summarizes the writer's main points. The report includes a complete list of the writer's sources.

Writing Prompt

Write a five-paragraph research report about an idea, issue, or event related to animals. Be sure to use relative pronouns in adjective clauses correctly.

① Prewrite Select a topic that interests you. Make sure the topic is narrow enough to cover in five paragraphs. Then write a question to direct your research. Possible research sources include books about your topic, newspapers, magazines, encyclopedias, and approved websites. Take notes and list your sources. Examine the quality of your research by discussing it with your classmates or teacher.

List and Organize Ideas and Details Use your notes to create an outline. A student named Evan decided to write about endangered species. Here is the outline he prepared:

WB 225

I. Introduce the problem of species endangerment
   A. Animals slow to adapt to surroundings
   B. Humans quick to alter environment
II. How many endangered species are in the world today?
   A. Total amount of endangered species: 25,821
   B. 76% of species in Lake Victoria Basin at risk
III. What are some reasons for animal endangerment associated with human interaction?
   A. Deforestation
   B. Poaching
   C. Toxic chemicals
IV. What are some organizations and activities that promote wildlife protection?
   A. European Wildlife
   B. Endangered Species Act passed in 1973 in U.S.A.
V. Conclude on species endangerment
   A. Enforcement of laws needed to preserve wildlife
   B. Combined efforts of lawmakers, experts, and public

② Draft

Use the model on pages 440–441 and your outline to help you write a first draft. Remember to begin with a paragraph that clearly presents your topic. Be sure to use your own words when you write your report. If you use exact words from a source, punctuate the quotation correctly. List all your sources accurately at the end of your report.

Citing Sources Use these examples as models of style, punctuation, and order of information.

> **Book**
> Stanchak, John. Civil War. New York: Dorling Kindersley, 2000.
>
> **Magazine article**
> Giovannini, Joseph. "Museums After Bilbao." *Architectural Record*. March 2008: 83—85. Print.
>
> **Internet website**
> Ramirez, Patricia. "Building an Eco-Aquarium." Patricia Ramirez Builds Things. 8 May 2018. <http://www.patriciabuildsthings75234.com.>
>
> **Encyclopedia article**
> Siple, Paul A. "Antarctica." World Book Encyclopedia. 1991 ed.

③ Revise

Read over your draft. As you do so, ask yourself the questions in the writing checklist. Use the questions to help you revise your report.

> **Six Traits of Writing Checklist**
>
> ☐ **Ideas:** Does my first paragraph introduce my topic in an engaging way?
> ☐ **Organization:** Do facts, examples, and details support the main idea in each paragraph?
> ☐ **Voice:** Are my tone and style appropriately formal?
> ☐ **Word Choice:** Do I use transitions to connect ideas?
> ☐ **Sentence Fluency:** Do my sentences vary in length and rhythm?
> ☐ **Conventions:** Does my writing follow the rules of grammar, usage, and mechanics?

Put It All Together

Here are the changes Evan plans to make when he revises his first draft:

Endangered Species

Over the last couple of centuries, steadily advancing technology has greatly improved the lives of people at the expense of plant and animal species. The endangerment of plants and animals, along with the fragile ecosystem*s* on which they depend, *is* a widespread problem ~~is. It has~~ *that* has sparked much debate. Plants and animals adapt to changes in their surroundings only over an extended period of time, while humans can change their environment very quickly to suit their needs. [*Revised to improve flow.* / *Revised to combine sentences.*]

Data for the number of endangered species is published yearly in a pamphlet called the Red Data Book by the International Union for the Conservation of Nature and Natural Resources (IUCN). According to the IUCN's statistics the total number of endangered species was 25,821 in the year 2018. It is also interesting to note that in places that once had a wide diversity of species, such as the Lake Victoria Basin in East Africa, over seventy-five percent of freshwater species are in danger. Catherine Sayer, IUCN Programme Officer, said, "The Lake Victoria Basin is home to hundreds of species which haven't yet been described, and this means the number of species at high risk of extinction may be even greater than we currently realize." ("Livelihoods at risk as freshwater species in Africa's largest lake face extinction—IUCN Report").

One human activity that has a negative effect on wildlife is deforestation. Since 1980, over 580,000 square kilometers of Amazon forest in Brazil has been destroyed. The forests are destroyed for purposes such as logging, cattle ranching, and agriculture (Butler). The rainforest in Africa has also been destroyed. In both places, the species that live in the rainforests are becoming extinct. ("Why Are They Being Destroyed?") Hunting also extremely damaging ~~is~~, [is] especially illegal hunting by poachers. A third activity that threatens many species is the use of toxic chemicals such as DDT. ~~It~~ [which] works by "hitching a ride on the food chain, first getting into plants, then the animals that eat plants, then animals that eat animals (Lampton 50).

Revised to correct placement of verb.

Revised to combine sentences.

Several international groups, such as European Wildlife, made significant progress in raising awareness of endangered animal and plant life. [In addition to the efforts of conservation groups,] Laws have been passed ~~for protecting~~ [to protect] endangered species. An example is the endangered species act of 1973, which officially prohibited any endangered or potentially threatened species from being brought into the united States (Stefoff 97).

Revised for clarity and flow.

Revised to correct capitalization.

Wildlife endangerment has received much attention but not enough has been done about it. Yet there is still hope. For example, in the case of rainforests, expanding protected areas, changing land policies, and increasing law enforcement are good ways to take action on this problem. [However,] With the help of lawmakers, scientific experts, and the public, the idea of a peaceful coexistence between humans and other living things could become closer to a reality.

Revised to combine sentences and clarify contrast.

Put It All Together

Writing Workshop

> **Works Consulted List**
>
> Butler, Rhett. "Deforestation in the Amazon." MongaBay 7 July 2014 <https://data.mongabay.com/brazil.html>
>
> International Union for Conservation of Nature <https://www.iucn.org/news/species/201804/livelihoods-risk-freshwater-species-africa's-largest-lake-face-extinction---iucn-report>
>
> Lampton, Christopher. Endangered Species. New York: Franklin Watts, 200.
>
> "Livelihoods at risk as freshwater species in Africa's largest lake face extinction – IUCN Report." 30 April 2018
>
> Stefoff, Rebecca. Extinction. New York: Chelsea House Publishers, New York, 1992.
>
> "Why Are They Being Destroyed?" Rainforest Concern. 18 June 2018. <http://www.rainforestconcern.org/rainforest_facts/why_are_they_being_destroyed/>

4 Edit and Proofread Check your work for errors in grammar, usage, mechanics, and spelling. Then trade essays with a partner and complete (✓) the Peer Review Checklist below to give each other constructive feedback.

Edit your final draft in response to feedback from your partner and your teacher.

Peer Review Checklist

- ☐ Could changes be made to improve the research report?
- ☐ Does the first paragraph introduce the research report in an engaging way?
- ☐ Does the concluding paragraph sum up the main ideas?
- ☐ Does each paragraph focus on one main Idea?
- ☐ Do the details in each paragraph support the main idea?
- ☐ Are appropriate quotations used correctly?
- ☐ Is the source of each quotation clear?
- ☐ Is the Works Consulted List formatted correctly?
- ☐ What changes could be made to improve the research report?

Evan Arbogast

Endangered Species

Over the last couple of centuries, steadily advancing technology has greatly improved the lives of people at the expense of plant and animal species. Plants and animals adapt to changes in their surroundings only over an extended period of time, while humans can change their environment very quickly to suit their needs. The endangerment of plants and animals, along with the fragile ecosystems on which they depend, is a widespread problem that has sparked much debate.

Data for the number of endangered species is published yearly in a pamphlet called the Red Data Book by the International Union for the Conservation of Nature and Natural Resources (IUCN). According to the IUCN's statistics, the total number of endangered species was 25,821 in the year 2018. It is interesting to note that in places that once had a wide diversity of species, such as the Lake Victoria Basin in East Africa, over seventy-five percent of freshwater species are in danger. Catherine Sayer, IUCN Programme Officer, said, "The Lake Victoria Basin is home to hundreds of species which haven't yet been described, and this means the number of species at high risk of extinction may be even greater than we currently realize." ("Livelihoods at risk as freshwater species in Africa's largest lake face extinction—IUCN Report").

Revised to add comma.

One human activity that has a negative effect on wildlife is deforestation. Since 1980, over 580,000 square kilometers of Amazon forest in Brazil have been destroyed. The forests are destroyed for purposes such as logging, cattle ranching, and agriculture (Butler). The rainforest in Africa has also been destroyed. In both places, the species that live in the rainforests are becoming extinct. ("Why Are They Being Destroyed?") Hunting is also extremely damaging, especially illegal hunting by poachers. A third activity that threatens many species is the use of toxic chemicals such as DDT, which works by "hitching a ride on the food chain first getting into plants, then the animals that eat plants, then animals that eat animals (Lampton 50).

Revised to remove comma.

Put It All Together

Several international groups, such as European Wildlife, made significant progress in raising awareness of endangered animal and plant life. In addition to the efforts of conservation groups, laws have been passed to protect endangered species. An example is the Endangered Species Act of 1973, which officially prohibited any endangered or potentially threatened species from being brought into the United States (Stefoff 97).

Wildlife endangerment has received much attention, but not enough has been done about it. Yet there is still hope. For example, in the case of rainforests, expanding protected areas, changing land policies, and increasing law enforcement are good ways to take action on this problem. However, with the help of lawmakers, scientific experts, and the public, the idea of a peaceful coexistence between humans and other living things could become closer to a reality.

Revised for capitalization and to add a comma.

Works Consulted List

Butler, Rhett. "Deforestation in the Amazon." MongaBay 7 July 2014 <https://data.mongabay.com/brazil.html>brazil.html>

International Union for Conservation of Nature <https://www.iucn.org/news/species/201804/livelihoods-risk-freshwater-species-africa's-largest-lake-face-extinction---iucn-report>

Lampton, Christopher. Endangered Species. New York: Franklin Watts, 2000.

"Livelihoods at risk as freshwater species in Africa's largest lake face extinction – IUCN Report." 30 April 2018

Stefoff, Rebecca. Extinction. New York: Chelsea House Publishers, New York, 1992.

"Why Are They Being Destroyed?" Rainforest Concern. 18 June 2018. <http://www.rainforestconcern.org/rainforest_facts/why_are_they_being_destroyed/>

5 Publish Obtain feedback from your teacher and classmates; then prepare your final draft. Share your research report with the class.

Test Preparation

Unit 6 Practice

Read the following test sample. Study the tips in the boxes. Work with a partner to answer the questions.

Morning

I stretch and lick the momma's face.
Come on, dear mom, pick up the pace.
The momma's moving slow today
I think it must be Saturday.
I'm sitting here and waiting while
She grabs her shoes out of the pile.
I cannot fathom why she's tired.
It's very nearly light outside.
She tries to hitch me up to go
Outside to make my tracks in snow.
But momma's moving far too slow.
Her eyes are falling closed, I know.
She opens up the door, by Gosh,
And I go running like a shot.
I run up to my favorite spot
And sniff and sniff and sniff a lot.
And suddenly, I realize
It's really, really cold outside.
And past the momma's back I fly.
Back into bed I jump and sigh.
It was quite a day I've had.
But why's the momma look so mad?

1 What is the poem about?
    A A child who wants to play in the snow
    B A woman trying to get ready for work
    C A dog going for the first walk of the day
    D A holiday morning with family

2 Which best describes the overall tone of the passage?
    A Objective   **C** Passionate
    B Humorous   **D** Inspiring

Taking Tests
You will often take tests to show what you know. Study the tips below to help you improve your test-taking skills.

Tip
Poetry often uses sensory information to explain events. When reading a poem, try to visualize the events in your mind.

Tip
When poems rhyme, it is human nature to stop at the end of every line. Don't stop where the line stops. Stop where the image stops.

WB 227—228

Visual Literacy

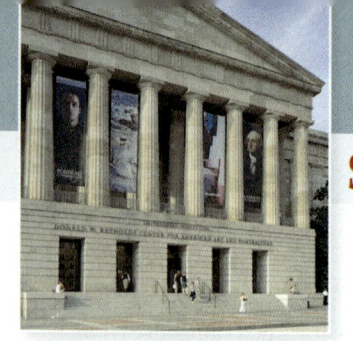

Smithsonian American Art Museum

Animals in Human Society

Artists have captured the animal world in many different ways. Some try to reproduce every detail so the creature seems alive and about to jump off the canvas. Others use fantastic colors and shapes to capture the essence or spirit of an animal. All want to celebrate or understand the other life forms that share planet Earth with us.

John Steuart Curry, *Ajax* (1936–37)

In *Ajax*, John Steuart Curry painted a lifelike portrait of an all-American bull. He deliberately placed the animal on a growing field, because so many farmers in the United States had lost their farms during the terrible economic depression of the 1930s. He wanted to capture hope and success, not failure.

Curry placed his bull on the crest of a hill in the center of the painting. The animal's huge brown side seems grand against the big, white clouds in the sky. Two small birds fly around the bull and eat insects off of its back. Their tiny size highlights the bull's enormous size. Fertile green fields stretch into the distance in the background. Curry's American landscape is one of energy, power, and bounty.

▲ John Steuart Curry, *Ajax*, 1936–37, oil, 36 x 48¼ in., Smithsonian American Art Museum

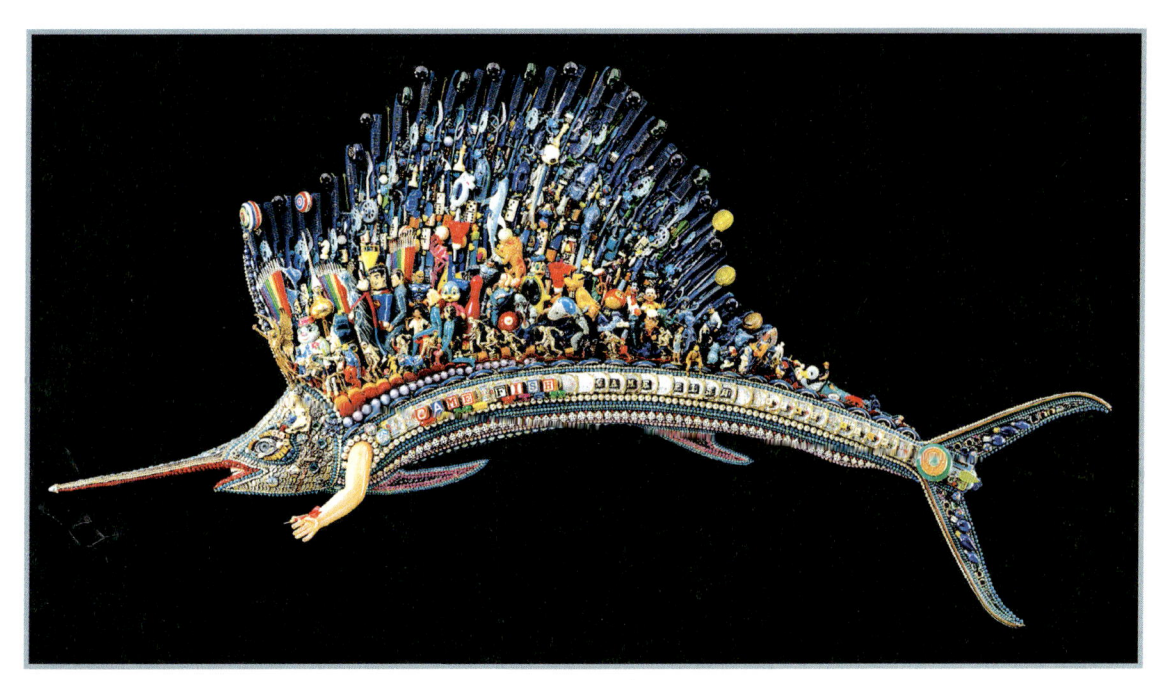

▲ Larry Fuente, *Game Fish*, 1988, mixed media, 51½ x 112½ x 10¾ in., Smithsonian American Art Museum

Larry Fuente, *Game Fish* (1988)

In *Game Fish*, Larry Fuente combines the real with the imaginary. He attached brightly colored beads, buttons, coins and game-related items onto a swordfish frame. He is making fun using the traditional trophy fish that fishermen often hang on the walls of their homes. On the fin he added dozens of plastic statues of some children's favorite play figures: Mickey Mouse, Superman, even monkeys from a popular game called Barrel of Monkeys. The work's title is repeated in individual letters from children's building blocks or word games and mounted on the curving arch of the fish's side.

A human arm pops out of the side of the fish near the head. The hand holds a red-tipped dart. The armed fish now becomes the hunter instead of the hunted!

Both of these artists focus on a single animal. But they use that animal to make different statements about people's relationship with nature.

Discuss What You Learned

1. Which of these artworks do you think tries to capture the essence or spirit of the animal? Explain.
2. Do you think these two artists have similar feelings about animals? Why or why not?

BIG QUESTION
In what way does each of these artworks make a statement about animals in human society?

229–230

Unit 6

Grammar Handbook

The Parts of Speech

In English there are eight **parts of speech**: nouns, pronouns, adjectives, verbs, adverbs, prepositions, conjunctions, and interjections.

Nouns

Nouns name people, places, or things. There are two kinds of nouns: **common nouns** and **proper nouns**.

A **common noun** is a general person, place, or thing.

> person   thing   place
> The **student** brings a **notebook** to **class**.

A **proper noun** is a specific person, place, or thing. Proper nouns start with a capital letter.

> person   place   thing
> **Joseph** went to **Paris** and saw the **Eiffel Tower**.

A noun that is made up of two words is called a **compound noun**. A compound noun can be one word or two words. Some compound nouns have hyphens.

> One word: **newspaper, bathroom**
> Two words: **vice president, pet shop**
> Hyphens: **sister-in-law, grown-up**

Articles identify nouns. *A*, *an*, and *the* are articles.

A and *an* are called **indefinite articles**. Use the article *a* or *an* to talk about one general person, place, or thing.

Use *an* before a word that begins with a vowel sound. Use *a* before a word that begins with a consonant sound.

> I have **an** idea.
> May I borrow **a** pen?

The is called a **definite article**. Use *the* to talk about one or more specific people, places, or things.

> Please bring me **the** box from your room.
> **The** books are in my backpack.

Pronouns

Pronouns are words that take the place of nouns or proper nouns. In this example, the pronoun *she* replaces, or refers to, the proper noun *Angela*.

> proper noun   pronoun
> **Angela** is not home. **She** is babysitting.

Pronouns can be subjects or objects. They can be singular or plural.

	Subject Pronouns	**Object Pronouns**
Singular	I, you, he, she, it	me, you, him, her, it
Plural	we, you, they	us, you, them

A **subject pronoun** replaces a noun or proper noun that is the subject of a sentence. A **subject** is who or what a sentence is about. In these sentences, *He* replaces *Daniel*.

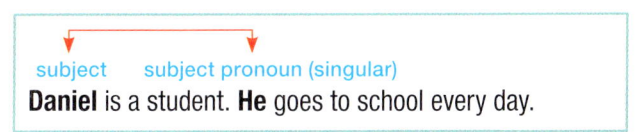

> subject   subject pronoun (singular)
> **Daniel** is a student. **He** goes to school every day.

An **object pronoun** replaces a noun or proper noun that is the object of a verb. A verb tells the action in a sentence. An **object** receives the action of a verb.

In these sentences, *him* replaces *Ed*, which is the object of the verb *gave*.

> object   object pronoun (singular)
> Lauren gave **Ed** the notes. Lauren gave **him** the notes.

Grammar Handbook

An object pronoun can also replace a noun or proper noun that is the **object of a preposition**. Prepositions are words such as *for*, *to*, and *with*. In these sentences, *them* replaces *José* and *Yolanda*, which is the object of the preposition *with*.

>   object of a preposition   object pronoun (plural)
> I went to the mall with **José and Yolanda**. I went to the mall with **them**.

Pronouns can also be possessive. A **possessive pronoun** replaces a noun or proper noun. It shows who owns something.

	Possessive Pronouns
Singular	mine, yours, his, hers, its
Plural	ours, yours, theirs

In these sentences, *hers* replaces the words *Kyoko's coat*. It shows that Kyoko owns the coat.

> It is **Kyoko's coat**. It is **hers**.

When an auxiliary verb (such as the verb *be*) follows a subject pronoun, it is usually contracted, especially in spoken English. In contractions, an apostrophe (') replaces the deleted letter.

Full Form		Contractions
I am		I'm
He She } is It		He's She's It's
You We } are They		You're We're They're

The **reciprocal pronouns** *each other* and *one another* are used in situations in which an action is carried out by two (or more) people at the same time. Use the reciprocal pronoun *one another* when referring to three or more people. Note that reciprocal pronouns can take the possessive form.

> Danny and David met **each other** when they were in eighth grade.
> When we were babies, my sisters and I looked similar to **one another**.
> Scientists believe that lions can recognize **one another's** roars.

Adjectives

Adjectives describe nouns. An adjective usually comes before the noun.

> **tall** grass   **big** truck   **two** kittens

An adjective can also come *after* the noun it describes.

> The bag is **heavy**. The books are **new**.

Do not add -*s* to adjectives that describe plural nouns.

> the **red** houses   the **funny** jokes   the **smart** teachers

Adjectives can also be possessive. A **possessive adjective** shows ownership.

	Possessive Adjectives
Singular	my, your, his, her, its
Plural	our, your, their

In these sentences, *their* shows who owns the car.

> It's **Sam and Paul's** car. It's **their** car.

Verbs

Verbs express an action or a state of being.

> subject verb   subject verb
> Jackie **walks** to school. The school **is** near her house.

An **action verb** tells what someone or something does or did.

Actions You Can See			Actions You Cannot See		
dance	sit	talk	know	remember	think
play	swim	write	name	sense	understand

Grammar Handbook

A **linking verb** shows no action. It links the subject of a sentence with information that describes the subject.

	Linking Verbs
Forms of *be*	am, is, are, was, were
Verbs related to the five senses	look, smell, sound, taste, feel
Verbs that reflect a state of being	appear, become, grow, remain, seem, turn

In this sentence, the adjective *tired* tells something about the subject, *cat*.

> Our cat **seems** tired.

In this sentence, the noun *friend* tells something about the subject, *brother*.

> Your brother **is** my friend.

A **helping verb** comes before the main verb. It adds to the main verb's meaning. Helping verbs can be forms of the verbs *be, do,* or *have.*

	Helping Verbs
Forms of *be*	am, is, are, was, were
Forms of *do*	do, does, did
Forms of *have*	have, has, had
Other helping verbs	can, must, could, have (to), should, may, will, would

In this sentence, *am* is the helping verb; *walking* is the action verb.

> helping action
> verb   verb
> I **am walking** to my science class.

In questions, the subject comes between a helping verb and a main verb.

>   subject
> **Did** Liang **give** you the CD?

Mood in verbs relates to the attitude of the speaker or writer. The **indicative** mood expresses factual statements. The **imperative** mood expresses commands, instructions, or requests. The **subjunctive** mood expresses something that is doubtful or not factual. This includes sentences that express things such as wishes, commands, emotion, possibility, necessity, or something that is contrary to fact.

Indicative mood	I am **reading** a book right now.
Imperative mood	**Read** Chapter 12 for Monday.
Subjunctive mood	She didn't understand the book. If she **were** older, she would have understood it better.

Adverbs

Adverbs describe the action of verbs. They tell *how* an action happens. Adverbs answer the question *Where? When? How? How much?* or *How often?*

Many adverbs end in *-ly*.

easily	slowly	carefully

Some adverbs do not end in *-ly*.

seldom	fast	very

In this sentence, the adverb *everywhere* modifies the verb *looked*. It answers the question *Where?*

> verb   adverb
> Nicole looked **everywhere** for her cell phone.

In this sentence, the adverb *quickly* modifies the verb *walked*. It answers the question *How?*

> verb   adverb
> They walked home **quickly**.

Grammar Handbook

Adverbs also modify adjectives. In this sentence, the adverb *very* modifies the adjective *dangerous*. It answers the question *How much?*

> adverb adjective noun
> This is **very** dangerous road.

Adverbs can also modify other adverbs. In this sentence, the adverb *fast* modifies the verb *runs*. The adverb *quite* modifies the adverb *fast*.

> verb adverb adverb
> John runs **quite** fast.

Prepositions

Prepositions can show time, place, and direction.

Time	Place	Direction
after	above	across
before	below	down
during	in	into
since	near	to
until	under	up

In this sentence, the preposition *above* shows place.

> preposition
> A bird flew **above** my head.

In this sentence, the preposition *across* shows direction.

> preposition
> The children walked **across** the street.

A **prepositional phrase** starts with a preposition and ends with a noun or pronoun.

In this sentence, the preposition is *near* and the noun is *school*.

> prepositional phrase
> The library is **near the new school**.

Conjunctions

A **conjunction** joins words, groups of words, and whole sentences.

Conjunctions			
and	for	or	yet
but	nor	so	

In this sentence, the conjunction *and* joins two proper nouns; the conjunction *or* joins two prepositional phrases.

> noun — noun — prepositional phrase — prepositional phrase
> Jonah **and** Teresa want to go to the movies **or** to the mall.

In this sentence, the conjunction *and* joins two independent clauses.

> ── independent clause ──   ── independent clause ──
> Amanda baked the cookies, **and** Eric made the lemonade.

Interjections

Interjections are words or phrases that express emotion.

Interjections that express strong emotion are followed by an exclamation point. Interjections that express mild emotion are followed by a comma.

> **Hey!** Watch out for that ball!
> **Hey,** I'm sorry that your team lost.

A Note about Case

Case refers to a word's grammatical role or function within a sentence. In English, nouns and pronouns have three cases: **nominative**, **objective**, and **possessive**. The nominative refers to the subject of the sentence; the objective refers to something that is the object of a verb or preposition; and the possessive refers to a noun that possesses or owns another noun. The nominative and objective cases of nouns are identical, but the possessive case takes a different form.

Case	Noun	Pronoun
Nominative	<u>Adam</u> has a new puppy.	<u>He</u> has a new puppy.
Objective	They gave <u>Adam</u> a puppy.	They gave <u>him</u> a puppy.
Possessive	<u>Adam's</u> puppy is cute.	<u>His</u> puppy is cute.

Grammar Handbook

Clauses

Clauses are groups of words with a subject and a verb. Some clauses form complete sentences; they tell a complete thought. Others do not.

Clauses that form complete sentences are called **independent clauses**.

> subject   verb
> Our **teacher smiled**.

Clauses that don't form complete sentences are called **dependent clauses**.

> subject   verb
> when the **class gave** her the present.

Clauses can be combined to form a sentence.

> ⌐independent clause⌐ ⌐— dependent clause —⌐
> Our **teacher smiled** when the class gave her the present.

Sentences

Sentences have a subject and a verb, and tell a complete thought. A sentence always begins with a capital letter. It always ends with a period, question mark, or exclamation point.

> subject action verb
> The **cheetah runs** very fast.
>
> helping
> verb   subject   action verb
> **Do you play** soccer?
>
> subject linking verb
> **I am** so late!

Simple, Compound, and Complex Sentences

Some sentences are called simple sentences. Others are called compound sentences. A **simple sentence** has one independent clause.

> ——independent clause——
> He sent the package to his grandmother.

Compound sentences are made up of two or more simple sentences, or independent clauses. They are joined together by a **conjunction**.

> ┌─ independent clause ─┐ ┌─ independent clause ─┐
> The band has a lead singer, **but** they need a drummer.

Complex sentences have an independent clause and one or more dependent clauses. In a complex sentence, the main idea is in the independent clause.

> ┌─ dependent clause ─┐ ┌─ dependent clause ─┐ ┌─ independent clause ─┐
> Although it's raining, and in spite of the cold, we still plan to go for a run.

Compound-complex sentences have more than one independent clause and at least one dependent clause.

> ┌─ dependent clause ─┐ ┌─ independent clause ─┐ ┌─ independent clause ─┐
> After the movie ended, we all said it was good, but secretly, we didn't like it.

Sentence Types

There are four types of sentences. All four have different purposes: **declarative** sentences are statements, **interrogative** sentences are questions, **imperative** sentences are commands, and **exclamatory** sentences express strong feelings.

Sentence Type	Example	Ending Punctuation
Declarative	We're going to the beach.	a period
Interrogative	Will you come with us?	a question mark
Imperative	Put on your jacket.	a period or exclamation point
Exclamatory	This is delicious!	an exclamation point

Grammar Handbook

Mechanics

End Marks

End marks come at the end of sentences. There are three kinds of end marks: periods, question marks, and exclamation points.

Use a **period** to end a statement (declarative sentence).

> The spacecraft *Magellan* took pictures of Jupiter.

Use a **period** to end a command or request (imperative sentence) that isn't strong enough to need an exclamation point.

> Please change the channel.

Use a **question mark** to end a sentence that asks a question. (interrogative sentence).

> Where does Mrs. Suarez live?

Use an **exclamation point** to end a sentence that expresses strong feeling (exclamatory sentence).

> That was a great party!
> Look at that huge house!

Use an **exclamation point** to end an imperative sentence that gives an urgent command.

> Get away from the edge of the pool!

Periods are also used after initials and many abbreviations.

Use a **period** after a person's initial or abbreviated title.

> Ms. Susan Vargas   Mrs. Fiske   J. D. Salinger
> Gov. Lise Crawford   Mr. Vargas   Dr. Sapirstein

Use a **period** after the abbreviation of streets, roads, and so on.

Avenue	Ave.	Road	Rd.
Highway	Hwy.	Street	St.

Use a **period** after the abbreviation of many units of measurement. Abbreviations for metric measurements do *not* use periods.

inch	in.	centimeter	cm
foot	ft.	meter	m
pound	lb.	kilogram	kg
gallon	gal.	liter	l

Commas

Commas separate, or set off, parts of a sentence, or phrase.

Use a comma to separate two independent clauses linked by a conjunction. In this sentence, the comma goes before the conjunction *but*.

⎡— independent clause —⎤ ⎡— independent clause —⎤
We went to the museum, **but** it is not open on Mondays.

Use commas to separate the parts in a series. A series is a group of three or more words, phrases, or very brief clauses.

	Commas in Series
To separate words	Lucio's bike is red, white, and silver.
To separate phrases	Today, he rode all over the lawn, down the sidewalk, and up the hill.
To separate clauses	Lucio washed the bike, his dad washed the car, and his mom washed the dog.

Use a comma to set off an introductory word, phrase, or clause.

	Commas with Introductory Words, Phrases, or Clauses
To set off a word	Yes, Stacy likes to go swimming.
To set off a phrase	In a month, she may join the swim team again.
To set off a clause	If she joins the swim team, I'll miss her at softball practice.

Grammar Handbook

Use commas to set off an interrupting word, nonrestrictive phrase, or nonrestrictive clause. (Note: A nonrestrictive phrase or clause can be left out of a sentence without changing the sentence's meaning.)

	Commas with Interrupting Words, Phrases, or Clauses
To set off a word	We left, finally, to get some fresh air.
To set off a phrase	Carol's dog, a brown pug, shakes when he gets scared.
To set off a clause	The assignment, I'm sorry to say, was too hard for me.

Use a comma to set off a contrasting expression.

> I like tea, not coffee.
> The exam is this Friday, not next Friday.

Use a comma to set off a speaker's quoted words in a sentence.

> Jeanne asked, "Where is that book I just had?"
> "I just saw it," said Billy, "on the kitchen counter."

In a direct address, one speaker talks directly to another. Use commas to set off the name of the person being addressed.

> Thank you, Dee, for helping to put away the dishes.
> Phil, why are you late again?

Use a comma between the day and the year.

> My cousin was born on September 9, 2003.

Use a comma between a city and a state and between a city and a nation.

> My father grew up in Bakersfield, California.
> We are traveling to Acapulco, Mexico.

Semicolons and Colons

Semicolons can connect two independent clauses. Use them when the clauses are closely related in meaning or structure.

> The team won again; it was their ninth victory.

Colons introduce a list of items or important information.

Use a colon after an independent clause to introduce a list of items.

> The following animals live in Costa Rica: monkeys, lemurs, toucans, and jaguars

Use a colon to introduce important information. If the information is in an independent clause, use a capital letter to begin the first word after the colon.

> There is one main rule: Do not talk to anyone during the test.

Dashes

Dashes are used to make a break in a sentence. They can be used as a replacement for commas, semicolons, colons, and parentheses. They appear more often in informal writing than formal writing.

Dashes are used to express added emphasis.

> There's only one person who can lead our team to victory—Steve.

Dashes are used to indicate an interruption.

> We were walking in the quiet park when—suddenly—we heard a loud noise over by the lake.

Dashes help to set off an abrupt change of thought.

> Could you please get me a—oh, never mind. I'll get it myself.

Grammar Handbook

Quotation Marks

Quotation marks set off direct quotations, dialogue, and some titles. A **direct quotation** is the exact words that somebody said, wrote, or thought.

Commas and periods *always* go inside quotation marks. If a question mark or exclamation point is part of the quotation, it is also placed *inside* the quotation marks.

> "Can you please get ready?" Mom asked.
> My sister shouted, "Look out for that bee!"

If a question mark or exclamation point is *not* part of the quotation, it goes *outside* the quotation marks. In these cases there is no punctuation before the end quotation marks.

> Did you say, "I can't do this"?

Conversation between two or more people is called **dialogue**. Use quotation marks to set off spoken words in dialogue.

> "What a great ride!" Pam said. "Let's go on it again."
> Julio shook his head and said, "No way. I'm feeling sick."

Writers will sometimes use quotation marks around a word or phrase to change its meaning from literal to ironic or sarcastic. Read this example of sarcasm:

> Our teacher gave us a "simple" homework assignment to do over the weekend. It's going to take me all weekend to finish it!

From context, we can infer that the writer was told an assignment was going to be simple, but he or she doesn't believe that it will be.

Now read this example of quotation marks used to indicate irony:

> The army fired shots at houses in the "safe haven" of the war zone.

Here the writer seems to be implying that even though an area is called a safe haven, it really isn't a safe place to be.

Use quotation marks around the titles of short works of writing or other art forms. The following kinds of titles take quotation marks:

Chapters	"The Railroad in the West"
Short stories	"The Perfect Cat"
Articles	"California in the 1920s"
Songs	"This Land Is Your Land"
Single TV episodes	"Charlie's New Idea"
Short poems	"The Bat"

Titles of all other written work and artwork are underlined or set in Italic type. These include books, magazines, newspapers, plays, movies, TV series, and paintings.

Apostrophes

Apostrophes can be used with singular and plural nouns to show ownership or possession. To form the possessive, follow these rules:

For singular nouns, add an apostrophe and an *s*.

Maria's eyes	hamster's cage	the sun's warmth

For singular nouns that end in *s*, add an apostrophe and an *s*.

her boss's office	Carlos's piano	the grass's length

For plural nouns that do not end in *s*, add an apostrophe and an *s*.

women's clothes	men's shoes	children's books

For plural nouns that end in *s*, add an apostrophe.

teachers' lounge	dogs' leashes	kids' playground

Apostrophes are also used in **contractions**. A contraction is a shortened form of two words that have been combined. The apostrophe shows where a letter or letters have been taken away.

> I will
> **I'll** be home in one hour.
>   do not
> We **don't** have any milk.

Grammar Handbook

Capitalization

There are five main reasons to use capital letters: to begin a sentence and in a direct quotation; to write the word I; to write a proper noun (the name of a specific person, place, or thing); to write a person's title; and to write the title of a work (artwork, written work, magazine, newspaper, musical composition, organization).

Use a capital letter to begin the first word in a sentence.

> Cows eat grass. They also eat hay.

Use a capital letter for the first word of a direct quotation.

> Carlos said, "We need more lettuce for the sandwiches."

Use a capital letter for the word *I*.

> How will I ever learn all these things? I guess I will learn them little by little.

Use a capital letter for a proper noun. Capitalize the important words in names.

> Robert E. Lee   Morocco   Tuesday   Tropic of Cancer

Capital Letters in Place Names	
Streets	Interstate 95, Center Street, Atwood Avenue
Cities and towns	Rome, Chicago, Fresno
States	California, North Dakota, Maryland
Regions	Pacific Northwest, Great Plains, Eastern Europe
Nations	China, Dominican Republic, Italy
Continents	North America, Africa, Asia
Mountains	Mount Shasta, Andes Mountains, Rocky Mountains
Deserts	Mojave Desert, Sahara Desert, Gobi Desert
Islands	Fiji Islands, Capri, Virgin Islands
Rivers	Amazon River, Nile River, Mississippi River
Lakes	Lake Superior, Great Bear Lake, Lake Tahoe
Bays	San Francisco Bay, Hudson Bay, Galveston Bay
Seas	Mediterranean Sea, Sea of Japan
Oceans	Pacific Ocean, Atlantic Ocean, Indian Ocean

Capital Letters for Specific Things	
Historical periods, events	Renaissance, Battle of Bull Run
Historical texts	Constitution, Bill of Rights
Days and months	Monday, October
Holidays	Thanksgiving, Labor Day
Organizations, schools	Greenpeace, Central High School
Government bodies	Congress, State Department
Political parties	Republican Party, Democratic Party
Ethnic groups	Chinese, Latinos
Languages, nationalities	Spanish, Canadian
Buildings	Empire State Building, City Hall
Monuments	Lincoln Memorial, Washington Monument
Religions	Hinduism, Christianity, Judaism, Islam
Special events	Boston Marathon, Ohio State Fair

Use a capital letter for a person's title if the title comes before the name. In the second sentence below, a capital letter is not needed because the title does not come before a name.

> I heard **S**enator Smith's speech about jobs. The **s**enator may come to our school.

Use a capital letter for the first and last word and all other important words in titles of books, newspapers, magazines, short stories, plays, movies, songs, paintings, and sculptures.

> Lucy wants to read *The **L**ord of the **R**ings.*
> The newspaper my father reads is *The **N**ew **Y**ork **T**imes.*
> Did you like the painting called ***W**ork in the **F**ields?*
> This poem is called "**T**he **B**irch **T**ree."

Grammar Handbook

Practice

The Parts of Speech

1. Choose the eight parts of speech from the list below and write them in your notebook. Then write an example sentence for each one, underlining the relevant part of speech.

nouns	adjectives	prepositions	pronouns
verbs	sentences	interjections	objects
subjects	adverbs	conjunctions	interrogatives

2. In your notebook, rewrite each sentence using the reciprocal pronoun *each other* or *one another*.
   a. Sandy gets along well with Laura, and Laura gets along well with Sandy.
   b. Elephants communicate with other elephants by using many different kinds of calls.
   c. At our school, students have to share the science lab with other students.
   d. The band has to listen to the orchestra's concerts, and the orchestra has to listen to the band's concerts.

3. In your notebook, rewrite the following paragraphs using contractions.

   > Hi Alejandra,
   > I have not seen you at school for a few days. Have you been sick? I hope you are OK. You are not missing much in social studies, but we are going to have a big exam in math next week, so I hope you will be back in school soon. There is a lot for you to catch up on!
   > Take care,
   > Melissa

   > Hi Melissa,
   > You are right—I have been sick for a couple of days. I am feeling much better today, so I will definitely be in school tomorrow. Let us get together this weekend to study math, OK? Maybe you can help me catch up! ☺
   > See you soon,
   > Alejandra

4. Copy the sentences into your notebook. After each one, say whether the underlined verb is in the indicative, imperative, or subjunctive mood.
   a. If I <u>were</u> you, I'd try to switch classes.
   b. <u>Call</u> me when you get home, OK?
   c. I usually <u>read</u> for half an hour before I go to sleep.
   d. I wish we <u>played</u> on the same team.

5. Copy the sentences into your notebook. After each one, say whether the underlined noun or pronoun is in the nominative, objective, or possessive case.
    a. Please give this book to <u>him</u>.
    b. <u>She</u> has beautiful eyes, doesn't she?
    c. Is this notebook <u>yours</u>?
    d. The <u>doctor's</u> office is on the second floor.

Clauses

6. Copy the sentences into your notebook. After each one, say whether the underlined clause is a dependent clause or an independent clause.
    a. <u>Whenever I go to bed late</u>, I feel tired the next day.
    b. If you win this race, <u>our team will be in first place</u>.
    c. I lost my gloves <u>before I got on the bus</u>.
    d. Since you don't have a ride, <u>you can come with us</u>.

Sentences

7. Copy the sentences into your notebook. After each one, say whether the sentence is compound, complex, or compound-complex. Underline the dependent clauses once, and the independent clauses twice.
    a. Before you can start, you have to read the instructions.
    b. When we first moved here, I didn't know anyone, but now I have a lot of friends.
    c. I'm still hungry even though I just ate a sandwich.
    d. While the rest of the class watched, my classmate and I gave our presentation, and the teacher videotaped us.
8. Copy the sentences into your notebook. After each one, say whether the sentence is declarative, interrogative, imperative, or exclamatory.
    a. Wow—what a nice-looking car!
    b. What time is it now?
    c. Matthew and Yolanda are leaving soon.
    d. Just leave your books in your locker.

Mechanics

9. Copy the sentences into your notebook. Add commas where appropriate.
    a. His kindergarten teacher Mrs. Richardson came to his graduation.
    b. They prefer rock not pop music.
    c. The paper she gave me if I can find it has all the information you need.
    d. My mom's car a four-door sedan doesn't have room for all of us.

Grammar Handbook

10. Copy the sentences into your notebook. Add dashes where appropriate. Be sure to adjust capitalization, as needed.
    a. If I could travel anywhere, I know where I would go. Spain.
    b. His goal in life is clear. He wants to become a musician.
    c. My best friend, Andrés Diaz, is the funniest person in the world.
    d. I wish I could find my . . . oh, never mind. Here it is.

11. Read the sentences. Notice how the quotation marks are used to indicate irony or sarcasm. Then choose a sentence that has the same meaning as the sentence with the quotation marks.
    a. Boy, that was an "easy" test. I'll be lucky if a get a C on it!
        1. The test was simple.
        2. The test was hard.
        3. The test was enjoyable.
    b. My "friend" Lisa never invites me to any of her parties.
        1. Lisa is not really my friend because she doesn't invite me to her parties.
        2. Lisa is my close friend even though she doesn't invite me to her parties.
        3. Lisa is the most popular girl in school.

12. Copy the following article into your notebook. Add the correct capitalization and punctuation where needed.

---

the biggest and the best

do you like shopping if so you should consider taking a trip to alberta canada thats the home of the biggest shopping center in the world the west edmonton mall this amazing entertainment center has more than 800 stores and services including an aquatic park a golf course and an ice rink

how would you like a little chocolate in july of 2006 nestlé singapore announced it had made the worlds largest chocolate bar the 2.668 ton bar surpasses the previous record of 2.28 tons according to the guinness book of records

you dont have to fly to the moon to experience weightlessness just go to six flags great adventure in new jersey usa where you can ride kingda ka the tallest and fastest roller coaster in the world this remarkable ride goes from 0 to 128 mph in 3.5 seconds and sends you 456 feet up into the sky hold onto your hats everyone

Editing and Proofreading Marks

To:	Use This Mark	Example:
add something	∧	We ate rice, bean⁀s and corn.
delete something	ℐ	We ate rice, beans, and corns.
close space	⌒	We ⌒ ate rice, beans, and corn.
start a new paragraph	¶	¶ We ate rice, beans, and corn.
add a comma	⍰	We ate rice, beans and corn.
add a period	⊙	We ate rice, beans, and corn⊙
switch letters or words	∽	We ate rice, baens, and corn.
change to a capital letter	a̳	we ate rice, beans, and corn.
change to a lowercase letter	⌿	WE ate rice, beans, and corn.
let the marked text stand	(stet)	We ate rice, beans, and corn. (stet)

Glossary

abandon to stop doing or planning to do something because of a problem

accurate exactly correct

adapt to gradually change behavior in order to become successful

address to speak directly to a person or group

adviser a person whose job it is to give advice about a specific topic

affect cause a person to feel strong emotions

alliance a union of countries or groups formed by agreement for some special purpose

alliteration the same sound used at the beginning of several words in a sentence

alternative something that you choose instead of another thing

analogy something that shows the relationship between a pair of words

analyze examine or think about something carefully in order to understand it

antagonist the character who tries to prevent the protagonist from reaching the goal

anticipation a feeling of excitement because something good or fun is going to happen

appreciation an understanding of the importance, meaning, or beauty of something

approached moved closer to

archetype a type of character that appears in literature often enough to be considered universal

armistice an agreement to stop fighting, usually for a specific period

arteries blood vessels that carry blood from the heart to the rest of the body

aside in a play, words spoken by a character to the audience

assassination the murdering of an important person, especially for political reasons

athletes individuals who excel in sports, or games

attached strongly connected to someone or something

attitude the opinions and feeling you have about something

author someone who writes a book, story, article, or play

author's purpose the reason for an author's writing

author's viewpoint the author's attitude toward a topic

beneficial good or useful

biased unfair because of a preference or dislike of something

biography a story of a person's life, based on facts

bitterness deep resentment; intense anger

bond a shared feeling or interest that unites people or animals

capability having the resources or skills to do something

category a group of the same kind of things

celestial relating to the sky or heaven

challenge something new, exciting, or difficult that needs a lot of skill and effort to do

Glossary

character foil a technique that an author uses to emphasize the differences between a main character and other characters

characterization the creation and development of a character in a story

circulation the way blood moves in a person in relation to one's heart

circumstances the conditions or facts that affect a situation

civilians people who are not members of any of the armed forces

classical literature books, plays, and poems of ancient Greece and Rome

clause a group of words that contains a subject and a predicate

collection a group of similar things that you get and keep together

colony an established grouping of animals or people

committed used all the time and energy that you could to achieve something

common noun names something general and should not be capitalized

communicate express your thoughts and feelings so that other people understand them

complexity the complicated nature of something

concave curved inward like a bowl

concept idea

conduct the way someone behaves

conflict a feeling of nervousness or unhappiness because you want to do two things at the same time

consequence something that happens as a result of a particular action

consult ask for advice from someone who might have the answer

context situation and conditions that surround something

contribute help make something happen

contribution something a person gives to the world that helps and is positive

controversy causing disagreement because people have strong opinions

convex curved outward like the surface of a ball

convince to persuade someone to do something

create make

credible believable, trustworthy

critique give your opinion on something

culture the art, literature, music, beliefs, and practices of a particular group of people

debate formal discussion of a subject in which people express differing opinions

declined became less in number or quality

defects faults or imperfections

define clearly show what something is or means

despite in spite of; regardless of

determined having a strong desire to succeed at something difficult

develop grow or change into something

device a piece of technology, or an item, with a specific function

devoted giving someone or something a lot of love, concern, or attention

dialogue a conversation in a book, play, or movie

Glossary

diction choice and use of words and phrases to express meaning, especially in literature and poetry

diplomat someone who officially represents his/her government in a foreign country

discrimination the practice of treating one group of people differently from another in an unfair way

distribution scattering or spreading of something over an area

document a piece of paper that has official information written on it

echolocation the system used by animals such as dolphins and bats to locate objects by emitting usually high-pitched sounds

ecosystems all living and non-living things in a particular environment

editorial a type of article that expresses an opinion

embryo the part of a seed that becomes the plant

entertain amuse or interest people in a manner that gives them pleasure

environment the land, water, and air in which plants and animals live

equipment the things that you need for a particular activity

equivalent something that has the same value or importance

estimate guess the value, size, number, etc., of something

ethical having to do with right and wrong

evaluate judge how good or successful something is

eventful full of events

evidence facts or signs that show that something is true

expand become larger, or to make something become larger

exploits brave and exciting actions

extinction a situation where something has died off and no longer exists

features parts of something that stand out because they seem important, interesting, or typical

figurative language language that expresses more than a literal meaning

flashback a scene that takes you back in time

foil a character, who, by contrast, highlights the qualities of another character

foreshadowing a plot device that reveals what will happen in the future

function the usual purpose of a thing OR what something, such as a part of your body, does

gender how a person identifies; most commonly male or female

germination the stage at which the embryo inside a seed starts to grow

heroism very great courage

honor do something to show publicly that someone is respected and admired

ignorance lack of knowledge or information about something

ignore pay no attention to someone or something

Glossary

imagery the use of vivid language to describe objects, ideas, or actions

imitate copy; make or do something like someone else

impact the effect that an event or situation has on someone or something

inactive not doing anything

indicate show that something is probably true

industry a collection of stores or places of business focusing on the same products or services

inform give information

informational text writing that gives facts about a subject

injury some damage caused to a body

instruct officially tell someone what to do or how to do something

integrity the quality of being honest and having high moral principles

internal conflict a struggle that takes place in a character's mind

interpret explain or decide what something means

investors people who spend money to support a business or business idea in order to later make money when the business suceeds

irony a contrast between appearance and reality

justify give a reasonable or acceptable explanation for something

lecture a talk given to a group of people about a particular subject

mammals animals such as cats and humans that drink their mothers' milk when they are young

marathon a competitive run that lasts for 26.2 miles, or close to 42 kilometers

metaphor an implied comparison in which one thing is spoken about as though it were something else

migrate when a group of people or animals move from one location to another

moral a lesson about what is right and wrong that you learn from a story

motivation the reason for a character's actions

mutual felt by two or more people toward one another

narrator a character who talks directly to the audience and tells about the characters on the stage

neutral not supporting either side in an argument, competition, or war

nocturnal active at night

objectively in a way that is not influenced by a person's feelings, beliefs, or ideas

onomatopoeia the use of words that imitate sounds

opaque unable to be seen through

organisms living things

organs a body part that is responsible for a specific action like breathing, or processing information

Glossary

patented a document which claims that within a certain time frame, a particular company is the only one allowed to sell a newly invented product

persistence the act of continuing firmly in some state, purpose, or course of action

personification a figure of speech in which something nonhuman is given human characteristics

persuade to make someone believe your viewpoint

phrase a group of related words that does not have a subject and predicate

plot the sequence of events that make up a story

poetry a form of writing in which language is used to create an emotional response

point of view the perspective from which a story is written

possessive pronoun indicates ownership

potential possible

prediction statement that something is going to happen

prey an animal targeted by a different animal for food

principle a moral set of ideas that makes you behave in a certain way

procedural text writing that tells you how to do something

process a series of actions, developments, or changes that happen in a sequence

protagonist the hero of a story, the character who must overcome obstacles to achieve a goal

protective used or intended for keeping someone or something safe from harm, damage, or illness

pursue continue doing an activity or trying to achieve something over a long time

racism when an entire race of people are openly discriminated against, or attacked

reaction something you say or do because of what has happened or been said to you

recognize to realize that you know a person when you see him or her

referees someone who enforces the rules of a particular game or sport while it is occuring

refugees people who have to leave their country, especially because of war

region fairly large area of a state or country, usually without exact limits

rejected not chosen

reluctance unwillingness to do something

repetition the act of saying or doing something again

resist to stop yourself from doing something you really want to do

resources all the money, property, and other goods that are available for use

reveal to uncover and show something

revolution one complete circular movement around a certain point

rover a vehicle used to explore a planet, moon, or other large area in space

sarcasm sharp language used to express scorn or disapproval

sensation a feeling

setting the time and place of a story's action

Glossary

significance importance or meaning of something

significant important; meaningful

similar almost the same

simile an expression that compares two things using the words *like* or *as*

smuggle to take something secretly and illegally from one place to another

soliloquy in a play, a speech spoken alone on stage by a character

sonnet a fourteen-line poem

source the cause of something or the place where it starts

species similar plants or animals that can reproduce

spirituals religious folk songs of African-American origin

stable unchanging

stage directions instructions that tell the actors what they should do and how they should do it

straighten become straight

stanza a group of lines that form a pattern in a poem

structure the way in which parts come together to make a whole

struggle something that takes a lot of effort over a long period of time

surrendered gave up fighting; admitted defeat

suspense a feeling of anxiety or excitement

symbol something that stands for or represents something else

sympathetic showing that you understand how sad, hurt, lonely, etc., someone feels

synthesize combine different things together

tangible able to be perceived through the sense of touch

technology the combination of all the latest knowledge, equipment, and methods used in scientific or industrial work

tenacity resilient, determined

tension the emotionally charged relationship between people or groups of people

terrestrial describing any of the four planets that are nearest to the sun and made mostly of rock

text the words in a printed piece of writing

theme the central idea or message of a work of literature

the wild an area that is completely uncivilized

thrive to become very successful, strong, or healthy

tone general feeling or attitude expressed in a piece of writing, activity, etc.

tradition a belief, custom, or way of doing something that has existed for a long time

tragic very sad and shocking

transformation a complete change in something or someone

translucent able to allow some light to pass through

transmit pass something through

transparent clear, able to be seen through

transport move or carry from one place to another

trenches long narrow holes dug in the earth to protect soldiers

universal existing everywhere or affecting everyone

Glossary

unsubstantiated opinion a belief not based on fact

vehicle writing, a piece of art, or an event used to transmit or express ideas

virtual able to be seen but not real

visible able to be seen

visual relating to seeing or sight

wavelength the distance between two waves of light

wingspan the distance from the end of one wing to the end of the other

wisdom knowledge gained over a long period of time

witness to see something happen, especially an accident or crime

Index of Skills

Further Readings, 67, 139, 213, 287, 357, 433

Grammar
Adjective clauses
  reduced to adjective phrases, 380
Adjectives
  adjectival phrases, 239, 283
  comparative, 118, 352
  order of, 16
  possessive, 238
  superlative, 208
  with too and enough, 119
Adverb clauses to describe a process, 269
Appositives, 312
Comparison structures, 352
Contrast and opposition, 326
Emphasis given by Italics, repetition, and more, 17
Gerunds, 426
Imperatives, 268
Infinitives, 427
Modals
  could, 179
  must, 164
  would, 165, 194
Nouns
  appositives, 312
  clauses with *that*, 397
Passive, 340
Prepositions
  combined with verbs, 47
  place and time, 46
  time, 313
Pronouns
  antecedents, 327
  indefinite, 192
  reciprocal and reflexive, 209
  relative, 396
Punctuation
  dashes to explain or clarify, 91
Quotations, 341
Restrictive and nonrestrictive clauses, 62, 63

Sentences
  compound and complex, 252, 253
  conditional, 135
  simple, 252
Sequence words, 90
Tense
  present and past progressive, 411
  past perfect, 105, 282
  present perfect, 104, 282
  passive voice, 33
  simple past, 104, 411
  simple present with when clause, 32
  Subjunctive, 195
  Transition words, phrases, and clauses, 178
Verbs
  have to, 134
  must, 164
Word order
  inverted in poems, 353
  inverted in prose, 381
  typical and atypical, 410
Would, 165, 194

Language Development
Language function
  comprehension, 14–15, 30, 44, 60, 88, 102–103, 116, 132, 162–163, 176, 192–193, 206, 236, 250–251, 266, 280, 310, 324, 338, 350–351, 378, 394, 408, 424
Language learning strategies
  cause-and-effect charts, 310
  dramatic reading, 250, 324, 350, 378, 408
  listening and speaking workshop, 68–69, 140–141, 214–215, 288–289, 358–359, 434–435
  reader's theater, 14, 44, 102, 132, 162, 192, 280, 424

Listening and Speaking
Dramatic reading, 250, 324, 350, 378, 408
Listening and speaking workshop
  description guessing game, 68–69
  how-to demonstration, 288–289
  oral report, 358–359
  radio commercial, 214–215
  skit, 140–141
  TV documentary, 434–435
Reader's theater, 14, 44, 102, 132, 162, 192, 280, 424

Literary Elements
Dramatic conventions
  narrator, 243
  soliloquy, 243
  stage directions, 243
Genre
  fable, 156–161, 186–191
  folktale, 86–87
  letters, 323
  myth, 8–13
  novel, 418–423
  play, 246–249
  poetry, 320, 321, 348, 349, 404–405, 406, 407
  science text, 24–29, 84–85, 112–115, 172–175, 260–264, 265, 388–393
  short story, 40–43, 98–101, 126–131, 276–279, 374–377
  social studies text, 54–59, 202–205, 230–235, 260–264, 265, 304–309, 334–337
  song, 322
Literary response and evaluation
  chart, 193
  comic strip, 163
  descriptive paragraph, 133, 409

Index of Skills

news article, 15, 251, 351
write from a different point of view, 45, 103, 281, 325, 379
write a new ending, 425
Literary terms
  antagonist, 371
  archetype, 371
  ballad, 345
  characterization, 123, 273
  dialogue, 123
  extended metaphor, 317
  figurative language, 37, 273, 317, 401
  flashback, 415
  foil, 371
  foreshadowing, 415
  imagery, 37, 345, 401
  internal conflict, 183
  irony, 5
  metaphor, 401
  moral, 153
  motivation, 153
  narrator, 243
  onomatopoeia, 5
  personification, 317
  plot, 95
  point of view, 95, 415
  protagonist, 371
  repetition, 5
  sarcasm, 123
  setting, 37, 415
  simile, 401
  soliloquy, 243
  sonnet, 345
  stage directions, 243
  suspense, 95
  symbol, 273, 345
  theme, 183

Media and Technology
Internet use, 68, 89, 133, 139, 214, 281, 287, 288, 357, 358, 395, 434
Library use, 68, 89, 133, 139, 214, 281, 357, 358, 395, 434

Reading
Comprehension, 14–15, 30, 44, 60, 88, 102–103, 116, 132, 162–163, 176, 192–193, 206, 236, 250–251, 266, 280, 310, 324, 338, 350–351, 378, 394, 408, 424
Critical thinking, 66, 138, 212, 286, 356, 432
Fluency, 31, 61, 66, 89, 117, 138, 177, 207, 212, 237, 267, 286, 311, 339, 356, 395, 432
Strategies
  analyze text structure, 245
  compare and contrast, 97
  connect ideas, 373
  distinguish fact from opinion, 171
  draw conclusions, 333
  evaluate new information, 387
  identify author's purpose, 185
  identify cause and effect, 303
  identify main idea and details, 229
  identify problems and solutions, 155
  make inferences, 125
  monitor comprehension, 259
  predictions, 7
  read aloud, 347, 403
  recognize sequence, 83
  recognize and analyze cultural context, 275
  recognize historical context, 319
  scan, 111
  sequence, 417
  skim, 23
  summarize, 201
  use visuals, 53
  visualize, 39
Text structure
  fable, 156–161, 186–191
  folktale, 86–87
  letters, 323
  myth, 8–13
  novel, 418–423
  play, 246–249
  poetry, 320, 321, 348, 349, 404–405, 406, 407
  science text, 24–29, 84–85, 112–115, 172–175, 260–264, 265, 388–393
  short story, 40–43, 98–101, 126–131, 276–279, 374–377
  social studies text, 54–59, 202–205, 230–235, 260–264, 265, 304–309, 334–337
  song, 322

Research and Study Skills
Internet use, 68, 89, 133, 139, 214, 281, 287, 288, 357, 358, 395, 434
Library use, 68, 89, 133, 139, 214, 281, 357, 358, 395, 434

Vocabulary
Academic words
  abandon, 244, 416
  accurate, 386
  address, 200
  adviser, 154
  alternative, 244
  affect, 96
  analyze, 184
  anticipation, 96
  appreciation, 402
  approached, 38
  attached, 372
  attitude, 402
  author, 6
  beneficial, 386
  biased, 170
  bond, 274, 346
  category, 402
  circumstances, 244
  collection, 154
  committed, 416
  communicate, 228
  complexity, 372

Index of Skills

concept, 228
conduct, 124
conflict, 244
consequence, 372
context, 318
contribute, 258
contribution, 52
controversy, 200
convince, 244
create, 318
culture, 6
debate, 170
define, 170
despite, 38
determined, 200
devoted, 274
discrimination, 96
distribution, 110
document, 332
environment, 82
equivalent, 38
estimate, 332
ethical, 184
evaluate, 258
expand, 110
exploits, 332
features, 386
function, 82, 258
ignorance, 386
ignore, 124
impact, 318
indicate, 346
injury, 52
instruct, 124
integrity, 332
interpret, 22
justify, 184
mutual, 274
neutral, 302
objectively, 170
persistence, 228
potential, 82
prediction, 110
principle, 184
process, 82
reaction, 96
recognize, 154

region, 110
rejected, 52
reluctance, 124
resist, 416
resources, 302
reveal, 416
significance, 274
significant, 51
similar, 318
source, 258
struggle, 258
sympathetic, 332
technology, 302
tension, 302
text, 6
thrive, 372
tradition, 6
tragic, 346
transformation, 228
transmit, 22
universal, 346
vehicle, 302, 402
virtual, 22
visible, 22
visual, 38
wisdom, 154
witness, 200
Key words
  alliance, 301
  armistice, 301
  arteries, 257
  assassination, 301
  athlete, 199
  attitude, 423
  bitterness, 227
  capability, 199
  celestial, 169
  cholesterol, 257
  circulation, 257
  civilians, 301
  colony, 109
  concave, 21
  consulate, 331
  convex, 21
  decline, 109
  defects, 227
  develop, 81

device, 51
diplomat, 331
echolocation, 385
embryo, 81
equipment, 51
eventful, 227
gender, 199
germination, 81
heroism, 331
honor, 331
imitate, 227
inactive, 81
industry, 51
investors, 51
lecture, 331
mammals, 385
marathon, 199
migrate, 109
nocturnal, 385
opaque, 21
organs, 257
patented, 51
prey, 385
protective, 81
racism, 199
referee, 199
refugees, 331
revolution, 169
rover, 169
sensation, 227, 257
species, 109
stable, 109
straighten, 81
surrendered, 301
survive, 109
tangible, 227
tenacity, 51
terrestrial, 169
the wild, 385
translucent, 21
transparent, 21
trenches, 301
wavelength, 21
wingspan, 385
Literary terms
  antagonist, 371
  archetype, 371

477

Index of Skills

ballad, 345
characterization, 123, 273
dialogue, 123
extended metaphor, 317
figurative language, 37, 273, 317, 401
flashback, 415
foil, 371
foreshadowing, 415
imagery, 37, 345, 401
internal conflict, 183
irony, 5
metaphor, 401
moral, 153
motivation, 153
narrator, 243
onomatopoeia, 5
personification, 317
plot, 95
point of view, 95, 415
protagonist, 371
repetition, 5
sarcasm, 123
setting, 37, 415
simile, 401
soliloquy, 243
sonnet, 345
stage directions, 243
suspense, 95
symbol, 273, 345
theme, 183

Word Study
Antonyms, 39
Compound words, 7
Frequently misspelled words, 417
Homographs, 97
Homophones, 319
Hyphenated words, 387
Idioms, 125
Irregular plurals, 155
Long *a, i, o* Spelling Patterns, 111
Long and short vowels, 185
Prefixes, 171
Related words, 83, 259
Root, 303
Sound /z/, 275
Spelling Long *e*, 347
Suffix *-ful*, 229
Suffix *-ness*, 333
Suffixes, 53, 373
Synonyms, 201, 245
Words with double letters, 403
Words with /el/ spelled *-le* and *-el*, 23

Writing
Applications
  Descriptive writing
    essay, 70–74
    character, 18
    experience, 64
    object, 34
    place, 48
  Expository writing
    essay, 290–294, 360–364
    cause-and-effect, 314
    compare and contrast, 328
    critical analysis, 284
    critique, 240
    instructions, 270
    interpretative response, 430–431
    news article, 342
    summary, 254
    support a position, 354
  Narrative writing
    fictional narrative, 142–146
    personal letter, 120
    personal narrative, 136
    rewriting a familiar story, 106
    story with starter, 92
  Persuasive writing
    advertisement, 210
    letter to the editor, 180
    paragraph, 196
    review, 166
    speech, 216–220
  Research report
    classifying paragraphs, 396
    interpretive response, 430
    introductory paragraph, 382
    main idea support, 412
    report, 436–440
Organization
  cause and effect, 314
  chronological order, 64, 92
  classify, 396
  compare and contrast, 328
  gather and organize information, 68, 140, 214, 288, 358, 434
  graphic organizers, 18, 34, 48, 64, 70, 92, 106, 120, 136, 142, 166, 180, 196, 210, 216, 240, 254, 270, 284, 290, 314, 328, 342, 354, 360, 382, 398, 412, 430, 436
  logical order, 290
  outline, 436
  spatial order, 48
  step-by-step instructions, 270
  story chart, 142
Skills and strategies
  Description
    character traits, 18
    physical traits, 18
    sensory details, 34, 48, 64, 70–74
    spatial order, 48
  Expository
    5Ws, 342, 360–364
    cause and effect, 314
    compare and contrast, 328
    personal response, 284
    sequence of steps, 270
    standards, 240
    supporting main idea with details, 290–294, 412

Index of Skills

Narrative
  dialogue, 140
  fictional, 142–146
  mood, 64
  point of view, 106
  sequence words, 92
  voice, 120
Persuasive
  opinions, 166, 180, 216
  supporting main idea with facts and detail, 196, 216
  supporting reasons and examples, 216
Research
  classifying, 396
  gathering and organizing information, 434
  interpretive response, 430
  narrowing a topic, 382, 434
  presenting information, 382
  supporting main idea with examples and explanations, 412, 436–440
  supporting main idea with facts and details, 412, 436–440
Traits of writing
  Checklists, 19, 35, 49, 65, 71, 93, 107, 121, 137, 143, 167, 181, 197, 211, 217, 241, 255, 271, 285, 291, 315, 329, 343, 355, 361, 383, 399, 413, 431, 437
Writing workshop
  descriptive essay, 70–74
  fictional narrative, 142–146
  speech, 216–220
  expository essay, 290–294
  expository essay, 360–364
  research report, 436–440

Index of Authors, Titles, Art, and Artists

"Abuela Invents the Zero" (Cofer), 126–131
Aesop's Fable (Riches), 153
Ajax (Curry), 444
Allston, Washington, 297
"Anthem for Doomed Youth" (Owen), 321

"The Beggar King," 156–161
Benton, Thomas Hart, 148
"Birdfoot's Grandpa" (Bruchac), 407
Bruchac, Joseph, 407
Butterfield, Deborah, 222

Cadeau (Serie II) (Ray), 223
"To Capture the Wild Horse," 246–249
"Climate Change Puts Nature on the Move," 112–115
Cofer, Judith, 126–131
Curry, John Steuart, 444

"Daybreak" (Kinnell), 406
Diary: December 12, 1941 (Shimomura), 367
Dickinson, Emily, 404
Dove, Arthur, 77

Earley, Frank, 323

"In Flanders Fields" (McCrae), 320
Fuente, Larry, 445

Game Fish (Fuente), 445
"A Game of Light and Shade" (Vivante), 40–43
"Getting to Know Real Bats" (Pringle), 388–393
Gilliam, Sam, 223
"Ginger for the Heart" (Yee), 276–279
"The Golden Serpent" (Myers), 186–191
Goodwin, Joe, 322

"Grandmother Spider Brings the Sun" (Keams), 8–13
Hanley, James F., 322
"The Heart's Wisdom," 260–264
"He Died at His Post" (Holman), 349
Hermia and Helena (Allston), 297
Holman, J.W., 349
Hopper, Edward, 76
"How Seeds and Plants Grow," 84–85

"In the Name of His Father" (Tasker), 334–337

Keams, Geri, 8–13
Keller, Helen, 230–235
Kinnell, Galway, 406

"Letter Home" (Earley), 323
"Light," 24–29
London, Jack, 418–423
Love Poem - Poem by Michael Hannon (Wiley), 296–297
Lupin Wedding Crown (Seppä), 149

MacDonald, Ballard, 322
Mars: Pro and Con, 172–175
McCrae, John, 320
Meltzer, Milton, 48–55
Monekana (Butterfield), 222
Myers, Walter Dean, 186–191

"A Narrow Fellow in the Grass" (Dickinson), 404
"Nourishing Your Heart and Your Brain," 265

Owen, Wilfred, 321

Plate #753 (Sperry), 77
Portrait of Giovanni Arnolfini and His Wife (van Eyck), 31
Pringle, Laurence, 388–393

"Providing Light in the Darkness," 54–59

Ray, Man, 223
Riches, Lizzie, 153
Rockwell, Norman, 366
Ryder's House (Hopper), 76

Save Freedom of Speech (Rockwell), 366
Seppä, Heikki, 149
Shimomura, Roger, 367
"Sonnet to My Brother, a Soldier," 348
Sperry, Robert, 77
from *The Story of My Life* (Keller), 230–235
Sun (Dove), 77
Swing (Gilliam), 223

"A Tale of Two Brothers," 86–87
"The Talking Bird," 374–377
Tasker, Fred, 334–337
"Three Wonderful Letters from Home" (Goodwin, MacDonald & Hanley), 322

Untitled (Mixed Flowers) (Walcott), 149

van Eyck, Jan, 31
Vivante, Arturo, 40–43

Walcott, Mary Vaux, 149
Wheat (Benton), 148
from *White Fang* (London), 418–423
"When Is a Winner a Hero?" 202–205
Wiley, William T., 296–297
"World War I," 304–309

Yee, Paul, 276–279

Acknowledgments

UNIT 1
"Grandmother Spider Brings the Sun" Rising Moon an imprint of Cooper Square Publishing.

Excerpt from "A Game of Light and Shade" Copyright © 1979 by Arturo Vivante. First appeared in RUN TO THE WATERFALL, published by Charles Scribner & Sons. Used by permission of Curtis Brown, Ltd.

UNIT 2
"How Seeds and Plants Grow." Copyright © Pearson Education, One Lake Street, Upper Saddle River, NJ, 07458.

"Abuela Invents the Zero" From AN ISLAND LIKE YOU: THE STORIES OF THE BARRIO by Judith Ortiz Cofer. Copyright © 1995 by Judith Ortiz Cofer. Scholastic, Inc/Orchard Books. Copyright © 1995 by Judith Ortiz Cofer. Reprinted by permission.

UNIT 3
"The Golden Serpent" The Golden Serpent © 1980 by Walter Dean Myers.

UNIT 4
Excerpt from The Story of My Life by Helen Keller.

"Ginger for the Heart" from Tales from Gold Mountain. Copyright © 1989 by Paul Yee. Reproduced with permission from Groundwood Books Inc. Toronto. www.groundwoodbooks.com

UNIT 5
"In Flanders Fields" by John McCrae.

"Anthem for Doomed Youth" by Wilfred Owen.

"Three Wonderful Letters From Home" by Goodwin, MacDonald, and Hanley.

"Letter Home" by Frank Earley.

"In the Name of His Father" The Miami Herald, 24 January © 2000 McClatchy. All rights reserved. Used by permission and protected by the Copyright Laws of the United States. The printing, copying, redistribution, or retransmission of this Content without express written permission is prohibited.

"He Died at His Post" by J.W Holman.

UNIT 6
Excerpt from "Getting to Know Real Bats" © LAURENCE PRINGLE, 1991

"A narrow fellow in the grass". THE POEMS OF EMILY DICKINSON: VARIORUM EDITION, edited by Ralph W. Franklin, Cambridge, Mass.: The Belknap Press of Harvard University Press, Copyright © 1998 by the President and Fellows of Harvard College. Copyright © 1951, 1955 by the President and Fellows of Harvard College. Copyright © renewed 1979, 1983 by the President and Fellows of Harvard College. Copyright © 1914, 1918, 1919, 1924, 1929, 1930, 1932, 1935, 1937, 1942 by Martha Dickinson Bianchi. Copyright © 1952, 1957, 1958, 1963, 1965 by Mary L. Hampson.

"Daybreak" from MORTAL ACTS, MORTAL WORDS by Galway Kinnell. Copyright © 1980, renewed 2008 by Galway Kinnell. Reprinted by permission of Houghton Mifflin Harcourt Publishing Company. All rights reserved.

"Birdfoot's Grandpa" from Native American Stories by Joseph Bruchac. Copyright © 1991 by Joseph Bruchac. Reprinted by permission of Fulcrum Publishing.

London Jack, White Fang (1906). By: Jack London: Novel, as published by Macmillan.

Credits

Illustrators: Aptara 86–87; Eldon Doty 163; Julie Downing 374, 375, 376, 377; Keith Favazza 98–99, 100, 101, 107; Luigi Galante 40, 42; Adam Gustavson 127, 128–129, 130, 276, 278–279; Carol Heyer 186–187, 188, 189, 190, 191; Dani Jones 157, 158, 159, 160, 161, 167; Dom Lee 334, 335, 336, 337; Tom Leonard 24–25, 27, 29; Joseph Qiu 419, 420, 422, 431; Val Paul Taylor 8, 11, 12, 13, 19.

FM: vi Photo by Tim Hursley/Smithsonian American Art Museum; viii Sonia.eps/Shutterstock; ix Photo12/Ann Ronan Picture Library/Alamy Stock Photo; xi Stmilan/Shutterstock; xii Triff/Shutterstock; xiii Denis Doyle/Getty Images; xiv (T) AP Images; xiv (B) Mariait/Shutterstock; xvi (T) The Picture Art Collection/Alamy Stock Photo; xvi (B) Everett Historical/Shutterstock; xvii Muratart/Shutterstock; xviii Merlin D. Tuttle/Science Source

UNIT 1: 002–003 Ninetyonefoto/Shutterstock; 002 (BC) Wides & Holl/The Image Bank/Getty Images; 002 (BR) Juan Enrique del Barrio/Shutterstock; 003 Chronicle/Alamy Stock Photo; 004 Simon J Byrne/Moment/Getty Images; 005 Caiti Borruso/Moment Open/Getty Images; 006 Luc Novovitch/Alamy Stock Photo; 007 Ronnie Kaufman/Larry Hirshowitz/Blend Images/Getty Images; 015 Kypros/Moment/Getty Images; 016 George H.H. Huey/Alamy Stock Photo; 020 Joon_T/Shutterstock; 021 Ulrich Niehoff/Image Broker/Alamy Stock Photo; 022 Werner Layer/Mauritius images GmbH/Alamy Stock Photo; 024 Wides & Holl/The Image Bank/Getty Images; 025 Sonia.eps/Shutterstock; 026 (TL) Optimarc/Shutterstock; 026 (TC) Huandi/123RF; 026 (TR) Koldunov Alexey/Shutterstock; 026 (B) Iakov Filimonov/Shutterstock; 028 Lorraine Swanson/Shutterstock; 031 (L) Art Collection 4/Alamy Stock Photo; 031 (R) Art Collection/Alamy Stock Photo; 035 Constantine Pankin/Shutterstock; 036 Sborisov/iStock/Getty Images; 037 Creative Travel Projects/Shutterstock; 038 Evgeny Kharitonov/123RF; 039 Ivan/Moment/Getty Images; 045 Juan Enrique del Barrio/Shutterstock; 049 GP232/E+/Getty Images; 050 Ian Dagnall Computing/Alamy Stock Photo; 054 Chronicle/Alamy Stock Photo; 054–059 (Bkgrd) Prisma Archivo/Alamy Stock Photo; 055 Prisma Archivo/Alamy Stock Photo; 057 Fotosearch/Archive Photos/Getty Images; 058 Photo12/Ann Ronan Picture Library/Alamy Stock Photo; 059 Everett Historical/Shutterstock; 061 John Parrot/Stocktrek Images/Getty Images; 065 Marko Poplasen/Shutterstock; 076 (T) Photo by Tim Hursley/Smithsonian American Art Museum; 076 (B) Edward Hopper/Smithsonian American Art Museum, Washington, DC/Art Resource, NY.; Hopper, Edward, V HOP, © 2018 Heirs of Josephine Hopper/Licensed by Artists Rights Society (ARS), NY; 077 (T) Arthur G. Dove/Smithsonian American Art Museum, Washington, DC/Art Resource, NY; 077 (B) Robert Sperry/Smithsonian American Art Museum, Washington, DC/Art Resource, NY

UNIT 2: 078–079 Mathisa/Shutterstock; 078 (BR) Stu Shaw/Shutterstock; 080 Sundaemorning/Shutterstock; 081 Singkham/Shutterstock; 082 Anton Foltin/Shutterstock; 084 (T) Madlen/Shutterstock; 084 (B) Designua/Shutterstock; 085 (TL) Janis Smits/Shutterstock; 085 (TR) Gerald A. DeBoer/Shutterstock; 085 (BL) Krasowit/Shutterstock; 085 (BR) Sergio99/Shutterstock; 088 Andrea Danti/Shutterstock; 089 Pam Walker/Shutterstock; 093 Dorling Kindersley ltd/Alamy Stock Photo; 094 File/AP Images; 096 Everett Historical/Shutterstock; 108 AndreAnita/Shutterstock; 109 Delmas Lehman/Shutterstock; 110 Sirtravelalot/Shutterstock; 112 Stmilan/Shutterstock; 112–115 (Bkgrd) Stephen VanHorn/Shutterstock; 113 Stu Shaw/Shutterstock; 114 Menno Schaefer/Shutterstock; 115 Frans Lemmens/Alamy Stock Photo; 116 Cwhiteway/Shutterstock; 117 Mathisa/Shutterstock; 122 Abo Photography/Shutterstock; 123 Monkey Business Images/Shutterstock; 124 Somddr/Shutterstock; 133 Stockbroker/123RF; 137 Dmitry Naumov/Shutterstock; 148 (T) Photo by Tim Hursley/Smithsonian American Art Museum; 148 (B) Smithsonian American Art Museum, Washington, DC/Art Resource, NY; © 2018 T.H. and R.P. Benton Testamentary Trusts/UMB Bank Trustee/Licensed by VAGA at Artists Rights Society (ARS), NY; 149 (T) Smithsonian American Art Museum, Washington, DC/Art Resource, NY; 149 (B) Smithsonian American Art Museum, Washington, DC/Art Resource, NY

UNIT 3: 150–151 Bannafarsai_Stock/Shutterstock; 150 (BC) MediaPunch Inc/Alamy Stock Photo; 151 Darren McCollester/Getty Images; 152 De Agostini/Biblioteca Ambrosiana/De Agostini Picture Library/Getty Images; 153 Private Collection/Portal Painters/Lizzie Riches/Bridgeman Art Library; 168 Christos Georghiou/123RF; 169 StockTrek/Purestock/Alamy Stock Photo; 170 Pavliha/E+/Getty Images; 171 Joel Kowsky/NASA;

Credits

172 Gorodenkoff/Shutterstock; 172–175 (Bkgrd) MediaPunch Inc/Alamy Stock Photo; 173 Triff/Shutterstock; 174 MediaPunch Inc/Alamy Stock Photo; 175 U3d/Shutterstock; 181 Iamluckylee/Shutterstock; 182 Interfoto/Alamy Stock Photo; 183 Ilya Images/Shutterstock; 184 Leremy/Shutterstock; 191 Charles Sykes/AP Images; 198 Â© Simon Bellis/Sportimage/Cal Sport Media/ZUMA Press, Inc./Alamy Stock Photo; 199 M. Anthony Nesmith/Icon Sportswire/Getty Images; 200 SeventyFour/iStock/Getty Images; 202 Paul Connell/The Boston Globe/Getty Images; 202–205 (Bkgrd) Darren McCollester/Getty Images; 203 Darren McCollester/Getty Images; 204 Denis Doyle/Getty Images; 205 Maxisport/Shutterstock; 211 Baibaz/123RF; 222 (T) Photo by Tim Hursley/Smithsonian American Art Museum; 222 (B) Smithsonian American Art Museum, Washington, DC/Art Resource, NY; © 2018 Deborah Butterfield/Licensed by VAGA at Artists Rights Society (ARS), NY; 223 (T) Smithsonian American Art Museum, Washington, DC/Art Resource, NY; © 2018 Sam Gilliam/Artists Rights Society (ARS), New York; 223 (B) Man Ray/Digital Image/The Museum of Modern Art/Licensed by SCALA/Art Resource, NY; © Man Ray 2015 Trust/Artists Rights Society (ARS), NY/ADAGP, Paris

UNIT 4: 224–225 Jennifer McCallum/Shutterstock; 224 (BL) Library of Congress/Corbis/VCG/Getty Images; 224 (BC) Mariait/Shutterstock; 224 (BR) Rawpixel.com/Shutterstock; 226 (L) Alsu/Shutterstock; 226 (R) PhotoQuest/Archive Photos/Getty Images; 228 Oleksandr Rybitskiy/Shutterstock; 230 Library of Congress/Corbis/VCG/Getty Images; 231 Album/Alamy Stock Photo; 232 AP Images; 233 Historical/Corbis/Getty Images; 234 Bettmann/Getty Images; 235 Hulton-Deutsch Collection/Corbis/Getty Images; 237 Bettmann/Getty Images; 241 Bettmann/Getty Images; 242 Diane Garcia/Shutterstock; 244 Natalia Mels/Shutterstock; 246 Mariait/Shutterstock; 247 Ronnie Howard/Shutterstock; 248 Jackson Stock Photography/Shutterstock; 249 Wavebreakmedia/Shutterstock; 251 Proma1/Shutterstock; 256 GraphicsRF/Shutterstock; 257 Rido/Shutterstock; 260 Rawpixel.com/Shutterstock; 260–264 (Bkgrd) Jennifer McCallum/Shutterstock; 262 Westend61/Getty Images; 263 Antonio Guillem/Shutterstock; 264 Jules Selmes/Pearson Education Ltd; 265 (T) Hong Vo/Shutterstock; 265 (B) Joshua Resnick/123RF; 268 Arne Beruldsen/Shutterstock; 271 Kasia/Shutterstock; 274 Eric Simard/123RF; 281 AP Images; 285 Amarita/Shutterstock; 296 (T) Photo by Tim Hursley/Smithsonian American Art Museum; 296 (B) Smithsonian American Art Museum, Washington, DC/Art Resource, NY; © William T. Wiley; 297 Smithsonian American Art Museum, Washington, DC/Art Resource, NY

UNIT 5: 298–299 Miroslav110/Shutterstock; 298 (BL) Sueddeutsche Zeitung Photo/Alamy Stock Photo; 298 (BC) Everett Historical/Shutterstock; 299 Muratart/Shutterstock; 301 Chronicle/Alamy Stock Photo; 302 Sueddeutsche Zeitung Photo/Alamy Stock Photo; 304 Sueddeutsche Zeitung Photo/Alamy Stock Photo; 304–309 (Bkgrd) David Persson/Shutterstock; 305 (T) Marcio Machado/ZUMA Press, Inc./Alamy Stock Photo; 305 (B) Pictorial Press Ltd/Alamy Stock Photo; 306 Milagli/Shutterstock; 307 (TL) The Picture Art Collection/Alamy Stock Photo; 307 (TR) David Persson/Shutterstock; 307 (C) Historical Images Archive/Alamy Stock Photo; 307 (B) Everett Historical/Shutterstock; 308 Everett Historical/Shutterstock; 309 Everett Collection Inc/Alamy Stock Photo; 315 James Montgomery Flagg/Library of Congress Prints and Photographs Division Washington, D.C. 20540 USA [LC-DIG-ppmsc-03521]; 316 Mondadori Portfolio/Getty Images; 318 Photo 12/Alamy Stock Photo; 320 (Bkgrd) Menzl Guenter/Shutterstock; 320 Historic Collection/Alamy Stock Photo; 321 (Bkgrd) Everett Historical/Shutterstock; 321 Lebrecht Music & Arts/Alamy Stock Photo; 322 Gado Images/Alamy Stock Photo; 323 (Bkgrd) The Picture Art Collection/Alamy Stock Photo; 323 Prisma by Dukas Presseagentur GmbH/Alamy Stock Photo; 324 Prisma by Dukas Presseagentur GmbH/Alamy Stock Photo; 325 Everett Historical/Shutterstock; 329 Sueddeutsche Zeitung Photo/Alamy Stock Photo; 330 Shawshots/Alamy Stock Photo; 331 Horizon Images/Motion/Alamy Stock Photo; 332 Fabrizio Troiani/Alamy Stock Photo; 334–337 (Bkgrd) Lars Poyansky/Shutterstock; 339 The Asahi Shimbun/Getty Images; 343 Ross Bell/Shutterstock; 344 (L) Library of Congress Prints and Photographs Division Washington, D.C. 20540 USA [LC-DIG-ppmsca-36464]; 344 (R) Library of Congress Prints and Photographs Division Washington, D.C. 20540 USA [LC-DIG-ppmsca-37159]; 346 RossHelen/Shutterstock; 348 Muratart/Shutterstock; 349 Fay 2018/Alamy Stock Photo; 351 Everett Collection Historical/

Credits

Alamy Stock Photo; 366 (T) Photo by Tim Hursley/Smithsonian American Art Museum; 366 (B) Printed by permission of the Norman Rockwell Family Agency Copyright ©1943 the Norman Rockwell Family Entities; 367 Smithsonian American Art Museum, Washington, DC/Art Resource, NY; © Roger Shimomura

UNIT 6: 368–369 Andrea Izzotti/Shutterstock; 368 (BC) Merlin D. Tuttle/Science Source; 368 (BR) Raimonds Kalva/Shutterstock; 370 Martinho Smart/Shutterstock; 371 Denis Roger/Shutterstock; 372 Maradon 333/Shutterstock; 373 Frank60/Shutterstock; 378 Anekoho/Shutterstock; 379 Aphotostory/Shutterstock; 384 Sarun T./Shutterstock; 385 Nature Collection/Alamy Stock Photo; 386 Merlin D. Tuttle/Science Source; 388 (L) Independent birds/Shutterstock; 388 (R) Tjakab/Shutterstock; 388–393 (Bkgrd) Ivo Antonie de Rooij/Shutterstock; 389 Merlin D. Tuttle/Science Source; 390 (L) G. Ronald Austing/Science Source/Science Source; 390 (R) Merlin D. Tuttle/Science Source; 391 Avalon/Photoshot License/Alamy Stock Photo; 392 (T) Merlin D. Tuttle/Science Source; 392 (B) Rick & Nora Bowers/Alamy Stock Photo; 393 Linda Kennard/Alamy Stock Photo; 394 (T) Merlin D. Tuttle/Science Source; 394 (B) Merlin D. Tuttle/Science Source; 395 123RF; 398 Nitin Chandra/Shutterstock; 399 Boonchuay Promjiam/Shutterstock; 400 Robertharding/Alamy Stock Photo; 401 Horsemen/Shutterstock; 402 Warakorn Harnprasop/123RF; 404–405 (Bkgrd) Raimonds Kalva/Shutterstock; 405 IanDagnall Computing/Alamy Stock Photo; 406 (Bkgrd) Rudchenko Liliia/Shutterstock; 406 Alden Pellett/AP Images; 407 (Bkgrd) Pakorn Sungkapukdee/123RF; 407 Michael Greenlar/The Image Works; 408 Jason Batterham/Shutterstock; 409 (L) Neelsky/Shutterstock; 409 (TR) Andrea Izzotti/Shutterstock; 409 (BR) Peter Fodor/Shutterstock; 413 LaDonna Brezik/Shutterstock; 414 Everett Historical/Shutterstock; 416 Critterbiz/Shutterstock; 423 Adoc-photos/Corbis Historical/Getty Images; 444 (T) Photo by Tim Hursley/Smithsonian American Art Museum; 444 (B) John Steuart Curry/Smithsonian American Art Museum, Washington, DC/Art Resource, NY; 445 Larry Fuente/Smithsonian American Art Museum, Washington, DC/Art Resource, NY

Smithsonian American Art Museum List of Artworks

Unit 1 Capturing the Power of Contrasts
Page 76
Edward Hopper
Ryder's House
1933
oil on canvas
36⅛ x 50 in.
Smithsonian American Art Museum, Bequest of Henry Ward Ranger through the National Academy of Design

Page 77
Arthur Dove
Sun
1943
wax emulsion on canvas
24 x 32 in.
Smithsonian American Art Museum, Bequest of Suzanne M. Smith

Robert Sperry
Plate #753
1986
stoneware, white slip over black glaze
4 x 27⅝ in. diam.
Smithsonian American Art Museum, Gift of the James Renwick Alliance

Unit 2 Cycles of Nature
Page 148
Thomas Hart Benton
Wheat
1967
oil on wood
20 x 21 in.
Smithsonian American Art Museum, Gift of Mr. and Mrs. James A. Mitchell and museum purchase

Page 149
Mary Vaux Walcott
Untitled (Mixed Flowers)
1876
watercolor on paper
5⅛ x 2⅜ in.
Smithsonian American Art Museum, Gift of the artist

Heikki Seppä
Lupin Wedding Crown
1982
18k gold, sterling silver, and diamond
4 x 8 x 8 in.
Smithsonian American Art Museum, Gift of the James Renwick Alliance
© Smithsonian American Art Museum

Artworks (continued)

Unit 3 That's Art?
Page 222
Deborah Butterfield
Monekana
2001
bronze
96 x 129½ x 63½ in.
Smithsonian American Art Museum, Gift of the American Art Forum, Mr. and Mrs. Frank O. Rushing, Shelby and Frederick Gans and museum purchase
© 2001 Deborah Butterfield

Page 223
Sam Gilliam
Swing
1969
acrylic and aluminum on canvas
119⅝ x 283½ in.
Smithsonian American Art Museum, Gift of Mr. Edwin Janss Jr.

Man Ray
Cadeau (Serie II)
1970
flat iron
6⅛ x 4⅛ x 3½ in.
Smithsonian American Art Museum, Gift of Juliet Man Ray

Unit 4 Bonding or Breaking?
Page 296
William T. Wiley
Love Poem—Poem by Michael Hannon
1997
watercolor on paper
41 x 27 in.
Smithsonian American Art Museum, Gift of the artist
© 1997 William T. Wiley

Page 297
Washington Allston
Hermia and Helena
before 1818
oil on canvas
30⅜ x 25¼ in.
Smithsonian American Art Museum, Museum purchase through the Smithsonian Institution Collections Acquisition Program and made possible by Ralph Cross Johnson, the Catherine Walden Myer Fund, and the National Institute

Smithsonian American Art Museum List of Artworks

Unit 5 Citizens on the Home Front
Page 366
Norman Rockwell
Publisher: Office of War Information
Printer: Government Printing Office
Save Freedom of Speech
1943
color lithograph on paper
56 x 48 in.
Smithsonian American Art Museum, Gift from the Steven L. Block Collection
©1943 The Norman Rockwell Family Trust

Page 367
Roger Shimomura
Diary: December 12, 1941
1980
acrylic on canvas
50¼ x 60 in.
Smithsonian American Art Museum, Gift of the artist
© Smithsonian American Art Museum

Unit 6 Animals in Human Society
Page 444
John Steuart Curry
Ajax
1936–37
oil on canvas
36 x 48¼ in.
Smithsonian American Art Museum, Gift of Peter and Paula Lunder

Page 445
Larry Fuente
Game Fish
1988
mixed media
51½ x 112½ x 10¾ in.
Smithsonian American Art Museum, Gift of the James Renwick Alliance and museum purchase through the Smithsonian Institution Collections Acquisition Program
© 1988 Larry Fuente